The Pronunciation of English

The Pronunciation of English

Principles and Practice

M.A. Yadugiri

Viva Books

New Delhi | Mumbai | Chennai | Kolkata | Bengaluru | Hyderabad | Kochi | Guwahati

Publisher's note

Every possible effort has been made to ensure that the information contained in this book is accurate at the time of going to press, and the publisher and author cannot accept responsibility for any errors or omissions, however caused. No responsibility for loss or damage occasioned to any person acting, or refraining from action, as a result of the material in this publication can be accepted by the editor, the publisher or the author.

Every effort has been made to trace the owners of copyright material used in this book. The author and the publisher will be grateful for any omission brought to their notice for acknowledgement in the future editions of the book.

First Published 2013

Viva Books Private Limited

- 4737/23, Ansari Road, Daryaganj, New Delhi 110 002
  Tel. 42242200, 23258325, 23283121, Email: vivadelhi@vivagroupindia.net
- 76, Service Industries, Shirvane, Sector 1, Nerul, Navi Mumbai 400 706
  Tel. 27721273, 27721274, Email: vivamumbai@vivagroupindia.net
- Jamals Fazal Chambers, 26 Greams Road, Chennai 600 006
  Tel. 28294241, 28290304, Email: vivachennai@vivagroupindia.net
- B-103, Jindal Towers, 21/1A/3 Darga Road, Kolkata 700 017
  Tel. 22816713, Email: vivakolkata@vivagroupindia.net
- 7, GF, Sovereign Park Aptts., 56-58, K. R. Road, Basavanagudi, Bengaluru 560 004
  Tel. 26607409, Email: vivabangalore@vivagroupindia.net
- 101-102, Moghal Marc Apartments, 3-4-637 to 641, Narayanguda, Hyderabad 500 029
  Tel. 27564481, Email: vivahyderabad@vivagroupindia.net
- First Floor, Beevi Towers, SRM Road, Kaloor, Kochi 682 018
  Tel. 0484-2403055, 2403056, Email: vivakochi@vivagroupindia.net
- 232, GNB Road, Beside UCO Bank, Silpukhuri, Guwahati 781 003
  Tel. 0361-2666386, Email: vivaguwahati@vivagroupindia.net

www.vivagroupindia.com

ISBN: 978-81-309-1777-1

Published by Vinod Vasishtha for Viva Books Private Limited, 4737/23 Ansari Road, Daryaganj, New Delhi 110 002.

Printed and bound by Raj Press, R-3, Inderpuri, New Delhi 110 012.

L0100

Contents

Symbols used in this book

This symbol indicates material that you can listen to on the CD.

These symbols indicate important differences between American and British pronunciation.

This symbol highlights characteristic features of Indian pronunciation.

This symbol emphasizes crucial points about English pronunciation that you should remember.

(T) This symbol indicates technical information dealing with Phonetics and Phonology.

(A) This symbol indicates advanced exercises.

Acknowledgements

I would like to thank Mr Sreetilak, General Manager Publishing, Viva Books, for suggesting this project and Mr T.V. Madhu, Viva Books, Bangalore, for his support and encouragement throughout.

A number of people have helped me with the recordings for the Audio CD that goes with this book. Many British, American and Indian speakers willingly recorded reading texts and listening exercises that form the basis of this course and I am grateful to them. I would like to thank these speakers individually.

British speakers

David Clark
Glenys Clark
Susan Elaine
Rebecca Poston
Lesly Williams

American speakers

Erik Byker
Susan Downey
Sylvia Giger-Taylor
Colby Green
Hilary Greer
Nancy Harris
Frank Iacopelli
Aaron Krumins
Amandeep Kullar
Surabhi Pandit
Dennis Ross

Indian speakers

Geetha Bhasker
Aparna Chandrashekar
Taarika Chandy
Usha Gopinath
Madhuri Jagadeesh
Joseph Joachim
Mary Mathew
Varun Mathew
Lakshmi Devi Nair
Shireen Nedungadi
Anita John Ninan
Komal S.K.
S.J. Singh
Ravi Srinivasan
Sujaya Sundaram

I would also like to thank the many friends who took an interest in the project and introduced me to the British and American speakers who recorded exercises and texts for the Audio CD.

Shantha Chandran
Iris Devadason
Pratima Iengar
Surabhi Pandit
Vijaya Pandit
Varghese P.M.
Rashmi B.T.
Suresh Gopi

A considerable part of the material on the Audio CD was recorded in The Music Mint, Bangalore and my thanks to S.R. Ramakrishna, Suchitra and Gokul Abhishek of this studio.

Several exercises for the Audio CD were recorded in the studios of the Department of Communication Studies, Mount Carmel College, Bangalore and the Department of Media Studies, Christ University, Bangalore and my thanks to Ms Sahana Das, Mount Carmel College and Father Biju, Christ University.

I would also like to thank Dr Paul F. Meekin, Head Master, Trio World School, Bangalore and Mr Bud Chapman for their help.

Introduction

Why is it important to learn English pronunciation?

English teaching in the past, especially in India, focused almost exclusively on reading and writing and little attention was given to listening or speaking. But in today's world listening and speaking have become much more important than they were because of globalization that has revolutionized technology and communication and given rise to a large number of new professions and careers, e.g., the outsourcing of various business, legal, and financial processes (just to name a few). Another outcome of globalization is the opening up in the field of higher education that has made it possible for a student to study the course of his/her choice in any university anywhere in the world. The language skills needed, if you wish to succeed now, either as a student or a professional, undoubtedly include both speaking and listening skills. A very important component of learning English today is therefore learning to speak English well. In fact many English courses taught now have a stronger focus on speaking than writing.

If you want to speak English well, learning English pronunciation is as important as learning its vocabulary and grammar, However good your command over vocabulary and grammar may be, you will not be able to speak English well, if you have problems with your pronunciation. Pronunciation problems will come in the way of your being able to speak clearly so that people may not understand you and may fail to get the message you wish to convey or what is worse, may misunderstand you and get the wrong message. And if you cannot make yourself understood when you speak, your communication will be ineffectual and as a result, your performance academic or professional is likely to be assessed negatively.

If you are a student taking a national or an international test to gain admission to an academic course, to get a certificate of proficiency, or to secure a job, some component of the test will involve speaking and your pronunciation will be crucial in how you will be assessed. Tests such as IELTS have a speaking component in which pronunciation is one of the skills that is tested and assessed. Other tests such as CAT may be written, but are followed by group discussions and interviews where your ability to speak clearly and effectively will make a big difference. The importance of clear speech in job interviews is obvious, especially now that many of these interviews are conducted on the phone.

If you are a professional, success and improvement in the performance of your functions as well as the assessment of your performance will depend on your ability to speak clearly and effectively. It may be presentations, meetings, progress reports, consultations, or negotiations, if you are a business or technical professional, or it may be interaction with patients, discussions with professionals in other fields, consultations and speaking at conferences, if you are a medical professional. Whatever may be your profession, a great deal of your work involves speaking and an inability to speak clearly will have a negative impact on your performance and your future career.

Another very important factor you have to consider is that in today's world you need to speak to a variety of people, often from different countries and professions, and for different purposes. This means that you have to make yourselves understood to native as well as non-native speakers of English. It is up to you that you speak in such a way that other people can easily follow you. You cannot expect that others should make an extra effort to follow you. The success of your communication depends on how listener-oriented it is, i.e. to what degree it takes into account the needs and expectations of the listeners. Another requirement if you want to communicate effectively is that you have to be able to understand what other people, both native and non-native speakers are saying. You may have to listen to a variety of accents, British, American or Indian and understand what is being said without difficulty. You will not be able to understand what different speakers are saying without an awareness of the important features of English pronunciation and will not be able to make yourself understood to them without an ability to use these features.

Pronunciation problems affect your speech and performance in another way too. People react to not only what you say but also how you say it. If you yourself think of the various speakers, e.g., colleagues, friends, teachers, news readers, disc jockeys, politicians etc. that you have listened to, you will be able to say which of them sound good/ok and which don't. 'Sounding good or not' is an expression that is used to describe the overall impression that one has of a speaker. If you examine further why a particular speaker does not sound good, you'll probably recognize that it is mostly due to some pronunciation problems, whether you are able to identify the exact problem/s or not. Thus whether we like it or not, the way we speak, of which our pronunciation is an integral part, does influence people's opinions about us. The question you should therefore ask yourself is 'How do I sound when I speak? Good or not good?' It's easy to find out. Record yourself speaking or reading and listen to the recording. When you listen to yourself, you may be able to identify what is good and what is not about your speech. You could also play the recording to your friends and ask them for their impressions.

All this means that if you have pronunciation problems, they negatively affect your social and professional standing and undermine your confidence and self esteem, apart from interfering with your ability to communicate clearly and effectively with speakers from different linguistic and professional backgrounds. It is therefore essential that you draw up a profile of your pronunciation in terms of your abilities and problems and try to overcome the problems and further develop your abilities.

Which variety of English pronunciation should you learn?

The two major varieties of English pronunciation that most of you hear are basically British and American (though there are various sub-varieties depending on where the speaker is from, e.g., British English from North or South of England, American English from New York or California, and Indian English of people who are either influenced by or trained to speak British English or American English). As far as teaching and learning materials are concerned, British course books describe standard British English (as heard on the BBC, which is called *Received Pronunciation*), whereas American course books describe standard North American English (also called American English). You can choose either as a model to improve your English pronunciation. The main factor you have to take into account is whether the people you will be communicating with socially, academically or professionally speak British or American English.

There is a very important distinction that has to be made here. The model you choose is a guide to follow and not a goal to be aimed at. It is not possible for a non-native speaker, an Indian, a Nigerian, a Chinese, or any other, to acquire a native-speaker pronunciation, either British or American (described in the course books and heard on the accompanying CDs), unless he/she is brought up in England or America. Trying to acquire a perfect British or American pronunciation is not only unrealistic, it is also undesirable. You don't have to sound like a British or American speaker of English. What you should aim at is speaking like an Indian, a Nigerian, or a Chinese with a good English pronunciation, which may be modelled on British or American pronunciation. The essential requirement is that you are clear and intelligible to both native and non-native speakers when you speak English and that you can communicate effectively in English in different situations and for different purposes. In order to achieve this goal, you need to develop an awareness of the important features of the model of pronunciation you choose (British or American) and try to acquire the ability to use these features.

A crucial point here is that it is acceptable as well as desirable to speak English like an Indian but not to speak English like you speak an Indian language. Speaking English like an Indian means that you speak using features of English pronunciation, but retaining your identity as an Indian. But speaking English like you speak an Indian language means that you speak English using features of pronunciation of an Indian language, and not of English. In fact most of the pronunciation problems English speakers of other languages have are because the speech habits of their own language are so deep and strong that they continue to use pronunciation features of this language even when speaking English. For example, two noticeable differences between many Indian Languages and English are that (1) in Indian languages there is a close correspondence between writing and speech, but in English there is a wide disparity between spelling and pronunciation, and (2) Indian languages have a rhythm based on the number of syllables, where as the rhythm of English is based on the number of stressed syllables, there being a marked contrast between stressed and unstressed syllables. A lack of awareness of these distinguishing features of English pronunciation results in many Indian speakers pronouncing English words according to their spelling and also not differentiating between stressed and unstressed syllables. What is essential therefore is for you to be aware of the characteristic features of English pronunciation and to be able to use them when you speak English. This means that you have to make a conscious effort to overcome the strong tendency to speak English the same way as you would your own language and to learn English pronunciation so that you are able to speak English the way English is spoken. But this does not mean that you have to try to learn to speak English like a British or an American speaker. The British or American model that you choose will help you to develop an awareness of the important features of British or American English pronunciation and conscious and intense practice will help you acquire the ability to use these features when you speak English.

What are the important features of English pronunciation that you should learn?

Sounds

It is essential to know what the 44 sounds, 24 consonants and 20 vowels of English are, i.e. how each of them is produced as well as how each of them sounds. In other words you have to be aware of the articulatory and auditory features of the individual sounds used in English. Which of these sounds you need to practise carefully so that you use them correctly in speech depends on two factors (1) the crucial differences between English sounds and the sounds of your language and (2) the problems that you have with particular sounds of English, both of which may come in the way of your being able to speak English clearly and intelligibly. For example, Indian speakers do not distinguish between the initial sounds in *vine* and *wine*, /v/ and /w/, because they are used to the sound /ʋ/ in their languages, which they tend to produce in English too for both /v/ and /w/. Another feature that occurs in the speech of many Indians is the pronunciation of 'qu' as /k/ and not /kw/ in words such as *question* and *quality*. As for the vowels, Indian speakers do not often distinguish between /ə/ and /ɜː/, and /ɒ/ and /ɔː/. Also some Indians tend to use what sounds like /ɑː/ in place of /ɔː/. These problems are likely to affect intelligibility because there are many words in English that are distinguished by the use of /v/ or /w/ as in *vine* and *wine*, and *vet* and *wet* and /ɒ/ or /ɔː/ as in *cot* and *caught*, and *tot* and *taught*. The use of /ə/ in place of /ɜː/ also needs to be avoided because /ə/ occurs only in unstressed syllables, whereas /ɜː/ occurs in stressed syllables. Pronouncing 'qu' as /k/ and not as /kw/ could lead to confusion because the words *coat* and *quote* will sound the same. If words such as *lord* and *cord* are pronounced with a sound more like /ɑː/ instead of /ɔː/, they are likely to be mistaken for *lard* and *card*. It is therefore necessary to identify the problems that you have with the pronunciation of sounds that may affect the intelligibility of your speech and try to overcome them by conscious practice.

Syllables

As the concept of the syllable is very important in understanding pronunciation, you need to know what a syllable is and how it is structured in English. A characteristic feature of English is the occurrence of consonant clusters at the beginning and the end of syllables (and words). You have to be able to pronounce these clusters correctly. There is often a tendency to omit a consonant in a cluster, e.g., *shink* for *shrink*, *deth* for *depth* or to insert a vowel between the consonants, e.g., *spiring* /spɪrɪŋ/ for *spring* /sprɪŋ/ or at the beginning, e.g., *ischool* /ɪsku:l/ for *school* /sku:l/ in a cluster. You should identify which of the clusters are difficult for you to pronounce and practise words that have these clusters carefully to get their correct pronunciation. Another problematic feature is the pronunciation of syllabic consonants such as those at the end of words like *handle, bottle, button,* and *cotton*, where there is no vowel between 'd' and 'l', 't' and 'l' and 't' and 'n'. Indian speakers frequently insert a vowel in this position, which should be avoided.

Word Stress

In spoken English words are identified mainly by their stress pattern, i.e. the placement of stress on the right syllable and the clear distinction between the stressed syllable and the other syllables. A very important part of learning English pronunciation is therefore learning the stress patterns of words. This involves learning (a) where to place stress in words and (b) how to make a clear distinction between stressed and unstressed syllables in speech. In order to learn correct stress placement in words, you need to study the rules regarding stress placement in specific types of words, such as words with two or three syllables, words functioning as nouns, adjectives, or verbs, phrasal verbs, words with prefixes or suffixes and compound words and practise the correct pronunciation of a number of words of different types. In order to make a clear distinction between stressed and unstressed syllables, you need to be aware of the different ways vowels are produced in stressed and unstressed syllables, particularly how vowels are often reduced to /ə/ or sometimes to /ɪ/ in unstressed syllables and practise the pronunciation of words with two or more syllables taking care to pronounce unstressed syllables with reduced vowels. As Indian speakers have a strong tendency to follow the spelling of words in their pronunciation, many of them pronounce words such as *police* and *motor* using full vowels in both the syllables and therefore hardly make a distinction between the stressed and unstressed syllables. This is due to a lack of awareness of the feature of word stress, which is not found in Indian languages.

As word stress is what helps listeners to identify a word correctly, not using word stress or using an incorrect stress pattern with a word will make your speech unclear and in cases even unintelligible. For example, in the word *cassette*, which has the stress on the second syllable, the first syllable is pronounced with the reduced vowel /ə/. If this word is pronounced with the vowel /æ/ as if the first syllable is stressed, it may be difficult for the listener to identify the word correctly and it may even be heard as *casket* (which has the stress on the first syllable and is pronounced with /ɑ:/ or /æ/) resulting in confusion. There will be more and more confusion and difficulties for the listener if words are continuously pronounced with incorrect stress patterns. It is therefore absolutely necessary to learn about word stress in English, what it is and how it is used, and to acquire the ability to pronounce different types of words with right stress patterns.

Features of connected speech

In addition to learning to pronounce the sounds and words of English correctly, it is essential to know what features characterize speech when words are connected to form longer utterances.

Firstly, there are features such as rhythm and certain adjustments in pronunciation that occur in fluent and natural speech. You need to understand how these features work in order to follow fluent speech and also learn to use them naturally in order to speak fluently. As mentioned earlier, English rhythm is marked by the occurrence of stressed syllables at regular intervals irrespective of the number of unstressed syllables between them. The contrast between stressed and unstressed syllables is crucial in this rhythm. In order to preserve such a rhythm, English speakers tend to compress unstressed syllables more and more as their number increases so that they can move from one stressed syllable to another very smoothly. Linking, assimilation, elision, and contraction are some of the adjustments in pronunciation they make, which help their speech to flow naturally and smoothly. Weak forms and contractions are important means by which they move over unstressed syllables quickly, which helps to mark the contrast between stressed and unstressed syllables. If you want your speech to be natural and fluent, you need to be aware of these features of connected speech and acquire the ability to use them appropriately.

Secondly, there are three features that give English speech its distinctive quality. They are division of longer utterances into identifiable stretches called tone units, placement of prominence on a particular stressed syllable in a tone unit, and use of an appropriate tone in the tone unit to convey the intended meaning. All these features are crucial to the communication of precise meanings and if you are not able to use them appropriately, your speech will be confusing or unintelligible. For example, an utterance such as *Youngsters who get restless very quickly want to have variety in everything* has two meanings depending on whether the speaker says *Youngsters who get restless very quickly // want to have variety in everything* or *Youngsters // who get restless very quickly // want to have variety in everything* (// marks a tone unit boundary). In such an utterance if no tone boundary is marked, the meaning will not be clear and since it has two meanings depending on where this boundary is marked, incorrect marking of the tone boundary will result in misunderstanding. And in a sentence such as *She bought a new computer in Germany last year*, different meanings can be conveyed depending on whether prominence is placed on *new, computer, Germany, last,* or *year*. As for the tone to be used, if a statement such as *He is a hard worker* is said with a falling tone, it indicates definiteness, but if a falling-rising tone is used instead, it suggests that the speaker has reservations about the statement. Speaking English clearly therefore means that you are able to use these features of connected speech appropriately to convey the precise meanings you wish to communicate.

What should you do to learn these features of English pronunciation and acquire the ability to speak English clearly?

Sounds

In order to learn about the articulatory and auditory features of English sounds, i.e. how they are produced and how they sound, you need to listen to these sounds individually and practise producing them following the different steps in their articulation. As British English and American English are different in the case of some sounds, it is necessary that you listen and practise the variety you wish to have as a model. There are some excellent websites you can go to for this purpose.

If you wish to have British pronunciation as a model, go to the website

http://www.teachingenglish.org.uk/try/resources/pronunciation/phonemic-chart-0

and listen to the individual sounds of English, both consonants and vowels. You can hear each of the sounds by clicking on the corresponding symbol. You can download and install the chart on your computer and listen to the sounds whenever you want to practise the sounds.

Another very interesting website is

http://www.bbc.co.uk/worldservice/learningenglish/grammar/pron/sounds/index.shtml

Here you learn about both sounds and the phonetic symbols used for them and also see videos of how these sounds are produced and hear how words with each of these sounds are produced. There are also very useful tips on the pronunciation of sounds.

If you wish to have American pronunciation as a model, go to the website

www.uiowa.edu/~acadtech/phonetics/english/frameset.html

and listen to the individual sounds of English as they are pronounced in American English. When you click on the symbol for a sound, you hear the sound and also see the animation and the video for the sound. The manner in which the sound is produced is clearly shown in the animation and the video. You can also hear the pronunciation of words in which the sound occurs in different positions.

After familiarizing yourself with the 44 sounds of English and the manner of their production, you should focus on those sounds that you have problems with, particularly the pairs of sounds that you tend to pronounce alike, such as /v/ and /w/, /s/ and /z/, or /ɜ:/ and /ə/. In addition to doing the exercises in this book on such pairs, you can make lists of words with these sounds that you are likely to use frequently and practise their pronunciation. It is a good idea to record yourself as you are practising and listen carefully to see if you have learnt to pronounce them correctly. You can also compare your pronunciation with standard pronunciations given by two online dictionaries,

http://www.macmillandictionary.com/ and www.howjsay.com

Both these dictionaries give British as well as American pronunciations of words.

What is more important than learning to pronounce individual sounds correctly is learning to pronounce correctly the words with the sounds that have problems for you, because factors like the other sounds in the same word, the grammatical function of the word, and the spelling of the word bring about changes in the pronunciation of individual sounds.

Syllables

Here you should focus on words with consonant clusters in different positions and words with syllabic consonants. In order to learn the correct pronunciation of such words, you should be aware of the common errors found in the speech of English learners such as inserting a vowel between consonants in a cluster or at the beginning or end of a cluster, and pronouncing syllabic consonants with a vowel. You should record your pronunciation of words with consonant clusters and syllabic consonants and listen to the recording very carefully to identify any errors. Again you could listen to the standard pronunciation of these words and try to correct any errors found and thus improve your pronunciation of these words.

Word Stress

First, you should understand what word stress is and how it works. It is useful to listen to the pronunciation of a number of words with two syllables where one syllable is stressed and the other is not. (In addition to the words in the various exercises in this book, you should make a list of a number of other words of two syllables and listen to their pronunciation on the online dictionaries mentioned above.) You will notice that in some words the first syllable is stressed or to put it very simply, pronounced with greater force, whereas in others, it is the second syllable that is stressed. Another difference that you should notice is that the vowel in the unstressed syllable is often reduced to /ə/ or /ɪ/, whatever the spelling may indicate. It is these differences in the pronunciation of the two syllables that give the word its distinctive stress pattern and helps the listener to identify the word correctly. It is only when you learn to pronounce these words with the right stress patterns that you will have learnt their right pronunciation.

Next, you should study words of three and more syllables to understand the difference between strong or primary stress and weak or secondary stress and practise the pronunciation of these words with the right stress patterns.

Then it is necessary to learn about the rules for stress placement in different types of words such as words functioning as nouns, adjectives, or verbs, phrasal verbs, words with prefixes or suffixes and compound words so that you will be able to pronounce the different types of words correctly.

The exercises in Chapter 6 will give you some practice in stress placement in different types of words but you may use many more such words in different situations and you have to learn to pronounce them with correct stress patterns. When you have to use a new word or a word the pronunciation of which you are not sure, check its stress pattern, listen to its correct pronunciation, and practise pronouncing it correctly. Learning the correct pronunciation of a word with the right stress pattern is as important as learning its correct spelling and usage.

Features of connected speech

Once you have learnt to pronounce individual words correctly with the right sounds and stress patterns, you should focus on how words are combined together to form longer stretches in speech. For this (apart from working through the exercises in this book) you should listen to a number of samples of different types of connected speech. Today you have plenty of opportunities to listen to newscasts, news reports, discussions, interviews, readings, demonstrations, how-to programmes, etc. on the radio, the TV and the Internet. You can also watch English films (both British and American). Generally you pay attention to meaning when you listen to these speech samples. In order to develop an awareness of how the features of connected speech such as linking, assimilation, elision, contraction and weak forms are used to contribute to the rhythm of English speech, you should try to identify these features in the samples of speech that you listen to. Constant listening will help you familiarize yourselves with these features and also move towards acquiring their use in your speech. You can monitor your progress by recording yourself reading short passages and speaking and listening to the recording.

The other three features of connected speech, namely, pausing at tone unit boundaries, placing prominence appropriately in a tone unit, and using the right tone to convey the meaning you wish to, require developing an awareness of how they work as well as rigorously practising their use. You should pay attention to grammar as well as meaning in learning to pause at the right places to mark tone unit boundaries in speech. Placing prominence or nuclear stress (sentence stress) will depend on the meaning you wish to convey and you should practise this carefully in different types of utterances. As for the tones, you should learn how to produce the three important tones, the fall, the rise and the fall-rise and also when to use them, i.e. what meanings they are used to convey. Here again you should begin by carefully listening to different types of dialogue and conversation, British or American or both, and noticing how these three features are used. You could practise repeating (as best as you could) single utterances of questions, exclamations and statements in what you listen to and compare yourself with the original speaker by recording yourself to find out if you are using these features right, especially placement of prominence and tone. It is only constant practice that can help you use these features appropriately.

But you should not expect to be able to sound exactly like a British or American speaker of English, as far as the use of tones is concerned. A native speaker, British or American uses a variety of tones with very subtle differences and you will not be able to use all of them unless you live in England or America for a number of years. It may not be necessary either to try to learn all the subtle variations in intonation found in British or American speech. What you should aim at learning is to make important distinctions in tone that are crucial for intelligibility so that you will not be misunderstood. Placement of prominence appropriate to the meaning intended and pausing at the right places are more important and you should try to acquire the ability to use these features in speech.

General tips

There are important points you should remember about learning pronunciation, which apply to all the different features discussed above.

- ***You should listen to as many speech samples of different varieties as possible.*** You can choose British, American or/and Indian speakers to listen to, but make sure that their pronunciation is clear and intelligible. It is by focusing on the different features of pronunciation while listening that you can develop an awareness of how these features are used in clear and intelligible speech. If you listen with friends and teachers, discussions with them will be of help.

- ***You should practise speaking (producing words, sentences and longer stretches of connected speech) as much as possible.*** You can get feedback from friends and teachers about your pronunciation, when they listen to you live. It is also very important that you can listen to yourself and be able to assess your pronunciation. You should therefore record yourself when you do the practice exercises in this book and listen to the recordings carefully focusing on the different features of pronunciation. This has another advantage in that your friends, teachers, or yourself can listen to any part/s of your speech repeatedly and thus be able to identify any problems that need to be worked on.
- ***You should always check the correct pronunciation of words you are not familiar with and words about the pronunciation of which you are not sure in a dictionary.*** You can listen to the correct pronunciation of such words given by the online dictionaries mentioned earlier and learn to pronounce them correctly. Do not hesitate to check the pronunciation of a word. It is better to check and learn the correct pronunciation of a word than to assume that you know and pronounce the word incorrectly.
- ***You should remember that in any sample of speech that you listen to or produce, all features of pronunciation (individual sounds, word stress, and features of connected speech) work together.*** It is only for purposes of learning that these features are focused on and studied separately. For example, when you listen to words that begin with different consonants, you focus on the pronunciation of these consonant sounds, but these words are pronounced with a distinctive stress pattern too. This is noticeable particularly when a word has more than one syllable. Similarly, when you listen to a sentence where the focus is on a word with a consonant cluster, the sentence may be spoken with some contractions or weak forms. It is therefore necessary to practise contextualized speaking activities in addition to practising individual words, phrases and sentences and listening to their recordings to find out how the various pronunciation features are incorporated in your speech.

What will you find in this book?

The book has 9 chapters. Chapter 1, ‘Towards an awareness of English Pronunciation’, has (a) a short questionnaire that will help you think about your pronunciation, (b) a few listening exercises that will help you become aware of some important differences between British and American English pronunciation and (c) a few practice exercises that will help you identify the features of pronunciation you should focus on.

Chapter 2 introduces you to speech sounds in general, the organs used to produce these sounds, and also the sounds of English, how they are identified and represented in writing. There are exercises focusing on speech organs, classification of speech sounds on the basis of their manner of production, divergence between spelling and pronunciation in English and the symbols used in the International Phonetic Alphabet (IPA) to represent sounds of English.

Chapters 3 to 8 deal with the different features of English pronunciation, namely consonants, vowels, syllables, word stress, and connected speech in English. Except for Chapter 1, all chapters have a similar organization. They begin with a few quotations highlighting the features presented and a preview of the contents of the chapter and their importance. They are divided into Units each of which has detailed descriptions of the features in focus and a variety of exercises that require learners to listen to and identify and also practise using these features. The descriptions include a number of examples to make for easy understanding. The IPA symbols are used to represent individual sounds and also to show the pronunciation of words.

In addition to descriptions of the pronunciation features in general terms, there is interesting and essential information about (i) important differences between British and American pronunciation, (ii) characteristic features of Indian pronunciation, (iii) crucial factors in the pronunciation of certain features, and (iv) useful technical terms and distinctions, all of which are highlighted by being presented separately. This information will help you understand better how English is pronounced differently by different groups of people and also what you should focus on in your pronunciation practice.

The salient points about the pronunciation features in focus are summed up at the end in a Chapter Summary.

Chapters 3 and 4 that deal with consonants and vowels give not only detailed descriptions of individual sounds and the manner of their production but also discuss how other sounds, grammar and spelling affect their pronunciation in speech.

Throughout the book, the exercises facilitate improving (1) awareness of important pronunciation features and (2) ability to use these features. The focus in Chapters 3, 4, 5, and 6 is mostly on listening to and then repeating words and sentences so that you get adequate practice in identifying and using the relevant pronunciation features. Many of these exercises require you to know what the words and phrases in focus mean and how they are used. Since you practise a number of different types of words and phrases in these exercises, you have an opportunity to improve your vocabulary too. In doing these exercises, you learn about many pairs of words that differ only in one sound but have very different meanings (minimal pairs), words in which identical letter/s are pronounced differently, nouns, verbs and adjectives that appear the same in writing but differ only in pronunciation (in word stress), words formed by the addition of prefixes and suffixes, phrasal verbs, and compound words. Some of the vocabulary you will find is quite challenging and some taken from the fields of business, finance and computers.

Chapters 3, 4, and 6 also have exercises focusing on the important differences between British and American pronunciation described in these chapters.

The exercises in Chapter 7 present stretches of language that illustrate the rhythm of English, different ways of linking words, and use of contractions, elision, and weak forms for listening and practice. Chapter 8 has exercises on tone unit boundaries, placement of prominence, and use of different tones and step-ups and step-downs in pitch and therefore mostly consist of exchanges between two speakers to provide appropriate contexts that make the meaning of tones clear. These exercises mainly help you to develop an awareness of the important features of connected speech and give you some practice in using them. But it is only constant listening and practice that will help you to acquire the ability to use these features appropriately.

A unique feature of this book is that at the end of every chapter, you get an opportunity to listen to one or two jokes and a fable or a passage on a topic of general interest read by three speakers, a British English speaker, an American English speaker and an Indian speaker. These jokes, fables and passages have been carefully selected so that they illustrate the particular feature/s focused on in the chapter. They enrich your study of English pronunciation as they have several advantages.

- ➢ They are interesting as well as entertaining.
- ➢ They'll help you see how particular features of pronunciation are used in the context of a meaningful self-contained text.
- ➢ They'll show you the differences between British, American and Indian pronunciation.
- ➢ Reading, recording and listening to your readings of these texts will give you useful practice in pronunciation.
- ➢ You can go back to the readings of these texts anytime to study how the different features of pronunciation you learnt and practised in different chapters work together in connected speech.

Chapter 9 has a few contextualized speaking activities that are designed to help you integrate the pronunciation features you have learnt in the earlier chapters and incorporate them into contextualized speech.

The Appendix deals with the problems many Indian speakers have in pronouncing certain types of words such as *shortage, surface, literature, beneficial, cautious* and *technology.*

There is a Glossary that gives explanations of the terms specific to the subject of pronunciation that are used in this book.

At the end of the book, you'll find a Key with answers to the exercises.

Audio CD

The audio CD has recordings of (a) the passages for listening, (b) words, phrases, sentences and exchanges given as illustrations of different features of pronunciation and (c) the listening exercises. The symbol in the book indicates what you'll find on the audio CD.

(a) The listening passages (jokes, fables and others) in all the chapters are read by three speakers, a British English speaker, an American English speaker and an Indian speaker. You'll hear different voices in each category.

(b) Illustrations and (c) listening exercises are read by British, American or Indian speakers. Here again you'll hear different voices.

As the key to learning correct pronunciation lies in listening and practising, the audio CD is a very useful aid. The more you use it the more you get out of it. You can listen to any passage, illustration or exercise any number of times, pausing wherever you wish. Listening in itself is not enough. It is very important that you practise and record what you practise so that you can compare your pronunciation with what you hear on the CD. Listening to yourself and getting feedback from others are equally important if you want to improve your pronunciation.

1

Towards an awareness of English pronunciation

1. Before beginning a systematic study of English pronunciation, it is useful to spend a few minutes thinking about your pronunciation. The questions and exercises below will help you consider some important aspects of your pronunciation, which will make your study of English pronunciation interesting and useful.

   (i) How would you describe your pronunciation when you speak English?

   (a) Very good ☐

   (b) Good ☐

   (c) OK ☐

   (d) Haven't thought about it ☐

   (ii) Do you think your mother tongue affects your pronunciation of English?

   (a) Very much ☐

   (b) A little ☐

   (c) Very little ☐

   (d) Can't say ☐

   (iii) Do you wish to improve your pronunciation? If yes, why?

   (a) Because you want to go to UK, USA or some other English speaking country to study or work ☐

   (b) Because you are working in an American, British or some other foreign company in India ☐

   (c) Because you feel that your chances of getting a good job will be better ☐

   (d) Because you wish to speak English well in both professional and social contexts ☐

(e) Because you are in or want to choose a profession where communication skills are very important ☐

(iv) In your attempts to improve your pronunciation, which model of English pronunciation would you choose?

(a) American ☐

(b) British ☐

(c) Any other ☐

If you choose (c) specify what model you would have.

____

(v) Do you think improving your pronunciation will be

(a) difficult ☐

(b) very difficult ☐

(c) impossible ☐

(d) possible with a lot of practice? ☐

L 1.1 You will hear two texts, first a short passage on coffee and then an anecdote about Einstein, read by three speakers, a British English speaker, an American English speaker and an Indian speaker. Identify which reading is British, which American and which Indian.

Coffee	*Indian*	*British*	*American*
Reading 1			
Reading 2			
Reading 3			

Einstein	***Indian***	***British***	***American***
Reading 1			
Reading 2			
Reading 3			

(i) Which accent, British or American are you more familiar with?

(ii) Which accent, British or American do you find easier to understand?

(iii) Read the transcripts of the two texts on page 20 and listen to the readings again. Are there particular words or expressions whose pronunciation sounds unfamiliar to you in any of the readings? Make a note of them below.

Coffee

Reading 1			
Reading 2			
Reading 3			

Einstein

Reading 1			
Reading 2			
Reading 3			

L 1.2 You will hear two more texts read by a British English speaker, an American English speaker and an Indian speaker. The first is 'Arthur the Rat' and the second is 'The Rainbow'.

(i) Read the transcripts of the two texts on pages 20–21 and listen to the readings again.

(ii) Can you describe whether the pronunciation of the words, expressions and sentences given below is different or not in the three readings? If different, can you describe how?
You can listen to the expressions and sentences in which they occur separately as they are spoken by the different speakers at the end of the readings.

'Arthur the Rat'
Arthur
asked
answer
"I don't know"
"yes" or "no" either
shirk
aunt
"Now look here"
"This won't do"
search
new
a calf
"Stop," he ordered coarsely. "You are coming, of course?"
"...Right about face. March!"
half in and half out of his whole
shirker
due
'The Rainbow'
The rainbow
colors
a long round arch
path
apparently
the pot of gold
a miracle
physical explanation
...the gods passed from earth to their home in the sky
The actual primary rainbow
the effect of superpositioning of a number of bows

L 1.3 Listen to a British English speaker and an American English speaker read two passages. The first is a short passage on lies and the second is a joke.

(i) Read the two passages aloud (transcripts given on pages 21–22) and record your readings.

(ii) Listen to your readings. Do you think your reading is closer to the British or the American reading?

(iii) Is your pronunciation of the words, expressions and sentences given below similar or different to British or American English? If different, can you describe how?

Lies

lies

"omits the truth"

start

...the use and power of language

malicious

manipulated

a child's environment

...not a big deal at all

folks

pathological liars

a description, not a diagnosis

They lie to protect themselves, look good, gain financially or socially and avoid punishment

A joke

A postdoc, a grad student and their professor

when they come upon an old brass lamp

Out pops a genie!

my lamp-prison

I can grant you three wishes

...a crew of totally buffed-out, gorgeous guys

my Harley

a gang of beautiful women

disappears

"I'd like those two back in lab after lunch."

2. **What components or features of speech do you think are important in describing the pronunciation of a speaker? Choose from the list given.**

Individual sounds – Consonants	Individual sounds – Vowels
Words – Stressed words	Words – Unstressed words
Manner of combining words	Rhythms
Pauses	Speech tempo
Loudness of voice	Voice quality

3. (i) Read the following paragraph silently focusing on meaning.

Globalization is the result of unprecedented scientific and technological advances. Some of the key inventions that have made a fast-moving, interlinked world possible are microchips, jet planes, satellites and optical fibers. Further, the costs of computing, telecommunications and transport have plummeted over the past decade. These technological changes have combined with a huge boom in world trade and rapid economic growth. Some of the consequences of all this have been disastrous especially for the environment. Another undesirable consequence has been the dominance of a Western culture based on consumerism and individualism.

"The Chips are Down." *New Scientist* 27 April 2002:30

(ii) Read the paragraph aloud as naturally as possible and record your reading on a tape or CD.

(iii) Think of an interesting experience you had recently. Tell your friend about it and record yourself on a tape or CD.

(iv) Listen to the recordings (ii) and (iii) and identify

(a) the good points about your pronunciation and

(b) the points where you think you need to improve.

(v) Play the recordings (ii) and (iii) to your teacher or another friend and ask them for an opinion on your pronunciation.

(vi) Now list the features that you think you need to focus on in order to improve your pronunciation.

Coffee is one of the world's most popular beverages. It is primarily enjoyed for its taste and aroma, but also for its well-known positive effect on mental performance. Drinking coffee has been demonstrated to improve an individual's alertness and concentration so aiding better performance and also helping to reduce the feeling of tiredness and lethargy. The key ingredient demonstrated to be responsible for enhanced mental performance is caffeine, which is naturally contained in coffee but also in tea and cocoa.

http://www.positivelycoffee.org/%2Ftopic_performance_statement.aspx

Albert Einstein - When Albert Einstein was making the rounds of the speaker's circuit, he usually found himself eagerly longing to get back to his laboratory work. One night as they were driving to yet another rubber-chicken dinner, Einstein mentioned to his chauffeur (a man who somewhat resembled Einstein in looks & manner) that he was tired of speechmaking. "I have an idea, boss," his chauffeur said. "I've heard you give this speech so many times. I'll bet I could give it for you." Einstein laughed loudly and said, "Why not? Let's do it!"

When they arrived at the dinner, Einstein donned the chauffeur's cap and jacket and sat in the back of the room. The chauffeur gave a beautiful rendition of Einstein's speech and even answered a few questions expertly Then a supremely pompous professor asked an extremely esoteric question about anti-matter formation, digressing here and there to let everyone in the audience know that he was nobody's fool. Without missing a beat, the chauffeur fixed the professor with a steely stare and said, "Sir, the answer to that question is so simple that I will let my chauffeur, who is sitting in the back, answer it for me."

http://www.innocentenglish.com/best-funny-jokes/einstein-jokes-jokes-about-einstein.html

Once there was a young rat named Arthur, who could never make up his mind. Whenever his friends asked him if he would like to go out with them, he would only answer, "I don't know." He wouldn't say "yes" or "no" either. He would always shirk making a choice.

His aunt Helen said to him, "Now look here. No one is going to care for you if you carry on like this. You have no more mind than a blade of grass."

One rainy day, the rats heard a great noise in the loft. The pine rafters were all rotten, so that the barn was rather unsafe. At last the joists gave way and fell to the ground. The walls shook and all the rats' hair stood on end with fear and horror. "This won't do," said the captain. "I'll send out scouts to search for a new home."

Within five hours the ten scouts came back and said, "We found a stone house where there is room and board for us all. There is a kindly horse named Nelly, a cow, a calf, and a garden with an elm tree." The rats crawled out of their little houses and stood on the floor in a long line.

Just then the old one saw Arthur. "Stop," he ordered coarsely. "You are coming, of course?" "I'm not certain," said Arthur, undaunted. "The roof may not come down yet." "Well," said the angry old rat, "we can't wait for you to join us. Right about face. March!"

Arthur stood and watched them hurry away. "I think I'll go tomorrow," he calmly said to himself, but then again "I don't know; it's so nice and snug here."

That night there was a big crash. In the morning some men—with some boys and girls—rode up and looked at the barn. One of them moved a board and he saw a young rat, quite dead, half in and half out of his hole. Thus the shirker got his due.

http://alt-usage-english.org/arth_txt.html

When the sunlight strikes raindrops in the air, they act like a prism and form a rainbow. The rainbow is a division of white light into many beautiful colors. These take the shape of a long round arch, with its path high above, and its two ends apparently beyond the horizon. There is, according to legend, a boiling pot of gold at one end. People look, but no one ever finds it. When a man looks for something beyond his reach, his friends say he is looking for the pot of gold at the end of the rainbow.

Throughout the centuries men have explained the rainbow in various ways. Some have accepted it as a miracle without physical explanation. To the Hebrews it was a token that there would be no more universal floods. The Greeks used to imagine that it was a sign from the gods to foretell war or heavy rain. The Norsemen considered the rainbow as a bridge over which the gods passed from earth to their home in the sky. Other men have tried to explain the phenomenon physically. Aristotle thought that the rainbow was caused by reflections of the sun's rays by the rain. Since then physicists have found that it is not reflection, but refraction by the raindrops which causes the rainbow. Many complicated ideas about the rainbow have been formed. The difference in the rainbow depends considerably upon the size of the water drops, and the width of the colored band increases as the size, of the drops increases. The actual primary rainbow observed is said to be the effect of superpositioning of a number of bows. If the red of the second bow falls upon the green of the first, the result is to give a bow with an abnormally wide yellow band, since red and green lights when mixed form yellow. This is a very common type of bow, one showing mainly red and yellow, with little or no green or blue.

http://alt-usage-english.org/rainb_txt.html

Everybody lies. It may only be "white" lies, but everyone tells lies or "omits the truth" sometimes. We start lying at around age 4 to 5 when children gain an awareness of the use and power of language. This first lying is not malicious, but rather to find out, or test, what can be manipulated in a child's environment. Eventually children begin to use lying to get out of trouble or get something they want. White lies, those concocted to protect someone's feelings, are not a big deal at all. The person, however, who seems to feel compelled to lie about both the small and large stuff has a problem. We often call these folks pathological liars (which is a description, not a diagnosis). They lie to protect themselves, look good, gain financially or socially and avoid punishment.

http://today.msnbc.msn.com/id/4072816/p1/0/

A postdoc, a grad student, and their professor are taking a walk outdoors during lunch when they come upon an old brass lamp. They pick it up and dust it off. Poof! Out pops a genie!

"Thank you for releasing me from my lamp-prison," he says, "I can grant you three wishes- one for each of you."

The postdoc thinks a moment, and then she says, "I'd like to be out sailing a yacht across the Pacific, racing before the wind, with a crew of totally buffed-out, gorgeous guys."

"It is done," says the Genie, and Poof! the postdoc disappears.

The grad student thinks a moment and says, "I'd like to be riding my Harley with a gang of beautiful women throughout the American Southwest."

"It is done," says the Genie, and Poof! the grad student disappears.

The professor looks at where the other two had been standing and rubs his chin in thought. Then, he tells the Genie, "I'd like those two back in lab after lunch."

http://schooljokes.informationresourcenetwork.com/index.ph

2

Understanding speech sounds

Although the sounds we produce and hear and comprehend during speech are continuous, everyone throughout history who has attempted to analyse language has recognized that speech utterances can be segmented into individual units.

Victoria Fromkin and Robert Rodman *An Introduction to Language* 1993, 5th Edition p. 177

A sound is made by definite movements of the organs of speech, and if those movements are exactly repeated the result will always be the same sound;

J.D.O'Connor *Better English Pronunciation* 1981, 2nd Edition p. 9

Knowing a language means knowing what sounds are in that language and what sounds are not.

Victoria Fromkin and Robert Rodman *An Introduction to Language* 1993, 5th Edition p. 4

PREVIEW

We all know that the basic components of speech are sounds and that in order to be able to speak a language well, it is necessary to learn to pronounce the sounds of that language correctly. One way of beginning to do this is to list the individual sounds, the consonants and vowels of that language and practice their pronunciation individually and in combination with other sounds. But it would be very useful to think a little about the sounds of languages in general and about the sounds of a specific language like English in particular before we begin practising specific sounds. This would give us an awareness of what exactly we are trying to learn by helping us realize the significance of the individual sounds that make up speech in a language.

With this aim in view, this chapter attempts to answer four important questions about (a) sounds of languages in general and (b) the individual sounds of English in particular, namely,

2.1 Why individual sounds are important in learning pronunciation,

2.2 How we produce speech sounds,

2.3 How we identify sounds of English and

2.4 How we represent sounds of English in writing.

2.1 Why individual sounds are important

When we consider the sounds we hear around us, we notice that we produce and hear an amazing variety of sounds. We not only speak and hear others speak, but we also laugh, yawn, snore, cough, sneeze, shout with joy or cry in pain or sorrow and play various musical instruments or hum tunes. But the important thing is that even in the midst of such a variety of different sounds, we know which of these sounds make up speech or language and which do not. In other words, we know whether someone is speaking or merely laughing, shouting or crying. This is so obvious that we don't even think about it. But it means that we have a means of identifying and distinguishing speech sounds from all other types of sounds. We can do this not only when we know the language spoken, but even when we don't know the language. When we know the language, we recognize meaningful words in what we hear. When we don't know the language, we still perceive that the sounds we hear have certain features that help us to identify them as speech sounds, though we may not be able to recognize the words of the language. We may not consciously know what these features are but use their presence to distinguish speech sounds from other sounds. In any study of the pronunciation of a language, be it English or any other, it is essential to identify, describe and classify the individual sounds that constitute speech in that language because the distinctive features they possess give the language its unique character.

(i) The most important distinguishing feature of speech sounds is that they can be separated and identified as distinct entities. For example, when we hear words like *bus*, *tell* or *degree*, we can identify the different sounds which make up each of them, /b/, /ʌ/ and /s/ in *bus*, /t/, /e/ and /l/ in *tell* and /d/, /ɪ/, /g/, /r/ and /iː/ in *degree*. But when we hear someone laughing or coughing, we cannot divide what we hear into constituent sounds, because we cannot identify any separate entities that make up the sounds of laughing or coughing. A characteristic feature of language, therefore, is that it is made up of distinct sounds, which can be separated and differentiated from one another.

(ii) Dividing words into their constituent sounds shows another distinguishing feature of speech sounds. When we look at the sounds /b/, /ʌ/ and /s/ separately, we notice that individual speech sounds do not have any meaning, /b/ does not mean anything, nor do /ʌ/ and /s/ taken separately. But if we combine /ʌ/ and /s/, we have *us*, which means something. Similarly if we combine /b/, /ʌ/ and /s/ we have *bus*, which also has meaning. Thus we can say that the distinct sounds that make up language do not have any meaning in themselves.

(iii) The distinct sounds that do not have any meaning in themselves acquire meaning when they are combined in specific ways. For example, if the sounds /t/, /e/ and /l/, which do not mean anything when taken separately, are combined to form the sequences /tel/ or /let/, they acquire meaning. But if we combine them to form /tle/, /lte/, /elt/ or /etl/, they do not have meaning. This is because /tel/ and /let/ are words in English but /tle/, /lte/, /elt/ and /etl/ are not. Every language combines its sounds in different ways to form words with meaning and it is only when the sounds are combined in these ways that the combinations of sounds acquire meaning in that language.

(iv) Though individual sounds like /t/ or /e/ do not have any meaning in themselves, they have an important function in conveying meaning when they are combined with other sounds. If we consider the combinations /tel/ and /bel/, for example, we see that both have meaning but different meanings. What is it that signals the difference in meaning between these two words? The only difference in sounds between the two words is that one has /t/ in the initial position, where as the other has /b/ in the same position. The other sounds are the same. We can therefore say that the sounds /t/ and /b/, though not having any meaning in themselves, signal a difference in meaning, when they are combined with /el/. Similarly, in /tel/ and /tu:l/, we find that the only difference between the two words is in the middle sounds /e/ and /u:/, where as the initial and the final sounds are same. Here the sounds /e/ and /u:/ signal the difference in meaning between the words *tell* and *tool*. In /tel/ and /ten/, it is the final sounds /l/ and /n/, which are different, the first two sounds in both the words being /t/ and /e/. The difference in meaning between the two words *tell* and *ten* is, therefore, signalled by /l/ and /n/. Thus individual sounds of language signal differences in meaning, though they do not have any meaning in themselves.

We can say that speech sounds or sounds of language are unique because they have these four characteristic features, namely, (i) they are distinct entities, (ii) they do not have any meaning in themselves, (iii) they convey meaning only when they are combined in specific ways and (iv) in specific combinations they signal contrasts in meaning.

Learning the correct pronunciation of the individual sounds of a language is crucial in learning to speak that language because every language is unique in (a) the number and type of speech sounds used, (b) the specific ways in which they are combined to convey meaning and (c) the contrasts in meaning that the individual speech sounds signal when they are combined with other sounds.

Learning about the sound system of English, i.e., the individual sounds used, the specific ways they are combined and the contrasts in meaning they signal in English speech and mastering the correct pronunciation of the sounds of English are therefore essential prerequisites for being able to speak English well.

Exercises

1. Write down 5 simple words in your mother tongue.
   (i) Divide the words into the individual sounds that make up each. Separate the consonant and vowel sounds.
   (ii) Check to see that the individual sounds themselves do not convey meaning.
   (iii) Try different combinations of the sounds in each word and identify which combinations are meaningful and which are not. (You will notice that only some combinations of sounds can be pronounced, whereas some others cannot even be pronounced).

(iv) Try substituting the sound in a specific position in a word by another and check if this substitution results in a new word with a different meaning. Try this with sounds in different positions in each of the words.

Do you see that the sounds in your mother tongue also show the four features of speech sounds described above?

2.2 How we produce speech sounds

Sounds are concrete entities and can be described in terms of their physical features. There are three features that can be used in describing speech sounds:

(a) The manner in which a speaker produces these sounds,
(b) The manner in which they are transmitted from the speaker to the listener and
(c) The manner in which the listener perceives (hears) them.

> **T** A study of the physical features of speech sounds is known as ***Phonetics***. There are three branches of phonetics depending on which of these features is studied. The study of the production of speech sounds is ***Articulatory Phonetics***, the study of the transmission of speech sounds is ***Acoustic Phonetics*** and the study of the perception of speech sounds is ***Auditory Phonetics***.

In language descriptions, generally the focus is on the production of sounds and hence the manner in which the sounds of a language are produced is studied in detail. A description of the manner of production of the sounds of a language will help us in identifying and distinguishing between these sounds.

The sounds that we produce when we speak are the result of an air stream coming up from the lungs which passes through the windpipe (called the ***Trachea***) and the voice box (called the ***Larynx***) into a passage ending in the mouth or the nose. This passage from the larynx is called the ***Vocal Tract***. The air stream is originally produced by the muscles we use for breathing. There are various organs in the vocal tract which move to modify the shape and character of the air stream coming up from the lungs. The air stream which is modified in its journey through the vocal tract comes out of the speaker's mouth or nose and travels into the surrounding air. If it reaches the ears of another person, it is heard as language. Thus when someone speaks and another person hears what is spoken, it is essentially an air stream that comes out of the speaker's lungs and reaches the ears of the listener. This air stream acquires its unique character as speech because of the modifications it undergoes in the vocal tract of the speaker. The air stream is modified in the vocal tract either because it passes through spaces of various shapes or because the surfaces it meets in its passage have different properties so that it encounters different types and degrees of resistance or obstruction.

In order to understand how different speech sounds are produced we have to consider

(a) the various organs in the vocal tract which have an important function in modifying the character of the air stream and

(b) the various ways in which these organs move to alter the shapes of the spaces through which the air stream passes or to offer different types of resistance or obstruction to the air stream.

These organs that alter the shape and character of the air stream by modifying it are called ***Articulators***. Figure 1 shows the important articulators used in speech. It is a diagram of the human head as though it has been cut in half and is seen from the side.

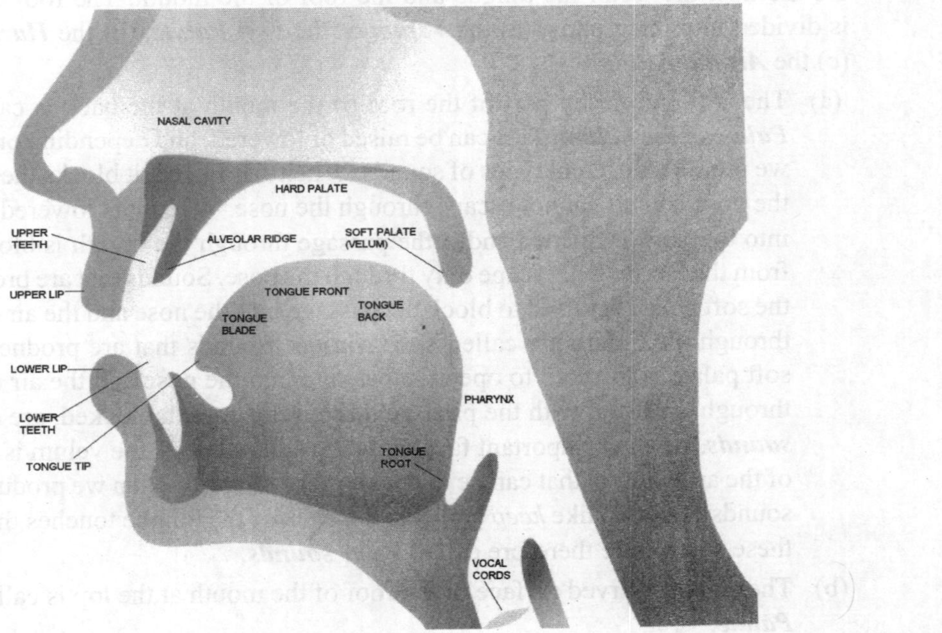

Figure 1

1. The larynx contains two thick flaps of muscle, which can produce a faint sound by vibrating. These are called ***Vocal Cords*** or ***Vocal Folds***. The space or the opening between the vocal cords is called the ***Glottis***. For some speech sounds, the larynx is open and the air passes through the slack vocal cords. For example, the initial sounds of *pet* and *fan* are produced with the air passing through slack vocal cords. Such sounds are called ***Voiceless sounds***. There is another type of speech sounds for which the vocal cords are brought close together and tightened, which results in the narrowing of the glottis. When air passes through the narrowed glottis, the vocal cords vibrate and make a faint sound, which is called a ***Vocal buzz***. This faint sound may be later amplified in the mouth or the nose. For example, the initial sounds of *bet* and *van* are produced with

the narrowed glottis and vibrating vocal cords. Such sounds are called ***Voiced sounds***. All vowels in English (and most other languages) are voiced, where as consonants may be voiced or voiceless. The difference between voiced and voiceless sounds is basic and is made as the air stream passes through the larynx into the vocal tract. It is in the vocal tract that the air stream undergoes important modifications to produce different speech sounds.

2. The ***Pharynx*** is a tube that begins just above the larynx and the air stream from the larynx passes through this tube into the vocal tract.
3. The organs in the mouth which play an important role in the production of speech sounds are the lips, the teeth, the tongue and the roof of the mouth. The roof of the mouth is divided into three parts, (a) the ***Velum*** or the ***Soft Palate***, (b) the ***Hard Palate*** and (c) the ***Alveolar Ridge***.
   (a) The soft and fleshy part of the roof of the mouth at the back is called the ***Soft Palate*** or the ***Velum***. This can be raised or lowered; and depending on its position, we produce different types of sounds. When it is raised, it blocks the passage into the nose and air cannot escape through the nose. When it is lowered, the passage into the nose is opened and if the passage through the mouth is blocked, the air from the larynx will escape only through the nose. Sounds that are produced when the soft palate is raised to block the passage into the nose and the air escapes only through the mouth are called ***Oral sounds***. Sounds that are produced when the soft palate is lowered to open the passage into the nose and the air escapes only through the nose, with the passage through the mouth blocked, are called ***Nasal sounds***. Another important fact about the soft palate or the velum is that it is one of the articulators that can be touched by the tongue. When we produce the initial sounds of words like *keep* and *give* the back of the tongue touches the velum and these sounds are therefore called ***Velar sounds***.
   (b) The smooth curved surface of the roof of the mouth at the top is called the ***Hard Palate***.
   (c) The bony part of the roof of the mouth between the hard palate and the top front teeth is called the ***Alveolar Ridge***. Sounds that are produced with the tongue touching this ridge are called ***Alveolar sounds***. For example, the initial sounds of *tin* and *din*.
4. The upper and lower teeth are both important in the production of speech sounds. The Figure above shows only the front teeth, which are immediately behind the lips.
5. The lips too have an important function in speech. They are used in different ways in producing different vowel and consonant sounds.
6. The tongue can take different positions and can be moved into different shapes and is therefore an important organ of speech. Generally it is divided into five different parts--the tip, the blade, the front, the back and the root.

Descriptions of how speech sounds are produced mainly deal with these articulators because they come directly into contact with the air stream from the lungs and modify it by their various movements and shapes before it passes through the mouth or the nose. Though the lower jaw also moves a lot when we speak, we generally do not consider it as an articulator because it does not directly come into contact with the air stream.

Consonants and Vowels

The basic distinction we make in describing the production of speech sounds is between ***Vowels*** and ***Consonants***. ***Vowels*** are sounds that are produced without any obstruction to the flow of air as it passes from the larynx through the vocal tract and escapes through the mouth or the nose. ***Consonants*** are sounds that are produced with a closure or a narrowing in the vocal tract, which causes an obstruction or a friction to the flow of air as it passes through the vocal tract. We can see this difference between vowels and consonants when we produce the initial sounds of *arm* or *eat* and *pit* or *fat*. When saying the initial sounds of *arm* or *eat*, we notice that the air flows easily and freely through the mouth. But in saying the first sounds of *pit* or *fat*, we notice that different articulators move to bring about a closure or a narrowing in the mouth, which results in an obstruction or a friction to the flow of air.

Exercises

1. Identify the different articulators with numbered arrows on the diagram.

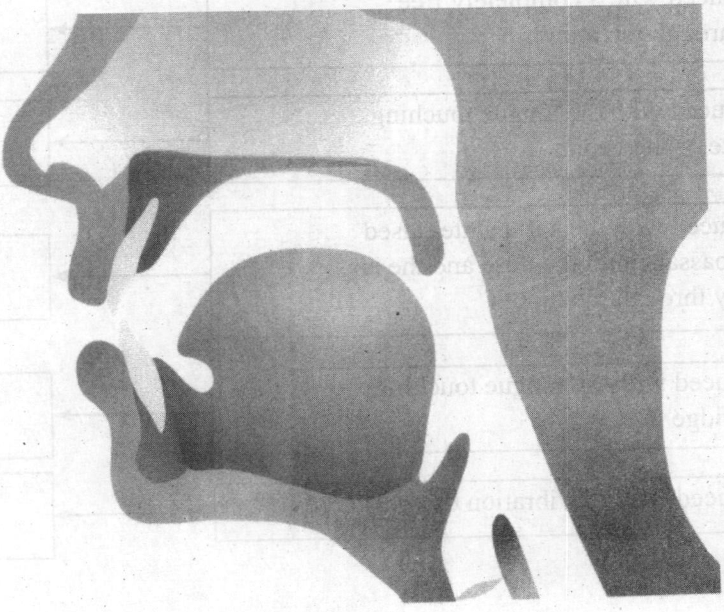

(i) Alveolar Ridge
(ii) Pharynx
(iii) Soft Palate (Velum)
(iv) Tip of the tongue
(v) Hard Palate
(vi) Root of the tongue
(vii) Hard Palate
(viii) Lower lip
(ix) Upper teeth
(x) Vocal cords
(xi) Lower teeth
(xii) Upper lip
(xiii) Back of the tongue
(xiv) Nasal cavity
(xv) Blade of the tongue

2. Choose the appropriate names of sounds to match the descriptions given.

Vowels	Oral sounds	Voiceless sounds	Velar sounds
Nasal sounds	Consonants	Alveolar sounds	Voiced sounds

Sounds produced with an obstruction or friction to the air flow in the vocal tract → ______

Sounds produced with vibration of vocal cords → ______

Sounds produced with the soft palate lowered to allow the air to pass through the nose and the passage through the mouth closed → ______

Sounds produced with a completely free flow of air through the mouth → ______

Sounds produced with the tongue touching the soft palate or the velum → ______

Sounds produced with the soft palate raised to block the passage into the nose and the air escaping only through the mouth → ______

Sounds produced with the tongue touching the alveolar ridge → ______

Sounds produced without vibration of vocal cords → ______

2.3 How we identify sounds of English

English, like other languages, has a distinct set of sounds. Some of the sounds used in English may be found in other languages also. Examples are the initial sounds in words like *pot, tin, keep, interest, egg* and *art*. But there are other sounds in English that may not be found in other languages like the initial sounds in *fool* or *zoo*. Many Indian languages, for example, do not have these sounds. Conversely Indian languages have sounds like /ɭ/ and /ɳ/, which are not found in English. It is, therefore, necessary to identify the distinct sounds of English separately.

In order to identify the sounds of a language, we make use of two of the distinctive features of speech sounds, namely they combine in specific ways to form words and individual sounds signal contrasts in meaning when they are combined to form words. When the substitution of one sound by another in a word results in a new word with a different meaning, we take the two sounds to be distinct sounds of that language. Thus, in the word, *pin*, if we substitute the sound /b/ for /p/ in the initial position, we get a new word, *bin*, and we can therefore conclude that /b/ and /p/ are distinct sounds of English. Similarly, /e/ and /ɪ/, the middle sounds in the words *set* and *sit* can be identified as distinct sounds of English, since the substitution of one in the place of another results in a different word. By repeating this process with a large number of words, we arrive at the complete set of distinct sounds in English. For example, words like *pin, bin, tin, kin, din, gin, thin, sin, shin, fin* and *chin* have different sounds only in the initial position with the second and third sounds being identical in all of them and therefore, we identify the initial sounds in these words as distinct sounds of English. Similarly, if we consider words like *hit, hat, hut, heat, hurt, hot, hoot, heart, hate* and *height*, we can identify the middle sounds in these words as distinct sounds of English. Using this procedure it has been found that there are 44 sounds in English; 24 of these are consonants like the beginning sounds of *pin, bin, tin, kin, din, gin, thin, sin, shin, fin* and *chin* and 20 are vowels like the middle sounds of *hit, hat, hut, heat, hurt, hot, hoot, heart, hate* and *height*.

> **T** The distinct sounds of a language are called ***Phonemes***. A ***Phoneme*** is the minimal unit of sound in a language. The pairs of words in which the substitution of one sound by another helps us to identify the distinctive sounds of a language are called ***Minimal Pairs***. A ***Minimal Pair*** is a pair of words that differ only in one sound. This sound, which marks the only difference between the two words, occurs in the same position in the two words, while the sounds in the other positions are the same. Some examples of minimal pairs in English are *bat* and *mat*, *chip* and *ship*, where the initial sounds are different, *sum* and *sun*, *seat* and *seed*, where the final sounds are different and *tan* and *tin* and *pen* and *pun*, where the middle sounds are different.

Exercises

L2.1 Listen to these groups of ten words and identify the words that form minimal pairs in each group.

(i) back trick clock sack walk sleek buck make bag kick
(ii) foam come room warm rude seem rhyme name zoom dome
(iii) goat not float cheat light spirit height meat cheap chat
(iv) train town won tone taught down twine drown doubt draft
(v) food wood shoot shall will should cool wool fruit spool
(vi) hang cling thing bring tuck thick long sing prick sung
(vii) pure queer year boor tore liar wear tear spire tour
(viii) just pest thirst must crest task moist thrust desk mist

Now listen and check your answers

1. Can you find three words that form minimal pairs with each of the following words?
big groom loss pitch add fad date myth rise thin
cup knack eat scent joy host chip own turn harm

2.4 How we represent sounds of English in writing

Once we have identified the sounds of a language, we need a means of representing these sounds in writing. The writing system we have, the alphabet we use, is not adequate for this purpose. If we take English, for example, there are only 26 letters in the alphabet, where as spoken English has 44 distinct sounds. Further, there are striking mismatches between the written letters and the spoken sounds in English.

In fact, there are four kinds of discrepancies between pronunciation and spelling in English:

(i) The same sound is sometimes represented by different letters,
(ii) The same letter is sometimes used to represent different sounds,
(iii) Some letters used in writing are not pronounced at all, and
(iv) Sometimes we pronounce extra sounds that do not have any representation in writing.

(i) The sound /ɪ/, for example, is represented by different letters in the following words.

village	the letter 'a'
pretty	the letter 'e'
city	the letter 'i'

women	the letter 'o'
busy	the letter 'u'

Similarly, the consonant sound /k/ is represented by different letters as in

copy	the letter 'c'
kind	the letter 'k'
chord	the letters 'ch'
queen	the letter 'q'

(ii) The following are examples of the converse type of relationship of the same letter representing different sounds.

man	the letter 'a' representing /æ/.
many	the letter 'a' representing /e/
make	the letter 'a' representing /eɪ/
mark	the letter 'a' representing /ɑː/
machine	the letter 'a' representing /ə/

With consonant sounds too, this is possible, as in

gun	the letter 'g' representing /g/
gem	the letter 'g' representing /dʒ/

Sometimes a letter within one word can represent different sounds as in *access*, where the letter *c* is first pronounced /k/ and then /s/.

(iii) Examples of words that contain letters that are not pronounced are

kneel	the letter 'k' is not pronounced
calm	the letter 'l' is not pronounced
debt	the letter 'b' is not pronounced
campaign	the letter 'g' is not pronounced
damn	the letter 'n' is not pronounced

Letters like 'k', 'l', 'b', 'g', and 'n' in the above words, which are used in spelling but are not pronounced in speech, are called ***Silent Letters***.

(iv) Examples of sounds pronounced in speech that do not have any representation in writing are found in the following words.

university	the sound /j/ in the beginning
once	the sound /w/ in the beginning

It is therefore necessary to have a different writing system where every speech sound can be represented separately by a different letter so that there is a one-to-one correspondence between the symbols used and the sounds they represent. Accordingly, a different alphabet has been designed to represent all the speech sounds used in all the languages of the world. This is known as the ***International Phonetic Alphabet***.

The International Phonetic Alphabet is based on the Roman alphabet. It uses some of the letters of the Roman alphabet like p, k, t, f, s, d, a, e, etc. In addition to these, it also has other letters that are either borrowed from other writing systems or modified from the existing letters. For example the letters θ and ð have been borrowed from the Greek writing system, the symbols ʌ and ə are modifications of v and e and the symbols tʃ and dʒ are combinations of two symbols.

The two major varieties of English, British and American are different in their accents. They differ more in vowel sounds than consonant sounds. The IPA symbols for the consonant and vowel sounds used in British and American English are given below.

Consonants – British and American		***Vowels***	***British***	***American***
pin	/p/	*feel*	/iː/	
bat	/b/	*sit*	/ɪ/	
ten	/t/	*bet*	/e/	
dog	/d/	*man*	/æ/	
cat	/k/	*father*	/ɑː/	
gun	/g/	*hot*	/ɒ/	/ɑː/
chip	/tʃ/	*saw*	/ɔː/	
jam	/dʒ/	*put*	/ʊ/	
fun	/f/	*fool*	/uː/	
van	/v/	*cut*	/ʌ/	
thin	/θ/	*bird*	/ɜː/	
that	/ð/	*about*	/ə/	
sit	/s/	*pay*	/eɪ/	
zoo	/z/	*fine*	/aɪ/	
shut	/ʃ/	*boy*	/ɔɪ/	
measure	/ʒ/	*now*	/aʊ/	
hat	/h/	*go*	/əʊ/	/oʊ/
mat	/m/	*fear*	/ɪə/	/ɪ/
nut	/n/	*pair*	/eə/	/e/
ring	/ŋ/	*pure*	/ʊə/	/ʊ/
like	/l/			
rose	/r/			
young	/j/			
win	/w/			

The vowels in words like 'hot', 'go', 'fear', 'pair' and 'pure', are different in British and American English and therefore have different symbols. We notice that the vowels in 'hot', 'fear', 'pair', and 'pure' in American English are the same as those in 'father', 'sit', 'bet', and 'put' respectively, whereas in British English these vowels are different from all other vowels. The vowel in 'go', on the other hand, is different from other vowels in both British and American English and therefore has a different symbol in both.

A major difficulty that Indian speakers have in learning English pronunciation is due to the mismatches between English spelling and pronunciation such as those illustrated above, particularly because such striking mismatches are not found in Indian languages. In most Indian languages, there is a close correspondence between the letters written and the sounds spoken and we pronounce a letter in the same way in whatever context it occurs. Further, there are neither silent letters nor extra sounds that are not represented in writing as in English. Indian speakers, therefore, tend to go by the spelling of a word in deciding how to pronounce it. This could result in mispronunciation of words such as *language* (where the letter 'a' following 'l' is pronounced the same way as it is in *large*), *determine* (where the letter 'i' following 'm' is pronounced the same way as it is in *mind*), *economy* (where the word is pronounced with an initial 'e' sound as in *editor*), *choose* (where the letter 's' is pronounced as it is in *chase*), and *honest* (where the word is pronounced with an initial 'h' sound). It is therefore essential that we learn the pronunciation of words independently and not be guided by their spellings.

Learning the 44 IPA symbols used to represent the sounds of English is essential because in order to learn the correct pronunciation of English words, (i) we have to be able to think of the sounds that combine to form these words independently, separating them from their spelling or written forms and (ii) we should be equipped to check the pronunciation of words in a dictionary, where IPA symbols are used.

Writing down speech sounds systematically and consistently using the symbols of IPA is known as ***Transcription***. Dictionaries generally give the transcriptions of words, indicating how the words should be pronounced. If we know the IPA symbols we can read these transcriptions i.e., we can find out how a word is to be pronounced, which is as important as knowing how a word is spelt. It is also useful to learn how to transcribe words using the IPA because this is how the spoken forms of words can be represented.

As there may be some differences in the IPA symbols used for some of the sounds of English in different dictionaries, you should compare the symbols given here with those used in your dictionary to find out if there are differences and what they are.

Consonant symbols	***In my dictionary***	***Vowel symbols***	***In my dictionary***
p		iː	
b		ɪ	
t		e	
d		æ	
k		ɑː	
g		ɒ/ɑː	
tʃ		ɔː	

dʒ		ʊ	
f		uː	
v		ʌ	
θ		ɜː	
ð		ə	
s		eɪ	
z		aɪ	
ʃ		ɔɪ	
ʒ		aʊ	
h		əʊ/oʊ	
m		ɪə/ ɪ	
n		eə/e	
ŋ		ʊə/ʊ	
l			
r			
j			
w			

Exercises

1. **Group the consonant and vowel symbols into two categories (i) those that are the same as the letters used in writing and (ii) those that are different from them.**
2. **Try the following to find out more about the mismatches between spelling and pronunciation in English. Look up the pronunciation of the given words in your dictionary.**

   (i) **The words *cut, but, hut, nut,* and *shut* are pronounced with the same vowel represented by /ʌ/. But the word *put* is pronounced with a different vowel, namely /ʊ/, though in writing the same letter 'u' is used in all these words.**

   The words *food, good, hood, mood,* and *wood* are all spelt with 'oo'. Are they all pronounced with the same vowel or different vowels?

   (ii) **The words *seed* and *seat* are spelt differently with 'ee' and 'ea', but in speech they are pronounced with the same vowel /iː/**

   Can you find three other pairs of words that are spelt with 'ee' and 'ea' but are pronounced with the same sound /iː/?

(iii) The words *champion* and *character* both begin with 'ch' but are pronounced differently, *champion* begins with the sound /tʃ/ as in *chair* and *character* with /k/ as in *cat*.

How is 'ch' pronounced in the words *cheap, chord, chore, church, chorus, chimp,* and *chronic*?

(iv) The words *cell* and *sell* are spelt differently but pronounced the same way with the same initial consonant /s/. Can you find two other pairs of words beginning with 'c' and 's' that are pronounced with the same consonant/s/?

(v) The letters 'l' and 'b' in the words *half* and *subtle* are silent letters as they are not pronounced in speech. Identify the silent letters in the words *wrong, psychology, palm, align, knowledge, tomb, doubt* and *Wednesday*.

(vi) The sound /j/ that occurs in the beginning of the word *unity* is an extra sound as it is not represented in the spelling of the word. What are the extra sounds found in the pronunciation of the words *queen, uniform, one, curious, computer* and *mutual*?

(vii) (a) How many sounds are there in the pronunciation of the following words?

ball	seed	free	butter
thumb	ring	trunk	simple
carry	kindle	bury	phone
neat	beauty	wheat	fear

(b) If the number of sounds does not match the number of letters, explain why.

3. The following will help you become familiar with the symbols for consonant sounds.

(i) Choose the right symbol for the sound used to pronounce the letter/s in bold in the following words.

(1)	carria**ge**	/z/ /g/ /dʒ/	(10)	feeli**ng**	/g/ /ŋ/ /k/	(19)	**z**oom	/ʒ/ /ʃ/ /z/
(2)	**d**entist	/t/ /d/ /θ/	(11)	expe**l**	/r/ /l/ /j/	(20)	plea**su**re	/ʃ/ /s/ /ʒ/
(3)	**ch**ampion	/dʒ/ /ʃ/ /tʃ/	(12)	**h**uman	/j/ /f/ /h/	(21)	**y**oung	/j/ /w/ /h/
(4)	**ph**oto	/f/ /p/ /b/	(13)	**kn**eel	/k/ /m/ /n/	(22)	**w**eather	/v/ /w/ /h/

(5)	**prize**	/z/ /s/ /ʃ/	(14)	**positive**	/p/ /b/ /v/	(23)	**through**	/ð/ /θ/ /t/
(6)	**surplus**	/ʃ/ /s/ /ʒ/	(15)	**proof**	/p/ /h/ /f/	(24)	**battle**	/b/ /v/ /p/
(7)	**tongue**	/g/ /k/ /j/	(16)	**thought**	/ð/ /t/ /θ/	(25)	**paid**	/b/ /p/ /f/
(8)	**sick**	/g/ /h/ /k/	(17)	**though**	/t/ /ð/ /d/	(26)	**this**	/t/ /θ/ /ð/
(9)	**memory**	/n/ /m/ /ŋ/	(18)	**publish**	/s/ /ʒ/ /ʃ/	(27)	**toss**	/d/ /ð/ /t/

(ii) Group the words below according to the symbols that represent the sounds used to pronounce the letter/s in bold.

cheap	**sh**eep	**j**eep	**s**eep	**z**ip	**ch**ip
lei**s**ure	i**s**	i**ss**ue	hed**ge**	tou**ch**	bea**ch**
shine	**j**am	**ch**at	**g**em	**sh**ut	**g**entle
bun**ch**	bo**ss**	gu**sh**	pic**tu**re	grud**ge**	ha**z**e
hu**sh**	clin**ch**	le**ss**	ma**tch**	ma**ch**ine	ma**j**or
zombie	**ch**ime	**J**une	**s**eat	**sh**iver	**j**acket
crun**ch**	cra**z**e	crin**ge**	free**z**e	fre**sh**	ki**ss**
gene	lo**s**e	lo**ss**	har**sh**	mer**c**y	ma**g**ic
/z/	/ʒ/	/tʃ/	/s/	/ʃ/	/dʒ/

L2.2 Close the book and listen to the words. Write the symbol for the first sound in each word on a sheet of paper.
Check your answers in the Key

chicken	....	watch	....
legal	....	zoom	....

hockey	....	circle	....
geometry	....	baggage	....
yellow	....	thief	....
design	....	temple	....
neat	....	pattern	....
photo	....	there	....
guard	....	wrong	....
cancel	....	mild	....
sugar	....	vacant	....

4. The following will help you become familiar with the symbols for vowel sounds.
   (i) Choose the right symbol for the sound used to pronounce the letter/s in bold in the following words.

(1)	**income**	/iː/ /ɪ/ /e/	(10)	**court**	/ɔː/ /ɒ/ /ɑː/	(19)	**clear**	/iː/ /ɪ/ /ɪə/
(2)	**admit**	/ʊ/ /ʌ/ /ə/	(11)	**pull**	/uː/ /ʌ/ /ʊ/	(20)	**sure**	/ʊə/ /uː/ /ʊ/
(3)	**article**	/ɒ/ /ɑː/ /ɔː/	(12)	**earth**	/e/ /ɑː/ /ɜː/	(21)	**cot**	/ɔː/ /ɒ/ /ɑː/
(4)	**action**	/e/ /æ/ /ɑː/	(13)	**bite**	/aɪ/ /ɪ/ /e/	(22)	**care**	/aɪ/ /eə/ /e/
(5)	**evening**	/ɪ/ /e/ /iː/	(14)	**cat**	/e/ /æ/ /ɒ/	(23)	**boat**	/ɔː/ /ɒ/ /əʊ/or/oʊ/
(6)	**ugly**	/ə/ /ʊ/ /ʌ/	(15)	**shut**	/ʌ/ /ʊ/ /ə/	(24)	**hate**	/eɪ/ /eə/ /aɪ/
(7)	**engine**	/e/ /æ/ /ə/	(16)	**out**	/ɒ/ /aʊ/ /əʊ/	(25)	**tour**	/uː/ /ʊ/ /ʊə/

(8)		/ʌ/	(17)		/ɔɪ/	(26)	/e/
	orange	/ɑː/		**say**	/aɪ/	**hair**	/eɪ/
		/ɒ/			/eɪ/		/eə/
(9)		/ʊ/	(18)		/eɪ/	(27)	/ɒ/
	boots	/ʌ/		**soil**	/ɔɪ/	**note**	/ɔː/
		/uː/			/aɪ/		/əʊ/or/oʊ/

(ii) Group the words according to the symbols that represent the sounds used to pronounce the letter/s in bold.

angry	army	equal	editor	item	ox
evil	idea	absent	office	argue	empty
set	pot	hand	beat	night	park
pen	treat	card	ninth	pack	cot
egg	eagle	identity	object	aunt	add
/e/	/aɪ/	/iː/	/ɑː/	/æ/	/ɒ/ or /ɑː/

cool	turn	gun	good	polite	lord
account	author	earn	about	umbrella	organ
love	short	put	collect	soon	bird
orbit	urgent	understand	obtain	afraid	affair
mood	money	wood	search	material	score
/uː/	/ʊ/	/ʌ/	/ə/	/ɜː/	/ɔː/

owl	ice	oil	aim	ear	old
coach	boil	dear	time	loud	same
kind	sound	day	tear	load	poison
idea	own	aid	open	oyster	ivory
gate	near	join	down	gold	kite
/ɪə/ or /ɪ/	/eɪ/	/aɪ/	/aʊ/	/ɔɪ/	/əʊ/ or /oʊ/

L2.3 Close the book and listen to the words. Write the symbol for the vowel sound/s in each word on a sheet of paper.
Check your answers in the Key.

net	....	poor	....
hurt	....	cop	....
cool	....	clear	....
nut	....	bear	....
hide	....	heart	....
seat	....	coil	....
tin	....	land	....
bore	....	great	....
sound	....	award	....
hood	....	coal	....

L2.4. Listen to two jokes read by a British English speaker, an American English speaker and an Indian speaker.
First listen without looking at the texts given below and then listen again following the texts.

Bubba and Becky are delighted when the adoption centre tells them they have a wonderful Russian baby. On the way home from the adoption centre they stop by the local college and enrol in night courses to learn Russian. 'You going to Russia on holiday?' asks the registration clerk. 'No,' replies Bubba. 'We just adopted a Russian baby. When he starts talking we'll want to know what he's saying.' (*Man walks into a bar* The Ultimate Collection of Jokes and One-liners Stephen Arnott and Mike Haskins p. 175)

A foreign visitor to England was having trouble with the pronunciation of words like 'enough', 'bough', and 'though'. He thought he was getting the hang of it until he saw the newspaper headline 'Fete pronounced success.' (*Man walks into a bar* The Ultimate Collection of Jokes and One-liners Stephen Arnott and Mike Haskins p. 279)

Read the two jokes and record your readings on a tape or CD and (b) play them to your teacher or friend/s and get their feedback on your readings.

Chapter summary

1. Speech is made up of series of sounds. It conveys meaning because speech sounds have four important features that distinguish them from other sounds, namely, (a) they are distinct entities that can be separated from one another, (b) they do not carry any meaning in themselves, (c) they convey specific meanings only in specific combinations and (d) they signal contrasts in meaning in these specific meaningful combinations.

2. (a) Though ***Phonetics***, the scientific study of speech sounds, deals with the production, transmission and perception of speech sounds, the main focus in learning pronunciation is on production of speech sounds, since the sounds of a language are generally described and classified in terms of their manner and place of production.

   (b) The organs of speech that play an important role in the production of speech sounds are the larynx that has the vocal cords and the glottis, the soft palate or the velum, the hard palate, the alveolar ridge, the teeth, the lips, the tongue that can be divided into five parts – the tip, the blade, the front, the back and the root – and the nasal cavity.

   (c) Speech sounds are produced when the air stream from the lungs enters the vocal tract through the pharynx (the windpipe) and undergoes changes by either passing through spaces of different sizes and shapes or by encountering different kinds and degrees of obstruction caused by the movement of various speech organs, before it comes out of the oral or nasal cavity.

   (d) Two main types of speech sounds are ***Vowels*** and ***Consonants***. ***Vowels*** are sounds that are produced without any obstruction to the flow of air as it passes from the larynx through the vocal tract and escapes through the mouth or the nose. ***Consonants*** are sounds which are produced with a closure or a narrowing in the vocal tract, which causes an obstruction or a friction to the flow of air as it passes through the vocal tract.

3. (a) When the substitution of one sound by another in a word results in a new word with a different meaning, we take the two sounds to be distinct sounds of that language. By following this process with a large number of words in English, we can identify 44 distinct sounds in English, 24 consonants and 20 vowels.

   (b) The distinctive sounds of a language are called ***Phonemes*** and the pairs of words which differ only in one sound in a specific position are called ***Minimal Pairs***.

4. (a) In English there are striking mismatches between pronunciation and spelling and therefore we cannot depend on spelling to decide the pronunciation of words.

(b) ***The International Phonetic Alphabet*** has been developed to represent in writing all the different sounds in all the languages, as no writing system has symbols to represent all these sounds. Representing speech sounds using the symbols of IPA is called ***Transcription***.

(c) Each of the 44 sounds of English is represented by a different symbol in IPA. As there are differences between American and British accents, there are differences in the pronunciation of certain sounds, particularly vowels, and therefore these vowels are given different symbols in American and British English.

(d) Learning the IPA symbols used to represent English sounds is very important as this helps us to read the transcription of words indicating their correct pronunciation in dictionaries.

3
English consonants

One way to think of consonant sounds is as the solid blocks with which we construct words, phrases, and sentences. These blocks are connected or held together by a more malleable or fluid material – the vowels of the language. Together, they provide the basic building materials we need to create the architecture of language.

Celce-Murcia M, Brinton D.M & Goodwin J.M *Teaching Pronunciation* 1996 p. 37

...the consonants form the bones, the skeleton of English words and give them their basic shape.

O'Connor, J.D *Better English Pronunciation* 1998, 2nd Edition p. 24

In most circumstances, substituting one consonant with another is more likely to lead to communication breakdown than when a wrong vowel is used.

Martin Hewings *Pronunciation Practice Activities* 2004 p. 15

PREVIEW

We have seen that in learning English pronunciation, it is useful to begin with the individual sounds of English, the consonants and the vowels. Which should we learn first, consonants or vowels? There is one good reason why we could begin with consonants. Consonants are produced when different articulators in the vocal tract move, come into contact and cause different degrees of obstruction to the flow of air. The place and manner of the obstruction to the air flow are obvious and therefore it is easy to describe how each consonant is produced and to distinguish between different consonants in terms of the place and manner of articulation.

We begin this chapter by describing and classifying English consonants.

In speech we combine sounds and when we do so, individual sounds undergo certain changes. After describing how individual consonants are produced, we'll examine how combining with other sounds affects their pronunciation.

There are a few changes in the pronunciation of consonants that are due to grammatical factors and we'll see what these changes are.

Finally, we'll consider how spelling affects the pronunciation of consonants.

Thus this chapter has four units, namely,

3.1 How we describe and classify English consonants
3.2 How combining with other sounds affects pronunciation of consonants
3.3 How grammar affects pronunciation of consonants
3.4 How spelling affects pronunciation of consonants.

3.1 How we describe and classify English consonants

Consonants are sounds that involve some obstruction to the flow of air in the vocal tract. It is as if the air moves through an obstacle course in the vocal tract when consonant sounds are produced. As the air encounters different degrees of obstruction, different consonant sounds are produced. We therefore distinguish consonant sounds from one another in terms of the degree of obstruction to the flow of air in the vocal tract. Different degrees of obstruction result because of difference in

(a) the manner of production of the sound and
(b) the place of production with different articulators moving in different ways.

In terms of the manner of production, consonants in English are divided into six groups.

(i) Plosives
(ii) Fricatives
(iii) Affricates
(iv) Nasals
(v) Laterals and
(vi) Approximants

Plosives

Plosives are sounds that are produced with a complete closure in the vocal tract, followed by a sudden release of air and a resulting plosion or noise (like a pop). There are six plosives in English, /p/, /b/, /t/, /d/, /k/, and /g/ as in *pat, bat, tin, din, cot* and *got*. The articulation of a plosive takes place in four stages.

(a) One articulator moves against another or two articulators move against each other in such a way that there is a complete closure in the vocal tract and no air is allowed to escape. This is called the closure phase.
(b) The air behind the closure in the vocal tract is compressed, as it cannot escape. This is called the hold phase.
(c) The two articulators forming the closure move apart and the compressed air behind is released with a plosion or noise (like a pop). This is called the release phase.
(d) The release of air is sometimes accompanied by aspiration in the case of some plosives. This is called the post-release phase.

Plosives are also called ***Stops*** because the flow of air is completely cut off or stopped by a complete closure in the vocal tract in the production of these sounds.

The six plosives are divided into three groups depending on the place of articulation and the two articulators involved.

The plosives /p/ and /b/ are produced with the two lips coming together to produce a closure that blocks the flow of air completely and the air being released when the lips move apart. The sounds /p/ and /b/ are therefore called ***Bilabial plosives***.

The plosives /t/ and /d/ are produced with the blade of the tongue pressed against the alveolar ridge to form a closure and the air getting released when the tongue moves away. The sounds /t/ and /d/ are therefore called ***Alveolar plosives***.

The plosives /k/ and /g/ are produced with the back of the tongue pressed against the soft palate or the velum to form a closure and the air getting released when the tongue moves away. The sounds /k/ and /g/ are therefore called ***Velar plosives***.

The two sounds in each of these three groups are distinguished from each other in terms of three features:

(i) the presence or absence of voicing,

(ii) the presence or absence of aspiration and

(iii) the length of a preceding vowel.

(a) In each pair of plosives, the first sound is always voiceless, where as the second is generally voiced, particularly when it occurs in the middle of a word. That is, the plosives /p/, /t/, and /k/ are always voiceless, but /b/, /d/, and /g/ are voiced, particularly when they occur in the middle of a word as in *rabid*, *ladder* and *bigger*. The presence of voicing in /b/, /d/, and /g/ in these words is the only feature by which they can be distinguished from the words *rapid*, *latter* and *bicker*, where /p/, /t/, and /k/ are voiceless.

(b) ***Aspiration*** is a phonetic feature that characterizes sounds that are produced with an audible puff of air, which sounds like 'h'. The plosives /p/, /t/, and /k/, when they occur in the initial position in a word, are aspirated. But /b/, /d/, and /g/ are never aspirated. This difference can be easily seen in words like *pat* and *bat*, *tin* and *din*, and *cot* and *got*. Another difference between /p/, /t/, and /k/ and /b/, /d/, and /g/ is that when these sounds occur in the initial position, /p/, /t/, and /k/ can be preceded by /s/ as in *spot*, *stop* and *skit*, but /b/, /d/, and /g/ cannot be preceded by any other consonant. But when /p/, /t/, and /k/ are preceded by /s/ in the initial position, they are not aspirated.

(c) Another difference is that vowels are longer when they occur before /b/, /d/, and /g/ than they are when they occur before /p/, /t/, and /k/, as in *cab* and *cap*, *need* and *neat*, *goad* and *goat* and *bag* and *back*.

Thus consonant sounds are described in terms of three features, (a) the manner of articulation, (b) the place of articulation and (c) the presence or absence of voicing and the description given to each consonant is unique to it. The six plosives are described as given below:

/p/ voiceless, bilabial plosive
/b/ voiced, bilabial plosive
/t/ voiceless, alveolar plosive
/d/ voiced, alveolar plosive
/k/ voiceless, velar plosive
/g/ voiced, velar plosive

Fricatives

Fricatives are sounds that are produced with the air passing through a very narrow passage in the vocal tract making a hissing sound. In the production of these sounds, two articulators come very close but do not touch each other, thus creating a narrow passage and there is friction as the air passes through this narrow passage. There are nine fricatives in English, and /f/, /v/, /θ/, /ð/, /s/, /z/, /ʃ/, /ʒ/, and /h/ as in *fan, van, thin, this, sip, zip, ship, measure* and *hat* (/ʒ/ cannot occur initially in English and in *measure* it occurs in the middle).

An interesting difference between plosives and fricatives is that fricatives are ***Continuant consonants*** i.e., sounds that we can continue making without interruption as long as we have air in our lungs. Plosives are not continuants as they are marked by a complete closure in the vocal tract. Fricatives, in contrast, are produced with an incomplete closure in the vocal tract, as there is only a narrowing of the passage through which the air passes.

The nine fricatives are divided into five groups depending on the place of articulation and the articulators involved.

The fricatives /f/ and /v/ are produced with the lower lip coming into contact with the upper teeth, thus forming a narrow passage through which the air escapes. The sounds /f/ and /v/ are therefore called ***Labio-dental fricatives***.

The fricatives /θ/ and /ð/ are produced with the tongue placed inside the teeth, the tip of the tongue touching the inside of the lower teeth and the blade touching the inside of the upper teeth and the air passing through the narrow gap between the tongue and the teeth. The sounds /θ/ and /ð/ are therefore called ***Dental fricatives***.

The fricatives /s/ and /z/ are produced with the tip and the blade of the tongue moving near the alveolar ridge and the air passing through the narrow passage between the tongue and the alveolar with audible friction. The sounds /s/ and /z/ are therefore called ***Alveolar fricatives***.

The fricatives /ʃ/ and /ʒ/ are produced with the tip and the blade of the tongue moving near the alveolar and the front of the tongue moving near the hard palate and the air escaping through the narrow passage between the tongue and the hard palate just behind the alveolar. The sounds /ʃ/ and /ʒ/ are therefore called ***Palato-alveolar fricatives***.

The fricative /h/ is produced with the air from the lungs passing through a narrow passage in the glottis (between the vocal cords) with friction and is therefore called a ***Glottal fricative***. The tongue can take different positions during the production of /h/ depending on the vowel that follows this sound in speech. Thus, for example, when we say the word *hat*, the tongue takes the position it takes for /æ/ even as we begin to produce the sound /h/ and similarly, when we say *hit*, the tongue takes the position for /ɪ/ in producing /h/. As a result of this influence of the following vowel on /h/, in speech the sound /h/ always acquires the characteristic features of the following vowel. But it is important to remember that /h/ is a consonant sound, though it sounds very much like the following vowel in speech.

Like the plosives, the fricatives in each of the groups mentioned above (except the glottal fricative /h/) can also be distinguished from each other in terms of the presence or absence of voicing. The first in each pair, /f/, /θ/, /s/, and /ʃ/ are voiceless fricatives and the second in each pair, /v/, /ð/, /z/ and /ʒ/ are voiced fricatives. /h/ is a voiceless fricative.

The nine fricatives can be described as given below:

/f/	voiceless, labio-dental fricative
/v/	voiced, labio-dental fricative
/θ/	voiceless, dental fricative
/ð/	voiced, dental fricative
/s/	voiceless, alveolar fricative
/z/	voiced, alveolar fricative
/ʃ/	voiceless, palato-alveolar fricative
/ʒ/	voiced, palato-alveolar fricative
/h/	voiceless, glottal fricative

Affricates

Affricates are sounds that begin as plosives but end as fricatives. There are two affricates in English, /tʃ/ and /dʒ/ as in *cheap* and *jeep*. The initial sound in *cheap*, /tʃ/ begins like the plosive /t/, with the articulators going through the closure and the hold phases, but instead of a rapid release of air with a plosion, the tongue moves to the position for the fricative /ʃ/. Thus the plosive is begun, but not completed and is followed by the fricative sound. The affricate is therefore composed of two sounds, a plosive /t/ and a fricative /ʃ/. Similarly the initial sound of *jeep*, /dʒ/ is a combination of /d/ and /ʒ/. This articulatory feature of affricates is indicated by using a combination of two symbols to represent these sounds /tʃ/ and /dʒ/.

Though affricates are considered to be composed of two sounds, a plosive and a fricative, they are independent phonemes (distinct sounds which signal contrasts in meaning) of English as seen in *tip*, *ship* and *chip*, *tot*, *shot* and *jot*, *dam* and *jam* and *chunk* and *junk*.

The affricates end with the fricative sounds /ʃ/ and /ʒ/ and are therefore described as palato-alveolar consonants. The first in the pair, /tʃ/ is voiceless and the second, /dʒ/ is voiced. The two affricates are therefore described as given below.

/tʃ/	voiceless, palato-alveolar affricate
/dʒ/	voiced, palato-alveolar affricate

> **T** Fricatives in English are often divided into two groups, ***Sibilants*** and ***Nonsibilants***. The sounds /s/, /z/, /ʃ/, and /ʒ/ are produced with a high pitched hissing sound and are called ***sibilants*** and the sounds /f/, /v/, /θ/, /ð/ and /h/ are produced with much less friction and energy and are called ***nonsibilants***. The two affricates /tʃ/ and /dʒ/ both have a sibilant release and are therefore considered sibilants.

Nasals

Nasals are sounds that are produced with the soft palate lowered to allow the air to pass through the nose and with a complete closure in the mouth to prevent the air from passing through the mouth. There are three nasals in English, /m/, /n/, and /ŋ/ as in *meat*, *neat* and *sing* (/ŋ/ cannot occur initially in English and in *sing* it occurs at the end). These three sounds can be distinguished from one another in terms of the place in the mouth where the complete closure takes place. In producing /m/, the two lips come together to form a closure, in producing /n/, the closure is between the tongue and the alveolar and in producing /ŋ/, the closure is between the back of the tongue and the soft palate or the velum. All the three nasal consonants in English are voiced sounds.

We see that the three nasals /m/, /n/, and /ŋ/ are produced with a closure at the same place as the plosives /p/ and /b/, /t/ and /d/ and /k/ and /g/. But the major difference is that, in the case of /m/, /n/, and /ŋ/, the air is allowed to pass through the nose with the soft palate lowered, where as, in the case of the plosives, the soft palate is raised to block the passage of air through the nose and there is a sudden release of the air through the mouth, which results in a plosion. Further, plosives can be voiceless as in /p/, /t/, and /k/ or voiced as in /b/, /d/, and /g/, where as all the three nasal consonants /m/, /n/, and /ŋ/ are voiced.

The three nasals are described as given below.

/m/	voiced, bilabial nasal
/n/	voiced, alveolar nasal
/ŋ/	voiced, velar nasal

The manner of production of the nasal consonants becomes clear if we try to produce the sounds /m/, /n/, and /ŋ/ pinching the nose closed. We find that /m/ sounds like /b/, /n/ sounds like /d/ and /ŋ/ sounds like /g/ because the nasal consonants are produced only when the air passes through the nose with the mouth closed.

Laterals

Laterals are sounds that are produced with a complete closure between the front of the tongue and some part of the hard palate and the air escaping along the sides of the tongue. There is one lateral consonant in English, /l/ as in *lap* and *lit*, which is produced with the closure formed between the front of the tongue and the alveolar ridge. The sound /l/ is voiced.

The actual pronunciation of /l/ differs depending on the context in which it occurs in speech. When /l/ occurs in the final position in a word as in *feel*, *fall* or *full* or before a consonant as in *gold*, *help* or *milk*, it is pronounced with the back of the tongue raised and has the quality of a back vowel like /ʊ/. This /l/ sound is called the dark /l/. In contrast, when /l/ occurs before a vowel as in *leap*, *loop*, *lap* or *lot*, it is pronounced with the front of the tongue raised and has the quality of a front vowel like /ɪ/. This /l/ sound is called the clear /l/.

/l/	voiced, alveolar lateral

Approximants

Approximants are sounds produced with the articulators approaching each other but not close enough to produce a closure or friction so that the air escapes freely through the gap between the articulators. There are three approximants in English, /r/, /w/, and /j/ as in *red*, *wet* and *yet*.

The sound /r/ is produced with the tip of the tongue approaching the back of the alveolar ridge but not actually making contact with it and the air escaping through the gap between. The tip of the tongue is in fact slightly curled backward in the direction of the hard palate during the production of this sound. Sounds that are produced with the tip of the tongue curled backward in this fashion are called ***Retroflex sounds***.

The sound /w/ is produced with the back of the tongue raised to take a position similar to the one in producing /ʊ/ and the lips getting rounded.

The sound /j/ is produced with the front of the tongue raised to take a position similar to the one in producing /ɪ/ and the lips being spread.

The sounds /w/ and /j/ have also been called semi-vowels because of their phonetic similarity to the vowels /ʊ/ and /ɪ/, but they are consonants and not vowels because like consonants, they occur before vowels.

The three approximants, /r/, /w/, and /j/ are all voiced sounds. They can be described as given below.

/r/	voiced, palato-alveolar approximant
/w/	voiced, bilabial approximant
/j/	voiced, palatal approximant

T Of the 24 consonants, 16 are listed in pairs, the first described as voiceless and the second as voiced. These are /p/ and /b/, /t/ and /d/, /k/ and /g/, /f/ and /v/, /θ/ and /ð/, /s/ and /z/, /ʃ/ and /ʒ/, /tʃ/ and /dʒ/. The second sound in each pair is not always voiced. The presence or absence of voicing in these sounds depends on the position in which they occur. When they occur in the final position, they are hardly voiced. Some phoneticians have, therefore, suggested that a different phonetic criterion could be used to distinguish between the two sounds in each pair. It is said that the first sound is produced with greater force than the second sound. So the voiceless first sounds in these pairs are called ***Fortis*** (meaning strong) sounds and the voiced second sounds are called ***Lenis*** (meaning weak) sounds. But the force used in producing sounds is very difficult to measure or define.

Table 3.1 shows the 24 consonants of English classified according to their manner of articulation, place of articulation and whether they are voiced or not.

Indian speakers need to practise a few consonants of English carefully as they are different from the sounds in Indian languages. There are three pairs of consonants in English, viz. /v/ /w/, /θ/ /ð/, and /t/ /d/, that are pronounced differently from similar sounds in Indian languages.

(i) A very important problem that Indian speakers have with English consonants is with the sounds /v/ and /w/, the first being a labio-dental fricative, while the second is a bilabial approximant. Indian speakers are familiar with only one similar sound /ʋ/, which is a voiced labio-dental approximant and which occurs in Indian languages. Indian speakers therefore tend to use this sound /ʋ/ in place of both /v/ and /w/ and are not able to differentiate clearly between pairs of words like *vice* and *wise*, *vine* and *wine*, and *vie* and *why*. But the distinction between /v/ and /w/ is crucial in English as there are a number of words that are different in meaning because of the use of one or the other of these two sounds. It is therefore essential for Indian speakers to learn to use these two sounds correctly in speech so that they are able to distinguish between words with /v/ and /w/.

(ii) /θ/ and /ð/ in English are dental fricatives unlike the similar sounds /t̪/ and /d̪/ that Indians use, which are dental plosives.

(iii) /t/ and /d/ in English are alveolar plosives unlike the similar sounds /ʈ/ and /ɖ/ that Indians use, which are retroflex plosives.

Table 3.1 Classification of English Consonants

Place of Articulation ------------- ***Manner of Articulation***	***Bilabial***	***Labiodental***	***Dental***	***Alveolar***	***Palato-Alveolar***	***Palatal***	***Velar***	***Glottal***
Plosive *Voiceless* *Voiced*	/p/ /b/			/t/ /d/			/k/ /g/	
Fricative *Voiceless* *Voiced*		/f/ /v/	/θ/ /ð/	/s/ /z/	/ʃ/ /ʒ/			/h/
Affricate *Voiceless* *Voiced*					/tʃ/ /dʒ/			
Nasal *Voiced*	/m/			/n/			/ŋ/	
Lateral *Voiced*				/l/				
Approximant *Voiced*	/w/				/r/	/j/		

Exercises

The following exercises are of two types, the first focusing on the description and classification of English consonants and the second on the correct pronunciation of English consonants.

Focusing on description and classification of English consonants

1. Match the consonant types with the features in the boxes by drawing connecting lines with arrows.

Composed of two sounds
Beginning as a plosive
Ending as a fricative

Complete closure
between two articulators
Air behind the closure
is compressed
The two articulators
forming the closure move
apart and the air escapes
with a plosion

Complete closure between
the centre of the tongue and
the alveolar ridge
Air escapes along
the sides of the tongue

APPROXIMANTS

NASALS

PLOSIVES

FRICATIVES

LATERALS

AFFRICATES

Complete closure
between two articulators
in the mouth
Soft palate is lowered
to allow the air to pass
through the nose

Two articulators
approach each other
No closure or
narrowing
Air escapes freely
through the gap
between the two
articulators

Air passes through a very
narrow passage
Air comes out with a hissing
sound

2. (i) (a) Write down words from columns A and B that begin with the same consonant.

A	B
market	thought
normal	phenomenon
politics	determine
unity	remember
begin	shiver
kitchen	zest
gallant	science
challenge	variety
generous	humour
welcome	lovely
terror	merit
dynamic	canal
shortage	pencil
thesis	knowledge
vehement	cheerful
certain	beautiful
them	government
feminine	jewelry
heredity	telephone
little	warmth
writing	yellow
zoom	therefore

(b) There are 22 words in columns A and B above that begin with 22 different consonants. Which are the 2 consonants that do not begin any of these words?

(ii) (a) For each word in column A, find a word from column B that ends with the same consonant as that which begins the word in column A.

A	B
board	soap
violet	polish
magic	contain
charming	safe
lazy	breathe
rain	solid
wish	league
temple	browse
citizen	room

kneel	permit
genuine	trick
usual	teach
pattern	derive
philosophy	south
diversion	long
theme	bottle
careful	notice
thus	damage
gaudy	rub
shooting	beige
zip	
hungry	

(b) There are 22 words in column A and 20 words in column B. 2 words in column B do not match any words in column A, i.e., 2 words in column B end with consonants that do not occur in the beginning of any words in column A. Find these 2 consonants.

(c) 4 words in column A do not match any words in column B, i.e., 4 words in column A begin with consonants that do not occur at the end of any words in column B. Find these 4 consonants.

(iii) For each word in column A, find a word from column B that begins with the same consonant as that which ends the word in column A.

A	B
youth	gate
model	sensitive
tribe	shield
captain	feast
lodge	theory
zip	vacation
poem	knife
phrase	kindness
cherish	there
soothe	patient
batch	deceive
knock	gentle
wig	luxury
grief	balance
dominate	zenith
justice	table

valid	choice
shave	mother

Notice that there are only 18 words here in columns A and B. The 6 consonants you identified above, 2 that do not occur in the beginning of words and 4 that do not occur at the end of words are not found here either at the end or the beginning of words.

(iv) Group the following words into the five categories given depending on the type of consonant that occurs in the beginning.

desire	wisdom	physics	thread	dominant	jubilant
manager	yesterday	generous	primary	round	number
grateful	writing	terrible	charge	circle	general
variety	chemistry	showman	character	gaudy	sacrifice
phenomenon	judicious	chivalry	wonderful	knife	pleasure
wings	chord	cancel	vegetable	charismatic	question
knowledge	pseudonym	psychology	yellow	qualify	kingdom
therefore	tremendous	breakable	hurricane	chafe	material

Plosive Fricative Affricate Nasal Approximant

(v) Group the following words into the six categories given depending on the type of consonant that occurs at the end

dialog	bottle	magic	reflect	belong	positive
mouth	strength	bottom	breathe	content	bomb
ideal	contrast	sandwich	egotism	plastic	triumph
bank	drawing	language	elephant	belief	inspect
hostage	hanging	flag	complex	insecure	monarch
divulge	civilize	attract	division	unique	exchange
graphic	excess	achieve	disguise	arrange	devise
polish	tough	package	fanfare	housewife	wise
teach	prize	spice	morpheme	long	house

Bilabial Labio-dental Dental Alveolar Palato-alveolar Velar

(vi) What is the difference between the following pairs of sounds?

/p/, /t/
/b/, /g/
/k/, /g/
/d/, /z/

(vii) (a) How does /ŋ/ differ from /n/ and /g/?
(b) How does /dʒ/ differ from /d/ and /ʒ/?
(c) How does /f/ differ from /p/ and /h/?

(viii) (a) /p/ is similar to _________ in the same way as /t/ is to /n/ and _________ to /ŋ/.
(b) /t/ is different from /s/ in the same way as _________ is from /z/.
(c) The difference between /tʃ/ and /dʒ/ is the same as that between _________ and /ð/, /ʃ/ and _________, _________ and /g/.

Focusing on correct pronunciation of English consonants

1. Fill in the blanks with the sound or sounds you produce if you follow the instructions given. Use the correct symbols for the sounds.
   (i) If you move the tip and blade of your tongue very near the alveolar ridge behind your teeth and let the air pass through the narrow passage, you produce _________ or _________.
   (ii) If you bring your lips together to block the air and then let the air escape through the nose, you produce _________.
   (iii) If you press the back of the tongue against the soft palate to block the air and then release the air suddenly by moving the tongue away, you produce _________ or _________.
   (iv) If you move the blade of your tongue to touch the inside of your upper teeth and let the air escape through the narrow passage between the tongue and the teeth, you produce _________ or _________.
   (v) If you move the tip of your tongue to approach the back of the alveolar ridge curling it backwards slightly and let the air escape through the gap between, you produce _________.
   (vi) If you open your mouth and breathe out, trying to make a noise, you produce _________.
   (vii) If you move the front of the tongue to touch the alveolar ridge and let the air escape along the sides of the tongue, you produce _________.
   (viii) If you press your lips together to block the air and then suddenly release the air through the mouth, you produce _________ or _________.
   (ix) If you move the blade of your tongue against the alveolar ridge to block the air and then let the air escape through the nose, you produce _________.
   (x) If you move your lower lip to touch your upper teeth and let the air pass through the narrow passage between the two, you produce _________ or _________.
   (xi) If you press the blade of your tongue against the alveolar ridge to block the air and then release the air suddenly through the mouth, you produce _________ or _________.

(xii) If you move the back of your tongue against the soft palate to block the air and then let the air escape through the nose, you produce __________.

L3.1 Close your book and listen to groups of 3 words. Decide whether the given sound occurs in the beginning, middle or end. Write B, M or E in the appropriate boxes in the table on page 58 to show the place of occurrence of the sound in the word. Check your answers in the Key.

/p/	surprise	paint	trip
	pass	hype	export
	group	compose	positive
/b/	rubbish	benefit	cherub
	bottom	problem	subvert
	tribe	robe	baker
/t/	tease	night	internal
	boot	time	motorist
	contain	tongue	table
/d/	hiding	mould	reduce
	round	delete	fluid
	donkey	India	danger
/k/	cattle	election	magnetic
	packing	comfort	kingdom
	attack	frolic	inspector
/g/	rogue	bargain	magazine
	girl	mug	log
	propagate	guest	gate
/tʃ/	touch	search	teach
	chirp	natural	cheat
	factual	channel	maturity
/dʒ/	gist	magic	jute
	dodge	gentle	engage
	vigilant	purge	jolly
/θ/	thief	teeth	south
	nothing	method	thump
	both	thesis	truthful

/f/	mischief	scientific	signify
	inform	function	finger
	foolish	leaf	safe
/v/	voice	reveal	improve
	service	vague	favourite
	have	leave	vote
/s/	listing	mistake	separate
	simple	greatness	famous
	promise	circle	disturb
/ʃ/	sharp	furnish	special
	polish	concession	shape
	bashful	shining	English
/l/	life	allot	liquid
	release	model	shallow
	vowel	loud	control

SOUND	***1***	***2***	***3***	***4***	***5***	***6***	***7***	***8***	***9***
/p/									
/b/									
/t/									
/d/									
/k/									
/g/									
/tʃ/									
/dʒ/									
/θ/									
/f/									
/v/									
/s/									
/ʃ/									
/l/									

In order to get the pronunciation of consonant sounds right, it is useful to practise them in pairs in such a way that the distinctive features of the sounds are focused on and learnt correctly. The following exercises deal with some of the pairs of consonant sounds that need to be distinguished clearly in speech.

(1) /p/ /t/

L3.2 Listen to pairs of words and decide which sound each word begins with. Write 1 or 2 to show whether the first or the second word in each pair begins with the sound given.

/p/	/t/
....	....
....	....
....	....
....	....
....	....
....	....

2. Repeat the pairs of words in L3.2 (given in the Key) making a clear distinction between the two sounds.

L3.3 Listen to the sentences and decide whether the words in A or B were used to complete the sentences.

	A	B
(i) She doesn't know much about computers; she can only cut and _________ things.	paste	taste
(ii) The workers decided to _________ outside the gates of the factory.	picket	ticket
(iii) The _________ of dishonesty harmed his career.	paint	taint
(iv) The performance of the new recruits is on _________ with the senior engineers.	par	tar
(v) You should not _________ into the personal lives of others.	pry	try

3. Repeat the sentences in L3.3 taking care to pronounce the appropriate words in the blanks correctly.
4. Work in pairs. First student 1 reads the sentence using one of the words given in the blank and student 2 gives the appropriate response. Next student 2 reads the sentence using the other word in the blank and student 1 gives the appropriate response.

(i) What do you do when you have _______________? (pests/tests)

We study all night.
We use this powder.

(ii) What about this _______________? (pile/tile)

I'll answer all those letters today.
It's broken. We'll have to replace it.

(iii) Why don't we use a different _______________? (pipe/type)

This is easy to read.
The others cannot withstand the heat.

(iv) They told us about the _______________. (poll/toll)

It gave us an idea of what people thought.
We didn't know we had to pay to cross the bridge.

(v) The child dropped the _______________. (pin/tin)

It was sealed and no harm done.
You won't be able to find it. It is too small.

(A)

5. Match each of the word definitions with the correct word and check its pronunciation in a dictionary and practise it.

A person who is successful in business or industry and has become rich and powerful	tenant
A person who sells tickets for popular events illegally at a higher price	techie
A person who makes illegal copies of video tapes, computer programmes, books etc.	punter
A person who is the first to study and develop a particular area of knowledge	tout
A person whose job is to receive and pay out money in a bank	plaintiff
A person who owns a business, a hotel land or buildings	tycoon
A person who buys or uses a particular product or service	teller
A person who pays rent for the use of a building or land to its owner	proprietor
A person who knows a lot about or is very interested in technology, especially computers	pioneer
A person who makes a formal complaint against somebody in court	pirate

(2) /p/ /f/

L3.4 Listen to pairs of words and decide which sound each word begins with. Write 1 or 2 to show whether the first or the second word in each pair begins with the sound given.

/p/	/t/
....	....
....	....
....	....
....	....
....	....
....	....

6. Repeat the pairs of words in L3.4 (given in the Key) making a clear distinction between the two sounds.

L3.5 Listen to the sentences and decide whether the words in A or B were used to complete the sentences.

		A	B
(i)	We don't want to push the children too much; it is better for them to work at their own ______________.	pace	face
(ii)	His mother asked him not to drive very ______________.	past	fast
(iii)	He was looking through a huge ______________ of papers trying to find the missing letter.	pile	file
(iv)	He is so ______________ that I can't think of depending on him.	pickle	fickle
(v)	The computer has another ______________ where you can connect a modem.	port	fort

7. Repeat the sentences in L3.5 taking care to pronounce the appropriate words in the blanks correctly.

8. Work in pairs. First student 1 reads the sentence using one of the words given in the blank and student 2 gives the appropriate response. Next student 2 reads the sentence using the other word in the blank and student 1 gives the appropriate response.

   (i) We have received the ______________ (packs/fax) you sent us.

   Hope that is the information you wanted.
   Hope the cigarettes are what you wanted.

(ii) What about the ________________? (pine/fine)

I'm afraid you'll have to pay.
I'm afraid it will have to be cut down.

(iii) I told her about the ________________. (pair/fair)

She wanted to know more about the antiques exhibited.
She wanted to know when the two of them were coming.

(iv) There is no ________________ here. (pork/fork)

Let us get one from the kitchen.
We can try for some in the other shop.

(v) The ________________ here are ok. (peas/fees)

Yes, they are quite reasonable.
Yes, they look quite fresh.

(A)

9. Match each of the word definitions with the correct word and check its pronunciation in a dictionary and practise it.

A group of documents stored in a computer	format
A piece of equipment that is connected to a computer	protocol
A very small amount of money, especially paid to somebody as wages	peripheral
A person, an organization or a system that is new and without experience	freeware
A description of somebody or something that gives useful information	folder
A right that somebody buys from a company that allows them to sell the company's goods and services in a particular area	fledgling
The way in which information is stored on a computer, disk, tape etc.	pittance
A set of investments owned by a particular person or organization	portfolio
Software that is offered free for anyone to use	franchise
A set of rules that control the way data is sent between computers	profile

(3) /b/ /d/

L3.6 Listen to pairs of words and decide which sound each word begins with. Write 1 or 2 to show whether the first or the second word in each pair begins with the sound given.

/b/	/d/
....	....
....	....
....	....
....	....
....	....
....	....

10. Repeat the pairs of words in L3.6 (given in the Key) making a clear distinction between the two sounds.

L3.7 Listen to the sentences and decide whether the words in A or B were used to complete the sentences.

	A	B
(i) She ________________ with painting water-colors when she was a girl.	babbled	dabbled
(ii) There is a ________________ in cell phone sales this year.	boom	doom
(iii) He could not ______________ the heat and decided to go for a swim.	bear	dare
(iv) After the accident there was a large ______________ on the front door of the car.	bent	dent
(v) You hear a ______________ when you switch on the micro-oven.	beep	deep

11. Repeat the sentences in L3.7 taking care to pronounce the appropriate words in the blanks correctly.

12. Work in pairs. First student 1 reads the sentence using one of the words given in the blank and student 2 gives the appropriate response. Next student 2 reads the sentence using the other word in the blank and student 1 gives the appropriate response.

    (i) Have you forgotten the ________________(bet/debt)?

    No, I'll pay it back next week.

    No, I'm sure I'll win it.

(ii) Did you find the missing ______________ (bead/deed)?

Yes, it was with the other papers on the lawyer's desk.
No, it must have got detached from the ring and fallen.

(iii) Nobody liked the ______________ (bust/dust).

Yes, we thought we had to wear masks to protect ourselves.
Yes, the expression on the face was totally wrong.

(iv) Do you think it is just a ________________ (bubble/double)?

Certainly, it'll burst very soon.
Certainly, it's too dangerous for the famous actor.

(v) Is she ____________ (busy/dizzy)?

Yes, I don't think you can see her now.
Yes, it looks as if she might collapse any moment.

(A)

13. Match each of the word definitions with the correct word and check its pronunciation in a dictionary and practise it.

A measurement of the amount of information that an Internet connection can send in a particular time	download
An amount of the profits that a company pays to its shareholders	barcode
What happens or appears on a computer if you do not make any other choice or change	buffer
A programme that lets you read documents on the Internet	debenture
A screen on a computer which shows the icons of the programmes and files that can be used	dividend
A pattern of thick and thin lines that is printed on things we buy in a shop, which contains information a computer can read	broadband
A loan for a long period of time on which a company promises to pay a fixed rate of interest	bandwidth
A system that can send large amounts of electronic data at a very fast speed	default
An extra quantity of goods that is kept in case it is needed	desktop
The act or process of copying data from a larger computer system to a smaller one	browser

(4) /b/ /v/

L3.8 **Listen to pairs of words and decide which sound each word begins with. Write 1 or 2 to show whether the first or the second word in each pair begins with the sound given.**

/b/	/v/
....	....
....	....
....	....
....	....
....	....
....	....

14. **Repeat the pairs of words in L3.8 (given in the Key) making a clear distinction between the two sounds.**

L3.9 **Listen to the sentences and decide whether the words in A or B were used to complete the sentences.**

	A	B
(i) The price mentioned on the label doesn't include ____________.	bat	vat
(ii) Her hopes of getting a good job ___________.	banished	vanished
(iii) Thousands of ___________ of cotton were destroyed in the fire.	bales	vales
(iv) ___________ is the unit used for measuring the force of an electric current.	bolt	volt
(v) After the Principal spoke, some teachers spoke in a similar ___________.	bane	vein

15. **Repeat the sentences in L.3.9 taking care to pronounce the appropriate words in the blanks correctly.**

16. **Work in pairs. First student 1 reads the sentence using one of the words given in the blank and student 2 gives the appropriate response. Next student 2 reads the sentence using the other word in the blank and student 1 gives the appropriate response.**

(i) His ______________ (boat/vote) doesn't count.

Yes, he has been suspended.

Yes, it has sprung a leak and cannot be used.

(ii) He has been ________________ (bending/vending) copper wire.
He plans to use it for electrical wiring.
He has been making good profit, as copper is expensive.

(iii) Are you ________________ (buying/vying) for the new house?
Yes, we thought all the furniture should be new.
Yes, I like it very much and don't want anyone else to get it.

(iv) She broke the________________ (bow/vow).
Yes, she was not strong enough to resist temptation.
Yes, she was frustrated that she couldn't learn to play the violin.

(v) What will they do about the ________________ (ban/van)?
They will take it to the garage to be repaired.
They will appeal against it in the High Court.

A

17. Match each of the word definitions with the correct word and check its pronunciation in a dictionary and practise it.

A programme written with the purpose of causing damage or causing a computer to behave in an unusual way	vendor
A set of share prices that are used to judge the performance of other shares	bubble
A copy of a file, programme, etc. that can be used if the original is lost or damaged	venture
A document that shows that money has been paid for something	Bluetooth
Money or property that you ask to be given to a particular person when you die	backup
A form of something that is slightly different from or newer than the original thing	virus
A technology that allows data to be transferred between mobile phones, mobile computers and other devices over short distances without the use of wires	voucher
A company or person that sells something	benchmark
A situation that cannot last in which prices rise very quickly and many people make a lot of money	bequest
A business project or activity, especially one that involves taking risks	version

(5) /tʃ/ /dʒ/

L3.10 Listen to pairs of words and decide which sound each word begins with. Write 1 or 2 to show whether the first or the second word in each pair begins with the sound given.

/tʃ/	/dʒ/
....	....
....	....
....	....
....	....
....	....
....	....

18. **Repeat the pairs of words in L3.10 (given in the Key) making a clear distinction between the two sounds.**

L3.11 Listen to the sentences and decide whether the words in A or B were used to complete the sentences.

	A	B
(i) Everyone was looking at her ___________.	choker	joker
(ii) He wants not a cup but a ___________ of coffee.	char	jar
(iii) It was quite ___________ and we decided to stay home and play cards.	chill	Jill
(iv) The archeologist recovered several ___________ from the site they were excavating.	chugs	jugs
(v) She had a toothache and found it difficult to ________.	chew	Jew

19. **Repeat the sentences in L3.11 taking care to pronounce the appropriate words in the blanks correctly.**

20. **Work in pairs. First student 1 reads the sentence using one of the words given in the blank and student 2 gives the appropriate response. Next student 2 reads the sentence using the other word in the blank and student 1 gives the appropriate response.**

    (i) Is she ____________________ (choking/joking)?

    I don't think so. She is trying not to laugh.

    No, she is dead serious.

(ii) What shall I do with this ________________ (chunk/junk)?

Throw it out, of course.

I think it would be better if you rewrote that part.

(iii) How do you like the ________________ (chest/jest)?

It is beautiful, especially the carving on the lid.

I think it was not in good taste and might have hurt him.

(iv) Are the spectators ________________ (cheering/jeering)?

Yes, there is thunderous applause to greet his double century.

Yes, they are very unhappy at the way he's got out.

(v) What about the ________________ (chin/gin)?

No, there're no scars there.

He had finished drinking it.

(A)

21. Match each of the word definitions with the correct word and check its pronunciation in a dictionary and practise it.

A stage in the development of a product or system, usually a technical one	chip
Communication, usually about one particular topic, between people in a special area on the Internet	junk
A method or system that people use to get information or to communicate	generation
An object-oriented computer programming language	joystick
A written statement describing the rights that a particular group of people should have	chat
Anxiety about whether something bad is about to happen	channel
The amount of money somebody asks for goods or services	jitters
Term used to show that a company or government has a low credit rating	charter
A very small piece of a material that is used inside a computer, etc. in order to carry a complicated electronic circuit	Java
A cursor control device in the form of a moveable stick that is usually used for controlling computer games	charge

(6) /t/ /θ/

L3.12 Listen to pairs of words and decide which sound each word begins with. Write 1 or 2 to show whether the first or the second word in each pair begins with the sound given.

/t/	/θ/
....	....
....	....
....	....
....	....
....	....
....	....

22. **Repeat the pairs of words in L3.12 (given in the Key) making a clear distinction between the two sounds.**

L3.13 Listen to the sentences and decide whether the words in A or B were used to complete the sentences.

		A	B
(i)	She gave his sleeve a sharp ___________ to warn him.	tug	thug
(ii)	Why don't you look for the message in the ________ folder?	trash	thrash
(iii)	Plato is remembered as a great ____________.	tinker	thinker
(iv)	He'll return within ____________ days.	tree	three
(v)	The fuel _________ holds 40 liters.	tank	thank

23. **Repeat the sentences in L.3.13 taking care to pronounce the appropriate words in the blanks correctly.**

24. **Work in pairs. First student 1 reads the sentence using one of the words given in the blank and student 2 gives the appropriate response. Next student 2 reads the sentence using the other word in the blank and student 1 gives the appropriate response.**

   (i) **What do you think of the ___________ (team/theme)?**
   Well, they are all sincere workers, but not original thinkers.
   Well, it is an unusual one, but not treated very well.

(ii) I asked her to use the ____________ (tongs/thongs) that she had.
That was the best thing to do, as the vessel was very hot.
There was nothing else to fasten the bags.

(iii) The ______________ (trust/thrust) was useful.
Yes, it was necessary to make the rocket lift off.
Yes, it helped many poor students to continue their studies.

(iv) What is that __________________ (ting/thing)?
Oh, that is actually a radio that looks like a car.
Oh, that is the sound of the micro-oven.

(v) What about the _________________? (ticket/thicket)
I have it in my pocket, don't worry.
Nothing can be hidden in those bushes, I have checked.

(A)

25. Match each of the word definitions with the correct word and check its pronunciation in a dictionary and practise it.

A MS Windows desktop component that indicates what programmes are being currently used and allows the user to switch between them	tab
The level at which something starts to happen, change or have an effect	terminal
The computer keyboard key that is used to move the cursor to the next tabulation point in a word processor programme	taskbar
Goods produced cheaply and intended to be thrown away after use	tariff
A tax that is paid on goods coming into or going out of a country	threshold
The habit of not spending too much money	throwaway
A piece of equipment, usually consisting of a keyboard and a screen that joins a user to a central computer system	thread
The amount of data that passes through a system in a given period of time	thrift
A thing that is used as a model for producing other similar examples	throughput
A series of connected messages on a message board on the Internet which have been sent by different people	template

(7) /v/ /w/

L3.14 **Listen to pairs of words and decide which sound each word begins with. Write 1 or 2 to show whether the first or the second word in each pair begins with the sound given.**

/v/	/w/
....	....
....	....
....	....
....	....
....	....
....	....

26. **Repeat the pairs of words in L3.14 (given in the Key) making a clear distinction between the two sounds.**

L3.15 **Listen to the sentences and decide whether the words in A or B were used to complete the sentences.**

	A	B
(i) I asked her __________ she was late.	vie	why
(ii) He keeps changing houses at the __________.	vim	whim
(iii) She took a __________ that she would work in a village two months every year.	vow	wow
(iv) His enthusiasm began to __________ very soon.	vane	wane
(v) I try to __________ the activities so that the children are not bored.	vary	wary

27. **Repeat the sentences in L.3.15 taking care to pronounce the appropriate words in the blanks correctly.**

28. **Work in pairs. First student 1 reads the sentence using one of the words given in the blank and student 2 gives the appropriate response. Next student 2 reads the sentence using the other word in the blank and student 1 gives the appropriate response.**

(i) Is that a ______________ (veil/whale)?

Yes, you could use it to cover your head

Yes, why did you think it was a shark?

(ii) What about the __________________ (vine/wine)?
Don't worry, I have got the best available in the cellar
It has overgrown; we'll have to cut it.

(iii) Anything wrong with the ______________ (veal/wheel)?
No, the axle may be broken.
I don't think it is fresh.

(iv) Why do you call him a ______________ (viper/wiper)?
Because he loves to harm people.
Because he loves drying the dishes after they are washed.

(v) What do you like about the ____________ (vest/west)?
Its colour and design.
The freedom and the opportunities there.

A

29. Match each of the word definitions with the correct word and check its pronunciation in a dictionary and practise it.

A magazine that is published on the Internet, not on paper	windfall
A form of communication over a network that uses video cameras so that people taking part can see and hear each other	watershed
A written agreement in which a company selling something promises to repair or replace it if there is a problem within a particular period of time	validity
A space that is completely empty of all substances, including all air or other gas	venue
An amount of money that somebody wins or receives unexpectedly	veteran
A person or group of people whose job is to check that companies are not doing anything illegal and to protect people's rights	webzine
The state of being legally or officially acceptable	vacuum
An event or period of time that marks an important change	warranty
A place where people meet for an organized event	watchdog
A person who has a lot of experience in a particular area or activity	videocon-ferencing

(8) /v/ /f/

L3.16 **Listen to pairs of words and decide which sound each word begins with. Write 1 or 2 to show whether the first or the second word in each pair begins with the sound given.**

/v/	/f/
....	....
....	....
....	....
....	....
....	....
....	....

30. **Repeat the pairs of words in L3.16 (given in the Key) making a clear distinction between the two sounds.**

L3.17 **Listen to the sentences and decide whether the words in A or B were used to complete the sentences.**

		A	B
(i)	I got a nice ____________ cheque as a gift for my birthday.	fat	vat
(ii)	He tried in ____________ to break open the door.	feign	vain
(iii)	The lights went off because a ____________ had blown.	fuse	views
(iv)	There is no reason for the brakes to ____________.	fail	vale
(v)	She was left to ______________ for herself in the new apartment.	fend	vend

31. **Repeat the sentences in L3.17 taking care to pronounce the appropriate words in the blanks correctly.**

32. **Work in pairs. First student 1 reads the sentence using one of the words given in the blank and student 2 gives the appropriate response. Next student 2 reads the sentence using the other word in the blank and student 1 gives the appropriate response.**

(i) The numbers were ____________ (fast/vast).
Yes, they never sing slow songs.
Yes, we had to work hard to take care of all of them.

(ii) The ______________ (figure/vigor) they displayed was amazing.
Yes, none of us had seen a statue like that.
Yes, we couldn't imagine where they got the energy.

(iii) What is she doing about the ________________ (fine/vine)?

She has to pay it, of course.
She is thinking of cutting it down.

(iv) Where is the ________________ (fault/vault)?

I think something is wrong with the motor.
They have constructed it in the basement.

(v) Did you buy the __________ (fan/van) you saw yesterday?

No, I thought it would be better to buy an air cooler instead.
No, we decided to buy a small car instead.

(A)

33. Match each of the word definitions with the correct word and check its pronunciation in a dictionary and practise it.

A flat disc inside a plastic cover that is used to store data in the form that a computer can read, and that can be removed from the computer	verdict
All the words in a particular language	flag
A material that is made from a mass of natural or artificial threads	vanguard
The right to refuse to allow something to be done, especially the right to stop a law from being passed	vocabulary
A system for sending documents in an electronic form along telephone wires and then printing them	floppy
A unit for measuring the force of an electric current	fiber
A special mark that you put next to information, an email, etc. that you think is important	firewall
A decision that is made by a jury in court, stating that somebody is considered guilty of a crime or not	veto
Combination of hardware and software used to control the data going into and out of a network and to prevent unauthorized access to the network by hackers	volt
Those who introduce and develop new ways of thinking, new technologies etc.	fax

(9) /θ/ /s/

L3.18 **Listen to pairs of words and decide which sound each word begins with. Write 1 or 2 to show whether the first or the second word in each pair begins with the sound given.**

/θ/	/s/
....	....
....	....
....	....
....	....
....	....
....	....

34. **Repeat the pairs of words in L3.18 (given in the Key) making a clear distinction between the two sounds.**

L3.19 **Listen to the sentences and decide whether the words in A or B were used to complete the sentences.**

	A	B
(i) They have used very ________ paper in this book.	thin	sin
(ii) They asked her to ____________ a song.	thing	sing
(iii) The sound of __________ frightened the children.	thunder	sunder
(iv) They should have a __________ here so that visitors can wash their hands.	think	sink
(v) They applied the paint _________ on the outer surface.	thickly	sickly

35. **Repeat the sentences in L.3.19 taking care to pronounce the appropriate words in the blanks correctly.**

36. **Work in pairs. First student 1 reads the sentence using one of the words given in the blank and student 2 gives the appropriate response. Next student 2 reads the sentence using the other word in the blank and student 1 gives the appropriate response.**

(i) **Did you notice the ____________ (thump/sump)?**
Yes, I heard the sound as the iron bar hit the wall.
Yes, I could see it though they had tried to cover it up.

(ii) What about the ______________(theme/seam)?

Oh, it was very unusual and made the play very interesting.
Oh, it is almost invisible because of the fineness of the thread used.

(iii) Do you think it is _________________ (thick/sick)?

Yes, it has not been able to eat anything we gave it.
Yes, it is enough to cover the old paint.

(iv) What is it? Is it a ________________ (thimble/symbol)?

Yes, it represents peace and prosperity.
Yes, you should use it when sewing.

(v) What do we do with this ________________ (thong/song)?

We could use it to fasten this bundle.
We'll try to set it to a different tune.

(A)

37. Match each of the word definitions with the correct word and check its pronunciation in a dictionary and practise it.

The programmes and data used in a computer	therapy
Plays considered as entertainment	slump
Unsolicited email sent to large numbers of people indiscriminately usually advertising or trying to sell a product	server
The study of religion and beliefs	theatre
A period when a country's economy or a business is doing very badly	software
The treatment of a physical problem or illness	theology
A main computer that provides a service on a network	spam
A device that measures or controls the temperature of a machine or room	throttle
A clever and dishonest plan for making money	scam
A device that controls the amount of fuel that goes into the engine of a vehicle	thermostat

(10) /ʃ/ /s/

L3.20 Listen to pairs of words and decide which sound each word begins with. Write 1 or 2 to show whether the first or the second word in each pair begins with the sound given.

/ʃ/	/s/
....	....
....	....
....	....
....	....
....	....
....	....

38. Repeat the pairs of words in L3.20. (given in the Key) making a clear distinction between the two sounds.

L3.21 Listen to the sentences and decide whether the words in A or B were used to complete the sentences.

	A	B
(i) I knew that she was very ____________.	shy	sigh
(ii) They threatened to ____________ us for damages.	shoe	sue
(iii) Do you call it a ____________?	shin	sin
(iv) The guide wanted to ____________ us all the paintings.	show	sow
(v) We decided to ____________ the house.	shell	sell

39. Repeat the sentences in L3.21 taking care to pronounce the appropriate words in the blanks correctly.

40. Work in pairs. First student 1 reads the sentence using one of the words given in the blank and student 2 gives the appropriate response. Next student 2 reads the sentence using the other word in the blank and student 1 gives the appropriate response.

(i) Would you like to take this ____________ (sheet/seat)?
Yes, I think the view is good from here.
Yes, I think it can be used to cover all the stuff.

(ii) The young man was advised to ____________ (shave/save).
He had to because he looked unkempt with his beard.
He has to because now he has a family to take care of.

(iii) We need to ________________ (shift/sift) out the useless items.

Yes, there is no room here for everything.
Yes, we need to know what is important and what is not.

(iv) How about a ________________ (ship/sip)?

Yes, but really very little, I cannot drink more now.
Yes, going by sea would be exciting.

(v) What about that ________________ (shack/sack) of yours?

Oh, that has to be pulled down; it's very old.
Oh, I threw it away; it was no good.

(A)

41. Match each of the word definitions with the correct word and check its pronunciation in a dictionary and practise it.

- The shares of a particular company
- The main inner part of an operating system
- The part of a graphical user interface window that allows the user to move through a document by clicking or dragging with the mouse
- Software that is distributed freely and only paid for if the user decides to keep it
- An extra share that a company gives to shareholders instead of a dividend
- A key on a computer keyboard that allows capital letters or a different set of characters to be keyed
- An optical input device that copies text or graphics into a computer
- A fault in somebody's character, a plan, a system etc.
- A fixed amount of money that is paid regularly to somebody as wages or money to live on
- An excellent example of something that people are meant to see and admire

- stipend
- scanner
- shortcoming
- shell
- stocks
- scrollbar
- scrip
- shareware
- showpiece
- shift

(11)	/ʃ/	/tʃ/

L3.22 Listen to pairs of words and decide which sound each word begins with. Write 1 or 2 to show whether the first or the second word in each pair begins with the sound given.

/ʃ/	/tʃ/
....	....
....	....
....	....
....	....
....	....
	....

42. Repeat the pairs of words in L3.22 (given in the Key) making a clear distinction between the two sounds.

L3.23 Listen to the sentences and decide whether the words in A or B were used to complete the sentences.

		A	B
(i)	She said the price was ______________.	sheep	cheap
(ii)	I helped him wear his ______________.	shoes	choose
(iii)	He wanted to ______________ up his job.	shuck	chuck
(iv)	The news was a big ______________ to all of us.	shock	choc
(v)	Their constant ______________ was annoying.	shatter	chatter

43. Repeat the sentences in L.3.23 taking care to pronounce the appropriate words in the blanks correctly.

44. Work in pairs. First student 1 reads the sentence using one of the words given in the blank and student 2 gives the appropriate response. Next student 2 reads the sentence using the other word in the blank and student 1 gives the appropriate response.

(i) What about his______________(share/chair)?

He gave it all to his sister saying he already had enough money.
He wanted it to be repaired because of his long attachment to it.

(ii) Is it a new ______________ (ship/chip)?

Yes, it is on its first voyage.
Yes, we threw away the old one and put in a brand new one.

(iii) Is there a ______________ (sheet/cheat)?
Yes, you can use it to move to the next stage of the game.
Yes, it is clean and fresh.

(iv) Would you like a ______________ (sherry/cherry)?
Yes, I love fruits.
Yes, I always have a drink before dinner.

(v) Can you show us where the __________ (shin/chin) is in this picture?
Yes, it is below the knee here.
Yes, it is below the mouth here.

(A)

45. Match each of the word definitions with the correct word and check its pronunciation in a dictionary and practise it.

A change from one system or method of working to another	charger
A system that is not as good or true as it seems to be	changeover
The place where you pay for the things you are buying in a supermarket	sham
A number of pieces of paper tied or held together	checkout
A piece of equipment for loading a battery with electricity	shuttle
A place where people come to worship because it is connected with a holy person or event	chime
A situation in which somebody has been completely defeated	shrine
A plane, bus or train that travels regularly between two places	sheaf
A ringing sound, especially one that is made by a bell	checkmate
A soft smooth shiny quality	sheen

(12) /l/ /r/

L3.24 Listen to pairs of words and decide which sound each word begins with. Write 1 or 2 to show whether the first or the second word in each pair begins with the sound given.

/l/	/r/
....	....
....	....
....	....
....	....
....	....
....	....

46. Repeat the pairs of words in L.3.25 (given in the Key) making a clear distinction between the two sounds.

L3.25 Listen to the sentences and decide whether the words in A or B were used to complete the sentences.

	A	B
(i) She said she didn't know the ________________.	late	rate
(ii) The journey didn't take ________________.	long	wrong
(iii) I asked them to ______________ up the presents.	lap	wrap
(iv) ______________ of sleep made him irritable.	lack	rack
(v) He did not want to ______________ her.	lob	rob

47. Repeat the sentences in L3.26 taking care to pronounce the appropriate words in the blanks correctly.

48. Work in pairs. First student 1 reads the sentence using one of the words given in the blank and student 2 gives the appropriate response. Next student 2 reads the sentence using the other word in the blank and student 1 gives the appropriate response.

(i) How about a ________________(lamp/ramp)?

Yes, we know we have to build one.
I don't know if it would be a good gift.

(ii) Is there a ________________ (lift/rift)?

Yes, you don't have to climb the steps.
Yes, nothing can be done to bring the two parties together.

(iii) What about the ______________ (liver/river)?

Oh, the water is badly polluted.
It is slightly sluggish, but nothing serious.

(iv) Do you think it is __________________ (light/right)?

No, you won't be able to carry it.
No, but there is nothing else we can do under the circumstances.

(v) What about the ___________________ (lock/rock)?

It is solid and will be difficult to drill through.
It is old but we could use it on the front door.

(A)

49. Match each of the word definitions with the correct word and check its pronunciation in a dictionary and practise it.

A record of when an event happened	retail
A programme that extracts songs from a CD and turns them into WAV files	lull
A small mistake, especially one that is caused by forgetting something or by being careless	rigging
An electronic device that links different networks or parts of a network	levy
A legal agreement that allows you to use a building, a piece of equipment or some land for a period of time, usually in return for rent	rally
A rise in prices after a period of falling prices	ripper
An extra amount of money that has to be paid, especially as a tax to the government	lapse
The selling of goods to the public, especially through shops	log
A quiet period between times of activity	router
The act of working to cause an artificial rise or fall in prices, in order to make a profit	lease

3.2 How combining with other sounds affects pronunciation of consonants

The description of English consonants given above shows how these sounds are pronounced in isolation, i.e., when each of them is pronounced by itself. When they are pronounced with other sounds in words and longer stretches of language, some changes take place, because of the other sounds before or after. These changes are determined by the rules of the language and are called ***Phonological Rules***. The phonological rules of a language determine (i) what sounds can occur in which positions, (ii) what sounds can combine with what other sounds, and (iii) how the sounds are pronounced when they combine with other sounds. Thus the phonological rules of English give rise to some positional restrictions on the occurrence of English consonants and also variations in their pronunciation.

1. All the consonants except two /ʒ/ and /ŋ/ occur freely in different positions, the initial, the middle and the final. Both /ʒ/ and /ŋ/ do not occur in the initial position. /ʒ/ is rare compared with /ʃ/ and /ŋ/ is not as freely distributed as the other nasals /m/ and /n/.
2. An important feature of English consonants is the manner in which the pronunciation of certain sounds varies depending on the positions in which they occur. This is most noticeable in the case of plosives.

(a) In the initial position, the voiceless plosives /p/, /t/, and /k/ are aspirated, but the voiced plosives, /b/, /d/, and /g/ are not. The initial sounds in *pack, pie, pay, tin, town, team, cap, came*, and *coat* are aspirated but those in *back, buy, bay, din, down, deem, gap, game*, and *goat* are not. Thus aspiration is an important distinguishing feature between the two words in these pairs.

pack-back	*tin-din*	*cap-gap*
pie-buy	*town-down*	*came-game*
pay-bay	*team-deem*	*coat-goat*

(b) In other positions, the middle and the final, there is no aspiration even with the voiceless plosives. Thus the sounds /p/, /t/, and /d/ are not aspirated when they occur in the middle and final positions as in

copy	*hockey*	*stick*	*deep*	*sick*
meter	*speed*	*skit*	*late*	

(c) In the final position, the plosives are generally not released, i.e., the articulators that form a closure do not move apart with a release of compressed air and there is no consequent plosion. Thus in the production of the final sounds of words like

lip	*job*	*meet*	*food*	*peek*	*dog*
jeep	*tub*	*night*	*loud*	*dark*	*fig*

the two articulators that form a closure do not move apart. This is particularly seen in casual speech.

(d) Further, when plosives occur in the final position, it may be difficult to distinguish between the final consonants in minimal pairs like

rope *robe* *seat* *seed* *leak* *league*
tap *tab* *fat* *fad* *sack* *sag*

because there is neither aspiration nor voicing in the final position as /p/, /t/, and /k/ are not aspirated in the final position and /b/, /d/, and /g/ are not voiced when they occur in the final position. In such cases, it is vowel length which helps to distinguish between the two words in these minimal pairs. As noted before, one of the differences between voiceless and voiced consonants is that vowels are shorter before voiceless consonants than they are before voiced consonants. Thus the vowel in the first word in each of the above pairs is shorter than it is in the second and this is what is crucial in distinguishing between the two words.
Affricates and fricatives are also similar to plosives in terms of vowel length. Vowels occurring before voiceless fricatives and affricates are shorter than those occurring before voiced ones. This is what distinguishes pairs of words like

safe *save* *price* *prize* *lunch* *lunge*
leaf *leave* *race* *raze* *search* *surge*

3. An example of how the pronunciation of certain consonants is affected by the nature of the sounds with which they combine is seen in the pronunciation of the letters 's' or 'es' occurring in the final position of words, particularly in plural forms of nouns and present tense forms of verbs with third person singular subjects.
When we make nouns plural, we generally add –s or –es to the singular forms of nouns as in *books, bags, cups, pubs, bats, rods, pens, bills, churches, judges, dresses, bushes* and *roses*. Similarly, when we use verbs in the present tense with third person singular subjects, we add –s or –es to the verbs as in *drinks, jogs, eats, reads, laughs, saves, cries, goes, catches, smudges, crosses, pushes* and *closes*. The pronunciation of the plural suffix, –s / -es in nouns, or the marker of the third person singular verb in the present tense, –s or –es, depends on the final sound in the singular form of the noun or the final sound of the base form of the verb.

(a) If the singular form of the noun or the base form of the verb ends in a voiceless consonant other than, /s/, /ʃ/, and /tʃ/, the suffix –s or –es is pronounced as /s/ as in

Nouns	**Verbs**
books	*drinks*
cups	*eats*
bats	*laughs*

(b) If the singular form of the noun or the base form of the verb ends in a voiced sound other than /z/, /ʒ/, and /dʒ/ (all vowels are voiced sounds), the suffix –s or –es is pronounced as /z/ as in

Nouns	**Verbs**
bags	*jogs*
pubs	*reads*
rods	*saves*
pens	*cries*
bills	*goes*

(c) If the singular form of the noun or the base form of the verb ends in /s/, /ʃ/, /tʃ/, /z/, /ʒ/, or /dʒ/, the suffix –s or –es is pronounced as /ɪz/ as in

Nouns	**Verbs**
churches	*catches*
judges	*smudges*
dresses	*crosses*
bushes	*pushes*
roses	*closes*

4. Another example of how the pronunciation of a consonant sound is affected by the sounds with which it combines is seen in the pronunciation of the past tense suffix –d/-ed. When we use verbs in the past tense, we add –d or –ed to the present tense form of the verb as in *kicked, grouped, laughed, dressed, pushed, gagged, robbed, loved, closed, called, applied, played, shouted, loaded, plotted, pleaded, voted* and *grounded.* The pronunciation of this past tense suffix –d or –ed also depends on the final sound of the present tense form of the verb.

   (a) If the present tense form of the verb ends in a voiceless consonant other than /t/, the past tense suffix –d or –ed is pronounced as /t/ as in

   kicked *grouped* *laughed* *dressed* *pushed*

   (b) If the present tense form of the verb ends in a voiced sound other than /d/ (all vowels are voiced sounds), the past tense suffix –d or –ed is pronounced as /d/ as in

   gagged *loved* *called* *played*
   robbed *closed* *applied*

   (c) If the present tense form of the verb ends in /t/ or /d/, the past tense suffix –d or –ed is pronounced as /ɪd/ as in

   shouted *loaded* *plotted* *pleaded* *voted* *grounded*

It is necessary that Indian speakers be aware of these two features of the pronunciation of English consonants, viz. (a) the pronunciation of certain consonants varies depending on the positions in which they occur and (b) the pronunciation of certain consonants is affected by the nature of the sounds with which they combine.

(1) (i) An important difference between Indian languages and English is in the way aspirated and unaspirated plosives are used. In Indian languages, each of the unaspirated and aspirated plosives, /p/, /p^h/, /b/, /b^h/, /ʈ/, /ʈ^h/, /ɖ/, /ɖ^h/, (as mentioned earlier, these four sounds are retroflex plosives in Indian languages) /k/, /k^h/, /g/, and /g^h/ is an independent sound, i.e., a different phoneme and therefore makes for difference in meaning between words. For example, in Hindi, the words *pal* and *p^{h}al* are different with different meanings and this difference in meaning is signaled only by the presence or absence of aspiration with the initial plosive. But in English, aspiration is a feature that occurs only in a certain position with voiceless plosives and it does not distinguish between different phonemes as it does in Indian languages. As we have seen, only the voiceless plosives /p/, /t/ and /k/ in the initial position are aspirated. In other positions, they are not aspirated. Further, the voiced plosives, /b/, /d/, and /g/ are never aspirated. Indian speakers, who tend to produce unaspirated voiceless plosives, /p/, /t/, and /k/ in all positions, need to be aware of this difference between their language and English in any attempt to learn correct English pronunciation.

(ii) The tendency to go by the spelling of words makes some Indian speakers produce plosive sounds in the final position also the same way they produce them in the initial position. Sometimes their pronunciation of words such as *beep*, *keep*, *site*, *right*, *pack*, *lack* etc. sounds a little strange because they try to articulate the final plosives fully.

(iii) The pronunciation of the nasal consonant /ŋ/ also has some problems for Indian speakers because words that have this sound in the final position are spelt with '*ng*'. Again, guided by the spelling, Indian speakers tend to add /g/ after /ŋ/ in the final position in words such as *king*, *bang*, *long*, *wing* etc. They need to practice the pronunciation of such words taking care to produce only /ŋ/ and not /ŋg/ at the end.

(iv) (a) Some Indian speakers have difficulty in pronouncing the sound /h/, particularly in the initial position in words such as *human*, *handle*, *honey* etc. They need to practice this sound carefully in order to get the correct pronunciation of such words.

(b) The more noticeable problem is with words such as *heir*, *honest*, *honour*, and *hour* where the letter 'h' that occurs initially is not pronounced. Many Indian speakers, going by the spelling, tend to pronounce an initial /h/ in these words also. They need to be aware of the mismatch between spelling and pronunciation in these words and learn to pronounce them with an initial vowel.

(2) (i) Variation in vowel length before voiced and voiceless consonants is another feature that Indian speakers need to pay particular attention to because in Indian languages, generally a sound is pronounced the same way in whatever environment it occurs.

(ii) The varying pronunciation of the plural and the past tense suffixes in English depending on the nature of the preceding sound is another feature that Indian speakers need to practice, as no such feature is found in Indian languages.

Exercises

A

L3.26 Listen to the following words and decide in which word the initial consonant is aspirated. Write A in the blank to indicate the word that begins with an aspirated consonant. Leave the blank unfilled if the initial sound is not aspirated.

package	....	topic	....	table	....
batch	....	coffee	....	danger	....
camel	....	gallon	....	bicycle	....
kindness	....	public	....	ticket	....
guidance	....	damp	....	picture	....
borrow	....	culture	....	custom	....
district	....	beauty	....	taxi	....
pension	....	guard	....	target	....
college	....	budget	....	guest	....
doubt	....	paint	....	google	....

1. Practise the correct pronunciation of the words above, paying attention to see that you aspirate the initial consonant where necessary.

A

L3.27 Listen to the following words and decide in which word /p/, /t/, or /k/ is aspirated. Write A in the correct box showing which sound is aspirated.

tackle	surprise	doubt	palace
repeat	patient	direct	secret
contest	fabric	subject	technical
skilful	keyboard	mountain	polish
remote	stable	cabinet	flop
studio	topic	happen	kitchen
gallant	pencil	focus	discount
colour	special	pursuit	rocket
gipsy	tourist	merit	country
habit	detail	gossip	perfect
daughter	grope	forest	temper
sputnik	capture	mistake	better

	/p/	/t/	/k/
tackle			
repeat			
contest			
skilful			
remote			
studio			
gallant			
colour			
gipsy			
habit			
daughter			
sputnik			
surprise			
patient			
fabric			
keyboard			
stable			
topic			
pencil			
special			
tourist			
detail			
grope			
capture			
doubt			
direct			
subject			
mountain			
cabinet			
happen			
focus			
pursuit			
merit			

gossip			
forest			
mistake			
palace			
secret			
technical			
polish			
flop			
kitchen			
discount			
rocket			
country			
perfect			
temper			
better			

2. (i) Practise the correct pronunciation of the words above, paying attention to see that you aspirate the right consonant in the right position.

(ii) When a word ends in a plosive, try practising its pronunciation without a release at the end.

3. Notice that the words used in Listening exercises L.3.2 to L.3.25 and exercises 2 to 49 above all begin with the consonant sounds that are in focus. Practise again those words that begin with a voiceless plosive taking care to aspirate the initial sound.

L3.28 Listen to the pairs of sentences and decide which of the two words given is used in the blank in each sentence. Write A or B in the blank.

	A	B
(i) A ______________ is a web site, usually maintained by an individual, with regular entries of commentary and descriptions of events.	**block**	**blog**
Lack of funds has been a ____________ to progress in this important project.		
(ii) The _______________ would not slide and we were not able to open the door.	**bolt**	**bold**
To type words in ______________, click on the letter 'B' at the top.		

(iii)	We could hear the ____________ of the drums from a long distance. She found the ____________ that was missing from the necklace.	beat	bead
(iv)	You can use this ____________ to get money from any ATM. She was pushing a ____________ loaded with packets of various sizes.	cart	card
(v)	The government has put a ____________ on the rate of interest the banks can charge on the loans they give. It is better to take a bus to the new airport than to spend a lot of money on a ____________.	cap	cab
(vi)	The sky is clear and blue and there isn't a ____________ anywhere. He has a lot of political ____________ though he doesn't hold any office.	clout	cloud
(vii)	She has been given a high ____________of morphine on doctor's advice. The journey was long and as he was feeling sleepy, he had a ____________ on the bus.	dose	doze
(viii)	Starting a business of her own marked the beginning of a new ____________ in her life. The malls have completely changed the ____________ of this quiet and peaceful locality.	face	phase
(ix)	The mountaineers planted their country's ____________ on Mount Everest. The move to hike fuel prices came in for a lot of ____________ from the public and the press.	flak	flag
(x)	They told us what to do if there is a gas ____________. The residents of this town have agreed to form a ____________ for clean environment.	leak	league
(xi)	The young man made a ____________ for the bowl as it fell from the shelf. The young people were discussing where to go for ____________.	lunch	lunge

(xii)	There isn't a single ____________ on the tree now. They get both paid and unpaid ____________.	leaf	leave
(xiii)	The interview was done in front of a ____________ audience. He has lived all his ____________ in big cities and doesn't know anything about living in a village.	life	live
(xiv)	The dress was very ____________ and I exchanged it. They didn't want to ____________ their money by investing in unknown companies.	loose	lose
(xv)	Our school won the first ____________ in the science quiz. The ____________ of oil has been falling steadily.	price	prize
(xvi)	The boy chose to ____________ himself on the wall so that he could watch the game better. We need to ____________ the system of the corruption that is everywhere.	perch	purge
(xvii)	He sat in front of a ____________ of folders that contained the project reports of a decade. We decided to ____________ a campaign to reduce air pollution.	mount	mound
(xviii)	The doctors tried their best to ____________ the life of the accident victim. These days it is not ____________ to keep all your jewelry at home.	save	safe
(xix)	The ____________ cause of the problem is lack of commitment on the part of the government. His ____________ behavior shocked everyone there.	root	rude
(xx)	The critics said that his article was wholly ____________ and need not be given any attention. The people of the ____________ living on this island do not want the place to be modernized.	tripe	tribe

4. Repeat the pairs of sentences above and practice the pronunciation of the pairs of words. Note the varying length of the vowel in the two words in each pair.

L3.29 Listen to the following words and decide if the plural suffix at the end is pronounced as /s/, /z/, or /ɪz/. Write 's', 'z' or 'iz' in the blank.

computers	....	charities	....	missiles	....
curtains	....	students	....	memos	....
currencies	....	museums	....	colleges	....
maps	....	shelves	....	horses	....
degrees	....	pitches	....	drugs	....
months	....	washes	....	husbands	....
ratings	....	mouths	....	windows	....
breaks	....	surprises	....	props	....

5. Practise the pronunciation of the words taking care to pronounce the plural suffix correctly.

L3.30 Listen to the following words and decide if the past tense suffix at the end is pronounced as /t/, /d/, or /ɪd/. Write 't', 'd', or 'id' in the blank.

promised	....	selected	....	demanded	....
bagged	....	kicked	....	lapped	....
logged	....	compared	....	sustained	....
survived	....	provided	....	permitted	....
tapped	....	attached	....	lodged	....
married	....	helped	....	travelled	....
maimed	....	arrested	....	polished	....
flattered	....	boiled	....	attacked	....

6. Practise the pronunciation of the words taking care to pronounce the past tense suffix correctly.
7. Practise asking and answering the following questions. This can be done either in pairs or groups of 3 to 4 people. Take care to pronounce words ending in *–ing* correctly.
   (i) What are you planning to do this weekend?
   (ii) What is your sister doing in Switzerland?
   (iii) Where were you working before you joined the university?
   (iv) Which position are you applying for and in which companies?
   (v) What is the government doing to control inflation?

(vi) Are the children sleeping or playing?
(vii) Is she going to study further or take up a job?
(viii) Were they enjoying the show or getting bored?
(ix) Are you coming out with us or staying at home and studying?
(x) Are we driving down to Mysore or taking a bus?

One of the most noticeable differences between British English and American English is the omission of /r/ in British English in three positions, (a) after the vowels /ɑː/, /ɔː/, /ɜː/, and after diphthongs, (b) before a consonant, and (c) in the final position. Thus the letter 'r' in words such as those below is not pronounced in British English but is pronounced in American English.

art	*father*	*better*	*order*	*cur*	*bird*	*bar*	*bark*	*bore*	*born*
first	*mother*	*butter*	*armour*	*err*	*curd*	*car*	*card*	*core*	*corn*
earn	*sister*	*teacher*	*perform*	*beer*	*bear*	*tire*	*tired*	*sure*	*pure*
garden	*brother*	*doctor*	*farmer*	*fear*	*dear*	*care*	*fare*	*cure*	*lure*

We notice that, in many of these words, more than one of the above three conditions hold good.

In connected speech, however, if a word ending in 'r' is followed by a word beginning with a vowel, the 'r' at the end of the first word is pronounced in British English. This /r/ is called the **linking** /r/. Thus in

They have fur overcoats
The doctor is out
The bar is open,

the 'r' at the end of the words *fur*, *doctor*, and *bar* is pronounced.

Indian speakers tend to produce the /r/ sound in all positions. If they wish to learn British pronunciation of English, they need to practise leaving out the sound /r/ in the three positions mentioned above, when these words are not followed by a word beginning with a vowel.

L3.31 Listen to the following words, first in British pronunciation and then in American pronunciation. What is the difference between the two?

(i)

anchor	answer	author	blunder	chapter	clever
color	computer	consumer	corner	culture	eager
fever	future	honour	lawyer	member	officer
October	paper	remember	rumour	scooter	similar
sugar	summer	vulgar	water	weather	wonder

(ii)	afford	allergy	apartment	argue	award
	bargain	birth	burn	burden	carbon
	certain	charge	course	comfort	commerce
	concern	conserve	court	darling	divorce
	energy	first	forbid	force	forget
	formal	fortune	fourth	furnace	garbage
	govern	harvest	margin	market	merchant
	morning	nervous	normal	organize	pardon
	parcel	party	percent	perfect	person
	portfolio	purpose	sharp	short	shirt
	source	sports	start	storm	superb
	support	surface	target	thermal	Thursday
	university	urban	urgent	version	virtual
	warden	warning	world		

8. Depending on whether you wish to learn British or American pronunciation, practise the pronunciation of these words as you heard them.
9. Practise the pronunciation of the following words taking care to pronounce the /r/ sound where it is necessary and leaving it out where it is not. (British English)

anger	angry	arm	army	computer	computerize
consumer	consumerism	cover	coverage	direct	director
discover	discovery	drive	driver	enter	entry
factor	factory	fair	fairy	favour	favourite
fever	feverish	flower	flowery	hunger	hungry
tour	tourist	insure	insurance	lecture	lecturer
minister	ministry	murder	murderer	nature	natural
occur	occurrence	offer	offering	prefer	preference
prior	priority	pure	purity	recover	recovery
refer	reference	score	scorer	structure	structural
suffer	suffering	terror	terrorist	tire	tiring

3.3 How grammar affects pronunciation of consonants

In English there are a number of words whose grammatical classification, that is, whether they are nouns or verbs is indicated by the pronunciation of the final consonant. Nouns end in a voiceless fricative such as /s/, /θ/, or /f/, whereas the corresponding verbs end in /z/, /ð/, or /v/.

Nouns	**Verbs**
/s/	/z/
use	*use*
house	*house*
abuse	*abuse*
excuse	*excuse*
spouse	*espouse*
loss	*lose*
advice	*advise*
choice	*choose*
/θ/	/ð/
bath	*bathe*
teeth	*teethe*
mouth	*mouth*
cloth	*clothe*

(Notice the difference in spelling between the two words. The noun mostly ends in 'th', whereas the verb ends in 'the'.)

Nouns	**Verbs**
/f/	/v/
shelf	*shelve*
life	*live*
grief	*grieve*
half	*halve*
safe	*save*
belief	*believe*
relief	*relieve*
proof	*prove*

(Here again the nouns end in 'f' or 'fe', whereas the verbs end in 've'.)

Indian speakers need to be aware of these differences in pronunciation between nouns and verbs, especially when there is no difference in spelling and should practise the pronunciation of such words carefully.

Exercises

L3.32 Listen to the pairs of sentences and decide which of the two words given is used in the blank in each sentence. Write A or B in the blank.

		A	B
(i)	Does she have a ______________ ? Yes, she can ______________ any dress she likes.	choose	choice
(ii)	Please ______________ me from attending the lecture this evening. What ______________ will you give?	excuse(/s/)	excuse(/z/)
(iii)	He didn't open his ______________ throughout the meeting. Nobody knew that she was asked only to ______________ the words of the song.	mouth(/θ/)	mouth(/ð/)
(iv)	He put the report on the ______________ and forgot all about it. I suspected that they were going to ______________ the project.	shelve	shelf
(v)	She has another ______________, a big one in London. They decided to ______________ the flood victims in school buildings.	house(/z/)	house(/s/)
(vi)	More than ______________ the movie is just singing and dancing. They have offered to ______________ the price/s of everything.	halve	half
(vii)	Everyday she has a ______________ before going to bed. He helps her to ______________ the baby in the morning.	bath	bathe
(viii)	I took your ______________ and applied for an extension. The instructor should ______________ him not to drive fast.	advise	advice

(ix) You have to ___________ that it was an accident. proof prove

They have no ___________ whatsoever to show that he is guilty.

(x) The ___________ you have is not enough to make a dress for you. clothe cloth

The money that she earns is just enough to feed and ___________ the family.

1. Repeat the pairs of sentences and practise the pronunciation of the pairs of words, giving particular attention to the consonants in the final position.

3.4 How spelling affects pronunciation of consonants

In Chapter II, Unit 4, we saw some of the discrepancies between English spelling and pronunciation.

(1) One such discrepancy is where the same letter is pronounced differently in different words. The consnant letters whose pronunciation depends on the spelling of the words in which they occur are (i) C, (ii) G, (iii) Q, (iv) X, (v) N, and (vi) S.

(a) **C**

Before the letters E, I, and Y, C is usually pronounced /s/ and everywhere else it is pronounced /k/ as the following examples show.

Where C is pronounced /s/

cell *cement* *centre* *century* *certain* *certificate*
cinema *circle* *circus* *city* *civil* *citizen*
cyber *cyanide* *cycle* *cynical* *cypher* *cyst*

Where C is pronounced /k/

cable *calculate* *calendar* *camera* *capital* *clever*
climate *climb* *close* *cluster* *coach* *coffee*
coin *college* *colour* *common* *cream* *craft*
credit *critic* *cube* *cucumber* *culprit* *culture*

(b) **G**

Before the letters E, I, and Y, G is mostly pronounced /dʒ/, and sometimes /g/. (This often depends on the etymology of the word. If the word is of Latin origin, G is pronounced /dʒ/ and if it is of Germanic origin, it is pronounced /g/.) Everywhere else it is pronounced /g/.

Where G is pronounced /dʒ/

gender *general* *gentle* *genuine* *geology*
gesture *giant* *gibber* *gin* *ginger*
giraffe *gybe* *gym* *gypsy* *gyrate*

Where G is pronounced /g/

gear *get* *gift* *girl* *give*
gallery *gamble* *game* *gather* *glass*
glimmer *globe* *glory* *goal* *good*
google *gossip* *graduate* *grand* *grateful*
grave *guard* *guess* *guide* *guitar*

(c) **Q**

The letter Q usually combines with U and is pronounced /kw/ before A, E, I, and O.

quake *quality* *queen* *question* *quiet*
equal *equipment* *frequent* *request* *vanquish*

But in words of foreign origin, the letter sequence QU can also be pronounced /k/, particularly in the final position, as in

antique *oblique* *unique* *clique* *pique*

There are a few other words which show a similar pronunciation of the sequence QU, such as

mosquito *conquer* *liquor* *bouquet* *coquettish*

(d) **X**

The letter X is pronounced /ks/ in middle and final positions as in

box *text* *fax* *extra* *six* *toxic*

But when X occurs between two vowels before a stressed syllable, it is pronounced /gz/ as in

exact *exam* *exempt* *exist* *exotic* *exult*

The letter X occurs rarely in the initial position in words and when it does, it is pronounced /z/.

xenon *xerox* *xylophone* *xenophobia*

(e) N

The letter N is pronounced /n/ in initial, middle and final positions except when it is followed by G, or K, C and CH pronounced /k/.

Some words in which N is pronounced /n/ are

nation *noise* *second* *final* *bacon* *heaven*

When N is followed by G, it is pronounced /ŋ/, as in

sing *long* *gang* *swing* *acting*

where G is not pronounced.

But in words such as

angle *finger* *single* *hungry* *bungle* *mingle*

G is also pronounced and we have /ŋg/.

When N is followed by K or C and CH pronounced /k/, it is again pronounced /ŋ/ and we have /ŋk/ as in

bank *think* *anchor* *canker* *concrete* *tinkle*

(f) S

The letter S has four different pronunciations, namely /s/, /z/, /ʃ/, and /ʒ/.

It is pronounced /s/ in words such as

soon *settle* *mistake* *history* *false* *bus*

But in quite a number of words, it is pronounced /z/ as in

noise *please* *propose* *design* *position* *visit*

It is pronounced /ʃ/ in words such as

insure *pressure* *tension* *compulsion* *discussion* *mansion*

where -SURE or -SION follows a consonant letter such as N, S, or L.

It is pronounced /ʒ/ in words such as

pleasure *treasure* *vision* *explosion* *confusion* *usual*

where -SURE, -SION, or -SUAL follows a vowel.

(2) Like the single consonant letters, there are a few consonant letter sequences that are also pronounced differently in different words. These are (i) CH, (ii) GH, and (iii) TH.

(a) CH

CH is often pronounced /tʃ/ as in

chat *check* *child* *chip* *choice* *church*
each *touch* *much* *rich* *inch* *bunch*

Another pronunciation of CH is /k/ which we find in words such as

character *chorus* *anchor* *technical* *ache* *echo*

In some words of French origin, CH is pronounced /ʃ/

chivalry *machine* *crèche* *cache*

(b) GH

In the initial position, GH is pronounced /g/ as in

ghastly *ghetto* *ghost* *ghee* *Ghana*

In the final position, GH is pronounced /f/ in words such as

cough *enough* *laugh* *rough* *tough*

but is silent in words such as

through *though* *caught* *bought* *light* *tight*

(c) TH

It is pronounced /θ/ in words such as

thank *think* *thing* *path* *moth* *tooth*

and /ð/ in words such as

than *that* *this* *brother* *rather* *tether*

But in names like

Thomas *Thames* *Thompson*

it is pronounced /t/.

The letter sequences SH and PH are pronounced /ʃ/ and /f/ respectively.
Letter sequences such as CH, GH, TH, SH, and PH, which consist of a pair of letters that represent a single sound are called ***digraphs***.

(3) As mentioned in Chapter II Unit 4, there are some consonant letters that are not pronounced in certain words and are called silent letters. In all these cases we find two letter sequences in which one of them is silent. These silent letters occur initially, medially as well as finally.

(a) Initial position

(i) When a consonant letter occurs immediately before N, this first consonant is not pronounced and the word begins with /n/.

knack ***knee*** ***knife*** ***knock*** ***know*** ***knuckle***

gnarled ***gnash*** ***gnat*** ***gnaw*** ***gnome*** ***mnemonic***

pneumatic ***pneumonia***

(ii) When words begin with PS, P is silent and the word begins with /s/.

psalm ***psephology*** ***pseudonym*** ***psyche***

(iii) When words begin with WR, W is silent and the word begins with /r/.

wrap ***wreck*** ***wrestle*** ***wrist*** ***write*** ***wrong***

(b) Middle position

(i) When L occurs after A and immediately before F/V, K, or M, it is not pronounced.

calf ***half*** ***calves***

balk ***chalk*** ***talk***

balm ***calm*** ***palm***

(ii) L is not pronounced in modal verbs *could*, *should* and *would*.

(iii) When G occurs after a vowel and immediately before M or N, it is not pronounced.

align ***benign*** ***deign*** ***feign*** ***sign*** ***paradigm***

(iv) When T occurs after F or S and before –EN or –LE, it is not pronounced.

often ***soften*** ***glisten*** ***listen*** ***bustle*** ***hustle***

(c) Final position

(i) When B occurs in the final position after M, it is not pronounced.

bomb ***comb*** ***limb*** ***tomb*** ***thumb***

(ii) When N occurs in the final position after M, it is not pronounced.

autumn ***damn*** ***column*** ***solemn*** ***condemn***

Some of these silent letters in the middle and the final positions are pronounced when a suffix is added to derive a different word as in

paradigm *paradigmatic*
solemn *solemnity*
bomb *bombard*

In addition to these, there are other instances of words with silent letters such as *mortgage, sword, handsome, strength*, and *badge*. We have to learn the pronunciation of such words individually

(4) In Chapter II Unit 4 we saw that sometimes we introduce in speech a consonant sound that is not represented in spelling. The most noticeable example of this is the sound /j/ though there is no letter Y in the spelling.

(a) When the sequence EU or EW occurs in a word and is pronounced /u:/ and is not preceded by J, R, L, or CH, the sound /j/ occurs before /u:/.

EU (ju:)	EW (ju:)
feud	*few*
euphoria	*ewe*
heuristic	*pew*

But in words such as *chew, crew, jewel* and *threw*, the sound /j/ does not occur.

(b) The sound /j/ is inserted before the letter U also, when it is pronounced /u:/ and is not preceded by J, R, L, or CH.

U (ju:)
cute
music
human
unity

But in words such as *chute, junior, rule*, and *rude*, the sound /j/ does not occur.

(1) In words ending with UR or ER + SION such as *incursion*, *subversion*, *conversion* and *dispersion*, the letter S is pronounced /ʒ/ in American English, whereas it is pronounced /ʃ/ in British English.

(2) American English and British English are different in the way the sound /j/ is introduced in words where EU, EW, and U are pronounced /uː/. Americans do not insert the sound /j/ in words where EU, EW, or U are preceded by T, D, S, Z, N, L, and X. The pronunciation of words such as the following will be without /j/ in American English, whereas in British English it will be with /j/.

dew	*duty*
neutral	*tune*
new	*nude*

Indian speakers of English, whose pronunciation generally follows the spelling of words, have to give particular attention to the ways spelling affects pronunciation of consonants.

(1) Many Indian speakers tend to pronounce words beginning with QU such as *question*, *quiet*, and *quantity* with /k/ and not /kw/. They need to practise the correct pronunciation of such words with /kw/.

(2) Another feature that many Indian speakers are not aware of is the difference in the pronunciation of X in different contexts, particularly in words beginning with EX. Going by spelling they pronounce all such words with /eks/. They need to distinguish between words such as *exercise* and *exihibit*, which are pronounced with /eks/ and /ɪgz/ respectively.

(3) Indian learners need to be aware of the correct pronunciation of words in which the letter N is followed by G or K and practise these words carefully.

(4) The different pronunciations of the letter S in different words also pose problems for Indian speakers. They may have to learn the pronunciation of such words with great care.

(5) Pronouncing the silent letters in words such as *bomb*, *hedge*, *mortgage*, *Wednesday* etc is another feature found in Indian speech. Indian speakers need to be aware of the occurrence of silent letters in different contexts and practise the pronunciation of words with silent letters taking care not to pronounce these letters.

(6) Lack of awareness of the specific contexts where the sound /j/ is inserted in words leads to two different types of mispronunciation among Indian speakers. (i) They may pronounce words such as *menu*, *mutiny*, and *fuse* without /j/ or (ii) having learnt to insert /j/ in words such as *few*, *mute*, and *cute*, they may insert the sound even in words such as *chew*, *jury*, and *threw*. It is therefore necessary that they give particular attention to the pronunciation of words in which EU, EW and U are pronounced /uː/.

Exercises

1. Match each of the word definitions with the correct word and practise its pronunciation, giving special attention to the pronunciation of QU.

Make something four times bigger	quell
A piece of written criticism	quest
Shake with fear	physique
Feeling sick	quiet
Not done in a direct way	grotesque
A long search for something	quadruple
Strange in an unpleasant way	critique
Stop violent behaviour	queasy
Without much noise or activity	quake
Size and shape of a person's body	oblique

L3.33 Listen to these words and decide how X is pronounced in them and put a √ in the appropriate column.

2. Check the pronunciation of each word in a dictionary and practise the right pronunciation.

	/ks/	/gz/
excavate	....	....
example	....	....
exceed	....	....
excellent	....	....
exam	....	....
except	....	....
excess	....	....
exact	....	....
exchange	....	....
excite	....	....
exclaim	....	....
excise	....	....
exclude	....	....

execute	....	....
executive	....	....
exercise	....	....
exertion	....	....
exhale	....	....
excuse	....	....
exemption	....	....
exhaust	....	....
exhibit	....	....
exile	....	....
exist	....	....
exit	....	....
exotic	....	....
expand	....	....
expect	....	....
exorbitant	....	....
expel	....	....
expense	....	....
experience	....	....
expert	....	....
explain	....	....
explicit	....	....
explode	....	....
exploit	....	....
explore	....	....
export	....	....
exuberant	....	....
expose	....	....
express	....	....
exquisite	....	....
extend	....	....
extra	....	....
extinct	....	....
extreme	....	....
extricate	....	....

L3.34 Listen to these words and decide how N is pronounced in them. Put a √ in the appropriate column.

3. Check the pronunciation of each word in a dictionary and practise the right pronunciation.

	/n/	/ŋ/
ankle	....	....
answer	....	....
blanket	....	....
bland	....	....
bunker	....	....
bundle	....	....
drink	....	....
flannel	....	....
flank	....	....
hanker	....	....
handle	....	....
junk	....	....
junction	....	....
tanker	....	....
tangent	....	....

L3.35 Listen to these words and decide how S is pronounced in them. Put a √ in the appropriate column.

4. Check the pronunciation of each word in a dictionary and practise the right pronunciation.

	/ʃ/	/ʒ/
dimension	....	....
admission	....	....
decision	....	....
revulsion	....	....
extension	....	....
explosion	....	....
seclusion	....	....
concession	....	....

collision	....	....
expansion	....	....
evasion	....	....
profession	....	....
provision	....	....
occasion	....	....
aggression	....	....
compassion	....	....
corrosion	....	....
commission	....	....
invasion	....	....
precision	....	....
submission	....	....
succession	....	....
conclusion	....	....
recession	....	....
television	....	....
illusion	....	....
comprehension	....	....
confusion	....	....
revision	....	....
repression	....	....

L3.36 Listen to the following words, first in American English and then in British English. Decide if the pronunciation of the letter S in these words is the same or different in American and British English.

	American	***British***
excursion	....	....
expulsion	....	....
perversion	....	....
immersion	....	....
intermission	....	....
inversion	....	....
aspersion	....	....
emulsion	....	....

diversion	....	....
dissension	....	....
aversion	....	....

5. Depending on whether you wish to learn British or American pronunciation, practise the appropriate pronunciation of these words, with /ʃ/ or /ʒ/.

L3.37 Listen to these words and decide how CH is pronounced in them. Put a √ in the appropriate column.

6. Check the pronunciation of each word in a dictionary and practise the right pronunciation.

	/tʃ/	/k/	/ʃ/
chafe	....	....	....
chameleon	....	....	....
chancellor	....	....	....
chandelier	....	....	....
chagrin	....	....	....
chaos	....	....	....
chapter	....	....	....
chaperone	....	....	....
character	....	....	....
charity	....	....	....
charade	....	....	....
charisma	....	....	....
cheerful	....	....	....
chef	....	....	....
chemo-therapy	....	....	....
chivalry	....	....	....
choice	....	....	....
chauffeur	....	....	....
choir	....	....	....
chore	....	....	....
chauvinism	....	....	....
chord	....	....	....
choreography	....	....	....

chronology	....	....	....
chunk	....	....	....
churl	....	....	....
arch	....	....	....
architect	....	....	....
avalanche	....	....	....
bachelor	....	....	....
brochure	....	....	....
echo	....	....	....
achieve	....	....	....
launch	....	....	....
mechanic	....	....	....
niche	....	....	....
ochre	....	....	....

7. **(a) Each of the words given below has a letter missing which is not pronounced in speech. Insert this silent letter in each word and choose the right word to fill in the blanks in the sentences.**

   (b) Practise the correct pronunciation of these words taking care not to pronounce the silent letters.

soverei_n	_riggle	smu_ge	_nob	sta_k
we_ge	diaphra_m	crum_s	bau_k	whis_le
forei_ner	bu_get	yo_k	_rit	_now-how
sa_mon	gru_ge	dou_t	do_ge	qua_ms
_rinkle	ali_n	_not	cas_le	campai_n
hym_	ba_m	mali_n	condem_	nu_ge
fo_k	de_t			

(i) The children heard the ______________ of the train and ran out.

(ii) She tried to turn the ____________ of the door but it would not move.

(iii) They launched a new ____________ against racism in public life.

(iv) The ______________ for this year showed a huge deficit.

(v) Everyone liked the ______________ they sang.

(vi) There is no ______________ that they will get the contract.

(vii) The government announced a new scheme to help old ____________ live comfortably.

(viii) He had no ____________ whatsoever about cheating in the exams.

(ix) They are deep in ____________ and therefore have decided to sell their house.

(x) We did not want to ____________ ourselves with any of the political parties.

(xi) The mother asked the little boy not to ____________ around but to sit quiet.

(xii) Every ____________ entering the country should have a valid visa.

(xiii) She doesn't like any fish other than ____________.

(xiv) There were ____________ of cake on the girl's shirt which she didn't notice.

(xv) Their house was like a ____________; nobody could enter it easily.

(xvi) She tried to ____________ the oncoming car and hit the tree by the roadside.

(xvii) He tried to ____________ the old man in the night with the intention of robbing him.

(xviii) In telephones there is a ____________, which turns electronic signals into sound and sound into electronic signals.

(xix) All countries ____________ terrorism.

(xx) A ____________ has been issued against the company for breach of contract.

(xxi) He doesn't have a ____________ against any of the people who tried to harm him.

(xxii) The report in the newspapers intended to ____________ her.

(xxiii) The doctor asked him to use a skin ____________ to relieve the pain.

(xxiv) She wiped the ____________ on the little girl's chin with her handkerchief.

(xxv) The round yellow part in the middle of an egg is called the ____________.

(xxvi) They may ____________ at the idea of spending a thousand rupees on a pair of shoes.

(xxvii) We untied the ____________ and used the ribbon again.

(xxviii) They are a ____________ country and have a right to decide what type of government they should have.

(xxix) I gave him a ____________ to warn him to be careful in what he said.

(xxx) They didn't have the technical ____________ to take on this project.

(xxxi) She did not succeed in driving a ____________ between the two of us.

(xxxii) There is not a ____________ on her face which shows how good her skin is.

L3.38 Listen to the following words, first in British pronunciation and then in American pronunciation. What is the difference between the two?

	American	***British***
accuse	....	....
adduce	....	....
avenue	....	....
compute	....	....
conducive	....	....
confuse	....	....
deuce	....	....
dubious	....	....
dupe	....	....
duration	....	....
eunuch	....	....
euphemism	....	....
exude	....	....
exuberant	....	....
feudal	....	....
fusion	....	....
humorous	....	....
illusion	....	....
immune	....	....
impunity	....	....
neutralize	....	....
newspaper	....	....
nutrition	....	....
puny	....	....
ruse	....	....
tube	....	....
Tuesday	....	....

8. **Depending on whether you wish to learn British or American pronunciation, practise the pronunciation of these words as you heard them.**

L3.39 Listen to two jokes read by a British English speaker, an American English speaker and an Indian speaker.

First listen without looking at the texts given below and then listen again following the texts.

(i) A man goes into a bar with a lamp. After he's had a few drinks the man says to the barman, 'This lamp is magic y' know. If you rub it a genie comes out and grants you a wish.' 'Oh yes?' replies the barman. 'Let's have a go then.' He rubs the lamp with a bar cloth and out pops a genie. 'Fantastic,' says the barman. 'It works. Er, let's see. Can I have a million bucks, please,' 'As you wish,' replies the genie and the bar is suddenly full of ducks. 'I forgot to mention,' says the man. 'He's a little deaf.' (*Man walks into a bar* The Ultimate Collection of Jokes and One-liners Stephen Arnott and Mike Haskins p. 211-12)

(ii) A tramp knocks on the door of a large house and begs for a meal. 'Tell you what,' says the householder. 'If you go round the back and paint my porch with whitewash I'll give you all the food that you can eat.' The tramp agrees. He goes round the back, finds a tin of whitewash and a brush, and gets started. Ten minutes later the tramp knocks on the door for his reward. 'That was fast work,' says the householder. 'I thought it would take hours to paint the huge porch.' 'Oh, it wasn't so big,' replies the tramp. 'And, by the way, it isn't a Porsche. It's a BMW.' (*Man walks into a bar* The Ultimate Collection of Jokes and One-liners Stephen Arnott and Mike Haskins p. 61)

1. (a) Read the two jokes and record your readings on a tape or CD and (b) play them to your teacher or friend/s and get their feedback on your readings.

L3.40 (i) Listen to a fable read by a British English speaker, an American English speaker and an Indian speaker.

First listen without looking at the text given below and then listen again following the text.

An old woman having lost the use of her eyes, called in a physician to heal them, and made this bargain with him in the presence of witnesses: that if he should cure her blindness, he should receive from her a sum of money; but if her infirmity remained, she should give him nothing. This agreement being made, the physician, time after time, applied his salve to her eyes, and on every visit took something away, stealing all her property little by little. And when he had got all she had, he healed her and demanded the promised payment. The Old Woman, when she recovered her sight and saw none of her goods in her house, would give him nothing. The physician insisted on his claim, and as she still refused, summoned her before the judge. The Old

Woman, standing up in the court, argued: "This man here speaks the truth in what he says; for I did promise to give him a sum of money if I should recover my sight: but if I continued blind, I was to give him nothing. Now he declares that I am healed. I on the contrary affirm that I am still blind; for when I lost the use of my eyes, I saw in my house various chattels and valuable goods: but now, though he swears I am cured of my blindness, I am not able to see a single thing in it."

http://aesopfables.com/cgi/aesop1.cgi?3&TheOldWomanandthePhysician

(ii) In this fable you hear words that begin with 21 of the 24 consonants. (There may be more than one word in the case of some consonants)

/p/, /b/, /t/, /d/, /k/, /g/, /tʃ/, /dʒ/, /θ/, /ð/, /f/, /v/, /s/, /ʃ/, /h/, /m/, /n/, /l/, /w/, /r/, /j/

At the end of the readings, you'll hear sample words from the fable that have these consonants in the beginning.

You'll also hear two words with /z/ and /ŋ/ in the final position.

Listen again to the readings taking care to notice how these words and others with these consonants are pronounced.

(iii) Read the fable and record your reading on a tape or CD and (b) play it to your teacher or friend/s and get their feedback on your reading.

Chapter summary

1. Consonants are described and classified into different categories in terms of (a) the manner of their production, (b) the place of their production and (c) the presence or absence of voicing during their production.

   In terms of the manner of production, six types of consonants have been identified in English, namely, **(i)** ***Plosives*** (/p/, /b/, /t/, /d/, /k/, and /g/), **(ii)** ***Fricatives*** (/f/, /v/, /θ/, /ð/, /s/, /z/, /ʃ/, /ʒ/, and /h/), **(iii)** ***Affricates*** (/tʃ/ and /dʒ/), **(iv)** ***Nasals*** (/m/, /n/, and /ŋ/), **(v)** ***Laterals*** (/l/), and **(vi)** ***Approximants*** (/r/, /w/, and /j/).

   In terms of the place of production, eight types of consonants have been identified in English, namely, **(i)** ***Bilabial*** (/p/, /b/, /m/, and /w/), **(ii)** ***Labio-dental*** (/f/ and /v/), **(iii)** ***Dental*** (/θ/ and /ð/), **(iv)** ***Alveolar*** (/t/, /d/, /s/, /z/, /n/, /l/ and /r/), **(v)** ***Palato-alveolar*** (/ʃ/, /ʒ/, /tʃ/, and /dʒ/), **(vi)** ***Palatal*** (/j/), **(vii)** ***Velar*** (/k/, /g/, and /ŋ/), and **(viii)** ***Glottal*** (/h/).

   Each of the 24 consonants is given a unique 3-term description using the three features mentioned above.

2. There are certain restrictions on the occurrence of consonants in different positions and also a few variations in the pronunciation of consonants, which are due to the ***phonological rules*** of English.
   (a) The consonants /ʒ/ and /ŋ/ do not occur in the initial position in English.
   (b) The voiceless plosives /p/, /t/, and /k/ are aspirated in the initial position but the voiced plosives /b/, /d/, and /g/ are not.
   (c) The plosives /b/, /d/, and /g/, which are voiced in the initial position are not voiced in the final position.
   (d) The plosives are generally not released when they occur in the final position.
   (e) Vowels are shorter before voiceless consonants than they are before voiced consonants.
   (f) The suffix –s or –es, which is added to nouns to make them plural or to verbs in present tense is pronounced /s/, /z/, or /ɪz/ depending on the final sound in the nouns or the verbs.
   (g) The suffix –d or –ed, which is added to verbs in past tense is pronounced /t/, /d/, or /ɪd/ depending on the final sound in the verbs.
3. As for the effect of grammar on the pronunciation of consonants, there are a number of words in English which end in a voiceless fricative such as /s/, /θ/, or /f/ when they are nouns but in /z/, /ð/, or /v/ when they are verbs, e.g., *use* (N) and *use* (V), *teeth* and *teethe* and *grief* and *grieve*.
4. The effect of spelling on the pronunciation of consonants is seen in the different pronunciations of the letters C (/s/ or /k/), G (/g/ or /dʒ/), Q (/kw/ or /k/), X (/ks/ or /gz/), N (/n/ or /ŋ/), and S (/s/, /z/, /ʃ/, or /ʒ/) and of the letter sequences CH (/tʃ/, /k/ or /ʃ/, GH (/g/, /f/ or nothing), and TH (/θ/ or /ð/ in different words.

   Further, there are letters such as K, G, M, P, W, L, T, N, and B, which are not pronounced but are silent in a number of words, e.g., *knot*, *gnat*, *mnemonic*, *psychology*, *wrong*, *half*, *listen*, *hymn* and *numb*.

   Also, there are words in which an extra sound such as /j/ is inserted though there is no letter Y in their spelling, e.g., *unity*, *curious*, and *human*.

4

English vowels

...in many respects, vowels can be more clearly delineated in relation to one another than in relation to any external standard of classification.

Celce-Murcia M, Brinton D.M & Goodwin J.M *Teaching Pronunciation* 1996 p. 94

Vowels must be learned by ***listening and imitating****. I could tell you that the English vowel /ɔː/ as in* ***saw*** *is made by rounding the lips and placing the back of the tongue in a position midway between the highest possible and the lowest possible position, but it would be much more helpful if I could simply say the sound for you and get you to imitate me.*

O'Connor, J.D *Better English Pronunciation* 1981, 2nd Edition p. 79

PREVIEW

We saw that consonants are described and classified in terms of clearly perceived features such as the place and manner of production, voicing and aspiration. But describing and classifying vowels is not very simple because the articulators do not come into contact to produce any obstruction to the flow of air in the production of vowel sounds as they do in the production of consonant sounds. As for voicing, it is not a distinguishing feature since all vowels are voiced. Vowels are differentiated mainly through differences in the size and shape of the oral cavity as the air passes through the vocal tract. It is the different positions of the tongue and the lips that bring about the differences in the size and shape of the oral cavity to produce different vowel sounds. Though the different positions of the lips are easily seen, it is not very easy to see or feel the different positions of the tongue because they are relative to one another and cannot be described in clear-cut terms.

As in the case of consonants, we begin by describing and classifying Englsih vowels.

Vowels too show changes in their pronunciation when combined with other sounds in speech. We'll see what these changes are.

Grammar sometimes brings about changes in the pronunciation of some vowels. We'll consider which vowels are affected and how.

Finally we'll examine how pronunciation of vowels is related to spelling.

There are thus four units in this chapter.

4.1 How we describe and classify English vowels
4.2 How combining with other sounds affects pronunciation of vowels
4.3 How grammar affects pronunciation of vowels
4.4 How spelling affects pronunciation of vowels.

4.1 How we describe and classify English vowels

We find that though all the vowels are characterized by a free flow of air through the vocal tract, the size and the shape of the oral cavity change in different ways for different vowels. We can, therefore, distinguish between different vowels in terms of the way the size and the shape of the oral cavity change during their production. There are three factors that we have to take into account in specifying how the size and the shape of the oral cavity change during the production of different vowels:

(i) The vertical difference between the upper surface of the tongue and the roof of the mouth,

(ii) The part of the tongue which is raised highest and

(iii) The shape of the lips.

The third of these is easily describable but the first two are not so easy to perceive and describe.

In order to identify and describe the different vowels of English, let us consider the following words.

sit
seat
put
set
soon
apart
sun
sat
surf
sort
part
pot

In each of the above words the underlined part of the word represents a vowel. It is obvious that no two of these vowels are the same. These twelve words illustrate the twelve different vowels of English. Of the twelve, some are long and others are not. Using this feature of length, the twelve vowels of English are divided into two groups, (a) ***Long vowels*** and (b) ***Short vowels***.

Long vowels	**Short vowels**
seat	*sit*
soon	*put*
surf	*set*
sort	*apart*
part	*sat*
	sun
	pot

(i) (a) If we compare the vowels in the words *seat* and *part*, we can see how the position of the tongue changes in the production of different vowels. When we produce the vowel in *seat* the tongue is raised high so that the surface of the tongue is very close to the roof of the mouth. This position of the tongue is called ***Close*** and the vowel produced with the tongue raised close to the roof of the mouth is called a ***Close vowel***.

(b) In producing the vowel in *part*, however, the tongue is not raised high and there is a great distance between the surface of the tongue and the roof of the mouth. Actually, the mouth is wide open when we produce this vowel. This position of the tongue is called ***Open*** and the vowel produced with the tongue not raised high and the mouth open is called an ***Open vowel***. Using this criterion, we see that the vowel in *soon* is also a close vowel. ***Close vowels*** are also called ***High vowels*** because the tongue is raised high in producing them and ***Open vowels*** are called ***Low vowels*** because the tongue is kept low in producing them.

(c) In producing the vowels in *surf* and *sort*, the tongue is in a position that is neither close nor open but between the two extremes of close and open positions. This position is described as ***Mid*** and these two vowels are also called ***Mid***.

(d) Of the short vowels, the vowels in *sit* and *put* are produced with the tongue raised but not so much raised as in the close position but a little lower. These vowels are also called close or high vowels.

(e) The vowels in *sat*, *sun* and *pot* are produced with the tongue in a position very slightly higher than the open position and therefore these vowels are also called open or low vowels.

(f) The vowels in *set* and *apart* are like the vowels in *surf* and *sort*. They are produced with the tongue between the open and the close positions and are therefore described as mid vowels.

Thus three different positions of the tongue are identified in describing vowels and this criterion divides the twelve vowels in English to three different groups as shown.

Close or high vowels	/iː/, /uː/, /ɪ/, /ʊ/
Mid vowels	/ɜː/, /ɔː/, /e/, /ə/
Open or low vowels	/ɑː/, /æ/, /ʌ/, /ɒ/

(ii) The different positions taken by the tongue during the production of different vowels were described in (i) without any reference to the part of the tongue that is raised when the tongue takes these different positions. The shape of the vocal tract changes depending on which part of the tongue is raised during the production of a vowel. For example, the vowels in *seat* and *soon* are both close vowels since, in the production of both /iː/ and /uː/ the tongue is raised high so that the surface of the tongue is close to the roof of the mouth. But in producing /uː/ the back of the tongue is raised high, where as in producing /iː/ it is the front of the tongue that is raised high. The part of the tongue that is raised high is therefore the second criterion used in distinguishing between different vowels. Vowels like /iː/, which are produced with the front of the tongue raised high are called ***Front vowels*** and vowels like /uː/, which are produced with the back of the tongue raised high are called ***Back vowels***. The vowels in *surf* and *sun* are produced with the central part of the tongue raised high and these vowels are called ***Central vowels***. Thus using this second criterion of which part of the tongue is raised high, the twelve vowels of English are divided into three groups.

Front vowels	/iː/, /ɪ/, /e/, /æ/
Central vowels	/ɜː/, /ə/, /ʌ/
Back vowels	/uː/, /ʊ/, /ɔː/, /ɑː/, /ɒ/

(iii) The third criterion used in distinguishing between vowels is related to the shape of the lips during the production of a vowel. Again, a comparison of the /iː/ in *seat* with the /uː/ in *soon* shows how vowels differ in this respect. In producing /uː/ the lips are rounded, with the corners of the lips brought towards each other and the lips pushed forward. But in producing /iː/ the lips are spread (not rounded), with the corners of the lips moved away from each other. Thus we have two types of vowels, ***Rounded*** and ***Unrounded***. ***Rounded vowels*** are vowels produced with the rounding of lips and ***Unrounded vowels*** are those produced with no rounding of lips but with the lips spread. The twelve vowels of English are divided into two groups using this criterion.

Rounded vowels	/uː/, /ʊ/, /ɔː/, /ɒ/
Unrounded vowels	/iː/, /ɪ/, /ɑː/, /ɜː/, /e/, /ʌ/, /ə/, /æ/

As there are three criteria that are used to distinguish between different vowels, each vowel can be given a three-feature description, which is unique to that vowel. The vowel /ə/ has the same description as /ɜː/, but it is different from all the other vowels in English because it is always unstressed (See Chapter 6). The following list shows the twelve English vowels with their three-feature descriptions.

/iː/	Front,	Close,	Unrounded
/uː/	Back,	Close,	Rounded
/ɑː/	Back,	Open,	Unrounded
/ɔː/	Back,	Mid,	Rounded
/ɜː/	Central,	Mid,	Unrounded
/ɪ/	Front,	Close (slightly lowered),	Unrounded
/ʊ/	Back,	Close (slightly lowered),	Rounded
/e/	Front,	Mid,	Unrounded
/æ/	Front,	Open,	Unrounded

/ə/ Central, Mid, Unrounded

/ʌ/ Central, Open, Unrounded

/ɒ/ Back, Open, Rounded

We notice that each of these twelve vowels is pronounced in a different way and therefore, each has a unique description in terms of the height and position of the tongue and the shape of the lips. We also use a different symbol to represent each of them.

It is true that there are similar pairs of *short* and *long* vowels as in /ɪ/ and /iː/, /ʊ/ and /uː/, /ɒ/ and /ɔː/. But the two vowels in each pair are different in quality (in tongue height and position and lip position) as well as in length. We, therefore, use different symbols for each vowel in these pairs too. Length by itself is not a distinctive feature of any of these vowels.

Figure 2 shows the various positions in the mouth where the twelve vowels are produced.

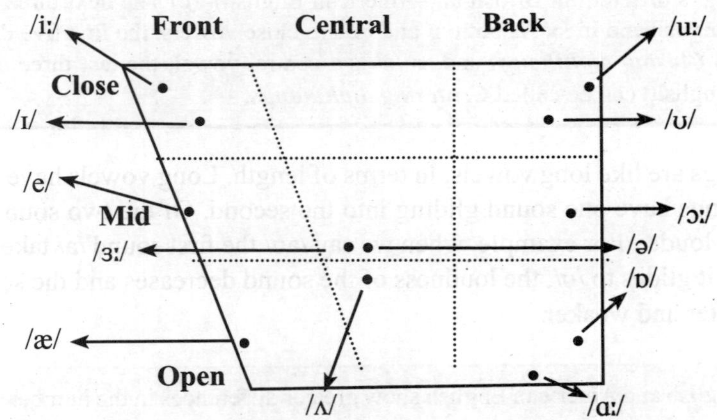

Figure 2

Diphthongs

Apart from the twelve vowels described above, English has other vowel sounds, which are characterized by a glide or movement from one vowel to another. These glides from one vowel to another are called ***Diphthongs***. In contrast the twelve single vowels described above are called Monophthongs. ***Monophthongs*** are constant and are not marked by a glide.

There are important differences between British and American English in the number of diphthongs used and sometimes also in the manner in which some diphthongs are pronounced.

The following words illustrate the diphthongs used in British and American English and the manner in which they are pronounced.

	British English	American English	
tail	/eɪ/	/eɪ/	Same diphthong
tile	/aɪ/	/aɪ/	Same diphthong
toil	/ɔɪ/	/ɔɪ/	Same diphthong
town	/aʊ/	/aʊ/	Same diphthong
toe	/əʊ/	/oʊ/	Different diphthongs
tear (liquid in the eyes)	/ɪə/	/ɪ/	Not a diphthong in Am Eng
tear (damage by pulling)	/eə/	/e/	Not a diphthong in Am Eng
tour	/ʊə/	/ʊ/	Not a diphthong in Am Eng

T Of these diphthongs, (a) the first three end in /ɪ/, and (b) the next two in /ʊ/ (though the fifth diphthong is different in British and American English). (c) The next three diphthongs in British English end in /ə/ As both /ɪ/ and /ʊ/ are close vowels, the first five diphthongs can be called ***Closing diphthongs*** and as /ə/ is a central vowel, the last three diphthongs (of British English) can be called ***Centering diphthongs***.

The diphthongs are like long vowels, in terms of length. Long vowels have only one sound, where as diphthongs have one sound gliding into the second. Of the two sounds involved, the first is longer and louder. For example, when we say /aʊ/ the first sound /a/ takes up most of the diphthong and as it glides to /ʊ/, the loudness of the sound decreases and the second part of the diphthong is shorter and weaker.

British English and American English show greater differences in the number and type of vowels used than of consonants.

(1) American English does not have the vowel /ɒ/. In words such as

dog *job* *coffee*
pocket *logic* *spot*

American speakers use the vowel /ɑː/, whereas British speakers use /ɒ/. Thus there are only 11 monophthongs in American English compared to 12 in British English.

(2) British English has 8 diphthongs, whereas American English has only 5. The pronunciation of words such as

fear *dear*
fare *care*
cure *lure*

in British English and American English is different not only in the vowels used but also in the presence or absence of the sound /r/, as we have seen earlier. These words are pronounced /fɪə/, /dɪə/, /feə/, /keə/, /kjʊə/ and /lʊə/ in British English

with a diphthong but no /r/. In American English they are pronounced /fɪr/, /dɪr/, /fer/, /ker/, /kjʊr/ and /lʊr/ with /r/ but not a diphthong.

(3) The diphthong used in words such as *show* and *open* are different in British and American English. British speakers use /əʊ/, where as American speakers use /oʊ/.

(4) Generally American English vowels are more glided than British English vowels, which is true not only of diphthongs but also of monophthongs, particularly of /iː/ and /uː/. (These sounds are sometimes represented by different symbols, viz., /iy/ and /uw/ to emphasize their glided quality in American English).

Indian English differs quite considerably from both British English and American English in the number and type of vowels used.

(1) Indian speakers mostly do not distinguish between the vowels /ʌ/, /ɜː/, and /ə/ and tend to use /ə/ in all the places where these vowels occur in British English. Thus there may be no difference between the vowels used in words such as *cut* and *curt*, *bun* and *burn*, *hub* and *herb*. The vowel used in all these words is similar to the unstressed /ə/ found in words such as *about*, *accept*, *general*, and *grammar*.

(2) Indian speakers do not distinguish between /ɒ/ and /ɔː/ and therefore there is often no difference in their pronunciation of pairs of words such as *cot* and *caught*, *tot* and *taught*, *not* and *naught*. They tend to use /ɒ/ in place of both /ɒ/ and /ɔː/.

(3) Of the diphthongs, /eɪ/ and /əʊ/ tend to be replaced by monophthongs /eː/ and /oː/. This is probably because of the similarity that Indian speakers perceive between these diphthongs and the sounds /eː/ and /oː/ that most Indian languages have. The inability to distinguish between the English diphthongs /eɪ/ and /əʊ/ and the Indian monophthongs /eː/ and /oː/ affects their pronunciation of common words such as *go*, *no*, *so*, *show*, *low*, *date*, *fate*, *gate*, *hate*, *late* and *rate*.

(4) Another factor that seems to affect Indian pronunciation of the vowel /ɔː/ and the diphthongs /ʊə/ and /eə/, particularly in words ending with the letter 'r' such as *bore*, *door*, *tore*, *sore*, *shore*, *more*, *poor*, *sure*, *tour*, *care*, *bare*, *dare*, *hair*, *pair*, *fare*, *fair*, etc. is their tendency to pronounce the sound /r/ at the end. In such words /ɔː/ becomes /ɒ/, /ʊə/ becomes /uː/ or /ʊ/, and /eə/ becomes /eː/.

Indian speakers, therefore, need to practice the vowels /ɒ/, /ɔː/, /ʌ/, /ɜː/, and /ə/ and the diphthongs /eɪ/, /əʊ/, /ʊə/ and /eə/ carefully and learn to distinguish between /ɒ/ and /ɔː/, /ʌ/, /ɜː/, and /ə/, and /eɪ/ and /eə/.

Exercises

As in the case of consonants, the following exercises are of two types, the first focusing on the description and classification of English vowels and the second on the correct pronunciation of English vowels.

Focusing on description and classification of English vowels

1. (i) Complete the following table by indicating the correct vowel in each of the blanks.
   (ii) Identify a word with this vowel and write it in the blank.

	Front	Central	Back
Close(High) *Rounded* *Unrounded*	 ……………… ………………		……………… ………………
Mid *Rounded* *Unrounded*	 ………………	 ……………… ………………	 ………………
Open (Low) *Rounded* *Unrounded*	 ………………	 ………………	 ……………… ………………

2. What is the difference between the following pairs of sounds?
   /iː/ and /uː/
   /ʌ/and /ɑː/
   /ɒ/ and /ɔː/

3. (i) How does /ɜː/ differ from /ɑː/ and /ɔː/?
   (ii) How does /ʌ/differ from /ɒ/ and /ə/?
   (iii) How does /e/ differ from /æ/ and /ɪ/?

4. Write down words from Columns A and B that have the same vowel.

A	B
foot	knot
dirt	judge
park	rule
bank	dead
teeth	form
tin	put
luck	pearl
box	card
set	beat
glue	live
torn	lax

5. (i) Complete the following table by indicating the correct diphthong in each of the blanks.
   (ii) Identify a word with this diphthong and write it in the blank.

Ending in /ɪ/	Ending in /ʊ/	Ending in /ə/
....	....	....
....	....	....
....		....

6. Indicate the diphthong/diphthongs
   (i) pronounced the same in both British English and American English
   ....
   (ii) pronounced differently in British and American English
   ....
   (iii) found only in British English.
   ....

7. Write down words from Columns A and B that have the same diphthong.

A	B
fight	near
cow	tone
noise	poor
hair	price
cake	praise
beer	buy
sure	care
nose	say
rise	house
raise	toy

Focusing on correct pronunciation of English vowels

L4.1 Listen to groups of four words and indicate in which of the words the given vowel is used. Use a √ or a ×. First listen without looking at the words given below. Then listen again looking at the words.

/ʌ/

(i)	bus	bud	boss	bug
(ii)	cult	cuff	cup	calf
(iii)	duck	dock	dull	dump
(iv)	fun	fund	fuss	fond
(v)	gone	gun	gum	gush
(vi)	luck	lock	lull	lunch
(vii)	pub	pump	pomp	puzzle
(viii)	tub	tug	top	tuck

(i)				
(ii)				
(iii)				
(iv)				
(v)				
(vi)				
(vii)				
(viii)				

1. Practise the pronunciation of the words you identified as having the vowel /ʌ/.

L4.2 Listen to groups of four words and indicate in which of the words the given vowel is used. Use a √ or a ×. First listen without looking at the words given below. Then listen again looking at the words.

/æ/

(i)	batch	bad	back	botch
(ii)	cat	cot	cap	catch
(iii)	flash	flap	flop	flat
(iv)	lack	lock	lad	lap
(v)	mop	map	mad	mat
(vi)	nap	nab	knob	nag
(vii)	sap	sop	sat	sad
(viii)	tap	tab	tag	top

(i)				
(ii)				
(iii)				
(iv)				
(v)				
(vi)				
(vii)				
(viii)				

2. Practise the pronunciation of the words you identified as having the vowel /æ/.

L4.3 Listen to groups of four words and indicate in which of the words the given vowel is used. Use a √ or a × . First listen without looking at the words given below. Then listen again looking at the words.

/ɒ/

(i)	cup	cop	cock	cog
(ii)	dot	dog	dug	dock
(iii)	hot	hop	hob	hub
(iv)	mop	mock	muck	mob
(v)	lock	luck	lot	log
(vi)	nut	not	knock	knob
(vii)	pot	posh	pup	pop
(viii)	sob	sock	suck	sop

(i)				
(ii)				
(iii)				
(iv)				
(v)				
(vi)				
(vii)				
(viii)				

3. Practise the pronunciation of the words you identified as having the vowel /ɒ/.

L4.4 Listen to groups of four words and indicate in which of the words the given vowel is used. Use a √ or a × . First listen without looking at the words given below. Then listen again looking at the words.

/ɔː/

(i)	port	part	pork	porch
(ii)	pore	bore	tore	tar
(iii)	core	car	gore	sore
(iv)	tall	ball	call	doll
(v)	pall	mall	roll	wall
(vi)	hawk	talk	walk	woke
(vii)	paw	saw	low	law
(viii)	lawn	pawn	dawn	darn

(i)				
(ii)				
(iii)				
(iv)				
(v)				
(vi)				
(vii)				
(viii)				

4. Practise the pronunciation of the words you identified as having the vowel /ɔː/.

L4.5 Listen to groups of four words and indicate in which of the words the given vowel is used. Use a √ or a ×. First listen without looking at the words given below. Then listen again looking at the words.

/ɜː/

(i)	bird	bard	birch	birth
(ii)	perk	perch	part	pert
(iii)	herd	hurt	heart	herb
(iv)	curd	card	curt	curb
(v)	girl	gird	guard	girth
(vi)	lurk	lark	learn	lurch
(vii)	dearth	dirge	dirt	dart
(viii)	mirth	mark	murk	merge

(i)				
(ii)				
(iii)				
(iv)				
(v)				
(vi)				
(vii)				
(viii)				

5. Practise the pronunciation of the words you identified as having the vowel /ɜː/.

L4.6 Listen to groups of four words and indicate in which of the words the given vowel is used. Use a √ or a × . First listen without looking at the words given below. Then listen again looking at the words.

/ɑː/

(i)	park	part	parch	porch
(ii)	barb	bard	board	barge
(iii)	carve	card	cart	court
(iv)	harsh	hoard	hard	harm
(v)	mark	march	mar	more
(vi)	force	farce	farm	fart
(vii)	lark	lard	lord	large
(viii)	dark	dork	darn	dart

(i)				
(ii)				
(iii)				
(iv)				
(v)				
(vi)				
(vii)				
(viii)				

6. **Practise the pronunciation of the words you identified as having the vowel /ɑː/**

L4.7 Listen to groups of four words and indicate which of the two diphthongs given is used in each of the words.

Diphthong 1 /aɪ/ Diphthong 2 /eɪ/

Write 1 or 2 to show whether the first or the second diphthong is used. First listen without looking at the words given below. Then listen again looking at the words.

(i)	bail	bile	bite	bait
(ii)	tile	tail	time	tame
(iii)	race	rice	raid	ride
(iv)	fail	file	fate	fight
(v)	pile	pale	pine	pane
(vi)	dame	dime	dine	dome
(vii)	mail	mile	mate	might
(viii)	late	light	lame	lime

(i)				
(ii)				
(iii)				
(iv)				
(v)				
(vi)				
(vii)				
(viii)				

7. **Practise the pairs of words that you identified as having the diphthongs /eɪ/ and /aɪ/.**

L4.8 Listen to groups of four words and indicate which of the two diphthongs given is used in each of the words.

Diphthong 1 /aʊ/ Diphthong 2 /aɪ/

Write 1 or 2 to show whether the first or the second diphthong is used.

First listen without looking at the words given below. Then listen again looking at the words.

(i)	down	dine	noun	nine
(ii)	bout	bite	tight	tout
(iii)	found	find	mind	mound
(iv)	rise	rouse	mouse	mice
(v)	how	high	bow	buy
(vi)	flout	flight	clown	cline
(vii)	proud	pride	crowd	cried
(viii)	sprite	sprout	trout	trite

(i)				
(ii)				
(iii)				
(iv)				
(v)				
(vi)				
(vii)				
(viii)				

8. Practise the pairs of words that you identified as having the diphthongs /aʊ/ and /aɪ/

L4.9 Listen to groups of four words and indicate which of the two diphthongs given is used in each of the words.

Diphthong 1 /ɔɪ/ Diphthong 2 /eɪ/

Write 1 or 2 to show whether the first or the second diphthong is used.

First listen without looking at the words given below. Then listen again looking at the words.

(i)	boil	bail	soil	sale
(ii)	tale	toil	foil	fail
(iii)	coin	cane	grain	groin
(iv)	join	loin	Jane	lane
(v)	voile	vale	ploy	play
(vi)	jay	joy	boy	bay

(i)				
(ii)				
(iii)				
(iv)				
(v)				
(vi)				

9. Practise the pairs of words that you identified as having the diphthongs /ɔɪ/ and /aɪ/.

L4.10 Listen to groups of four words and indicate which of the two diphthongs given is used in each of the words.

Diphthong 1 /əʊ/ or /oʊ/ Diphthong 2 /aʊ/

Write 1 or 2 to show whether the first or the second diphthong is used.

First listen without looking at the words given below. Then listen again looking at the words.

(i)	boat	bout	doubt	dote
(ii)	cowl	coal	foal	fowl
(iii)	goat	gout	flout	float
(iv)	now	no	woe	wow
(v)	hole	howl	how	hoe
(vi)	rout	rote	tote	tout
(vii)	tone	town	drown	drone
(viii)	coach	couch	load	loud

(i)				
(ii)				
(iii)				
(iv)				
(v)				
(vi)				
(vii)				
(viii)				

10. Practise the pairs of words that you identified as having the diphthongs /əʊ/ or /oʊ/ and /aʊ/.

L4.11 Listen to groups of four words and indicate which of the two diphthongs/vowels given is used in each of the words.

Diphthong 1 /ɪə/ or the vowel /ɪ/ Diphthong 2 /eə/ or the vowel /e/

Write 1 or 2 to show whether the first or the second diphthong is used.

First listen without looking at the words given below. Then listen again looking at the words.

(i)	fear	fare	deer	dare
(ii)	bare	beer	peer	pear
(iii)	cheer	chair	tear (cloth)	tear (eye)
(iv)	hare	hear	leer	lair
(v)	mare	mere	sheer	share
(vi)	clear	Claire	rear	rare

(i)				
(ii)				
(iii)				
(iv)				
(v)				
(vi)				

11. **Practise the pairs of words that you identified as having the diphthongs /ɪə/ or /ɪ/ and /eə/ or /e/.**

(1) /iː/ /ɪ/

L4.12 Listen to the pairs of words and decide which vowel is found in each. Write 1 or 2 to show whether the first or the second word in each pair has the sound given.

/iː/	/ɪ/
....	....
....	....
....	....
....	....
....	....
....	....

12. Repeat the pairs of words in L4.12 (given in the Key) making a clear distinction between the two sounds.

L4.13 Listen to the sentences and decide whether the words in A or B were used to complete the sentences.

	A	B
(i) The gas ___________ was the cause for the explosion.	leak	lick
(ii) The view from the top of the __________ was breathtaking.	heal	hill
(iii) As a rider you should know when to use the __________.	weep	whip
(iv) The _____________ of the college interviewed the short-listed candidates.	dean	din
(v) She was __________ on going on the trip.	keen	kin

13. Repeat the sentences in L4.13 taking care to pronounce the appropriate words in the blanks correctly.

14. Work in pairs. First student 1 reads the sentence using one of the words given in the blank and student 2 gives the appropriate response. Next student 2 reads the sentence using the other word in the blank and student 1 gives the appropriate response.

(i) What about the ______________ (bead/bid) that you were telling me about?
It was never found. It must have been swept away.
The company rejected it because they thought it was very low.

(ii) What did you think of the ______________ (meal/mill)?
Oh it was simply delicious.
It's ok but not worth investing on.

(iii) He thought that the ______________ (peach/pitch) was bad.
But he liked the grapes very much.
He said that it would become unplayable in two days.

(iv) What is the problem? I thought you had a good ___________ (lead/lid).
I don't think it is good enough to win the match.
It is too tight and might break if forced.

(v) Do you think she will _____________ (leave/live)?
I think she will. She is very unhappy with this job.
Can't say. Depends on how she responds to the treatment.

(2) /ɪ/ /e/

L4.14 **Listen to the pairs of words and decide which vowel is found in each. Write 1 or 2 to show whether the first or the second word in each pair has the sound given.**

/ɪ/	/e/
....	....
....	....
....	....
....	....
....	....
....	....

16. Repeat the pairs of words in L4.14 (given in the Key) making a clear distinction between the two sounds.

L4.15 Listen to the sentences and decide whether the words in A or B were used to complete the sentences.

	A	B
(i) You can pay your ____________ here.	bill	bell
(ii) The house is in a ______________.	miss	mess
(iii) He asked me to ______________ the bottle with water.	fill	fell
(iv) They came in the ________________ of time.	nick	neck
(v) This is my ____________ and I don't want anybody else here.	din	den

16. Repeat the sentences in L4.15 taking care to pronounce the appropriate words in the blanks correctly.
17. Work in pairs. First student 1 reads the sentence using one of the words given in the blank and student 2 gives the appropriate response. Next student 2 reads the sentence using the other word in the blank and student 1 gives the appropriate response.

    (i) Why are you complaining about the ________________ (disk/desk)?
    Well, it is too low for me.
    Well, it is Read only and can't be rewritten.

    (ii) What about the ________________ (pin/pen)?
    It has stopped writing. I should buy a refill for it.
    It is very loose. That is why the plug doesn't work.

(iii) What did you think of the ________________ (trick/trek)?

It's nothing new. I have seen many conjurers do the same thing.

It was wonderful, especially the part in the mountains.

(iv) Did they find the ________________ (will/well)?

No, they didn't though they walked for miles across the fields.

No, they didn't though they looked through all her papers.

(v) Do you like the ______________ (tint/tent)?

Yes, it will give us shelter for the night.

Yes, your hair looks beautiful with it.

(3) /e/ /æ/

L4.16 Listen to the pairs of words and decide which vowel is found in each. Write 1 or 2 to show whether the first or the second word in each pair has the sound given.

/e/	/æ/
....	....
....	....
....	....
....	....
....	....
....	....

18. Repeat the pairs of words in L4.16 (given in the Key) making a clear distinction between the two sounds.

L4.17 Listen to the sentences and decide whether the words in A or B were used to complete the sentences.

	A	B
(i) The captain gave him a ____________ on the back.	pet	pat
(ii) He tried to __________ into the company's computer network.	heck	hack
(iii) The doctor asked her to put up her right __________.	leg	lag
(iv) I don't have the ____________ for it.	neck	knack
(v) She didn't want to ____________ him any money.	lend	land

19. Repeat the sentences in L4.17 taking care to pronounce the appropriate words in the blanks correctly.

20. Work in pairs. First student 1 reads the sentence using one of the words given in the blank and student 2 gives the appropriate response. Next student 2 reads the sentence using the other word in the blank and student 1 gives the appropriate response.

(i) Where is the ______________ (leather/lather)?
This is hard water and you won't see much.
It is yet to come from the tanning section.

(ii) What did you do with the ________________ (mesh/mash)?
I fed the animals with it.
I fitted the front window with it.

(iii) Did you notice the ______________ (wreck/rack) at the back?
Yes, nobody can miss the new crockery arranged on it.
Yes, they seemed to think they can salvage something out of it.

(iv) What about the ______________ (trek/track)?
It is in good shape now and motor racing can start again.
We had to cancel it because of bad weather.

(v) Did you buy a ______________ (pen/pan)?
Yes, the old one had stopped writing.
Yes, the handle of the old one was broken.

(4) /ʌ/ /ɜː/

L4.18 Listen to the pairs of words and decide which vowel is found in each. Write 1 or 2 to show whether the first or the second word in each pair has the sound given.

/ʌ/	/ɜː/
....	....
....	....
....	....
....	....
....	....
....	....

21. Repeat the pairs of words in L4.18. (given in the Key) making a clear distinction between the two sounds.

L4.19 Listen to the sentences and decide whether the words in A or B were used to complete the sentences.

		A	B
(i)	I gave the child a jam ____________.	bun	burn
(ii)	We saw the boy ____________ up and go to sleep.	cull	curl
(iii)	She didn't want to ____________ the offer.	spun	spurn
(iv)	They asked him to ____________ for the information on the Internet.	such	search
(v)	He looked very ____________.	stun	stern

22. Repeat the sentences in L4.19 taking care to pronounce the appropriate words in the blanks correctly.

23. Work in pairs. First student 1 reads the sentence using one of the words given in the blank and student 2 gives the appropriate response. Next student 2 reads the sentence using the other word in the blank and student 1 gives the appropriate response.

(i) Did you see that ____________ (bird/bud)?
Yes, I wondered if it was a cuckoo.
Yes, I wondered when it would bloom.

(ii) Didn't he see the ____________ (kerb/cub)?
Obviously he didn't and that is why he stumbled and fell.
No, he didn't; he thought there was only the bear.

(iii) What about the ____________ (murk/muck) there?
Don't worry, I'll clean it up.
Don't worry, with the headlights on, we'll be able to manage.

(iv) Can you see the ____________ (girl/gull) there?
Yes, she looks very young.
Yes, it'll fly away if we go closer.

(v) What do you think of the ____________ (herb/hub) here?
Well, it seems very busy and is ideally located for air passengers.
It looks healthy and should soon be full of flowers.

(5) /e/ /eɪ/

L4.20 Listen to the pairs of words and decide which vowel is found in each. Write 1 or 2 to show whether the first or the second word in each pair has the sound given.

/e/	/eɪ/
....	....
....	....
....	....
....	....
....	....
....	....

24. Repeat the pairs of words in L4.20. (given in the Key) making a clear distinction between the two sounds.

L4.21 Listen to the sentences and decide whether the words in A or B were used to complete the sentences.

	A	B
(i) She bought a loaf of ____________ for breakfast.	bread	braid
(ii) We have a ____________ and therefore there is no problem for water.	well	whale
(iii) His is a ____________ of sorrow and suffering.	tell	tale
(iv) I hope I won't ____________ in my attempt to get his approval for the project.	fell	fail
(v) You haven't ____________ my brother.	met	mate

25. Repeat the sentences in L4.21 taking care to pronounce the appropriate words in the blanks correctly.

26. Work in pairs. First student 1 reads the sentence using one of the words given in the blank and student 2 gives the appropriate response. Next student 2 reads the sentence using the other word in the blank and student 1 gives the appropriate response.

   (i) What about the ____________ (bet/bait)?
   I lost it and had to pay him a thousand rupees.
   The fish just swallowed it and I got nothing.

   (ii) Why don't you have a ____________(cell/sale)?
   This is not the right time; we should have it during a festival.
   I don't wish to be bothered with phone calls wherever I go.

(iii) Let us sit in the ____________ (shed/shade).
Yes, it has been cleaned just this morning.
Yes, it must be cool under the tree.

(iv) How was the ______________ (test/taste)?
It was easy, we did well.
The food was simply delicious, we enjoyed it.

(v) What did they say about the ____________ (gel/jail)?
They said that it was good for the skin.
They said that it was overcrowded.

(6) /ʌ/ /ɒ/ or /ɑː/

L4.22 Listen to the pairs of words and decide which vowel is found in each. Write 1 or 2 to show whether the first or the second word in each pair has the sound given.

/ʌ/	/ɒ/ or /ɑː/
....	....
....	....
....	....
....	....
....	....
....	....

27. Repeat the pairs of words in L4.22 (given in the Key) making a clear distinction between the two sounds.

L4.23 Listen to the sentences and decide whether the words in A or B were used to complete the sentences.

	A	B
(i) I can't do anything about the ________ that has set in.	rut	rot
(ii) She tried to ______________ out.	lug	log
(iii) We watched them ______________ each other.	hug	hog
(iv) Where did you get this ____________ from?	cluck	clock
(v) I made myself a ______________ of tea.	cup	cop

28. Repeat the sentences in L4.23 taking care to pronounce the appropriate words in the blanks correctly.

29. Work in pairs. First student 1 reads the sentence using one of the words given in the blank and student 2 gives the appropriate response. Next student 2 reads the sentence using the other word in the blank and student 1 gives the appropriate response.

(i) What about the ________________ (cut/cot)?

It is very comfortable; I like it.

It is not painful though not completely healed.

(ii) What do you think of the ________________ (luck/lock) he had?

It is too small for this big door.

I think he deserved it after all that he's gone through.

(iii) Is there a problem with the ________________ (nut/knot)?

It is too tight and can't be untied.

It is too small and can't be used with this bolt.

(iv) Does she like the ________________ (bus/boss)?

No, she thinks he's not at all friendly.

Yes, she says it is posh and comfortable.

(v) Where is the ______________ (duck/dock)? I can't see it.

It is on the other side of the boat there.

Can you see the ship from which they are unloading the goods?

(7)	/ʌ/	/ɔː/ or /ɑː/

L4.24 Listen to the pairs of words and decide which vowel is found in each. Write1 or 2 to show whether the first or the second word in each pair has the sound given.

/ʌ/	/ɔː/ or /ɑː/
....	
....	....
....	....
....	....
....	....
....	....

30. Repeat the pairs of words in L4.24. (given in the Key) making a clear distinction between the two sounds.

L4.25 Listen to the sentences and decide whether the words in A or B were used to complete the sentences.

		A	B
(i)	She took a long time to __________ over things.	mull	maul
(ii)	Put a __________ after the given number.	nut	naught
(iii)	We watched the __________ of the space shuttle.	lunch	launch
(iv)	The __________ for the murderer has ended.	hunt	haunt
(v)	He had a __________ that he would find her at home.	hunch	haunch

31. Repeat the sentences in L4.25. taking care to pronounce the appropriate words in the blanks correctly.

32. Work in pairs. First student 1 reads the sentence using one of the words given in the blank and student 2 gives the appropriate response. Next student 2 reads the sentence using the other word in the blank and student 1 gives the appropriate response.

(i) What about the __________ (hull/hall)?
It is spacious and can hold at least a hundred people.
It is wood but that doesn't matter.

(ii) What do you think of the __________ (tuck/talk)?
It looks ok, I hope it doesn't come off after a wash.
It sounds interesting, I hope it will be useful to the students.

(iii) Do you think this is __________ (fun/fawn)?
Oh yes, it's really enjoyable.
I don't know. It looks brown to me.

(iv) What does he want to do about the __________ (punch/paunch)?
Well, he says he'll go to the gym regularly and try to reduce.
Well, he thinks he should add more juice to it.

(v) Where is the __________ (pun/pawn)?
You will see it if your vocabulary is good.
It is under the chair.

(8) /ɑː/ /ɔː/

L4.26 Listen to the pairs of words and decide which vowel is found in each. Write 1 or 2 to show whether the first or the second word in each pair has the sound given.

/ɑː/	/ɔː/
....	....
....	....
....	....
....	....
....	....
....	....

33. **Repeat the pairs of words in L4.26. (given in the Key) making a clear distinction between the two sounds.**

L4.27 Listen to the sentences and decide whether the words in A or B were used to complete the sentences.

	A	B
(i) This is an important ______________ of our programme.	part	port
(ii) This episode looks like a ______________ to me.	farce	force
(iii) I bought this in a department ____________.	star	store
(iv) The ____________ on the road melted in the heat.	tar	tore
(v) Did you see the ______________ there?	stark	stork

35. **Work in pairs. First student 1 reads the sentence using one of the words given in the blank and student 2 gives the appropriate response. Next student 2 reads the sentence using the other word in the blank and student 1 gives the appropriate response.**

(i) What about the ______________ (car/core)?
It is in the garage and I'll get it only tomorrow.
It is a very small number of people who are there.

(ii) What do you think of his ______________ (farm/form)?
He is playing very well after the training.
It is huge and very well maintained.

(iii) The best word in this context is ______________ (hard/hoard).
The work is difficult and tiresome.
The storekeepers aren't telling us the truth about their stocks.

(iv) What did she say about _______________ (lard/lord)?
She said that he was very pleasant and friendly.
She said that she always used a little of it.

(v) Why don't you use the _____________ (park/pork)?
I don't like to serve anything that is not fresh.
We could have the fair there.

(9) /ɑː/ /ɜː/

L4.28 Listen to the pairs of words and decide which vowel is found in each. Write 1 or 2 to show whether the first or the second word in each pair has the sound given.

/ɑː/	/ɜː/
....	....
....	....
....	....
....	....
....	....
....	....

36. Repeat the pairs of words in L4.28. (given in the Key) making a clear distinction between the two sounds.

L4.29 Listen to the sentences and decide whether the words in A or B were used to complete the sentences.

	A	B
(i) Have you seen her new ____________?	car	cur
(ii) She lost her ____________ when she went to the sale.	parse	purse
(iii) He found it __________ to settle down in the new school.	hard	herd
(iv) He was so mad that he decided to _________ all his papers.	barn	burn
(v) The children want to go to the ____________.	park	perk

37. Repeat the sentences in L4.29. taking care to pronounce the appropriate words in the blanks correctly.

38. Work in pairs. First student 1 reads the sentence using one of the words given in the blank and student 2 gives the appropriate response. Next student 2 reads the sentence using the other word in the blank and student 1 gives the appropriate response.

(i) Where is the ____________________ (card/curd)?
It is in his wallet.
It is in a bottle in the fridge.

(ii) What about her _________________ (farm/firm)?
It is being expanded with two new branches abroad.
She is growing flowers and vegetables there.

(iii) Did you see the _______________ (mark/murk)?
Yes, I made sure of the date of manufacture.
Yes, nobody could miss it, it was getting to be really dark.

(iv) Do you think it is _________________ (carved/curved)?
Yes, out of a single piece of stone.
No, it has a straight blade.

(v) Who is the __________________ (parson/person)?
He is new to the parish and came here just a month ago.
She is a well known nuclear scientist and is visiting our University.

(10) ɜː/ /ɔː/

L4.30 Listen to the pairs of words and decide which vowel is found in each. Write 1 or 2 to show whether the first or the second word in each pair has the sound given.

/ɜː/	/ɔː/
....	....
....	....
....	....
....	....
....	....

39. Repeat the pairs of words in L4.30. (given in the Key) making a clear distinction between the two sounds.

L4.31 Listen to the sentences and decide whether the words in A or B were used to complete the sentences.

	A	B
(i) The __________ was wet and the match had to be cancelled.	curt	court

(ii) We had some chairs on the ______________. perch porch

(iii) Do you want to buy this colourful _________? shirt short

(iv) She gave _____________ answers to all the questions. pert port

(v) He loves all forms of _______________. spurt sport

40. Repeat the sentences in L4.31 taking care to pronounce the appropriate words in the blanks correctly.

41. Work in pairs. First student 1 reads the sentence using one of the words given in the blank and student 2 gives the appropriate response. Next student 2 reads the sentence using the other word in the blank and student 1 gives the appropriate response.

(i) Where is the _______________ (bird/board)?
It will get ready only tomorrow; it is with the painters.
It is in the backyard; the children are playing with it.

(ii) What do you think of this _________________ (stir/store)?
It is great; it stocks all the famous brands.
It is quite understandable, but of no use.

(iii) Did you see the __________________ (herd/hoard)?
Yes, the animals looked healthy and well fed.
Yes, I wondered for how long he has been putting away the gold.

(iv) Could you tell me which __________________ (word/ward) it is?
It is the first one to the right as you get off the lift.
It begins with the letters 'str'.

(v) What about the ________________ (hearse/horse)?
The undertakers will arrange for it.
Now that I know riding, I will bring it myself.

4.2 How combining with other sounds affects pronunciation of vowels

The description of English vowels above shows how these sounds are pronounced in isolation, i.e., when each of them is pronounced by itself. As we have seen earlier in the case of consonants, vowels too are affected when they are pronounced with other sounds in words and longer stretches of language because of the other sounds before or after. There are phonological rules of English that determine (a) in what positions the vowels can occur and (b) how they are pronounced when they are combined with other sounds. Some of the positional restrictions on the occurrence of English vowels and some important variations in their pronunciation are given here.

(1) Of the twelve vowels, some can occur in all positions in a word, the initial, middle and final positions, where as others can occur only in some of these positions. For exampleand /iː/, /uː/, /ɑː/, /ɔː/, /ɜː/, /ɪ/, and /ə/ occur in all positions, as in

each,	*seed,*	*see*
ooze,	*soon,*	*true*
arm,	*park,*	*far*
ought,	*caught,*	*saw*
earth,	*burn,*	*fur*
if,	*bit,*	*pity*
above,	*control,*	*finger*

But /ʌ/, /æ/, /e/, /ɑ/, and /ʊ/ occur only in some positions and not others, as in

up,	*but*	—
am,	*mat,*	—
egg,	*pet,*	—
ox,	*dog,*	—
—	*put,*	*to*

(2) As we have seen earlier, vowels are longer when they are followed by a voiced consonant than when they are by a voiceless consonant. They are longer when they occur in the final position in a word in the same way as they are when followed by a voiced consonant. This is true of monophthongs as well as diphthongs. For example, the vowel /iː/ in *bee* and *bead* is longer than it is in *beat*. There is a similar difference between *see* and *seed* and *seat* and *fee* and *feed* and *feet* and *bride* and *bright* and *cloud* and *clout*. Pairs of words like *sad* and *sat*, *log* and *lock*, *pig* and *pick* also show this difference in the length of the vowels.

(3) Vowels in English are oral sounds. But when these sounds precede nasal consonants, they get nasalized. Thus we find two types of vowels in English, oral and nasal vowels. Nasal vowels occur when a vowel precedes a nasal consonant, whereas oral vowels occur in all other positions. We can see the two types of vowels in the following pairs of words.

tip	*tin*
type	*time*
fight	*fine*
pet	*pen*
cup	*come*
boot	*boom*
sick	*sing*
fitter	*finger*

In the words in the left column, the vowels precede oral consonants and therefore these are pronounced as oral sounds. But in the words in the right column, the vowels precede nasal consonants and therefore pronounced as nasal sounds. This difference in the pronunciation of the same vowel in each pair becomes obvious if, in saying these words, we pinch our noses closed. We will notice that when the vowel precedes an oral consonant, pinching the nose closed does not affect its pronunciation, but when it precedes a nasal consonant, blocking the passage through the nose makes a striking difference to its pronunciation.

(4) A striking feature of English is the way the pronunciation of vowels varies depending on whether they occur in stressed or unstressed syllables especially in content words. Vowels in stressed syllables do not vary much in their pronunciation. But vowels in unstressed syllables are often reduced to /ə/ or sometimes to /ɪ/. This happens mostly in words with more than one syllable. For example, *adequate* is pronounced /ˈædɪkwət/ and *banana*, /bəˈnɑːnə/ or /bəˈnænə/. A few other examples of how vowels are pronounced differently in stressed and unstressed syllables are

add	/ˈæd/	*agent*	/ˈeɪdʒənt/	*argue*	/ˈɑːgjuː/ /ˈɑːrgjuː/	*alter*	/ˈɔːltə/ /ˈɔːltər/
addition	/əˈdɪʃn/	*agenda*	/əˈdʒendə/	*arise*	/əˈraɪz/	*aloof*	/əˈluːf/
/æ/ to /ə/		/eɪ/ to /ə/		/ɑː/ to /ə/		/ɔː/ to /ə/	

ceremony	/ˈserəməni/	*men*	/ˈmen/	*civil*	/ˈsɪvl/	*effort*	/ˈefət/ /ˈefərt/
ceramic	/səˈræmɪk/	*postmen*	/ˈpəustmən/ /ˈpoustmən/	*civility*	/səˈvɪləti/	*effect*	/ɪˈfekt/
/e/ to /ə/		/e/ to /ə/		/ɪ/ to /ə/		/e/ to /ɪ/	

supple	/ˈsʌpl/	*polish*	/ˈpɒlɪʃ/ /ˈpɑːlɪʃ/	*deprive*	/dɪˈpraɪv/
supply	/səˈplaɪ/	*police*	/pəˈliːs/	*deprivation*	/ˌdeprɪˈveɪʃn/
/ʌ/ to /ə/		/ɒ/ or /ɑː/ to /ə/		/aɪ/ to /ɪ/	

British English and American English differ more in the pronunciation of vowels than of consonants.

(1) A striking difference is the American pronunciation of words such as

answer	*dance*	*blast*	*pass*
half	*laugh*	*path*	*bath*

with the vowel /æ/, whereas the British pronunciation will have the vowel /ɑ:/ in these words. This difference occurs mostly in words that have the sounds /n/, /s/, /f/, and /θ/ following the vowel.

(2) As described in Unit 3, words beginning with the sound /t/, /d/, or /n/, which is followed by the vowel /u:/ represented by the letters 'u', 'ew', or 'eu' such as

tune	*tutor*	*dew*
duke	*news*	*neurotic*

are pronounced with only /tu:/, /du:/, or /nu:/ in American English, where as in British English they are pronounced with /tju:/, /dju:/, or /nju:/.

(3) Words that end in –ile such as

facile	*fragile*	*fertile*
hostile	*missile*	

are pronounced with /əl/ in American English, where as in British English they are pronounced with /aɪl/.

(4) There are quite a number of frequently used words that are pronounced differently in American and British English mainly because a vowel in these words is pronounced differently. For example

	American English	British English
clerk	/klɜ:rk/	/klɑ:k/
derby	/dɜ:rbi/	/dɑ:bi/
either	/i:ðər/	/aɪðə/
neither	/ni:ðər/	/naɪðə/
vase	/veɪs/ or /veɪz/	/vɑ:z/
tomato	/təˈmeɪtoʊ/	/təˈmɑ:təʊ/
leisure	/ˈli:ʒər/	/ˈleʒə/

In words with more than one syllable such as *agenda*, *banana*, *ceremony* and *civility* where the spelling shows more than one occurrence of 'a', 'e', or 'i', Indian speakers tend to pronounce a full vowel in all the positions where they find 'a', 'e', or 'i', because (i) their pronunciation is largely guided by spelling and (ii) they generally do not distinguish between stressed and unstressed syllables and are not familiar with the concept of reduced vowels that occur in unstressed syllables. As a result, their pronunciation of multisyllabic words often sounds strange and may even cause misunderstanding. It is essential that Indian learners of English make a careful study of word stress in English and learn to pronounce multisyllabic words with the right stress and appropriate use of reduced vowels.

Exercises

L4.32. Listen to these words and try to identify the reduced vowels that occur in them and indicate where a reduced vowel occurs by underlining the letter.

In some words more than one reduced vowel may occur.

Practise the pronunciation of these words taking care to pronounce the reduced vowels.

support	carbon	honour	forget	garbage	author
apartment	parcel	thermal	excellent	person	humorous
alimony	exuberant	matrimony	order	formal	purpose
advertisement	ceremony	urban	exorbitant	ordinarily	doctor
monastery	arbitrary	sugar	fever	conserve	lawyer

L4.33. Listen to the following words, first in British English and then in American English. Notice the difference in pronunciation.

afternoon	chancellor	trance	bask	plant	chancery
basket	branch	bathroom	fasten	passport	master
graft	glance	plaster	slander	draft	brass
craft	task	vast	castle	ghastly	slant
mask	chance	casket	clasp	grasp	last
bastard					

1. Depending on whether you wish to learn British or American pronunciation, practice the appropriate pronunciation of these words, with /ɑː/ or /æ/.

We often use a number of vowels either alone or in combination to convey various meanings suggesting particular feelings or emotions. For example, we say /ɑː/ (either quite short or long depending on the situation) when we want to express satisfaction or appreciation. It may be when you have been trying to find out why your printer is not working and you see that it has become unplugged or when you come home very tired and are given a cup of hot coffee. The sounds that we use to convey particular emotions and the meanings we convey by the use of specific sounds vary depending on our mother tongue and culture. Here are two lists of vowels with communicative meaning in English, the first, British and the second, American.

	Common meaning	Pronunciation	Written	Example
1.	Now I understand	/ɑː/ (short falling tone)	ah	'It's not working because it's not plugged in!' 'Ah, of course.'
2.	That's really pretty or nice.	/ɑː/ (long falling tone)	ah or aah	'And here's a photo of my baby daughter.' 'Ah, isn't she pretty.'
3.	That hurts.	/aʊ/ (falling tone)	ow	'Ow, I've cut myself.'
4.	I'm disappointed.	/əʊ/ (falling tone)	oh	'Sorry, Jim's already left.' 'Oh, what a pity.'
5.	I'm thinking about what to say next.	/ɜː/ (level tone)	er	'What do you want to do now?' 'Er, I'm not sure.'
6.	That's horrible/ disgusting.	/ɜːː/ or /iːː/ (both long; falling tone)	urgh ee	'This cheese has gone mouldy. Look!' 'Urgh, it smells revolting.'
7.	I'm looking forward to something.	/uː/ (falling tone)	ooh	'Shall we go out for a meal?' 'Ooh, that would be nice.'
8.	Angrily getting someone's attention usually to stop them doing something they shouldn't.	/ɔɪ/ (falling tone; usually said loudly)	oi	'Oi! Get off my bike'.

(From *Pronunciation Practice Activities* by Martin Hewings p.59)

Written	Pronounced	Used to express	In response to/situation
Ahhh!	/ɑː/ (/ɑːː/)	Satisfaction, relaxation	(You step into a nice hot tub./ You take a sip of refreshing iced tea on a hot day.)
Aw.	/ɔː/	Sympathy, disappointment	"My dog just died."
Ow!	/aw/ (/aʊ/)	Pain	(A door slams on your finger)
Oh?	/ow/ (/oʊ/)	Mild surprise, interest	"The new Woody Allen movie is opening tonight."
Oh.	/owː/ (/oʊː/)	Comprehension	"You have to plug it in before it'll work."
Uh-oh.	/ʔʌʔow/ (/ʔʌʔoʊ/)	Trouble	(You're driving over the speed limit and you see a police car in your rear-view mirror.)
Ooh!	/uwː/(/uː/)	Disgust	"Look! There's a fly in your soup."
Oops!	/uwps/ (uːps/)	Recognition of problem	(You spill your coffee while pouring.)
Aha!	/ehɑ/ (əhɑː/)	Discovery	(You finally understand the math problem you've been working on.)
Huh?	/hʌ/ (nasal)	Lack of understanding	(You don't hear what someone says to you, or you think you heard incorrectly.)
Boo!	/buw/ (/buː/)	Frightening someone	(You sneak up behind someone and want to scare him or her.)
Uh-uh.	/ʔʌʔə/ (nasal)	No	"Have you ever read this book?"
Uh-huh.	/əhʌ/ (nasal)	Yes	"Can I tell you?"

(From *Teaching Pronunciation* by Marianne Celce-Murcia, Donna M. Brinton and Janet M. Goodwin p.122)

2. What are the differences between the sounds and their meanings given in these two lists and the sounds you make in your language to convey these meanings?

4.3 How grammar affects pronunciation of vowels

A number of words in English that end in *–ate* such as *advocate*, *delegate*, and *intimate* function as both verbs and nouns or verbs and adjectives. When these words are used as verbs they are pronounced /eɪt/ at the end, but when they are used as nouns or adjectives, they are pronounced /ət/ with a reduced vowel at the end.

	Verb	**Noun**	**Adjective**
advocate	/ædvəkeɪt/	/ædvəkət/	....
delegate	/delɪgeɪt/	/delɪgət/	....
intimate	/ɪntɪmeɪt/	....	/ɪntɪmət/

Other words ending in *–ate*, which function only as verbs, such as

dominate
educate
fascinate
rotate
terminate

are also pronounced /eɪt/ at the end, whereas words ending in *–ate*, which function only as adjectives such as

accurate
adequate
delicate
passionate

are pronounced /ət/ at the end.

As Indian speakers go by the spelling of words, they tend to pronounce these words the same way with a strong vowel both as verbs and nouns or as verbs and adjectives and do not distinguish between the two uses in their pronunciation. Here again it is important to be aware of the fact that the strong vowel is used only when these words are used as verbs and that when they are used as nouns or adjectives, they need to be pronounced with a reduced vowel.

Exercises

A

L4.34 Listen to the pairs of sentences and decide which of the two words given is used in the blank in each sentence. Write A or B in the blank.

	Sentences	A	B
(i)	The ____________ of the scores in the different rounds will decide the winner. They decided to ____________ the total losses from the different quarters.	aggregate (/ət/)	aggregate (/eɪt/)
(ii)	The company asked the engineers to ____________ coming to the office with working from home on a weekly basis. Parking is allowed here on ____________ days.	alternate (/ət/)	alternate (/eɪt/)
(iii)	It was interesting to see how the new topic could ____________ her. This applies only to ____________ creatures.	animate (/ət/)	animate (/eɪt/)
(iv)	He is a very ____________ person. We told her to ____________ her views clearly.	articulate (/ət/)	articulate (/eɪt/)
(v)	I would always ____________ grey skies and gloomy days with my stay in London. He is the ____________ director of the award winning film.	associate (/ət/)	associate (/eɪt/)
(vi)	It was a ____________ attempt to deceive them. They needed more time to ____________ on the proposal before making a decision.	deliberate (/ət/)	deliberate (/eɪt/)
(vii)	Would you like to be thought a ____________ person? It is important to see that the meeting doesn't ____________ into chaos.	degenerate (/ət/)	degenerate (/eɪt/)

(viii) I don't want to ______________ what you have already done. duplicate (/ət/) duplicate (/eɪt/)

You have to submit the form in ______________.

(ix) The system is too ______________ for us to understand easily. elaborate (/ət/) elaborate (/eɪt/)

We asked her to ______________ on her answer.

(x) I ______________ that this project would cost more than 5 million dollars. estimate (/ət/) estimate (/eɪt/)

This is only a rough ______________ of the money we would need.

(xi) She is a science ______________ and will easily follow this procedure. graduate (/ət/) graduate (/eɪt/)

He will ______________ in two years.

(xii) She should ______________ to her parents her intention to move out. intimate (/ət/) intimate (/eɪt/)

He was on quite ______________ terms with all his classmates.

(xiii) The prices are ______________ and the quality is good. moderate (/ət/) moderate (/eɪt/)

She was asked to ______________ the discussion on the new measures to control drug abuse.

(xiv) Even the fear of an epidemic did not ______________ them into action. precipitate (/ət/) precipitate (/eɪt/)

His advice was not to be ______________ but to think carefully before doing anything.

(xv) You should always ______________ politics from religion. separate (/ət/) separate (/eɪt/)

Public health and family welfare are ______________ issues.

1. Repeat the pairs of sentences and practise the pronunciation of the pairs of words, giving particular attention to the pronunciation of *–ate* at the end in the different sentences.

2. Fill in the blanks with the appropriate word and repeat the sentences, taking care to pronounce correctly the words you choose.
   (i) You are ____________ to be selected as your country's ____________ at the conference. (*delegate, fortunate*)
   (ii) The figures indicating the company's assets in the ____________ presented were highly ____________. (*estimate, exaggerated*)
   (iii) Let us ____________ these claims to find out which of them are ____________. (*legitimate, investigate*)
   (iv) They were ____________ because they could not get anyone suitable to ____________ the big event. (*despearate, coordinate*)
   (v) It was not ____________ for you to ____________ the conversation in such a way. (*dominate, appropriate*)
   (vi) It was a ____________ situation and they had to be careful about how they should ____________ this unpleasant decision. (*communicate, delicate*)
   (vii) Their decision to ____________ the contract would definitely ____________ everyone in our company. (*exasperate, terminate*)
   (viii) They should ____________ the evidence given to find out if it is ____________ to obtain a conviction. (*adequate, evaluate*)
   (ix) She was determined to ____________ her daughter and was very happy when the girl became a ____________ in law. (*graduate, educate*)
   (x) The data is not ____________; I'm sure it is ____________. (*fabricated, accurate*)

4.4 How spelling affects pronunciation of vowels

In English we use six letters, A, E, I, O, U, and Y to represent more than twelve different vowel sounds.

(1) There are certain regularities in the pronunciation of these six letters when they occur in words with only one vowel sound. Such words can have either a vowel letter followed by one or two consonants at the end or a vowel letter followed by a consonant plus a word-final E. There may be one or two consonants in the initial position before the vowel letter.

(a) **A**

In words where the letter A is followed by one or two consonants at the end, it is pronounced /æ/, whereas in words where A is followed by a consonant plus a word-final E, it is pronounced /eɪ/.

Vowel letter followed by one or two consonants	Vowel letter followed by a consonant and a word-final E
bad	*bade*
cap	*cape*
dam	*dame*
fat	*fate*
man	*mane*
sham	*shame*
spat	*spate*
tap	*tape*
mat	*mate*
mad	*made*
pan	*pane*

(b) **E**

In words where the letter E is followed by one or two consonants at the end, it is pronounced /e/, whereas in words where E is followed by a consonant plus a word-final E, it is pronounced /iː/

Vowel letter followed by one or two consonants	Vowel letter followed by a consonant and a word-final E
gen	*gene*
pet	*Pete*
met	*mete*
them	*theme*
	these
	cede
	scheme

(c) **I**

In words where the letter I is followed by one or two consonants at the end, it is pronounced /ɪ/, whereas in words where I is followed by a consonant plus a word-final E, it is pronounced /aɪ/

Vowel letter followed by one or two consonants	Vowel letter followed by a consonant and a word-final E
bit	*bite*
pin	*pine*
pip	*pipe*
rid	*ride*
rip	*ripe*
shin	*shine*

(d) **O**

In words where the letter O is followed by one or two consonants at the end, it is pronounced /ɒ/ or /ɑː/, whereas in words where O is followed by a consonant plus a word-final E, it is pronounced /əʊ/ or /oʊ/

Vowel letter followed by one or two consonants	Vowel letter followed by a consonant and a word-final E
cop	*cope*
dot	*dote*
lob	*lobe*
mod	*mode*
pop	*pope*
slop	*slope*

(e) **U**

In words where the letter U is followed by one or two consonants at the end, it is pronounced /ʌ/, whereas in words where U is followed by a consonant plus a word-final E, it is pronounced (/j/)/uː/.

Vowel letter followed by one or two consonants	Vowel letter followed by a consonant and a word-final E
cub	*cube*
cut	*cute*
dun	*dune*
jut	*jute*
plum	*plume*
tub	*tube*

There are some exceptions like *give*, *have*, and *come*.

(2) Another regularity in the pronunciation of the six vowel letters is found in words where the letter R comes immediately after the vowel letter. In such words R may or may not be followed by another consonant letter.

(a) **A**

In words where A is immediately followed by R, it is pronounced /ɑː/.

bar	*bark*
car	*card*
	dart
	garb
	hard
par	*part*
tar	*tart*

(b) **E, I, and U**

In words where E, I, or U is immediately followed by R, the letters are pronounced /ɜː/.

her
per

sir
cur
fur

fern
herb
perk
pert
term
bird
birth
dirt
firm
girl

curb
furl
hurt
lurch
murk
purge

(c) **O**

In words where O is immediately followed by R, it is pronounced /ɔː/. In many of these words R is followed by E.

bore
core
more

born
corn

force
lord
porch

In all these words R is pronounced in America English but not in British English.

(3) A characteristic feature of English is that in many words pairs of vowel letters occur together and these pairs of letters or digraphs represent different sounds in different words.

AI	Generally pronounced /eɪ/	*bait, chain, mail, pain, sail, train, complain*
	Sometimes pronounced /ɪ/ or /ə/ (especially in unstressed syllables)	*captain, mountain, fountain*

AU	Generally pronounced /ɔː/	*caution, clause, daunt, fault, launch*
	Sometimes pronounced /ɑː/ or /æ/	*laugh, aunt*
EA	Generally pronounced /iː/	*beat, cheat, east, heal, lean, peace reach, seam, tea*
	Sometimes pronounced /e/	*death, head, bread, breath, tread*
	Sometimes pronounced /eɪ/	*break, great, steak*
	Sometimes pronounced /ɜː/	*earth, heard, learn, yearn*
	Sometimes pronounced /ɑː/	*heart, hearth*
	Sometimes pronounced /ɪə/ or /ɪ/	*fear, hear, near, tear*
	Sometimes pronounced /eə/ or /e/	*bear, pear*
EI	Generally pronounced /eɪ/	*deign, rein, neighbor*
	Sometimes pronounced /iː/	*ceiling, seize, receive*
	Sometimes pronounced /aɪ/	*height, sleight*
EE	Generally pronounced /iː/	*beep, deem, fee, green, heed, meet need, peep, queen, reef, seed, teem*
IE	Generally pronounced /aɪ/	*die, lie, tie, pie*
	Sometimes pronounced /iː/	*belief, piece, shield, thief*
OA	Generally pronounced /əʊ/ or /oʊ/	*boat, cloak, foam, groan, hoax, soap*
	Pronounced /ɔː/ when followed by R	*boar, board, hoard, soar*
OE	Generally pronounced /əʊ/ or /oʊ/	*doe, foe, hoe, toe*
	Sometimes pronounced /uː/	*shoe*
OI	Generally pronounced /ɔɪ/	*boil, coin, foible, hoist, moisture, noise*
OU	Generally pronounced /aʊ/	*bout, blouse, count, flout, house, mouse*
	Sometimes pronounced /əʊ/ or /oʊ/ (when followed by L)	*soul, shoulder, smoulder*
	Sometimes pronounced /ɔː/ (when followed by R)	*court, mourn, pour, source*
	Sometimes pronounced /uː/	*group, soup*
	Sometimes pronounced /ʌ/	*couple, cousin, double, trouble*
OO	Generally pronounced /uː/	*cool, doom, food, goose, hoof, noon, root*
	Sometimes pronounced /ʊ/	*book, good, hood, foot*
	Sometimes pronounced /ʌ/	*blood, flood*

(4) There are also sequences where a vowel letter occurs with W or Y, which together represent single vowel sounds.

AW	Generally pronounced /ɔː/	*claw, draw, law, raw, saw*
AY	Generally pronounced /eɪ/	*day, gay, hay, jay, lay, pay*

EW	Generally pronounced /uː/ or /juː/	*dew, few, new, pew, brew*
	Sometimes pronounced /əʊ/	*sew*
EY	Generally pronounced /eɪ/	*fey, grey, prey, obey, they*
	Sometimes pronounced /iː/	*key*
OW	Generally pronounced /əʊ/ or /oʊ/	*low, mow, row, tow, sow*
	Sometimes pronounced /aʊ/	*cow, how, now, town, crown*
OY	Generally pronounced /ɔɪ/	*boy, coy, toy*

An interesting fact about English letters is that when we pronounce them individually to spell names and words, we produce a vowel sound with each of them. 24 letters of the English alphabet can be divided into five groups depending on the vowel sound we produce with them.

/iː/	/e/	/eɪ/	/uː/	/aɪ/
B, C, D, E, G, P, T, V	F, L, M, N, S, X	A, H, J, K	Q, U, W	I, Y
Z (American English)	Z (British English)			

The letters O and R are pronounced with very different vowels.

The letter Z is pronounced /ziː/ in American English and /zed/ in British English.

It is very important that we learn to pronounce the letters of the alphabet correctly because we are often asked to spell names and words.

Exercises

L4.35 Listen to the following words and check if their pronunciation follows the rule described under (1) (a), (b), (c), (d) and (e) above. Use a √ or a × in the blanks.

1. Practise the correct pronunciation of the words.

bang ..... blame ..... base ..... bale ..... bash ..... brake .....
blab ..... blaze ..... brag ..... brat ..... cage ..... catch .....
crab ..... crane ..... dad ..... date ..... drape ..... drab .....
fag ..... fade ..... fake ..... fan ..... flat ..... flap .....
flash ..... game ..... gang ..... gas ..... gaze ..... gram .....
glad ..... glaze ..... grab ..... grade ..... hack ..... ham .....
lake ..... lag ..... lame ..... lane ..... lap ..... lash .....
map ..... man ..... male ..... make ..... mate ..... maze .....
nab ..... knack ..... name ..... nap ..... nape ..... plan .....

plane ….. place ….. pan ….. pale ….. page ….. pal …..
rap ….. rag ….. rate ….. rage ….. rash ….. sane …..
shade ….. shape ….. shake ….. shack ….. sham ….. slab …..
tab ….. tan ….. tame ….. tag ….. tale ….. tram …..
trap ….. trade ….. beg ….. bed ….. bet ….. fetch …..
gel ….. gem ….. get ….. hem ….. jet ….. mesh …..
leg ….. shed ….. sled ….. then ….. mete ….. ten …..
blip ….. brick ….. bride ….. bring ….. chide ….. chip …..
click ….. cline ….. crib ….. crime ….. dip ….. dive …..
drive ….. fig ….. five ….. fine ….. fish ….. gig …..
give ….. glitch ….. glide ….. glib ….. grim ….. grime …..
hide ….. hip ….. hit ….. hitch ….. hive ….. king …..
kick ….. kite ….. kith ….. life ….. live ….. lick …..
mike ….. mile ….. mine ….. mix ….. nil ….. nine …..
pig ….. pile ….. pitch ….. pride ….. rich ….. rife …..
ship ….. sine ….. size ….. sing ….. slime ….. sling …..
thing ….. tide ….. tin ….. time ….. trip ….. trite …..
bode ….. bold ….. blog ….. bone ….. both ….. cog …..
cope ….. come ….. cone ….. clone ….. clock ….. close …..
drop ….. don ….. done ….. dose ….. dot ….. drone …..
fob ….. fog ….. flop ….. gone ….. globe ….. glove …..
hog ….. hope ….. host ….. home ….. job ….. joke …..
log ….. lone ….. love ….. lose ….. mob ….. mole …..
mop ….. mope ….. most ….. move ….. nod ….. node …..
none ….. notch ….. knob ….. posh ….. pop ….. pole …..
pose ….. post ….. rock ….. rod ….. role ….. rose …..
soft ….. sole ….. some ….. stone ….. stock ….. sop …..
tot ….. tote ….. tone ….. ton ….. those ….. top …..
bud ….. bush ….. cub ….. cube ….. duck ….. duke …..
dupe ….. flute ….. flush ….. fluke ….. fun ….. fuse …..
jug ….. June ….. jute ….. lush ….. lute ….. mug …..

mute	much	nude	nun	nut	pub .....
puke	pulp	push	put	rub	rude .....
rule	rust	such	truce	truth	truck .....

A

2. (i) Each of the words given below has a pair of vowels or a vowel digraph missing. Choose form the list of digraphs to complete the word and fill in the blanks with the right word.

(ii) Practise the correct pronunciation of the words.

w__d	pr__st	h__x	r__ch	s__th	b__m
h__ght	t__ch	sw__t	br__f	f__m	m__ld
tr__t	w__ght	h__d	c__rse	j__rney	d__t
c__ch	b__t	pr__f	d__l	dec__ve	d__f
p__ce	w__nd	f__d	s__ge	p__sant	b__ge
ea	ei	ie	oa	ou	oo

(i) I was asked to produce some ____________ of identity by the bank manager.

(ii) The train ____________ was long and very boring.

(iii) The police said that the bomb threat was a ____________ and that there was no need to worry.

(iv) The teacher desired to ____________ her students into good musicians.

(v) Arrangements have been made to provide ____________ and shelter to all the refugees.

(vi) He consulted the ____________ about the wedding ceremony.

(vii) The players thanked their ____________ for the support and encouragement that he had given them.

(viii) He had a bullet ____________ in his right leg.

(ix) They selected five chidren of the same ____________ for the dance.

(x) The workers got a good ____________ on overtime payment.

(xi) The boys asked their father for a special ____________.

(xii) It is warmer in the ____________ than in the north.

(xiii) Different communities live in ____________ in our country.

(xiv) The ____________ in the IT sector has provided jobs to thousands of people.

(xv) ____________ children find it difficult to learn to speak.

(xvi) The doctor advised her to be careful about her ____________.

(xvii) I did not like the cloth because I found it ____________.

(xviii) All their furniture was made of ____________.

(xix) The ____________ woman left her child under a tree and went to work in the field.

(xx) A crowd of young people had gathered to watch the wrestling ____________.

(xxi) They asked the speaker to make his presentation ____________.

(xxii) The guests in the hotel felt they were under ____________ because the police did not allow anyone to go out.

(xxiii) Please do not ____________ the exhibits.

(xxiv) She was looking for a coat with a ____________.

(xxv) He wiped the ____________ off his face as he came in.

(xxvi) In spite of the heavy rains she managed to ____________ the airport in time.

(xxvii) I checked the ____________ of the suitcases before locking them.

(xxviii) He said that he never tried to ____________ anyone.

(xxix) I said that the colour was ____________ but she said it was light brown.

(xxx) We bought a ____________ mattress for the guest room.

L4.36. Listen to two jokes read by a British English speaker, an American English speaker and an Indian speaker.

First listen without looking at the texts given below and then listen again following the texts.

(i) An Englishman, Mr. Blake, felt thirsty and tired when he was visiting the Great Wall in Beijing. At that moment, he heard the guide suggesting that they should go to the beer house. Mr. Blake was full of gratitude thinking of drinking beer soon, but the guide took him to the bear house to see the bear's performances, which really disappointed Mr. Blake. (Adapted from www.34914.com/xsq/jokes.htm)

(ii) Teacher, 'Johnny, give me a sentence starting with "I".' Little Johnny replies, 'I is ...' Teacher interrupts, 'No, Johnny. Always say "I am".' Johnny replies, 'Okay. I am the ninth letter of the alphabet.' (*Man walks into a bar* The Ultimate Collection of Jokes and One-liners Stephen Arnott and Mike Haskins p.146)

1. (a) Read the two jokes and record your readings on a tape or CD and (b) play them to your teacher or friend/s and get their feedback on your readings.

L4.37. (i) Listen to a fable read by a British English speaker, an American English speaker and an Indian speaker.

First listen without looking at the text given below and then listen again following the text.

A slave named Androcles once escaped from his master and fled to the forest. As he was wandering about there he came upon a lion lying down moaning and groaning. At first he turned to flee, but finding that the lion did not pursue him, he turned back and went up to him. As he came near, the lion put out his paw, which was all swollen and bleeding, and Androcles found that a huge thorn had got into it, and was causing all the pain. He pulled out the thorn and bound up the paw of the lion, who was soon able to rise and lick the hand of Androcles like a dog. Then the lion took Androcles to his cave, and every day used to bring him meat from which to live. But shortly afterwards both Androcles and the lion were captured, and the slave was sentenced to be thrown to the lion, after the latter had been kept without food for several days. The Emperor and all his Court came to see the spectacle, and Androcles was led out into the middle of the arena. Soon the lion was let loose from his den, and rushed bounding and roaring towards his victim. But as soon as he came near to Androcles he recognised his friend, and fawned upon him, and licked his hands like a friendly dog. The Emperor, surprised at this, summoned Androcles to him, who told him the whole story. Whereupon the slave was pardoned and freed and the Lion let loose to his native forest.

Gratitude is the sign of noble souls.

http://aesopfables.com/cgi/aesop1.cgi?1&Androcles

(ii) In this fable you hear words that have the diphthongs /aɪ/, /aʊ/, /əʊ/ or /oʊ/, and /eɪ/ and words that have the vowels /iː/, /uː/, /ɑː/, /ɔː/, /ɜː/, /e/, /ɪ/, /ʊ/, /æ/, /ɒ/, and /ʌ/. (There may be more than one word in the case of some diphthongs and vowels)

At the end of the readings you'll hear sample words from the fable that have these diphthongs and vowels.

Listen again to the readings taking care to notice how these words and others with these diphthongs and vowels are pronounced.

(iii) Read the fable and record your reading on a tape or CD and (b) play it to your teacher or friend/s and get their feedback on your reading.

Chapter summary

1. Vowels are described and classified into different categories in terms of (a) the vertical distance between the surface of the tongue and the roof of the mouth, (b) the part of the tongue that is raised highest and (c) the shape of the lips, whether rounded or not, at the time of the production of a particular vowel.

   In terms of the distance between the surface of the tongue and the roof of the mouth, vowels are of three types, namely (i) ***Close*** or ***High vowels*** (/iː/, /uː/, /ɪ/, and /ʊ/), (ii) ***Mid vowels*** (/ɜː/, /ɔː/, /e/, and /ə/), and (iii) ***Open*** or ***Low vowels*** (/ɑː/, /æ/, /ʌ/, and /ɒ/).

   In terms of the part of the tongue that is raised highest, vowels are again of three types, namely (i) ***Front vowels*** (/iː/, /ɪ/, /e/, and /æ/), (ii) ***Central vowels*** (/ɜː/, /ə/, and /ʌ/), and (iii) ***Back vowels*** (/uː/, /ʊ/, /ɔː/, /ɑː/, and /ɒ/).

   In terms of the shape of the lips, vowels are of two types, namely (i) ***Rounded vowels*** (/uː/, /ʊ/, /ɔː/, and /ɒ/) and (ii) ***Unrounded vowels*** (/iː/, /ɪ/, /ɑː/, /ɜː/, /e/, /ʌ/, /ə/, and /æ/).

   In terms of the length of the sound, there are 5 long vowels and 7 short vowels. Each of these 12 vowels is given a unique 3-term description using the three features mentioned above.

   These 12 vowels are single sounds and are called ***Monophthongs***.

   British English and American English show differences in the number and type of vowels used. American English does not have the vowel /ɒ/ as /ɑː/ is used instead and therefore has only 11 monophthongs.

   In addition to monophthongs, English also has vowels that are glides from one sound to another, which are called ***Diphthongs***. There are important differences between British and American English in the number of diphthongs used and sometimes also in the manner in which some diphthongs are pronounced. British English has 8 diphthongs, namely /eɪ/, /aɪ/, /ɔɪ/, /aʊ/, /əʊ/, /ɪə/, /eə/, and /ʊə/, whereas American English has 5, namely /eɪ/, /aɪ/, /ɔɪ/, /aʊ/, and /oʊ/. American English uses /ɪ/, /e/, and /ʊ/ instead of /ɪə/, /eə/, and /ʊə/.

2. As with consonants, there are certain restrictions on the occurrence of vowels in different positions and also a few variations in the pronunciation of vowels, which are due to the ***phonological rules*** of English.

   (a) The vowels /iː/, /uː/, /ɑː/, /ɔː/, /ɜː/, /ɪ/, and /ə/ occur in all positions, whereas /ʌ/, /æ/, /e/, /ɑ/, and /ʊ/ occur only in some positions

   (b) Vowels are longer in the final position and when followed by voiced consonants than when followed by voiceless consonants, e.g. *bee* and *bead* compared with *beat*.

(c) Vowels are nasalized when they precede nasal consonants, e.g. the vowel /ɪ/ in *pin* is nasalized whereas it is not in *pit*.

(d) In words with more than one syllable, we often use reduced vowels such as /ə/ and /ɪ/ in unstressed syllables, e.g. the word *challenge* is pronounced /tʃæləndʒ/.

3. As for the effect of grammar on the pronunciation of vowels, words ending in *–ate* are pronounced with /eɪt/ at the end when they are verbs and with /ət/ when they are nouns or adjectives, e.g. *intimate* is pronounced /ɪntɪmeɪt/ when it is a verb but /ɪntɪmət/ when it is an adjective.

4. Spelling affects the pronunciation of vowels in different ways.

   (a) The letters A, E, I, O, and U are pronounced /æ/ or /eɪ/, /e/ or /iː/, /ɪ/ or /aɪ/, /ɒ/ or /ɑː/ or /əʊ/ or /oʊ/, /ʌ/ or (/j/) /uː/ depending on whether these letters are followed by one or two consonants or by a consonant plus the letter E, e.g. *fat* and *fate*, *gen* and *gene*, *sit* and *site*, *dot* and *dote*, and *cut* and *cute*.

   (b) When the letters A, E, I, O, and U are immediately followed by R, we produce longer vowels, namely, /ɑː/ in the case of A as in *part*, /ɜː/ in cases of E, I, and U as in term, *dirt* and *lurk*, and /ɔː/ in the case of O as in *fort*.

   (c) Apart from the individual vowel letters, pairs of them such as AI, AU, EA, EI, EE, IE, OA, OE, OI, OU, and OO have different pronunciations in different words.

   (d) Combinations of vowel letters with W or Y such as AW, AY, EW, EY, OW, and OY also have different pronunciations in different words.

5

English syllables

*English has a characteristic rhythm and listeners **expect** to hear all speakers use this rhythm.*

Joanne Kenworthy *Teaching English Pronunciation* 1987 p. 19

The basic unit of English rhythm is the syllable. A syllable is most simply explained as something with a vowel sound at its center.

Judy B. Gilbert *Teaching Pronunciation* 2008 p. 4

The syllable is a very important unit. Most people seem to believe that, even if they cannot define what a syllable is, they can count how many syllables there are in a given word or sentence. If they are asked to do this they often tap their finger as they count, which illustrates the syllable's importance in the rhythm of speech.

Peter Roach *English Phonetics and Phonology* 1991 2nd Edition p. 67

PREVIEW

After studying the individual sounds, consonants and vowels of English, we will look at how these sounds are combined in speech to form larger units. In speech the unit that is larger than the sound or phoneme is ***the syllable***. The syllable is a unit of sound and is more difficult to define and identify than the word, which is more familiar to us. The words we know are made up of one or more syllables. Generally we can decide fairly easily how many syllables a word has. For example, we know that words like *bill, come,* and *fool* have one syllable each, where as words like *become, comfort,* and *summer* have two syllables, *computer, cinema,* and *medicine* have three syllables and *democracy, application,* and *mechanical* have four syllables. Roughly speaking, we decide the number of syllables in a word by counting the number of vowels in it.

But it is much more difficult to decide where a syllable begins and ends in a word with more than one syllable. As the syllable is a unit of sound, we should look at the phonetic transcription of a word and not its spelling, when we are trying to divide it into constituent syllables or to decide how many syllables it has and how they are structured. For example, in a word like *exact*, the spelling does not help in deciding how we should divide the word into its constituent syllables, because the letter 'x' is actually pronounced as /gz/ and the two syllables in the word are /ɪg/ and /zækt/.

In this chapter we'll first consider how we define the syllable and analyse its structure in terms of the sounds, vowels and consonants, which make it up.

We often find more than one consonant occurring before and after a vowel in a syllable and this makes pronouncing certain words difficult for many learners of English. We'll examine what consonants or consonant sequences occur within a syllable and how to learn to pronounce them.

We'll also study another important feature of English, where a consonant, called ***a syllabic consonant***, occurs at the centre of a syllable that does not have any vowels.

The three units in this chapter are

5.1 How we define the syllable and analyse its structure

5.2 Consonant clusters and their pronunciation

5.3 Syllabic consonants and their pronunciation.

5.1 How we define the syllable and analyse its structure

The syllable being a unit of sound can be defined phonetically as well as phonologically. The phonetic definition will be in terms of how we produce a syllable, i.e., in terms of what type of sounds make up a syllable. The phonological definition will be in terms of how a syllable is structured in a particular language like English, i.e., in terms of the possible combinations of sounds that make up a syllable in a particular language like English.

Phonetic definition

Phonetically, a syllable is said to consist of a ***centre*** which has little or no obstruction to the flow of air and which sounds comparatively loud. Before and after the centre, there may be greater obstruction to the air flow and also the sound may be less loud.

According to this definition, at the centre of a syllable there is mostly a vowel and, at the beginning and end of a syllable, there may be consonants. This means that different types of syllables are possible.

(i) Syllables which consist of only a vowel like the ones found in words *I* or *eye*. In these words the vowel is neither preceded nor followed by any other sound.

(ii) Syllables where the vowel at the centre is preceded by one or more than one consonant but is not followed by any sound. For example, *bee, shoe, tree* and *fly*.
Syllables like these are called ***Open Syllables***. ***Open Syllables*** are syllables that have an ***onset*** but no ***termination***, because they have sounds before the centre but not after.

(iii) Syllables where the vowel at the centre is followed by one or more than one consonant but is not preceded by any sound. Examples are *ant, egg, ink, up,* and *ice.* Syllables like these are called ***Closed Syllables***. ***Closed Syllables*** are syllables that have no onset but have a termination, because they have no sounds before the centre but have one or more sounds after.

(iv) Syllables where the vowel at the centre is both preceded and followed by one or more than one consonant as in *book, case, step, felt, treat, strip, next* and *twelve*. These syllables have both an onset and a termination.

Thus the syllable has three positions, centre, onset and termination. The centre is also called the ***peak*** and another term used for termination is ***coda***.

The phonetic definition of a syllable seems satisfactory when we consider single syllables. But when we look at words with more than one syllable, problems arise, especially with the question of how exactly such words can be divided into constituent syllables. For example, in a word like *inspect*, we would all agree that there are two syllables. But when we think of how exactly we can divide the word into two syllables, there may be different answers. It is possible to divide the word into /ɪn/ and /spekt/, /ɪns/ and /pekt/, or /ɪnsp/ and /ekt/ or any other pair of syllables as long as each of them has a vowel. The phonetic definition of the syllable does not help us to find the correct answer. We need a definition of the syllable, which tells us what are the different ways in which a syllable may be structured i.e., what different combinations of sounds make up a syllable. In other words, we need a definition of the syllable in terms of its structure.

The syllable does not have the same structure in all languages. Sounds are combined in different ways in different languages and therefore, the syllable will have different structures in different languages. This means that the structure of the syllable is a phonological feature and we need a phonological definition of the syllable in order to account for the possible structures of a syllable.

Phonological definition

In order to describe the structure of the syllable in English, we need to know what sounds can occur at the beginning and end of a word, since the word is the smallest bit of language that we can use as a full utterance. We find that a word can begin with a vowel as in *apply, impress, under* or *end*, with one consonant as in *college, research, simple* or *thought*, with two consonants as in *present, flight, blue* or *school* or with three consonants as in *spring, strong, split* or *scream*. In the same way, when we look at what sounds occur at the end of a word, we find that a word can end with a vowel as in *pretty, shoe, cuckoo* or *boy*, with one consonant as in *cot, soap, cloth* or *touch*, with two consonants as in *cold, melt, bench* or *dance*, with three consonants as in *next, glimpse, twelfth* or *tempt* or with four consonants as in *texts* or *twelfths*.

Thus we see that a syllable is made up of two types of elements, vowels and consonants, the vowel being the obligatory element and the consonants being optional. A vowel by itself can be a syllable or it may be preceded by one, two or three consonants and/or it may be followed by one, two, three or four consonants. The vowel is the central element in the syllable and is called the ***Nucleus***. The consonants that precede the central vowel are called ***Releasing consonants*** and the consonants that follow the central vowel are called ***Arresting consonants.***

The structure of an English syllable can be shown symbolically as

$$\overrightarrow{(CCC)\,V\,(CCCC)}$$

where the consonants, Cs, are enclosed within brackets because they are optional. The arrow above indicates the order in which the vowel and the consonants can be combined in a syllable. The various structures possible in a syllable are

V *I*
CV *me*
CCV *true*
CCCV *spree*
VC *eat*
VCC *apt*
VCCC *amps*

VCCCC	
CVC	*sip*
CVCC	*gold*
CVCCC	*tempt*
CVCCCC	*texts*
CCVC	*truth*
CCVCC	*friend*
CCVCCC	*friends*
CCVCCCC	*twelfths*
CCCVC	*stream*
CCCVCC	*streets*
CCCVCCC	*splints*
CCCVCCCC	

The examples given here to illustrate syllables of different structures are full words. But we should note that a syllable does not always constitute a word and that it is often part of a word. For example, the word, *responsibility*, has six syllables, *re-spon-si-bil-i-ty,* which have the structures CV, CCVC, CV, CVC, V and CV and the word, *abstract,* has two syllables, *ab-stract*, which have the structures VC and CCCVCC.

It is essential to understand what the syllable is and how it is structured if we wish to understand the important features of spoken English and be able to speak English well. In fact, many of the characteristic features of English pronunciation are described in terms of the syllable.

(1) In Chapter 3 we saw how the pronunciation of English consonants changes depending on their positions and also on what sounds they combine with. For example, we saw that the voiceless plosives /p/, /t/, and /k/ are aspirated only in the initial position. The different positions, namely the initial, the final, and the middle have to be identified with reference to a syllable and not a word. In this case of aspiration in the initial position, another distinction is necessary. Syllables are either stressed or unstressed and the rule about the voiceless plosives being aspirated in the initial position applies only to stressed syllables. It is true that the examples we considered were all words, but they were mostly words with only one syllable that is stressed. This was only to make the description easier to follow. But we need to bear in mind that it is the concept of the syllable that is crucial here. The same is true of the feature of voicing, which also occurs only in specific positions.

(2) One of the most distinctive features of spoken English is word stress and to understand how and where English speakers use 'stress' in words and to learn to stress words correctly in our speech, we need to understand the syllabic structure of words. Further, the distinction between stressed and unstressed syllables is very important.

(3) Connected and fluent speech in English is marked by features such as contraction, elision and assimilation of sounds. These various strategies are also described in terms of syllabic structure and can be practised only with an understanding of the syllable and its structure.

(4) Finally, the distinctive tone patterns used in English and the ways in which speakers assign prominence to certain items of information in order to convey specific messages can also be understood and practised only if we are aware of the ways in which stressed and unstressed syllables are combined in English speech.

Exercises

A

L5.1. Listen to the following words. How many syllables are there in each of them?

national	students	umbrella	popular ......
saintly	angle	might	consult ......
idea	promise	season	smile ......
neither	twelfth	social	about ......
hastily	English	number	courtship ......
people	friendliness	textiles	pressurize ......
painfully	foreign	shrewd	attempt ......
occasion	baggage	eyes	stand ......
control	calm	pleasantly	heaven ......
callous	loyalty	lights	paper ......
flower	waterfall	college	wonderful ......
phonetics	history	paint	palmist ......

A

L5.2. Listen to the following words. Group them according to the number of syllables they have.

numerous	parliamentarian	student	computer
magnificent	humidity	organization	beautiful
temperature	stabilizer	international	apartment
comparison	passport	verification	graduation

certificate	degree	prominent	publisher
programming	argumentation	disallow	transport

2 syllables	3 syllables	4 syllables	5 syllables

L5.3. Listen to the following words. Write the syllabic structure of each of them.

strike	....	next	....	both	....	true	....
height	....	texts	....	first	....	count	....
joy	....	church	....	more	....	aim	....
clasps	....	push	....	catch	....	lamp	....
scream	....	prompt	....	third	....	hurt	....
ease	....	spine	....	queen	....	twist	....
kite	....	cough	....	ought	....	bike	....
swing	....	hanged	....	depth	....	thirst	....
self	....	float	....	pure	....	noise	....
please	....	child	....	dwell	....	warmth	....
widen	....	theirs	....	fifths	....	tempts	....
key	....	halves	....	axe	....	judge	....

L5.4. Listen to the following words and group them depending on the syllabic structure they have.

struck	surf	treat	love	mouse
bloom	hurt	plight	dark	queen
judge	king	crime	skirt	climb
fax	scream	lisps	shoes	squeeze
helps	drips	plant	keys	lock
charms	thief	pumps	sleeps	clasp
salt	drink	match	fifths	spasm

CVC	CCVC	CVCC	CCVCC	CCCVC	CVCCC

(A)

1. Where do syllable boundaries occur in the following words? Check your answers in a dictionary. (Remember that spelling can be misleading and therefore it is necessary to consider the pronunciation of the words)

responsibility	tolerance	phenomenon	gratitude
fundamentalism	university	industrialization	humorous
satisfaction	imperialistic	educational	prominence
independent	spectacular	illiterate	electrification
embarrassment	charismatic	judicious	correspondence
enormously	obedience	magnificent	triumphant

5.2 Consonant clusters and their pronunciation

As we have seen above, English syllables can have a variety of structures, which means that we need to learn to pronounce the different types of syllables correctly. Here again, we have to take into account how the vowels and consonants combine to form different types of syllables. It is mainly the number of consonants that can occur with a vowel either before or after or both before and after that gives rise to syllables that are quite difficult to pronounce. The various possibilities described above show that we need to practise three types of syllables.

(i) Syllables with two or three initial consonants,

(ii) Syllables with two, three or four final consonants, and

(iii) Syllables with more than two consonants in both the initial and final positions.

When two or more consonants occur together either initially or finally in a syllable they are said to form ***a consonant cluster***. Not all consonants can occur in either an initial or a final consonant cluster. The phonological rules of English determine what consonants can occur in these initial and final consonant clusters and also in what sequences they can occur.

Examples of the different types of consonant clusters possible at the beginning, the end and both the beginning and end are given below. These are words with one syllable (with only a few exceptions such as *beauty, duty, sclerosis* and *evolved*) and therefore, show consonant clusters at the beginning or the end of words.

(1) Initial clusters

(a) *With two consonants at the beginning*

(i) Those beginning with /s/

	/p/	/t/	/k/	/f/	/m/	/n/	/l/	/w/
/s/ +	*spin*	*stop*	*skit*	*sphere*	*smile*	*snack*	*slip*	*swipe*

(ii) Other two-consonant clusters

	/p/	/t/	/k/	/b/	/d/	/g/	/f/	/θ/	/ʃ/	/h/	/v/	/m/	/n/
/l/	*plot*	---	*clap*	*blue*	---	*glad*	*flat*	---	---	---	---	---	---
/r/	*price*	*trick*	*cry*	*bright*	*dry*	*greet*	*fry*	*three*	*shrink*	---	---	---	---
/w/	---	*twist*	*queen*	---	*dwell*	---	---	*thwart*	---	---	---	---	---
/j/	*pure*	*tube*	*queue*	*beauty*	*duty*	---	*few*	---	---	*huge*	*view*	*muse*	*news*

(b) *With three consonants at the beginning*

Here the possibilities are highly restricted. In three-consonant initial structures, the first sound can be only /s/. The possibilities in the second and the third positions are shown below.

/s/ +

	/p/	/t/	/k/
/l/	*split*	------	*sclerosis*
/r/	*spring*	*strike*	*scrap*
/w/	------	------	*squeeze*
/j/	*spew*	*stew*	*skew*

(2) Final clusters

There are many more consonant clusters in the final position than in the initial position.

(a) *With two consonants at the end*

(i) Where the first consonant is /m/, /n/, /ŋ/, /l/, or /s/

/mp/	/nt/	/nd/	/ŋk/	/lp/	/lt/	/lk/	/sp/	/st/	/sk/
jump	*dent*	*bind*	*thank*	*help*	*belt*	*milk*	*gasp*	*past*	*task*
camp	*lint*	*land*	*sink*	*gulp*	*tilt*	*bulk*	*lisp*	*fist*	*mask*
limp	*hunt*	*send*	*wink*	*pulp*	*halt*	*sulk*	*wasp*	*nest*	*husk*

(ii) Where the second consonant is /s/, /z/, /t/, /d/, or /θ/

/s/		/z/		/t/		/d/		/θ/	
lapse	/ps/	*ribs*	/bz/	*pact*	/kt/	*robbed*	/bd/	*depth*	/pθ/
false	/ls/	*fads*	/dz/	*kept*	/pt/	*loved*	/vd/	*tenth*	/nθ/
box	/ks/	*logs*	/gz/	*lift*	/ft/	*gold*	/ld/	*fifth*	/fθ/

(b) *With three consonants at the end*

(i) Where the final consonant is the plural noun suffix or the singular verb suffix /s/ or /z/ or the past tense suffix /t/ or /d/

/s/		/z/		/t/		/d/	
wasps	/sps/	*bands*	/ndz/	*pumped*	/mpt/	*ranged*	/ndʒd/

nests /sts/ *bulbs* /lbz/ *thanked* /nkt/ *singed* /ndʒd/
camps /mps/ *winds* /ndz/ *gasped* /spt/ *tinged* /ndʒd/
dents /nts/ *fields* /ldz/ *gulped* /lpt/ *evolved* /lvd/
belts /lts/ *sands* /ndz/ *sulked* /lkt/ *delved* /lvd/
gifts /fts/ *holds* /ldz/ *asked* /skt/ *shelved* /lvd/

(ii) Where the final consonant is /t/or /θ/

/t/ /θ/

text /kst/ *sixth* /ksθ/
tempt /mpt/ *twelfth* /lfθ/

(c) *With four consonants at the end*

These are formed when the suffix /s/ is added to words with three final consonants like the four words above in (b) (ii)

texts /ksts/ *sixths* /ksθs/
tempts /mpts/ *twelfths* /lfθs/

(3) *Clusters at both the beginning and end*

(a) *With two consonants at the beginning and end*

blunt *branch* *blast* *trust* *brink*
drunk *crest* *clump* *graft* *crept*

(b) *With two consonants at the beginning and three consonants at the end*

prompt *crafts* *twelfth* *crisps* *glimpse* *tracts*

(c) *With two consonants at the beginning and four consonants at the end*

prompts *twelfths* *glimpsed*

(d) *With three consonants at the beginning and two consonants at the end*

sprint *splint* *squint* *script* *strings* *streets*

(e) *With three consonants at the beginning and end*

sprints *splints* *squints* *scripts*

(4) *Clusters within words*

We find that two or more consonants can occur not only at the beginning and end of words but also within words. Some examples are given below.

(a) *With two consonants*

attraction *accelerate* *actual* *betray* *compare* *system*
sympathy *number* *mistake* *lecture* *fifteen*

(b) *With three consonants*

anxious *astronaut* *central* *compress* *describe* *disclaim*
fixture *improve* *install* *lustrous* *muscular* *obstinate*

(c) *With four consonants*

monstrous *inscribe* *demonstrate* *express* *extra* *explain*

(d) *With more than one instance of two or more consonants in a word*

inspector *transplantation* *prospectus* *obnoxious* *destructive*

T

In quite a few words, the consonants that occur together within a word belong to different syllables that make up the word. For example, in *fixture*, there are three consonants /kstʃ/ that occur together within the word. But when we consider the syllabic structure of this word, we find that it has two syllables, '*fix*' and '*ture*' and that two consonants /ks/ occur in the first syllable, where as the consonant /tʃ/ occurs in the second syllable. Similarly in the word *transplantation*, we find four consonants /nspl/ occurring together within the word. But the syllabic structure of the word shows that there are four syllables in the word and that the consonant /n/ occurs at the end of the first syllable, where as the consonants /spl/ occur at the beginning of the second syllable. The structure of these syllables that make up a longer word is in accordance with the phonological rules about how many consonants and which consonants can occur at the beginning and end of syllable. As we have seen, if three consonants occur together at the beginning of a syllable, the first has to be /s/, the second has to be /p/, /t/ or /k/ and the third is /l/, /r/, /w/, or /j/. So we have /spl/ at the beginning of the second syllable in *transplantation*.

Further, there are instances of consonants that sometimes occur together within a syllable and at other times together but in different syllables within a word. For example, let us look at the consonants /nt/ in *want* and *contest*. In *want* they occur together at the end of the single syllable that makes up the word. But in *contest* the consonant /n/ occurs at the end of the first of the two syllables in the word and the consonant /t/ occurs at the beginning of the second. Thus though the two consonants occur together within the word *contest*, they belong to different syllables here. When consonants such as /n/ and /t/ occur together in the same syllable as in *want*, they are said to form ***a consonant cluster***. But when they occur together but in different syllables within a word as in *contest*, they are called ***abutting consonants***.

Since in American English the sound /r/ is pronounced in all positions, words such as *heart, nerve, lord, sharp, blurb, lark, horn, warm* have a two consonant cluster at the end in American speech. But in British English, such words have only one consonant at the end since the sound /r/ is not pronounced before a consonant.

Indian languages do not have the same type of consonant clusters as English has and therefore, Indian speakers need to practise the pronunciation of English consonant clusters carefully. They may experience difficulties with

(1) words beginning with two consonant clusters such as /pl/, /bl/, gl/, /fl/, /tr/, /fr/, /kw/, /tw/, /kj/, /tj/ etc.,
(2) words beginning with three consonant clusters,
(3) words ending with two consonant clusters such as /lp/, /lt/, /lθ/, /lf/, /sp/, /st/, /sk/, /pt/, /kt/, /nd/ etc., and
(4) words ending in three consonant and four consonant clusters.

In practicing words with consonant clusters at the beginning, it is important that we should take care to avoid the common errors that occur in the speech of English learners. When we pronounce words with consonant clusters at the beginning, we

should not change any consonant in a cluster to a different consonant, as for example, using /r/ for /l/ in words such as *glass, clash,* and *plod* and saying *grass, crash,* and *prod* instead,

should not leave out any consonant in a cluster, as for example, leaving out /w/ in words such as *question* and *guava*,

should not add an extra vowel at the beginning of a word with an initial consonant cluster, as for example, adding /ɪ/ at the beginning of words such as *school, spring,* and *sport*, and

should not add an extra vowel between consonants in a cluster at the beginning of a word, as for example, adding /ɪ/ between /t/ and /r/ in words such as *travel, trade,* and *traffic*.

Pronouncing words with consonant clusters at the end

Words with consonant clusters at the end, especially those ending in three and four consonants are difficult to pronounce. Even speakers whose mother tongue is English sometimes find it difficult to pronounce such words. A strategy they use to make it easier to pronounce words such as *pacts, lumps, jumped, masked, minds* and *hints*, which have three consonant clusters at the end, is to leave out the middle consonant. Thus what we hear when these words are spoken is /pæks/, /lʊms/, /dʒʌmt/, /mɑːst/, /maɪns/ and /hɪns/ without the middle consonants /t/, /p/, /p/, /k/, /d/, and /t/.

(1) We have to note that it is the ***middle consonant*** that is left out and ***not the final consonant***. Leaving out the final consonant can cause misunderstanding, since in these words, the final consonant indicates the grammatical ending that marks the plural as in *pacts, lumps, minds* and *hints* or the past tense as in *jumped* and *masked*. When the final consonant is not a grammatical suffix, leaving out the final consonant can cause even greater confusion, as we can see in words such as *pact, hump, mind, guest,* and *mend*, where if the final consonant is left out, we have a different set of words, *pack, hum, mine, guess,* and *men*. It is therefore very important that we don't leave out the final consonant in words that end in consonant clusters.

(2) Words such as *jumped* and *masked* pose another problem for English learners, especially if their pronunciation is guided by spelling. It is important to note that there is no vowel between 'p' and 'd' in *jumped* and 'k' and 'd' in *masked*. Also the letter 'd' is pronounced /t/. Some learners have a tendency to insert a vowel between consonants in clusters in words such as *jumped, masked, watched, talked,* and *kicked*, mainly because of spelling and sometimes just to make the pronunciation of the cluster easier. This should be avoided.

(3) Another practice that should be avoided is adding a vowel at the end of words with a final consonant cluster such as *fast, bounce, gold, hint, crisp,* and *rift*, where some speakers add /ə/ at the end.

Divergence between spelling and pronunciation

There are two instances of where spelling suggests similar consonant clusters at the end but pronunciation shows a divergence.

(1) Words ending in 'mp' and 'mb' in the final position are pronounced differently. Those ending in 'mp' such as

camp	*dump*	*pump*
damp	*sump*	*lamp*
bump	*thump*	*jump*

are pronounced with a consonant cluster /mp/. But those ending in 'mb' such as

bomb	*comb*	*dumb*
thumb	*lamb*	*womb*

are pronounced with only /m/ at the end and 'b' is silent.

(2) Words ending in 'nk' and 'ng' in the final position are also pronounced differently. Those ending in 'nk' such as

bank	*sink*	*think*	*rank*
link	*pink*	*wink*	

are pronounced with a consonant cluster /ŋk/, whereas those ending in 'ng' such as

bang	*king*	*thing*
wing	*long*	

are pronounced with only /ŋ/ at the end.

But if 'ng' occurs in the middle of a word as in

anger *finger* *linger*

it is pronounced with the consonant cluster /ŋg/. In words derived from verbs such as

singer *hanger* *banger*

however, 'ng' is pronounced with only the consonant /ŋ/. (*See Chapter 3 Unit 4*)

Exercises

L5.5. **Listen to the pairs of sentences and decide which of the two words given is used in the blank in each sentence. Write A or B in the blank.**

		A	B
(i)	She did not sleep the whole night because of the ________. It would be better if you learn to use ________ language in all your letters.	pain	plain
(ii)	He is described as one of the greatest writers of English ________. They decided to ________ as security men and enter the building.	pose	prose
(iii)	I asked her to buy a loaf of ________. The children go to ________ at 9 o'clock.	bed	bread
(iv)	They wanted to ________ the modern and traditional styles of dancing. He could not ________ his left leg after the accident.	bend	blend
(v)	They thought that the future was ________. The bird caught the fish in its ________.	beak	bleak
(vi)	Her mother asked her to ________ her room. The young man was ________ on going abroad.	keen	clean
(vii)	The dress seems to ________ to her body. A large number of people had assembled to greet the ________ on his birthday.	king	cling
(viii)	My friend wanted me to ________ her books on the shelf. The burglar tried to ________ into the room noiselessly.	keep	creep
(ix)	Be careful, the paint may ________ on the floor. ________ it in hot water to remove the grease.	dip	drip
(x)	Do not ________ after drinking. The forecast was that the prices of shares could ________ low again.	dive	drive

(xi) Your next monthly installment is __________ now. do due

Please ____________ attend the meeting tomorrow.

(xii) The _____________ of new cars bought by
the company will be lined up for inspection. feet fleet

She has been on her______________ since
six o'clock in the morning.

(xiii) The ________________ was covered with
a beautiful carpet. four floor

There were _____________ children in the small room.

(xiv) The old woman looked very _____________. fail frail

We are aware that our attempts could _____________.

(xv) The girls appeared to _____________ down the steps. guide glide

We would like someone to _____________ us to the castle.

(xvi) This project helped me _____________ experience. gain grain

The government decided to ban _____________
exports for one year.

(xvii) There was not a _____________ of evidence against him. shed shred

The ____________ was used to store old machinery.

(xviii) The ____________ was visited by thousands of people. shine shrine

He did not ____________ as a musician but became
a very good actor.

(xix) They used a ______________ to fasten the bundles. thong throng

It was very difficult to make way through the
______________.

(xx) We could not see anything in the ___________. fog flog

It is a criminal offence to _____________ children.

1. Repeat the pairs of sentences and practise the pronunciation of the pairs of words.
2. Replace /l/ with /r/ or /r/ with /l/ as the case may be in the words below and practise the pairs of words you get.

(i)			(ii)		
	play	....		brand	....
	plod	....		blink	....
	pry	....		bloom	....

	prop	....		breach	....
	present	....		bright	....
(iii)	cram	....	(iv)	flame	....
	cloud	....		frank	....
	cramp	....		flesh	....
	clash	....		free	....
	clutch	....		flight	....
(v)	glow	....			
	grade	....			
	gland	....			
	groom	....			
	gloss	....			

3. Add two consonant sounds to the beginning of the words below and practice the pronunciation of the word/s that you get. You may be able to add different consonants to some of the words below and get more than one new word.
   You can choose from the list of two consonant clusters that occur in the initial position given in 5.2 (1) (a) (i) and (ii) on pages 172-73 and and refer to your dictionary to check the words you get. (***Remember you have to consider the pronunciation of the words given and not the spelling and also add two consonant sounds and not two letters at the beginning***)

air	/eə(r)/	....	....	....
ate	/eɪt/	....	....	....
ape	/eɪp/	....	....	....
and	/ænd/	....	....	....
ache	/eɪk/	....	....	....
ash	/æʃ/	....	....	....
ace	/eɪs/	....	....	....
am	/æm/	....	....	....
each	/iːtʃ/	....	....	....
end	/end/	....	....	....
ease	/iːz/	....	....	....
I	/aɪ/	....	....	....

ice	/aɪs/	………………	………………	………………
ill	/ɪl/	………………		………………
it	/ɪt/	………………		………………

4. (a) Find 5 words ending with each of the consonant clusters given and practise their pronunciation. You can refer to your dictionary to help you find the words. ***Remember you have to consider the pronunciation of the words given and not the spelling.***

(i) /nt/ paint	(ii) /nd/ fond	(iii) /nθ/ tenth
………………	………………	………………
………………	………………	………………
………………	………………	………………
………………	………………	………………
………………	………………	………………

(iv) /ŋk/ bank	(v) /lt/ halt	(vi) /ld/ child
………………	………………	………………
………………		………………
………………	………………	………………
………………	………………	………………
………………	………………	………………

(vii) /lk/ bulk	(viii) /sp/ gasp	(ix) /st/ dust
………………	………………	………………
………………	………………	………………
………………	………………	………………
………………	………………	………………
………………	………………	………………

(x) /sk/ risk	(xi) /ks/ wax	(xii) /kt/ sect
………………	………………	………………
………………	………………	………………
………………	………………	………………
………………	………………	………………
………………	………………	………………

(b) Divide the words you found above into nouns and verbs.

(i) Add the plural suffix to the nouns and practise the resulting words ending with three consonants, e.g., *paints, banks* etc.

(ii) Add the past tense suffix to the verbs and practise the resulting words ending with three consonants, e.g., *risked, gasped* etc.

L5.6. Listen to the pairs of sentences and decide which of the two words given is used in the blank in each sentence. Write A or B in the blank.

		A	B
(i)	The ___________ took off smoothly despite the bad weather. He spoke in ___________ and had no intention of hurting anyone.	jet	jest
(ii)	She complained of ___________ pain. The children are playing ___________.	chess	chest
(iii)	The school is organizing a summer ___________ for the high school children. His ___________ was blown away by the wind.	cap	camp
(iv)	The new books are on this ___________. They found an unexploded ___________.	shell	shelf
(v)	They measured the ___________ of the pool. The ___________ of the young actor shocked everyone.	death	depth
(vi)	The ___________ got filled in two hours. He worked out the ___________ in his head.	sum	sump
(vii)	The ice cream was beginning to ___________. I ___________ my old school teacher after many years.	met	melt
(viii)	It is time to cut the ___________. His ___________ was so tight that the boy could not run away.	grass	grasp
(ix)	It was his ___________ that he could break open any lock. We enjoyed the ___________ ride very much.	boat	boast

(x) Please take your ____________ with you. pass past

There is no use thinking about the ____________.

(xi) When she heard the good news, she ____________ for joy. wet wept

There was a notice cautioning people about the ____________ floor.

(xii) He worked in a ____________ mine. coal cold

It was very ____________ and we decided to stay at home.

(xiii) The ____________ between the rich and poor countries has widened. gull gulf

We saw the ____________ diving and coming up with the fish in its beak.

(xiv) She tried to ____________ the bag but it was too heavy for her. lit lift

The roads were well ____________ and driving was no problem.

(xv) The students listened to the professor with ____________ attention. rap rapt

____________ music is very popular these days.

5. Repeat the pairs of sentences and practise the pronunciation of the pairs of words.

L5.7. Listen to the pairs of sentences and decide which of the two words given is used in the blank in each sentence. Write A or B in the blank.

A B

(i) His colleagues gave him a nice ____________ when he retired. gift gifts

The child wanted to open all the ____________ she got on her birthday.

(ii) There was a fear that the school building would ____________ after the earthquake. collapse collapsed

The talks between the two companies ____________.

(iii) The people here don't stop working even in the ____________ of winter. depth depths

Do you know the ____________ of these oil wells?

(iv)	He works as a safety ____________ in a factory. The insurance people wanted to ___________ the vehicle.	inspect	inspector
(v)	She is looking quite _______________ now. Her sister is ________________ than she is.	plump	plumper
(vi)	Shares _____________ to their lowest value in more than a year. Power shut down will _______________ the whole city into darkness.	plunge	plunged
(vii)	Fill in the ______________ with appropriate prepositions. I left one ______________ unfilled because I did not know the answer.	blank	blanks
(viii)	The car company announced that they would _____________ the new model next month. The young men ______________ a campaign to help the old people living alone.	launch	launched
(ix)	Don't _______________ me, I am on a diet. She _________________ children giving them chocolates.	tempt	tempts
(x)	The principal said that they will have to stop their _____________. He was such a ________________ when he was in school.	pranks	prankster

6. Repeat the pairs of sentences and practise the pronunciation of the pairs of words.

5.3 Syllabic consonants and their pronunciation

In a syllable the nucleus is generally a vowel and this is preceded or followed by consonants, which are marginal elements. But there are some special cases where a consonant becomes the nucleus of the syllable. For example, the consonant /l/ in words such as *bottle, cattle, kettle, little,* and *subtle,* and the consonant /n/ in words such as *cotton, sudden, button,* and *mutton*, become vowel-like and function as the nucleus of unstressed syllables. When consonants like /l/ and /n/ function as the nucleus of unstressed syllables without a vowel, they are called ***Syllabic consonants***. These syllabic consonants are shown in dictionaries with a vertical line ˌ under the consonant or a ᵊ symbol before the consonant.

(1) Syllabic consonants /l̩/ and /n̩/ occur mostly after the following consonants at the end of stressed syllables.

	/l̩/		/n̩/
/t/	*battle, cattle, metal, rattle*	/t/	*cotton, mutton, button, rotten*
/d/	*pedal, muddle, fiddle, riddle*	/d/	*sudden, widen, garden, hidden*
/p/	*people, chapel, ripple, supple*	/p/	*happen, open, deepen, sharpen*
/b/	*pebble, bubble, dribble, trouble*	/s/	*listen, fasten, mason, person*
/s/	*parcel, bustle, castle, tussle*	/z/	*season, prison, reason, cousin*
/z/	*puzzle, muzzle, nuzzle, fizzle*	/f/	*roughen, toughen, soften, stiffen*
/k/	*fickle, heckle, buckle, knuckle*	/v/	*heaven, given, seven, driven*
/n/	*panel, funnel, kernel, tunnel*	/θ/	*heathen, python, lengthen, strengthen*
		/ʃ/	*mission, passion, ration, caution*
		/ʒ/	*fusion, vision, illusion, collision*

Most of these are spelt with *-le*, but some with *-al*, *-el*, or *-ol*.

Most of these are spelt with *-en*, *-on*, or *-ion*.

(2) In addition to words such as the above, past participle forms ending in *–en* such as

beaten *ridden* *eaten* *hidden* *written*

are also used with syllabic consonants in conversation

(3) Contracted negatives ending in *–nt* such as

didn't *couldn't* *wouldn't* *hadn't*

that frequently occur in conversation provide another instance of the use of syllabic consonants.

(4) Another consonant that functions as a syllabic consonant is /m/ in words ending in *-sm* such as

socialism *communism* *journalism* *criticism* *Hinduism*

> Pronouncing syllabic consonants
>
> In pronouncing syllabic consonants, it is important to remember that we should not pronounce a vowel + consonant sequence in words such as *bottle, trouble, cousin,* and *dozen*. These words should be pronounced
>
> (British) /bɒtl/ or (American) /bɑːtl/, /trʌbl/, /kʌzn/, and /dʌzn/
>
> **and not**
>
> /bɒtəl/ or /bɑːtəl, /trʌbəl/, /kʌzən/, and /dʌzən/.

Celce-Murcia et al (1996:77) explain how learners can practise pronouncing the syllabic consonants, /n̩/ and /l̩/ in words like *cotton* and *battle*. They suggest that learners should first say *cot* with the final sound /t/ unreleased. With the tongue still touching the alveolar ridge, they should transform the unreleased /t/ sound into an /n̩/ by releasing the air blocked in the mouth out through the nose to form the nasal sound. Similarly, in producing *battle*, they should say the first syllable *bat* and hold the front of the tongue on the ridge behind the upper front teeth. Then they should release the air blocked in the mouth out over the sides of the tongue to form /l̩/, never allowing the tongue to move away from the alveolar ridge.

Since Indian speakers mostly go by the spelling of words, they tend to produce a vowel + consonant sequence in the last syllable in words such as *cotton, sudden, metal,* and *pistol* that end with a syllabic consonant. It is necessary that they are aware of how syllabic consonants are pronounced and practise the correct pronunciation of words with syllabic consonants.

Exercises

L5.8. Listen and identify words with syllabic consonants.

(i) Global stocks tumble
(ii) Tourist arrivals double
(iii) Fresh troubles rattle stock markets
(iv) International models fumble
(v) Considerable changes in fiscal policy
(vi) Final stop for eternal delights
(vii) Tickle your grey cells
(viii) Special prizes for children
(ix) Heavy vehicles not allowed
(x) Abandon superstition
(xi) Garbage disposal to be outsourced
(xii) Professionals United beaten
(xiii) No place for Communalism in society
(xiv) Festival celebrations opened
(xv) Manned space programme planned
(xvi) Student activism criticised
(xvii) Incredible adventures on Disney Channel
(xviii) Mission impossible achieved
(xix) Anthology of articles by liberal writers
(xx) Enable the disabled

1. Practise each utterance focusing on the right pronunciation of syllabic consonants.

L5.9. Listen to these sentences. Notice the pronunciation of the contracted negatives.

(i) Why *didn't* you buy the laptop?
I *didn't* have the money to buy it.

(ii) Why *shouldn't* we protest?
You *shouldn't* break the rules.

(iii) *Wouldn't* they like to come for a picnic?
They *wouldn't* like to come if their neighbours are coming.

(iv) *Couldn't* you have asked for more time?
I *couldn't* have, because I *didn't* have any good reasons.

(v) *Didn't* they have to submit their assignments today?
Yes, some did but quite a few *didn't*.

(vi) I *didn't* get a bus, so I took a taxi thinking you *wouldn't* be here if I came late.
You *needn't* have hurried. I *wouldn't* have left before you came.

2. Practise the sentences focusing on the right pronunciation of the syllabic consonants in the contracted negatives.

A

L5.10. Listen to the words and put them into the appropriate group.

agnosticism casteism patriotism paganism feminism heroism

magnetism chauvinism atheism puritanism pragmatism liberalism

racism skepticism escapism dynamism theism secularism

You may wish to put some words in more than one group.

Qualities you will be praised for	Qualities you will be criticized for	Religious beliefs you may have	Social beliefs you may have

3. Practise the pronunciation of the words you grouped above taking care to pronounce the syllabic consonants correctly.

L5.11. Listen to three jokes read by a British English speaker, an American English speaker and an Indian speaker.

First listen without looking at the texts given below and then listen again following the texts.

(i) Use the word 'information' in a sentence: 'Geese sometimes fly information.' (*Man walks into a bar* The Ultimate Collection of Jokes and One-liners Stephen Arnott and Mike Haskins p. 151)

(ii) What does the word 'benign' mean?: 'Benign is what you will be after you be eight.' (*Man walks into a bar* The Ultimate Collection of Jokes and One-liners Stephen Arnott and Mike Haskins p. 152)

(iii) Susie is having trouble with her computer so she calls Harry, the computer guy, over to her desk. Harry clicks a couple of buttons and solves the problem. 'So, what was wrong?' asks Susie. Harry replies, 'It was an ID ten T error.' 'So what's that?' asks Susie. 'Write it down,' says Harry. 'You'll figure it out.' (*Man walks into a bar* The Ultimate Collection of Jokes and One-liners Stephen Arnott and Mike Haskins p. 277)

1. (a) Read the three jokes and record your readings on a tape or CD and (b) play them to your teacher or friend/s and get their feedback on your readings.

L5.12. (i) Listen to a fable read by a British English speaker, an American English speaker and an Indian speaker.

First listen without looking at the text given below and then listen again following the texts.

A MISER sold all that he had and bought a lump of gold, which he buried in a hole in the ground by the side of an old wall and went to look at daily. One of his workmen observed his frequent visits to the spot and decided to watch his movements. He soon discovered the secret of the hidden treasure, and digging down, came to the lump of gold, and stole it. The Miser, on his next visit, found the hole empty and began to tear his hair and to make loud lamentations. A neighbour, seeing him overcome with grief and learning the cause, said, "Pray do not grieve so; but go and take a stone, and place it in the hole, and fancy that the gold is still lying there. It will do you quite the same service; for when the gold was there, you had it not, as you did not make the slightest use of it."

http://aesopfables.com/cgi/aesop1.cgi?3&TheMiser&miser.jpg

(ii) Listen again and identify the words that have these consonant clusters

Final clusters		Initial clusters		Both initial and final clusters	
....ld	3 words	sp....		gr...nd	with 1 syllable
....mp		tr....		fr...nt	with 2 syllables
....nd		st....	3 words	sl...st	with 2 syllables
....nt		gr....	2 words		
....nts		pr....			
....kst		pl....			
		kw....			

(iii) Listen once again and identify the words with these syllabic consonants.

/....dn/

/....ʃns/

(iv) Read the fable taking care to pronounce correctly the words you have identified above in (ii) and (iii). Record your readings on a tape or CD and (b) play them to your teacher or friend/s and get their feedback on your reading.

Chapter summary

1. There have been two approaches to defining a syllable resulting in (1) a ***Phonetic definition*** in terms of how a syllable is produced and (2) a ***Phonological definition*** in terms of how a syllable is structured in particular languages.
   (1) Phonetically, a syllable is defined as a unit of sound with a centre which has little or no obstruction to the airflow and which may be preceded and/or followed by a greater degree of obstruction to the airflow. This means that at the centre of a syllable, there is a vowel that may be preceded and/or followed by consonants. Thus there can be different types of syllables, (i) those that consist of only a vowel at the centre like *I*, (ii) those in which the centre is preceded by consonants but not followed by any like *we* and *see*, which are called ***Open Syllables***, as they have an ***onset*** but no ***termination***, (iii) those in which the centre is not preceded but followed by consonants like *ice* and *eat*, which are called ***Closed Syllables***, as they have no onset but have a termination, and (iv) those in which the centre is both preceded and followed by consonants like *bag* and *kite*, which have both an onset and a termination.
   (2) Phonologically, a syllable is defined in terms of how it is structured in particular languages. In English, a syllable obligatorily has a vowel, which is its ***nucleus***. This can be preceded by one, two or three optional consonants called ***Releasing***

consonants and / or followed by one, two, three or four optional consonants called ***Arresting consonants***. The structure of a syllable in English can be shown as

$$\overrightarrow{\text{(CCC)V(CCCC)}}$$

2. When two or more consonants occur together either initially or finally in a syllable they form ***a consonant cluster***. The phonological rules of English determine what consonants can occur in these initial and final consonant clusters and also in what sequences they can occur.

   Syllables and words with initial or/and final consonant clusters are often difficult to pronounce and learners should practice their correct pronunciation taking care to avoid common errors such as changing or leaving out a consonant, adding an extra vowel either at the beginning or between consonants in initial consonant clusters and leaving out the final consonant, adding a vowel either in the middle or at the end in final consonant clusters.

3. In English there are special cases of syllables where a consonant functions as the nucleus. Such a consonant is called ***a syllabic consonant***. /l/ and /n/ function as syllabic consonants in unstressed syllables in words such as *battle*, *little*, *sudden*, and *button*. Syllabic consonants also occur in past participle forms ending in *–en* and contracted negatives ending in *–nt*, which occur frequently in conversation. /m/ also functions as a syllabic consonant in words such as *capitalism*. It is important that learners practice the correct pronunciation of words with syllabic consonants without inserting a vowel between the consonants in the second syllable in words such as *battle* and *sudden*.

6

Word stress

In English there is a special relationship between the different parts of a word.... in an English word of two or more syllables, one of these will have 'prominence' or 'stress' That syllable is perceived as more prominent because of a complex of features such as loudness, length of vowel, etc. If the learner doesn't stress one syllable more than another or stresses on the wrong syllable, it may be very difficult for the listener to identify the word. This is because the stress pattern of a word is an important part of its identity ...

Joanne Kenworthy *Teaching English Pronunciation* 1987 p. 18

Initially, learners need to understand that a basic characteristic of every English word containing more than one syllable is its stress pattern. They also need to understand that even if all the individual sounds are pronounced correctly, incorrect placement of stress can cause misunderstanding.

Celce-Murcia M, Brinton D.M & Goodwin J.M *Teaching Pronunciation* 1996 p. 143

PREVIEW

In our study of English pronunciation, we have so far focused on (1) the individual sounds, the vowels and consonants of English, and (2) the syllable and its structure in English. When we speak, we combine sounds and syllables into longer sequences that are recognizable as words and sentences and in connected speech, we find that certain features affect the manner in which individual sounds or syllables are pronounced. One such important feature is called ***Stress.***

When we consider how the following words are pronounced,

chapter	*admire*
sister	*surprise*
argue	*conclude*

we notice that all of them have two syllables, but the way we pronounce the two syllables is different in the words in the two columns. In the words in the left column, we pronounce the first syllable more strongly than the second, whereas in the words in the right column, it is the second syllable that is pronounced more strongly than the first. An important feature of spoken English is that when we use words of more than one syllable, we generally pronounce one syllable more strongly than the other syllables in the word, so that this syllable stands out from its background. The syllable that is pronounced more strongly than the other syllables in the same word is said to be ***stressed*** or ***accented*** or to receive the ***stress*** or ***accent.***

In this chapter we'll first see how stressed syllables are different from unstressed syllables. Then we'll consider the different degrees of stress found in words and also the conventions used to mark primary and secondary stress. The most important question about word stress is which syllable in a word gets primary or main stress. There are important features of words that decide where primary stress falls in a word and we'll examine these features with examples.

There are eleven units in this chapter.

6.1 How stressed syllables are different from unstressed syllables

When we say that in words a certain syllable is stressed or produced more strongly than other syllables which are unstressed, the question that comes up is how we can distinguish between stressed and unstressed syllables. We can look at this question in two ways, one from the point of view of the speaker and the second, that of the listener. We can ask what the speaker does in producing a stressed syllable or what the listener hears in recognizing a syllable as stressed. This means that we can consider stress either in terms of production or perception. The two perspectives may be closely related but are not identical.

Investigations into the processes of speech production have not been able to give clear and specific answers to the question of how stressed syllables are produced. The one difference that has been noticed is that a speaker uses more muscular energy or makes a greater muscular effort when producing stressed syllables than unstressed syllables. But it is difficult to measure the muscular energy used in speaking.

In contrast it is easier to identify the features that help a listener to recognize a syllable as stressed. From the point of view of perception, the stressed syllable is stronger than unstressed syllables because of specific features:

(i) Stressed syllables are louder than unstressed ones.

(ii) Stressed syllables are also perceived to be longer than unstressed ones.

(iii) ***Pitch*** and pitch movement are important features of speech. ***Pitch*** is related to the frequency of vibration of the vocal cords and every syllable is said on some pitch, high or low. If all syllables in a word are said on a pitch except one, on which the pitch falls from a high or rises from a low, then the syllable on which the pitch movement takes place is heard as stressed.

(iv) Generally, in English the stressed syllable has a vowel that is different in quality from the vowels in unstressed vowels. Unstressed syllables frequently have the vowels /ʊ/, /ɪ/ and /ə/ and also syllabic consonants. Stressed syllables, in contrast, often have long vowels or diphthongs, which are perceived to be stronger against the 'background' of the weaker unstressed syllables.

Generally, these four features combine to produce the effect of being strong, though sometimes syllables are made strong by only one or two of these features.

Exercises

L6.1. Listen to these words and identify and underline the stressed syllable in each. Notice the use of reduced vowels in the unstressed syllables.

begin	oppose	basket	belief	fulfill
number	protect	organ	structure	consult
surprise	signal	sponsor	prepare	foolish
climate	teacher	sterile	equal	silent
alarm	amuse	vacate	erase	contempt
system	harbour	immense	provoke	taboo
council	disgrace	promise	legend	disturb
crystal	mistake	derive	velvet	become
problem	polite	concern	protein	mature
				question

1. Practise the pronunciation of the words placing the stress on the right syllable and using reduced vowels in the unstressed syllable.

6.2 Word stress and degrees of stress within a word

We have said that in words of two or more syllables, one syllable is made stronger than other syllables i.e., one syllable is stressed, whereas other syllables are unstressed. Here we are looking at ***Word Stress*** or stress within the word. We should remember that in studying word stress, we are looking at words as they are said in isolation, though we know that we generally combine words when we speak. It is only a few words like *yes, no, please, who, what, why, how*, which we use by themselves as complete utterances. But in order to understand how word stress works and to find out where we place the stress in words, it is necessary to look at words in isolation.

Degrees of Stress

The distinction we have made between stressed syllables and unstressed syllables suggests that there is a simple distinction between the presence and the absence of stress. But often, in words with more than three or four syllables like, for example, *possibility* or *qualification*, there is one syllable, the third in *possibility* and the fourth in *qualification,* which gets the type of stress that has been described above and in addition to this, the first syllable in each word gets a stress that is weaker than this type of stress. What is noticeable is that the first syllable in these words is stronger than the other unstressed syllables, but not as strong as the stressed syllable. It is therefore necessary to recognize two degrees of stress, one, ***Primary or Strong stress*** and the other, ***Secondary or Weak stress***. Thus we can say that in English speech, we find three kinds of syllables in terms of stress, (a) syllables with primary or strong stress, (b) syllables with secondary or weak stress and (c) syllables with no stress. In *possibility*, the third syllable has the primary stress, the first syllable, the secondary stress and the other syllables, no stress and similarly, in *qualification*, the fourth syllable has the primary stress, the first, the secondary stress and the other syllables, no stress.

Conventions of representing stressed and unstressed syllables

When words are written using normal spelling, the convention is to use large capital letters, small capital letters, and lower case letters to represent strongly stressed syllables, weakly stressed syllables and unstressed syllables respectively. For example, POSSIBILity and QUALIfiCAtion.

When words are phonetically transcribed, the convention is to use a small vertical line just above and before the stressed syllable and just below and before the weakly stressed syllable. For example /ˌpɒsəˈbɪləti/ and /ˌkwɒlɪfɪˈkeɪʃn/.

The stress pattern in the two words is indicated by ooOoo and oooOo, where 'O' indicates a stressed syllable, 'o', a weakly stressed syllable and 'o', an unstressed syllable.

Exercises

A

L6.2. Listen to these words and mark the syllables with strong and weak stress in each. Rewrite the words using large and small capital letters to indicate strogly and weakly stressed syllables.

abbreviation	…………………	credibility	…………………
humanitarian	…………………	manifestation	…………………
productivity	…………………	sentimental	…………………
communication	…………………	verisimilitude	…………………
zoological	…………………	problematic	…………………

insensibility	....	biographical	....
contradiction	....	discontinuous	....
privatization	....	medication	....
elementary	....	consultation	....
transformation	....	conductivity	....

1. Practise the pronunciation of the words with the right stress patterns and appropriate use of reduced vowels in unstressed syllables.

L6.3. Listen to these words and group them according to their stress patterns.

betrayal	portrayal	register	develop	citizen
minimum	proportion	bifurcate	history	beautiful
calculate	deputy	prejudice	balcony	phonetics
tomorrow	delicate	companion	secular	behavior
suitable	department	professor	cinema	gradual
computer	demolish	telephone	terrible	survival
successful	practical	transparent	chemistry	detachment
momentum	collective	guardian	formula	benefit
decorate	important	molecule	fantasy	tentative
mechanic	feminine	manuscript	removal	barrister

Ooo　　　　　　　　　　oOo

2. Practise the pronunciation of the words with the right stress patterns and appropriate use of reduced vowels in unstressed syllables.

6.3 Important features in deciding word stress placement

In English, word stress does not always fall on the same syllable in words. For example, if we look at words like *quantity, polite, politician* and *responsibility*, we notice that the stress falls on the first syllable in /ˈkwɒntəti/, the second in /pəˈlaɪt/, the third in /pɒleˈtɪʃn/ and the fourth in /rɪˌspɒnsəˈbɪləti/. The important question, therefore, is how do we know which syllable should be stressed in a word? The way in which stress placement varies from word to word seems to suggest that we should learn stress placement for every word separately, just as we learn the spelling or the meaning and usage of every word. But a careful study of stress placement in

English words shows that there are certain features of words, which determine which syllable in the word should be stressed. There are five features that have been identified as crucial in deciding stress placement:

(i) the number of syllables in the word i.e., whether the word has one or more syllables,

(ii) the phonological structure of the syllables that make up a word i.e., the sequence of consonants and vowels that make up the syllables,

(iii) the grammatical category that the word belongs to i.e., whether the word is a noun, adjective or a verb etc.

(iv) the morphological structure of the word i.e., whether the word is ***simple***, or whether it is ***complex*** because it contains prefixes or suffixes or both, or whether it is ***compound***, formed by combining two, three or more words,

(v) whether the word is of a specific type like reflexive pronouns with *self/selves*, numbers such as *thiry* and *thirteen* or abbreviations such as *PC* and *USA*.

6.4 Stress in monosyllabic words

Generally words of one syllable are stressed, when they are nouns like *book, girl, fruit, phone, car, dog* etc., full verbs like *walk, hit, play, sing, eat, dance* etc., adjectives like *tall, big, cheap, clean, new, fast* etc., or adverbs like *well, here, now, out, too, yet* etc. But grammatical words that have one syllable like pronouns (*I, he, she, you, they, it*), prepositions (*to, for, in, with, at, of*), articles (*a, an, the*) or auxiliary verbs (*are, has, can, may, will, does*) are not usually stressed. All words of more than one syllable are stressed. In words of more than one syllable, features mentioned in (ii), (iii), (iv), and (v) become important in deciding which syllable should be stressed.

6.5 Stress in words of two or three syllables

When we consider the phonological structure of words, we notice that in many words of two or three syllables, the stress falls on the syllable that contains a long vowel or a diphthong or on the syllable that ends with more than one consonant.

Examples of a few verbs, nouns and adjectives are given here.

Listen to the words on the CD and notice how they are stressed.

(1) *Verbs*

proceed	proCEED	/prəˈsiːd/ or /proʊˈsiːd/
conclude	conCLUDE	/kənˈkluːd/
depart	dePART	/dɪˈpɑːt/ or /dɪˈpɑːrt/
combine	comBINE	/kəmˈbaɪn/
destroy	deSTROY	/dɪˈstrɔɪ/
resist	reSIST	/rɪˈzɪst/

determine	deTERmine	/dɪˈtɜːmɪn/ or /dɪˈtɜːrmɪn/
contradict	contraDICT	/ˌkɒntrəˈdɪkt/or/ˌkɑːntrəˈdɪkt/

(2) *Nouns*

canteen	canTEEN	/kænˈtiːn/
buffoon	buFFOON	/bəˈfuːn/
relief	reLIEF	/rɪˈliːf/
design	deSIGN	/dɪˈzaɪn/
control	conTROL	/kənˈtrəʊl/ or /kənˈtroʊl/
intent	inTENT	/ɪnˈtent/
synopsis	syNOPsis	/sɪˈnɒpsɪs/ or /sɪˈnɑːpsɪs/
marine	maRINE	/məˈriːn/

(3) *Adjectives*

serene	seRENE	/səˈriːn/
profuse	proFUSE	/prəˈfjuːs/
discreet	diSCREET	/dɪˈskriːt/
divine	diVINE	/dɪˈvaɪn/
profound	proFOUND	/prəˈfaʊnd/
correct	coRRECT	/kəˈrekt/
pervasive	perVAsive	/pəˈveɪsɪv/ or /pərˈveɪsɪv/
vicarious	viCArious	/vɪˈkeərɪəs/ or /vaɪˈkerɪəs/

But this rule has many exceptions like *intellect* (INtellect /ˈɪntəlekt/), *contemplate* (CONtemplate /ˈkɒntəmpleɪt/ or /ˈkɑːntəmpleɪt/), *excellent* (EXcellent /ˈeksələnt/), and *innovate* (INNovate /ˈɪnəveɪt/). This is because there are several factors that determine stress placement in English words and we cannot go by one criterion alone. Sometimes the word may be originally from a different language (for example, *contemplate* and *innovate*) or may have alternative stress patterns like *controversy* (either CONtroversy /ˈkɒntrəvɜːsɪ/, /kɑːntrəvɜːrsɪ/ or conTROversy /kənˈtrɒvəsɪ/) and *laboratory* (either laBOratory /ləˈbɒrətrɪ/ or LAboratory /ˈlæbrətɔːrɪ/). Generally, it is more difficult to predict where the stress falls in words of more than three syllables.

Exercises

L6.4. Listen to these words and identify the syllable that has the primary stress. Rewrite the words using large and small capital letters to indicate strogly and weakly stressed syllables (if any).

Which words do you think do not follow the rule about stress placement given above?

balloon	bargain	beacon
believe	bombard	borrow
campaign	casino	circumstance
climax	cohesive	collect
colleague	collide	combine
compete	complex	computer
concrete	constrict	continue
correspond	costume	courtesy
declare	defend	define
degree	delicate	depict
despair	difficult	direct
district	facile	fatigue
finance	focus	futile
genius	humour	machine
magnet	major	manoeuvre
marathon	maroon	master
mistake	monitor	nephew
perform	perfume	perfect
perplex	persist	perspective
persuade	perturb	police
polite	precise	predict
prepare	pretend	promote
protect	provide	pursue
receive	recruit	reduce
reflect	relax	request
resist	restrict	retire
salute	schedule	seduce
select	silence	stupid
sublime	suggest	support
suspect	thousand	transform

1. Practise the pronunciation of these words with the right stress placement and the appropriate use of reduced vowels.

6.6 Stress in nouns, adjectives and verbs

An interesting feature of English language is that there are several pairs of words in English, which have the same spelling but belong to different word classes (nouns, verbs or adjectives). For example the word *object* can be either a noun or a verb as seen in the following sentences:

These are familiar objects.

I object to his coming here.

The only difference between *object* as a noun and *object* as a verb is in the way it is pronounced. *Object* as a noun is pronounced with the stress on the first syllable, where as *object* as a verb is pronounced with the stress on the second syllable. Some of the other pairs of words that show the same type of difference in stress placement because of word class difference are given below. Listen to the words on the CD and notice how they are stressed.

Nouns		**Verbs**		
CONduct	/ˈkɒndʌkt/	conDUCT	/kənˈdʌkt/	British
	/ˈkɑːndʌkt/			American
CONflict	/ˈkɒnflɪkt/	conFLICT	/kənˈflɪkt/	British
	/ˈkɑːnflɪkt/			American
CONtest	/ˈkɒntest/	conTEST	/kənˈtest/	British
	/ˈkɑːntest/			American
CONtract	/ˈkɒntrækt/	conTRACT	/kənˈtrækt/	British
	/ˈkɑːntrækt/			American
CONtrast	/ˈkɒntrɑːst/	conTRAST	/kənˈtrɑːst/	British
	/ˈkɑːntræst/		/kənˈtræst/	American
CONvert	/ˈkɒnvɜːt/	conVERT	/kənˈvɜːt/	British
	/ˈkɑːnvɜːrt/		/kənˈvɜːrt/	American
CONvict	/ˈkɒnvɪkt/	conVICT	/kənˈvɪkt/	British
	/ˈkɑːnvɪkt/			American
DESert	/ˈdezət/	deSERT	/dɪˈzɜːt/	British
	/ˈdezərt/		/dɪˈzɜːrt/	American
INcline	/ˈɪnklaɪn/	inCLINE	/ɪnˈklaɪn/	
INcrease	/ˈɪnkriːs/	inCREASE	/ɪnˈkriːs/	
INsert	/ˈɪnsɜːt/	inSERT	/ɪnˈsɜːt/	British
	/ˈɪnsɜːrt/		/ɪnˈsɜːrt/	American
INsult	/ˈɪnsʌlt/	inSULT	/ɪnˈsʌlt/	

OBject	/ˈɒbdʒɪkt/	obJECT	/əbˈdʒekt/	
PERmit	/ˈpɜːmɪt/	perMIT	/pəˈmɪt/	British
	/ˈpɜːrmɪt/		/pərˈmɪt/	American
PROGress	/ˈprəʊgres/	proGRESS	/prəˈgres/	British
	/ˈprɑːgres/			American
PRODuce	/ˈprɒdjuːs/	proDUCE	/prəˈdjuːs/	British
	/ˈprɑːduːs/		/prəˈduːs/	American
PROject	/ˈprɒdʒekt/	proJECT	/prəˈdʒekt/	British
	/ˈprɑːdʒekt/		/prəˈdʒekt/	American
PROtest	/ˈprəʊtest/	proTEST	/prəˈtest/	British
	/ˈproʊtest/			American
REBel	/ˈrebəl/	reBEL	/rɪˈbel/	
RECord	/ˈrekɔːd/	reCORD	/rɪˈkɔːd/	British
	/ˈrekərd/		/rɪˈkɔːrd/	American
SUBject	/ˈsʌbdʒekt/	subJECT	/sʌbˈdʒekt/	
SURvey	/ˈsɜːveɪ/	surVEY	/səˈveɪ/	British
	/ˈsɜːrveɪ/		/sərˈveɪ/	American
SUSpect	/ˈsʌspekt/	suSPECT	/səˈspekt/	

With a word like *absent* it can be either an adjective or a verb as we see in the following sentences:

She was absent from the meeting.
She did not want to absent herself from the meeting.

In such cases the adjective has the stress on the first syllable and the verb on the second syllable. Some of the other words like *absent* are *present, abstract,* and *perfect.* Listen to the words on the CD and notice how they are stressed.

Adjectives		Verbs		
ABsent	/ˈabsənt/	abSENT	/abˈsent/	
ABstract	/ˈabstrskt/	abSTRACT	/abˈstrakt/	
PERfect	/ˈpɜːfɪkt/	perFECT	/pəˈfekt/	British
	/ˈpɜːrfɪkt/		/pərˈfekt/	American
PRESent	/ˈpreznt/	preSENT	/prɪˈzent/	

In general, we can say that in a number of words with two syllables, the difference in their grammatical function is indicated only by a change in stress placement. When the word is used as a noun or adjective, the stress is on the first syllable and when it functions as a verb, the stress falls on the second syllable.

Exercises

L6.5. Listen to the following pairs of sentences and decide from the stress pattern whether the underlined word is used as a verb or a noun or adjective.

(i) The abstract should not be longer than 150 words.
She tried to abstract the main points from the essay.

(ii) They decided to conduct a survey on this issue.
His conduct of the negotiations was criticised.

(iii) He decided to contest a seat in the Parliament.
She won the first prize in a beauty contest.

(iv) Nobody paid any attention to our protest.
We protest against the new rules about the exams.

(v) The ferment in the country caused a lot of hardship to the people.
He allowed his violent feelings to ferment inside him.

(vi) His object in life is to earn a lot of money.
They decided to object to the plan because they thought that it was expensive.

(vii) All great musicians perfect their art by constant practice.
He is a perfect example of a gentleman cricketer.

(viii) I consider what you said to be an insult.
She did not want to insult him.

(ix) The government refused him a permit to take the paintings out.
Please permit us to leave early.

(x) The contrast between the two colours was striking.
What do you contrast it with?

(xi) Rajasthan is mostly desert.
A true friend will not desert you in need.

(xii) He refused to sign the contract.
An important property of metals is that they contract.

(xiii) He wanted to escort his sister to Bombay.
They provided a police escort to the visiting players.

(xiv) Most of the students were present at the function.
I want to buy him a wedding present.

(xv) The rebel was shot dead in an encounter with the police.
It is difficult to rebel against long established conventions.

(xvi) The subject of this talk is non-violence.
They had no intention to subject her to this kind of harassment.

(xvii) A strict watch was kept over the convict.
The judge refused to convict her.

(xviii) They produce cars with state of the art technology.
The produce this summer is an all time record.

(xix) Her research project is very interesting.
The economists project a big increase in foreign trade.

(xx) The sisters have started to export garments.
The export of leather goods has come up.

(xxi) Her latest record sold more than a million copies.
He did not give us permission to record his speech.

(xxii) Japan has to import a lot of raw materials.
There is a ban on the import of gold.

(xxiii) Politicians should not be allowed to defect from one party to another.
There was a major defect in the new instrument supplied.

(xxiv) The American visitor went to the bank to convert his dollars into rupees.
She is the last convert to the cause of wild life protection.

(xxv) He was a suspect in the bank robbery case.
We suspect that he is not telling us the truth.

1. Repeat the sentences with the stress on the right syllable in the underlined words.

6.7 Stress in phrasal verbs

Phrasal verbs consist of two or three words and have a verb followed by an adverb or a preposition or both an adverb and a preposition as in *call off, depend on,* and *look up to*.

Stress placement in phrasal verbs follows the general rule about verbs and adverbs being stressed and prepositions being unstressed. In phrasal verbs that have a verb and an adverb as in *call off*, the verb *call* has secondary or weak stress and the adverb *off* has primary or strong stress. In phrasal verbs that have a verb and a preposition as in *depend on*, primary or strong stress is on a syllable in the verb, on the second syllable in *depend* and the preposition *on* is unstressed. In three word phrasal verbs like *look up to*, the verb *look* gets secondary or weak stress, the adverb *up* gets primary or strong stress and the preposition *to* is unstressed. A few other examples of phrasal verbs with adverbs or prepositions or both are given below with the stress patterns generally used. Listen to the phrasal verbs on the CD and notice how they are stressed.

(1) With adverbs

break down	BREAK DOWN	/ˌbreɪk ˈdaʊn/
call back	CALL BACK	/ˌkɔːl ˈbæk/
doze off	DOZE OFF	/ˌdəʊz ˈɒf/ or /ˌdoʊz ˈɑːf/
give in	GIVE IN	/ˌgɪv ˈɪn/
give up	GIVE UP	/ˌgɪv ˈʌp/
figure out	FIGURE OUT	/ˌfigər ˈaʊt/
mix up	MIX UP	/ˌmɪks ˈʌp/
write down	WRITE DOWN	/ˌraɪt ˈdaʊn/

(2) With prepositions

aim at	AIM at	/ˈeɪm ət/
approve of	aPPROVE of	/əˈpruːv əv/
come from	COME from	/ˈkʌm frəm/
deal with	DEAL with	/ˈdiːl wɪθ/
dream of	DREAM of	/ˈdriːm əv/
look for	LOOK for	/ˈlʊk fə/ or /ˈlʊk fər/
object to	obJECT to	/əbˈdʒekt tə/
read about	READ about	/ˈriːd əbaʊt/
result in	reSULT in	/rɪˈzʌlt ɪn/
take after	TAKE after	/ˈteɪk ɑːftə/ or /ˈteɪk æftər/

(3) With both an adverb and a preposition

catch up with	CATCH UP with	/ˌkætʃ ˈʌp wɪθ/
get ahead of	GET aHEAD of	/ˌget əˈhed əv/
go through with	GO THROUGH with	/ˌgəʊ ˈθruː wɪθ/ or /ˌgoʊ ˈθruː wɪθ/
grow out of	GROW OUT of	/ˌgrəʊ ˈaʊt əv/ or /ˌgroʊ ˈaʊt əv/
look down on	LOOK DOWN on	/ˌlʊk ˈdaʊn ɒn/ or /ˌlʊk ˈdaʊn ɑːn/
look forward to	LOOK FORward to	/ˌlʊk ˈfɔːwəd tə/ or /ˌlʊk ˈfɔːrwərd tə/

put up with	PUT UP with	/ˌpʊt ˈʌp wɪθ/
run away with	RUN aWAY with	/ˌrʌn əˈweɪ wɪθ/
talk down to	TALK DOWN to	/ˌtɔːk ˈdaʊn tə/
walk out on	WALK OUT on	/ˌwɔːk ˈaʊt ɒn/ or /ˌwɔːk ˈaʊt ɑːn/

It is important that when we learn a new phrasal verb, we should learn not only its meaning and use, but also whether it has an adverb or a preposition, so that we learn how to pronounce it with the right stress.

(4) Nouns derived from phrasal verbs

There are quite a number of compound nouns derived from phrasal verbs that have an adverb such as *break-down* and *mix-up*, which are derived from the corresponding phrasal verbs. These nouns have a different stress pattern from the corresponding phrasal verbs. As we have seen, in the phrasal verb there is secondary stress on the verb and primary stress on the adverb that follows. But in the compound noun, there is only one stress on the first syllable. Thus we pronounce the phrasal verbs *break down* and *mix up* /ˌbreɪk ˈdaʊn/ and /ˌmɪks ˈʌp/, but the nouns *break-down* and *mix-up* are pronounced /ˈbreɪkdaʊn/ and /ˈmɪksʌp/. Some of the other nouns derived from the corresponding phrasal verbs are

break-out	BREAKout	/ˈbreɪkaʊt/
cover-up	COVerup	/ˈkʌvərʌp/
get-together	GETtogether	/ˈgettəgeðə/ or /ˈgettəgeðər/
hold-up	HOLDup	/ˈhəʊldʌp/ or /ˈhoʊldʌp/
print-out	PRINTout	/ˈprɪntaʊt/
send-off	SENDoff	/ˈsendɒf/ or /ˈsendɑːf/
stop-over	STOPover	/ˈstɒpəʊvə/ or /ˈstɑːpoʊvər/
turn-out	TURNout	/ˈtɜːnaʊt/ or /ˈtɜːrnaʊt/
warm-up	WARMup	/ˈwɔːmʌp/ or /ˈwɔːrmʌp/
wash-out	WASHout	/ˈwɒʃaʊt/ or /ˈwɑːʃaʊt/

Listen to the words on the CD and notice how they are stressed.

Exercises

(A)

L6.6. Listen to the following sentences and decide from the stress pattern whether the underlined phrasal verb in each has an adverb or a preposition.

(i) I did not want to back down because I believed that there should be no compromise on principles.

(ii) The officers will have to answer for any losses that the company may suffer.

(iii) What brought about this complete change in the boy's behavior?

(iv) She carried on cutting vegetables in candle light when the lights went off.

(v) He is having a tough time and you have to bear with him.

(vi) The girl tried to figure out how she could retrieve the data that disappeared form the screen.

(vii) The speaker said that he would focus on three important issues related to global warming.

(viii) They met again today to iron out the problems they had about the agreement on water sharing.

(ix) The young man jumped at the chance of meeting the great financier.

(x) They had to put off their visit to China because of lack of funds.

(xi) She said that she would tell us how to come by a good job.

(xii) The child took to her new teacher very quickly.

(xiii) He messed up all the arrangements made by postponing his visit.

(xiv) They wanted to buy an SUV but had to settle for a small car.

(xv) We thought of going to Europe for a holday but it was very expensive.

(xvi) They did up their house so beautifully that you wouldn't believe that it is more than twenty years old.

(xvii) The doctor said that the patient would come round in about two hours.

(xviii) You should not laugh at everything he says and does.

(xix) All the students who appeared for the exam from our school got through.

(xx) The government decided to take over the company after the fraud became known.

1. Repeat the sentences taking care to pronounce the underlined phrsal verbs with the right stress pattern.

(A)

2. (i) Choose the appropriate three-word phrasal verb to fill in the blanks.
   (ii) Repeat the sentences taking care to pronounce the phrasal verbs you have chosen with the right stress pattern.

catch up on	get along with	go in for	reach out to	look down on
hit out at	shy away from	stand up to	end up with	watch out for

(i) Her father wanted her to ________________ tennis but she wants to play badminton.

(ii) They did not have the courage to ________________ the tyranny of the principal.

(iii) He could ________________ his roommates very well and they had great fun together.

(iv) I am not one to ________________ my responsibilities and you can trust me.

(v) The new teacher in the school knows how to ________________ small children and has become very popular.

(vi) The instructor asked me to ________________ sharp bends in the road and not to drive very fast.

(vii) The young member of Parliament ________________ corruption in the government in his speech, which was highly applauded.

(viii) You should not ________________ people just because they don't wear expensive and fashionable clothes.

(ix) She ________________ very low scores in social studies because she focused exclusively on science and mathematics.

(x) His mother helped him to ________________ his homework which had piled up because he missed school for a week.

(A)

L6.7. Listen to the following pairs of sentences and decide where a phrasal verb is used and where a noun derived from the phrasal verb is used.

(i) They asked for a generator as a <u>backup</u> because there were frequent power failures.
It is always useful to <u>back up</u> all your important files on the computer.

(ii) I cannot believe that at 30 years of age she is <u>burned out</u> and cannot play professional tennis anymore
The <u>burn-out</u> age in IT industry is much lower than it is in other fields.

(iii) He decided to <u>drop out</u> of the competition because of charges of lying about his age.
The government started the midday meal scheme to reduce the <u>drop-out</u> rate in schools especially in villages.

(iv) The <u>hand-over</u> to the newly elected government was without any problems.
The CEO decided to resign and <u>hand over</u> to an officer appointed by the government.

(v) The <u>hold-up</u> on the highway left hundreds of motorists stranded.
The delivery of the new computer is <u>held up</u> because the sales people are on strike.

(vi) The famous company decided to <u>lay off</u> five thousand workers because of huge losses.
There may be more <u>lay-offs</u> if the company cannot make a profit next year.

(vii) The protesters demanded that the government <u>roll back</u> the increase in fuel prices.
The government said that there would be no <u>roll-back</u> because the oil companies were suffering huge losses.

(viii) It is just a <u>start-up</u> and we'll have to watch how the company performs over the next two years.
The engine wouldn't <u>start up</u> whatever I did and I had to call the garage helpline.

(ix) Wait till the computer <u>shuts down</u> before switching off.
The <u>shut-down</u> of the factory continued for months and caused great misery to the workers and their families.

(x) He promised that as the new MD he would do his best to <u>turn around</u> the company in six months.
The economists warned that there would not be any <u>turn around</u> in the economy for at least a year.

3. Repeat the sentences taking care to pronounce the phrasal verb or the noun derived from the phrasal verb with the right stress pattern.

6.8 Stress in complex words-1

The morphological structure of words can be simple or complex. If a word consists of only one grammatical unit like *use, take* or *possible*, it is ***a simple word***. But words like *useful, usefulness, management, manager, impossible* or *possibility,* which have suffixes like *-ful, -ness, - ment, -er, -ity* or prefixes like *imp-* and which are thus made up of more than one grammatical unit are ***complex words***. In addition to simple and complex words, we also have words like *postman, overtake* and *waterproof,* which are made up of two independent words like *post* and *man, over* and *take* and *water* and *proof*. Such words are called ***compound words***.

Complex words can have more than one suffix and/or prefix and compound words can have more than two independent words combined together. Stress placement often depends on whether a word is simple or complex or compound. Further, in complex words, stress placement is determined by the type of suffix or prefix used and in compound words, by the grammatical class of the words combined and the sequence in which these words occur.

Complex words with prefixes

(1) Generally in words with prefixes, the first syllable of the ***root*** or the ***stem*** (the word to which a prefix or a suffix or both are added) is strongly stressed and the prefix is unstressed or sometimes weakly stressed. For example, *arrive* is pronounced aRRIVE or /əˈraɪv/, *dislike* is pronounced disLIKE or /dɪsˈlaɪk/, and *overtake* is pronounced overTAKE or /ˌəʊvəˈteɪk/ or /ˌoʊvərˈteɪk/. Other examples of words with prefixes that have similar stress placements are given below. Listen to the words on the CD and notice how they are stressed.

aboard	aBOARD	/əˈbɔːd/ or /əˈbɔːrd/
abroad	aBROAD	/əˈbrɔːd/
ahead	aHEAD	/əˈhed/
alone	aLONE	/əˈləʊn/ or /əˈloʊn/
award	aWARD	/əˈwɔːd/ or /əˈwɔːrd/
become	beCOME	/bɪˈkʌm/
before	beFORE	/bɪˈfɔː/ or /bɪˈfɔːr/
below	beLOW	/bɪˈləʊ/ or /bɪˈloʊ/
beside	beSIDE	/bɪˈsaɪd/
bewitch	beWITCH	/bɪˈwɪtʃ/
command	coMMAND	/kəˈmɑːnd/ or /kəˈmænd/
commit	coMMIT	/kəˈmɪt/
compel	comPEL	/kəmˈpel/

complain	comPLAIN	/kəmˈplaɪn/
compose	comPOSE	/kəmˈpəʊz/ or /kəmˈpoʊz/
decrease	deCREASE	/dɪˈkriːs/
default	deFAULT	/dɪˈfɔːlt/
degrade	deGRADE	/dɪˈgreɪd/
delay	deLAY	/dɪˈleɪ/
deport	dePORT	/dɪˈpɔːt/ or /dɪˈpɔːrt/
disable	disAble	/dɪsˈeɪbl/
disarm	disARM	/dɪsˈɑːm/ or /dɪsˈɑːrm/
disclose	disCLOSE	/dɪsˈkləʊz/ or /dɪsˈkloʊz/
displace	disPLACE	/dɪsˈpleɪs/
distrust	disTRUST	/dɪsˈtrʌst/
include	inCLUDE	/ɪnˈkluːd/
increase	inCREASE	/ɪnˈkriːs/
infect	inFECT	/ɪnˈfekt/
inflate	inFLATE	/ɪnˈfleɪt/
inform	inFORM	/ɪnˈfɔːm/ or /ɪnˈfɔːrm/
misjudge	misJUDGE	/ˌmɪsˈdʒʌdʒ/
mislead	misLEAD	/ˌmɪsˈliːd/
misplace	misPLACE	/ˌmɪsˈpleɪs/
misread	misREAD	/ˌmɪsˈriːd/
misuse	misUSE	/ˌmɪsˈjuːz/
outdo	outDO	/ˌaʊtˈduː/
outgrow	outGROW	/ˌaʊtˈgrəʊ/ or /ˌaʊtˈgroʊ/
outlive	outLIVE	/ˌaʊtˈlɪv/
outrun	outRUN	/ˌaʊtˈrʌn/
outwit	outWIT	/ˌaʊtˈwɪt/
overcome	overCOME	/ˌəʊvəˈkʌm/ or /ˌoʊvərˈkʌm/
overdraw	overDRAW	/ˌəʊvəˈdrɔː/ or /ˌoʊvərˈdrɑː/
overeat	overEAT	/ˌəʊvəˈiːt/ or /ˌoʊvərˈiːt/
overlook	overLOOK	/ˌəʊvəˈlʊk/ or /ˌoʊvərˈlʊk/
overtake	overTAKE	/ˌəʊvəˈteɪk/ or /ˌoʊvərˈteɪk/
unburden	unBURden	/ʌnˈbɜːdᵊn/ or /ʌnˈbɜːrdᵊn/

unfurl unFURL /ʌnˈfɜːl/ or /ʌnˈfɜːrl/
unlearn unLEARN /ʌnˈlɜːn/ or /ʌnˈlɜːrn/
unlike unLIKE /ʌnˈlaɪk/
unlock unLOCK /ʌnˈlɑk/ or /ʌnˈlɑːk/
underbid UNderBID /ˌʌndəˈbɪd/ or /ˌʌndərˈbɪd/
undercharge UNderCHARGE /ˌʌndəˈtʃɑːdʒ/or /ˌʌndərˈtʃɑːrdʒ/
undercut UNderCUT /ˌʌndəˈkʌt/ or /ˌʌndərˈkʌt/
underline UNderLINE /ˌʌndəˈlaɪn/ or /ˌʌndərˈlaɪn/
update upDATE /ʌpˈdeɪt/
upgrade upGRADE /ʌpˈgreɪd/
uplift upLIFT /ʌpˈlɪft/
upload upLOAD /ʌpˈləʊd/ or /ʌpˈloʊd/
uproot upROOT /ʌpˈruːt/

(2) Words with prefixes functioning as nouns

Some words with prefixes such as *out-, over-, up-,* and *under-* function as nouns. When words with these prefixes function as verbs, the primary stress is on the first syllable of the root or the stem and the prefix is only weakly stressed, as shown above. But when they function as nouns, it is the prefix or its first syllable that gets the primary stress and there is no stress on the root or the stem. Listen to the words on the CD and notice how they are stressed.

outlook OUTlook /ˈaʊtlʊk/
outline OUTline /ˈaʊtlaɪn/
output OUTput /ˈaʊtpʊt/
overcoat Overcoat /ˈəʊvəkəʊt/ or /ˈoʊvərkoʊt/
overdose Overdose /ˈəʊvədəʊs/ or /ˈoʊvərdoʊs/
overpass Overpass /ˈəʊvəpɑːs/ or /ˈoʊvərpæs/
underdog UNderdog /ˈʌndədɑg/ or /ˈʌndərdɔːg/
underpass UNderpass /ˈʌndəpɑːs/ or /ˈʌndərpæs/
underwear UNderwear /ˈʌndəweə/ or /ˈʌndərwer/
upkeep UPkeep /ˈʌpkiːp/
upstart UPstart /ˈʌpstɑːt/ or /ˈʌpstɑːrt/
upsurge UPsurge /ˈʌpsɜːdʒ/ or /ˈʌpsɜːrdʒ/

(3) Words that have a different stress because of a difference in meaning

The prefix *re-* is used with a number of words. Some of these words have different meanings depending on whether the prefix *re-* means 'again' or not. For example, *recover*('get well') and *recover*('cover again'). Though these words have the same spelling, they are pronounced differently with a different stress. The first is pronounced reCOVer or /rɪˈkʌvə/ or /rɪˈkʌvər/ and the second, RECOVer or /ˌriːˈkʌvə/ or /ˌriːˈkʌvər/.

Some of the other words that have a different stress because of a difference in meaning are

recount	reCOUNT	/rɪˈkaʊnt/	RECOUNT	/ˌriːˈkaʊnt/
reform	reFORM	/rɪˈfɔːm/ or /rɪˈfɔːrm/	REFORM	/ˌriːˈfɔːm/or/ˌriːˈfɔːrm/
remark	reMARK	/rɪˈmɑːk/ or /rɪˈmɑːrk/	REMARK	/ˌriːˈmɑːk/or/ˌriːˈmɑːrk/
resign	reSIGN	/rɪˈzaɪn/	RESIGN	/ˌriːˈsaɪn/

Listen to the words on the CD and notice how they are stressed.

Exercises

1. (i) Choose the appropriate word to fill in the blanks in the following sentences.

   (ii) Repeat the sentences taking care to pronounce the words you have chosen to fill in the blanks with the right stress pattern.

devalue	alive	over-ride	uncover	insight
beware	contain	outlast	mismatch	underlie
configure	debar	outweigh	inactive	disgrace
discolour	over-hear	apart	upturn	outshine
undermine	over-load	misfire	unclear	uphold

(i) The young man took the machine __________ to find out what was wrong.

(ii) This juice does not __________ any preservatives and has only fruit concentrates.

(iii) The journalists were not able to __________ the reasons for the attack on the famous actor.

(iv) The benefits of moving to a different location __________ the hardships we have to face.

(v) This setback is only a minor one and you should not allow it to __________ your confidence.

(vi) It is true that he has taken a break from his practice but he is by no means _____________.

(vii) She always wants to ______________ all the other students in her class in everything.

(viii) It is __________ why they did not take any precautions against the spread of the virus.

(ix) There is a _____________ between spelling and pronunciation in many English words.

(x) How he managed to stay ___________ for ten days without food and water is a mystery.

(xi) The water in the lake is beginning to _____________ because of the industrial waste that flows into it.

(xii) Her talk gave us an ____________ into how these tribal communities have been able to live untouched by modern civilization.

(xiii) I bet I can ______________ all of you on the tennis court.

(xiv) Were you able to ______________ anything about their future plans?

(xv) They did not expect their plan to _______________ and were sure that they would be able to evacuate all the refugees.

(xvi) It is a ______________ that there is such corruption even in the police department.

(xvii) He spoke in detail about the philosophical ideas that _______________ all his novels.

(xviii) The manager's decision to ______________ all our objections made us unhappy.

(xix) You can _____________ the program according to your preferences.

(xx) The teachers decided to _______________ the the decision made by the principal of the college.

(xxi) The courts can ____________ him from contesting in the elections.

(xxii) The police have warned people to ____________ of picking up strange parcels left in public places.

(xxiii) We should not _____________ the work done by labourers.

(xxiv) You cannot expect an _____________ in the economy at least for two more years.

(xxv) She tried not to _____________ the children with homework.

L6.8. Listen to the following pairs of sentences and decide whether the underlined word is used as a verb or a noun.

(i) There is an overlap between the responsibilities of the two executives.
The two lectures overlap and we cannot attend both.

(ii) You can upload your files by clicking here.
For a faster upload follow these steps.

(iii) This lecture hall is small and students often overflow into the corridor.
They tried their best to stop the overflow of water from the river.

(iv) The TV channel put out a news update every hour.
We have to update the data on the available service providers.

(v) I was told that it was necessary to overhaul the engine completely.
They decided to go in for a major overhaul of the accounting procedures.

(vi) The latest upgrade for the adobe reader is now available.
You can upgrade your computer whenever you think it is necessary.

2. Repeat the sentences taking care to pronounce the underlined words with the right stress pattern.

6.9 Stress in complex words-2

Complex words with suffixes

The various suffixes used in complex words can be divided into three groups depending on how they influence stress placement in the words in which they occur:

(1) Suffixes that do not affect stress placement when they are added to words.

(2) Suffixes that influence stress placement in the words to which they are added.

(3) Suffixes that carry the stress themselves.

(1) Suffixes that do not affect stress placement when they are added to words are

-able	REAson	/ˈri:zn/	REAsonable	/ˈri:znəbl/
-age	PATron	/ˈpeɪtrən/	PATronage	/ˈpeɪtrənɪdʒ/
-al	SEAson	/ˈsi:zn/	SEAsonal	/ˈsi:zənl/
-en	TIGHT	/ˈtaɪt/	TIGHTen	/ˈtaɪtn/
-ful	sucCESS	/səkˈses/	sucCESSful	/səkˈsesfl/
-fy	SIMple	/ˈsɪmpl/	SIMplify	/ˈsɪmplɪfaɪ/
-ing	enGAGE	/inˈgeɪdʒ/	enGAging	/inˈgeɪdʒiŋ/
-ish	FOOL	/ˈfu:l/	FOOlish	/ˈfu:lɪʃ/
-like	CHILD	/ˈtʃaɪld/	CHILDlike	/ˈtʃaɪldlaɪk/

-less	HELP	/ˈhelp/	HELPless	/ˈhelpləs/
-ly	QUICK	/ˈkwɪk/	QUICKly	/ˈkwɪkli/
-ment	aCHIEVE	/əˈtʃi:v/	aCHIEVEment	/əˈtʃi:vmənt/
-ness	GOOD	/ˈgʊd/	GOODness	/ˈgʊdnəs/
-ous	FAME	/ˈfeɪm/	FAmous	/ˈfeɪməs/
-wise	LIKE	/ˈlaɪk/	LIKEwise	/ˈlaɪkwaɪz/
-y	MILK	/ˈmɪlk/	MILky	/ˈmɪlki/

Listen to the words on the CD and notice how they are stressed.

(2) Suffixes that influence stress placement in the words to which they are added are

-eous	OUTrage	/ˈaʊtreɪdʒ/	outRAgeous	/aʊtˈreɪdʒəs/
-ial	PAlace	/ˈpæləs/	paLAtial	/pəˈleɪʃl/
-ic	Artist	/ˈɑ:tɪst/ /ˈɑ:rtɪst/	arTIStic	/ɑ:ˈtɪstɪk/ /ɑ:rˈtɪstɪk/
-cal	techNOlogy	/tekˈnɒlədʒi/ /tekˈnɑ:lədʒi/	TECHnoLOgical	/ˌteknəˈlɒdʒɪkl/ /ˌteknəˈlɑ:dʒɪkl/
-ion	EDit	/ˈedɪt/	eDITion	/ɪˈdɪʃn/
-ious	UProar	/ˈʌprɔ:/ /ˈʌprɔ:r/	upROArious	/ʌpˈrɔ:riəs/
-ity	CApable	/ˈkeɪpəbl/	CApaBILity	/ˌkeɪpəˈbɪlɪti/

In these words we see that the addition of the suffix moves the stress to the last syllable of the root or the stem from an earlier syllable.

Listen to the words on the CD and notice how they are stressed.

(3) Suffixes that carry the stress themselves are

-aire	QUEStion	/ˈkwestʃən/	QUEStioNNAIRE	/ˌkwestʃəˈneə/ /ˌkwestʃəˈner/
-ee	PAY	/ˈpeɪ/	PAYEE	/ˌpeɪˈi:/
-eer	ENgin	/ˈendʒɪn/	ENGiNEER	/ˌendʒɪˈnɪə/ /ˌendʒɪˈnɪr/
-ese	JOURnal	/ˈdʒɜ:nəl/	JOURnaLESE	/ˌdʒɜ:nəˈli:z/ /ˌdʒɜ:rnəˈli:z/
-esque	PICture	/ˈpɪktʃə/ /ˈpɪktʃər/	PICtuRESQUE	/ˌpɪktʃəˈresk/
-ique	TECHnical	/ˈteknɪkl/	techNIQUE	/tekˈni:k/
-ette	Kitchen	/ˈkɪtʃɪn/	KItcheNETTE	/ˌkɪtʃɪˈnet

In many of the words given above, we see that there is a secondary stress that falls on the initial syllable in root or the stem after the addition of the suffix.
Listen to the words on the CD and notice how they are stressed.

Changes in the pronunciation of a vowel or a vowel and a consonant when a suffix is added
Sometimes when a suffix is added to a word, the pronunciation of the vowel in the root word changes. Also, there are instances where there is a change in the pronunciation and sometimes the spelling of a consonant too. This happens (1) when the suffix changes the stress pattern and (2) also when it doesn't. We saw this in the examples of the suffixes *-cal, -ial,* and *-ion* above, where the stress pattern changes.

(1) A few other examples of vowel and vowel plus consonant change when suffixes change the stress pattern are

ORgan	/ˈɔːgən/ or /ˈɔːrgən/	orGANic	/ɔːˈgænɪk/ or /ɔːrˈgænɪk/
reVEAL	/rɪˈviːl/	reveLAtion	/ˌrevəˈleɪʃn/
reSIGN	/rɪˈzaɪn/	RESigNAtion	/ˌrezɪgˈneɪʃn/
LUxury	/ˈlʌkʃərɪ/	luXUrious	/lʌgˈʒʊərɪəs/or /lʌgˈʒʊrɪəs/

(2) Some examples when suffixes do not change the stress pattern are

TYPE	/ˈtaɪp/	TYpical	/ˈtɪpɪkl/
WISE	/ˈwaɪz/	WISdom	/ˈwɪzdəm/
SPHERE	/ˈsfɪe/ or /ˈsfɪr/	SPHErical	/ˈsferɪkl/
SANE	/ˈseɪn/	SANity	/ˈsænəti/
NAtion	/ˈneɪʃn/	NAtional	/ˈnæʃnəl/
NAture	/ˈneɪtʃə/ or /ˈneɪtʃər/	NAtural	/ˈnætʃrəl/
CLEAN	/ˈkliːn/	CLEAnliness	/ˈklenlɪnəs/
seREne	/səˈriːn/	seREnity	/səˈrenəti/
suPREme	/suːˈpriːm/	suPREmacy	/suːˈpreməsi/
DRAma	/ˈdrɑːmə/	DRAmatize	/ˈdræmətaɪz/
conSUme	/kənˈsjuːm/	conSUMPtion	/kənˈsʌmpʃn/
deTAIN	/dɪˈteɪn/	deTENtion	/dɪˈtenʃn/
SIGN	/ˈsaɪn/	SIGnature	/ˈsɪgnətʃə/ or /ˈsɪgnətʃər/
deDUCE	/dɪˈdjuːs/	deDUCtion	/dɪˈdʌkʃn/
inVERT	/ɪnˈvɜːt/ or /ɪnvɜːrt/	inVERsion	/ɪnˈvɜːʃn/ or /ɪnˈvɜːrʃn/
proVIDE	/prəˈvaɪd/	proVIsion	/prəˈvɪʒn/
deSCRIBE	/dɪˈskraɪb/	deSCRIPtion	/dɪˈskrɪpʃn/
BRIEF	/ˈbriːf/	BREvity	/ˈbrevətɪ/

There are quite a number of words like this where we find different types of changes in pronunciation. Interestingly, the words *pronounce* (proNOUNCE /prəˈnaʊns/) and *pronunciation* (proNUNciATION /prəˌnʌnsiˈeɪʃn/) also show a change in the pronunciation of a vowel with a change in the stress pattern. It is necessary, therefore, to check the pronunciation of multisyllabic words in a dictionary and learn to pronounce them with the right stress pattern. This is very important because, as we see above, the spelling does not indicate changes in pronunciation in most of these words.

Exercises

1. First fill in the blanks in the following pairs of sentences/sentences with the right word from those given.

L6.9. Listen to these sentences and notice the stress patterns used in the words chosen to fill the blanks.

(i) She always took an ____________ part in classroom discussions.
Her numerous ____________ left her little time to spend with her children.
(activities, active)

(ii) I did not ____________ her because of her short hair.
He has won international ________________ as a great singer.
(recognize, recognition)

(iii) This is a ______________ journey across the border.
He studied Indian ______________ in college.
(History, historic)

(iv) Water is _________________ of hydrogen and oxygen.
Scientists analysed the ________________ of the rocks from the moon.
(composed, composition)

(v) He says that he is a ______________ scientist, not a ____________.
(politician, political)

(vi) His ________________ of the data on food production was very good.
She was asked to do an ________________ report on dowry deaths.
(analytical, analysis)

(vii) She has a _________________ nature.
Her ________________ has won her many friends.
(generous, generosity)

(viii) Could you _________________ me a good book on phonetics?
I bought this book on the ________________ of a friend.
(recommendation, recommend)

(ix) He is so ______________ that anyone would think that he has the ________________ of ten people. *(energy, energetic)*

(x) The machine did not work because of a ________________ part.
No political system is without __________________.
(defective, defects)

(xi) What is your ________________?

The concept of ________________ is not new to Indians.

(*nationalism, nationality*)

(xii) She said that she was an ______________ and not a teacher.

Everyone admired her ______________ skill.

(*artistic, artist*)

(xiii) I am ________________ to know what happened yesterday.

I am dying with ______________ to know what happened yesterday.

(*curious, curiosity*)

(xiv) They refused to ________________ the results of the election.

The delay in the ________________ of the results made the people unhappy.

(*declaration, declare*)

(xv) The doctors decided to keep her under ___________________.

I ________________ him trying to open the locked door.

(*observed, observation*)

(xvi) The ticket is ________________ for the return journey too.

The___________________ of her claim was questioned.

(*validity, valid*)

(xvii) An ________________ is an expert in ________________.

An ________________ person knows how to practice ________________.

(*economical, economics, economist, economy*)

(xviii) A new ________________ of Newton has been published.

It is not easy to get ________________ information about dead writers.

(*biographical, biography*)

(xix) It is a highly ________________ position.

It means that she has to take on more ________________.

(*responsible, responsibilties*)

(xx) Law and order has been ________________.

The building is in need of ________________.

(*restored, restoration*)

(xxi) Doctors are also________________, they do make mistakes.

The terrorists were guilty of crimes against ________________.

(*humanity, human*)

(xxii) **It was a ________________ in skill as well as strength.**

Both the friends decided to ________________ for the top prize.

(compete, competition)

(xxiii) **The Moghul ____________ ruled over India for centuries.**

People protested against the ________________ rule of the country by one family.

(dynastic, dynasty)

(xxiv) **The country faces serious economic ________________.**

These measures to cut expenditure may be ________________.

(problematic, problems)

(xxv) **She is a very ________________ child.**

She has to be handled with tact and ________________.

(sensitivity, sensitive)

2. Repeat the sentences taking care to pronounce the words used to fill the blanks with the right stress pattern.

A

3. Add the appropriate suffix to the words given and write the newly formed words in the right columns.

Check the pronunciation of each pair of given and newly formed words and practise their pronunciation with the right stress pattern.

mountain	million	train	legal
auction	refuge	doctrine	puppet
divorce	journal	interview	commission
address	command	billion	musket

-aire	*-eer*	*-ee*	*-ese*

L6.10. Listen to these words and mark where the primary stress falls.

4. Practise the pronunciation of the words with the right stress pattern.

diskette	technique	grotesque	launderette	physique	cassette
burlesque	statuette	mystique	statuesque	oblique	boutique

L6.11. Listen to the following pairs of words and group them depending on whether the primary stress remains on the same syllable or not and whether there is a change in the pronunciation of a vowel or a consonant or both.

able – ability	absorb – absorption	academic – academician
acquire – acquisition	admire – admiration	analyze – analytical
approve – approval	assume – assumption	benefit – beneficial
botany – botanical	central – centrality	ceremony – ceremonial
Christ – Christian	collide – collision	combine – combination
condense – condensation	danger – dangerous	defame – defamatory
direct – direction	dissolve – dissolution	employ –employment
exhaust – exhaustion	expand – expansion	explain – explanation
formal – formality	grave – gravity	guide – guidance
hero – heroic	human – humanity	inform – information
introduce – introduction	invade – invasion	invite – invitation
local – locality	method – methodical	permit – permission
prescribe – prescription	reduce – reduction	resign – resignation
suggest – suggestion	technology – technological	theme – thematic
valid – validity	reason – reasonable	

<table>
<tr><th colspan="2">Primary stress remains on the same syllable</th><th colspan="2">Primary stress doesn’t remain on the same syllable</th></tr>
<tr><th>No change in pronunciation</th><th>With change in pronunciation of a vowel or a consonant or both</th><th>No change in pronunciation</th><th>With change in pronunciation of a vowel or a consonant or both</th></tr>
<tr><td></td><td></td><td></td><td></td></tr>
<tr><td></td><td></td><td></td><td></td></tr>
<tr><td></td><td></td><td></td><td></td></tr>
</table>

5. Practise the pronunciation of these pairs of words with the right stress patterns and appropriate changes in the pronunciation of a vowel or a consonant or both.

6.10 Stress in compound words

Though compound words are made up of two independent words, they are pronounced with only one primary stress as in simple words. Sometimes there may be a secondary stress on a syllable in the word that does not carry the primary stress. For example, *bookshelf* which is pronounced /ˈbʊkʃelf/, *lightweight* which is pronounced /ˈlaɪtweɪt/ and *backdate* which is pronounced /ˌbækˈdeɪt/. The problem in learning to pronounce a compound word correctly is deciding which of the two parts has the primary stress. This largely depends on the grammatical category to which the two parts belong and also what grammatical function the compound word has.

Compound words are divided into three main groups depending on their grammatical function, (1) Noun compounds, (2) Adjective compounds and (3) Verb compounds.

(1) Noun compounds

(a) Noun compounds are of different types depending on the words that make them up. Mostly the primary stress falls on the first part in these compounds.

Listen to the words on the CD and notice how they are stressed.

(i) Noun + Noun

guesthouse	GUESThouse	/ˈgesthaʊs/
timetable	TIMEtable	/ˈtaɪmteɪbl/
bookshop	BOOKshop	/ˈbʊkʃɒp/ or /bʊkʃɑːp/
post office	POSToffice	/ˈpəʊstɒfɪs/or /ˈpoʊstɔːfɪs/
keyboard	KEYboard	/ˈkiːbɔːd/ or /ˈkiːbɔːrd/
grape juice	GRAPEjuice	/ˈgreɪpdʒuːs/
bomb scare	BOMBscare	/ˈbɒmskeə/ or /ˈbɑːmsker/
laser printer	LAserprinter	/ˈleɪzəprɪntə/or/ˈleɪzərprɪntər/

(ii) Noun + -ing

channel surfing	CHAnnelsurfing	/ˈtʃænlsɜːfɪŋ/or/ˈtʃænlsɜːrfɪŋ/
job hunting	JOBhunting	/ˈdʒɒbhʌntɪŋ/or/ˈdʒɑːbhʌntɪŋ/
horse riding	HORSEriding	/ˈhɔːsraɪdɪŋ/ or /ˈhɔːrsraɪdɪŋ/
book learning	BOOKlearning	/ˈbʊklɜːnɪŋ/ or /ˈbʊklɜːrnɪŋ/
copy editing	COPyediting	/ˈkɒpiedɪtɪŋ/ or /ˈkɑːpiedɪtɪŋ/
gift wrapping	GIFTwrapping	/ˈgɪftræpɪŋ/
house hunting	HOUSEhunting	/ˈhaʊshʌntɪŋ/
finger printing	FINgerprinting	/ˈfɪŋgəprɪntɪŋ/or/ˈfɪŋgərprɪntɪŋ/

(iii) –ing + Noun

drawing board	DRAWingboard	/ˈdrɔːɪŋbɔːd/ or /ˈdrɔːɪŋbɔːrd/
walking stick	WAlkingstick	/ˈwɔːkɪŋstɪk/
washing machine	WAshingmachine	/ˈwɒʃɪŋməʃiːn/ or /ˈwɑːʃɪŋməʃiːn/
shopping bag	SHOppingbag	/ˈʃɒpɪŋbæg/ or /ˈʃɑːpɪŋbæg/
sleeping pill	SLEEpingpill	/ˈsliːpɪŋpɪl/
reading group	READinggroup	/ˈriːdɪŋgruːp/
writing paper	WRItingpaper	/ˈraɪtɪŋpeɪpə/ or /ˈraɪtɪŋpeɪpər/
playing card	PLAYingcard	/ˈpleɪɪŋkɑːd/ or /ˈpleɪɪŋkɑːrd/

(iv) Verb + Noun

ring tone	RINGtone	/ˈrɪŋtəʊn/ or /ˈrɪŋtoʊn/
search engine	SEARCHengine	/ˈsɜːtʃendʒɪn/ or /ˈsɜːrtʃendʒɪn/
control freak	conTROLfreak	/kənˈtrəʊlfriːk/or /kənˈtroʊlfriːk/
pay channel	PAYchannel	/ˈpeɪtʃænl/
show room	SHOWroom	/ˈʃəʊruːm/ or /ˈʃoʊruːm/
talk time	TALKtime	/ˈtɔːktaɪm/
call center	CALLcenter	/ˈkɔːlsentə/ or /ˈkɔːlsentər/
play thing	PLAYthing	/ˈpleɪθɪŋ/

(b) But in noun compounds that have adjective + noun, the primary stress falls on the second part and secondary stress on the first. Listen to the words on the CD and notice how they are stressed.

loudspeaker	LOUDSPEAker	/ˌlaʊdˈspiːkə/ or /ˌlaʊdˈspiːkər/
live action	LIVEACtion	/ˌlaɪvˈækʃn/
full house	FULLHOUSE	/ˌfʊlˈhaʊs/

old age	oldAGE	/ˌəʊldˈeɪdʒ/ or /ˌoʊldˈeɪdʒ/
legal aid	legalAID	/ˌliːglˈeɪd/
global village	globalVILLage	/ˌgləʊblˈvɪlɪdʒ/or/ˌgloʊblˈvɪlɪdʒ/
active service	activeSERvice	/ˌæktɪvˈsɜːvɪs/ or /ˌæktɪvˈsɜːrvɪs/
lost cause	lostCAUSE	/ˌlɒstˈkɔːz/ or /ˌlɑːstˈkɔːz/

(2) Adjective compounds

Adjective compounds are also of different types depending on the words that make them up.

(a) In the following three types, the primary stress falls on the first part.

Listen to the words on the CD and notice how they are stressed.

(i) Adjective compounds that are written as one word,

watertight	WAtertight	/ˈwɔːtətaɪt/ or /ˈwɔːtərtaɪt/
foolproof	FOOLproof	/ˈfuːlpruːf/
footloose	FOOTloose	/ˈfʊtluːs/
homesick	HOMEsick	/ˈhəʊmsɪk/ or /ˈhoʊmsɪk/
steadfast	STEADfast	/ˈstedfɑːst/ or /ˈstedfæst/
threadbare	THREADbare	/ˈθredbeə/ or /ˈθredber/

(ii) Noun + *-ing* adjectives

heart-warming	HEARTwarming	/ˈhɑːtwɔːmɪŋ/ or /ˈhɑːrtwɔːrmɪŋ/
hair-splitting	HAIRsplitting	/ˈheəsplɪtɪŋ/ or /ˈhersplɪtɪŋ/
pains-taking	PAINStaking	/ˈpeɪnzteɪkɪŋ/
globe-trotting	GLOBEtrotting	/ˈgləʊbtrɒtɪŋ/ or /ˈgloʊbtrɑːtɪŋ/
nerve-racking	NERVEracking	/ˈnɜːvrækɪŋ/ or /ˈnɜːrvrækɪŋ/
mind-blowing	MINDblowing	/ˈmaɪndbləʊɪŋ/or/ˈmaɪndbloʊɪŋ/

(iii) Noun + past participle adjectives

bedridden	BEDridden	/ˈbedrɪdn/
heartfelt	HEARTfelt	/ˈhɑːtfelt/ or /ˈhɑːrtfelt/
spellbound	SPELLbound	/ˈspelbaʊnd/
shell-shocked	SHELLshocked	/ˈʃelʃɒkt/ or /ˈʃelʃɑːkt/
water-logged	WAterlogged	/ˈwɔːtəlɒgd/ or /ˈwɑːtərlɑːgd/
air-cooled	AIRcooled	/ˈeəkuːld/ or /ˈerkuːld/

(b) But in adjective compounds of the following types, the primary stress falls on the second part whereas the first part gets the secondary stress.

Listen to the words on the CD and notice how they are stressed.

(i) Noun+ adjective

toll-free	TOLLFREE	/ˌtəʊlˈfriː/ or /ˌtoʊlˈfriː/
ice-cold	ICECOLD	/ˌaɪsˈkəʊld/ or /ˌaɪsˈkoʊld/
red-hot	REDHOT	/ˌredˈhɒt/ or /ˌredˈhɑːt/
sky-high	SKYHIGH	/ˌskaɪˈhaɪ/

(ii) Adjective + noun

full-size	FULLSIZE	/ˌfʊlˈsaɪz/
high-class	HIGHCLASS	/ˌhaɪˈklɑːs/ or /ˌhaɪˈklæs/
open-source	OPENSOURCE	/ˌəʊpnˈsɔːs/ or /ˌoʊpnˈsɔːs/

(iii) Adverb or Adjective + past participle

good-humored	GOODHUmored	/ˌgʊdˈhjuːməd/or/ˌgʊdˈhjuːmərd/
strong-willed	STRONGWILLED	/ˌstrɒŋˈwɪld/ or /ˌstrɑːŋˈwɪld/
top-rated	TOPRATed	/ˌtɒpˈreɪtɪd/ or /ˌtɑːpˈreɪtɪd/
full-grown	FULLGROWN	/ˌfʊlˈgrəʊn/ or /ˌfʊlˈgroʊn/

(iv) Adverb or Adjective +*-ing*

high-ranking	HIGHRANking	/ˌhaɪˈræŋkɪŋ/
low-lying	LOWLYing	/ˌləʊˈlaɪɪŋ/ or /ˌloʊˈlaɪɪŋ/
right-thinking	RIGHTTHINking	/ˌraɪtˈθɪŋkɪŋ/
tight-fitting	TIGHTFItting	/ˌtaɪtˈfɪtɪŋ/

(v) *self* + Adjective or past participle or *–ing*

self-centered	SELFCENtered	/ˌselfˈsentəd/ or /ˌselfˈsentərd/
self-conscious	SELFCONscious	/ˌselfˈkɒnʃəs/ or /ˌselfˈkɑːnʃəs/
self-contained	SELFconTAIND	/ˌselfkənˈteɪnd/
self-employed	SELFemPLOYED	/ˌselfɪmˈplɔɪd/
self-respecting	SELFreSPECting	/ˌselfrɪˈspektɪŋ/
self-serving	SELFSERVING	/ˌselfˈsɜːvɪŋ/ or /ˌselfˈsɜːrvɪŋ/

(3) Verb compounds

Verb compounds are mostly made up of a noun and a verb and carry the primary stress on the first part.

Listen to the words on the CD and notice how they are stressed.

brainwash	BRAINwash	/ˈbreɪnwɒʃ/ or /ˈbreɪnwɑːʃ/
daydream	DAYdream	/ˈdeɪdriːm/
earmark	EARmark	/ˈɪəmɑːk/ or /ˈɪrmɑːrk/
hoodwink	HOODwink	/ˈhʊdwɪŋk/

Exercises

A

1. Choose an item each from the two columns and combine them to form compound words. Decide what stress pattern the compound words will have and practice their pronunciation.

week	loving
cool	crafted
film	movie
high	lasting
brand	start
low	moving
back	stitched
fake	snack
wedding	free
bold	hotel
fashion	space
burglar	site
health	fisted
easy	oil
machine	editing
fun	day
horror	coat
long	designer
acting	mail
luxury	print

long	priced
water	wound
kick	box
tape	filter
light	currency
duty	sized
web	alarm
cooking	access
hot	school
tight	board
answering	print
medium	guest
voice	career
hard	escape
drawing	drink
narrow	working
hand	machine
finger	shop
bullet	recorder
fast	spring

2. Choose the appropriate compound word to match the definitions given. Practise the pronunciation of the compound words with the right stress pattern. The stress patterns may vary depending on whether the compound word is a noun, verb, or adjective.

jet lag	phone tapping	text message	download	live music
high flier	word processor	green party	childproof	shift key
watch dog	speaker phone	reality show	hair raising	hard sell
right click	bungee jumping	market driven	bottom line	soft copy

(i) An entertainment show based on real people in real situations

(ii) A person who has the desire and the ability to be highly successful

(iii) To move data from a larger computer system to a smaller one

(iv) Influenced by competitive buying and selling of goods

(v) Designed so that young children cannot open, use or damage it

(vi) The feeling of being tired and slightly confused after a long plane journey
(vii) A method of selling that puts a lot of pressure on the customer to buy
(viii) The most important thing we have to consider or accept
(ix) A written message that we send by using a mobile phone
(x) A party that supports the principle of protecting the environment
(xi) To press the right button on a mouse to choose a particular function or item on a computer screen
(xii) Extremely frightening but often exciting
(xiii) Music performed when people are watching, not recorded
(xiv) A sport in which a person jumps from a high place with a long rope that can stretch tied to their feet
(xv) A key on a computer keyboard or typewriter that allows capital letters or a different set of characters to be typed
(xvi) A person or group of people whose job is to check that companies are not doing anything illegal or ignoring people's rights
(xvii) The practice of connecting a piece of equipment to a telephone in order to listen secretly to other people's telephone conversations
(xviii) Information that is stored in a computer and can be read on a screen, and is not printed on paper
(xix) A computer programme that is used for creating and storing written documents
(xx) A telephone that can be used without being held because it contains a microphone and a loudspeaker

6.11 Stress in reflexive pronouns, numbers and abbreviations

(1) Reflexive pronouns have *self/selves* at the end and always have the primary stress on this final part.

Listen to the words on the CD and notice how they are stressed.

myself	mySELF	/maɪˈself/
yourself	yourSELF	/jɔːˈself/ or /jɔːrˈself/
himself	himSELF	/hɪmˈself/
herself	herSELF	/hɜːˈself/ or /hɜːrˈself/
itself	itSELF	/ɪtˈself/
ourselves	ourSELVES	/aʊəˈselvz/ or /aʊərˈselvz/
yourselves	yourSELVES	/jɔːˈselvz/ or /jɔːrˈselvz/
themselves	themSELVES	/ðəmˈselvz/

(2) Words such as *thirty* and *thirteen*, *forty* and *fourteen*, *fifty* and *fifteen*, *sixty* and *sixteen* *seventy* and *seventeen*, *eighty* and *eighteen*, and *ninety* and *nineteen* are distinguished in speech mainly by the use of different stress patterns. The first word in each of these pairs has the primary stress on the first syllable, where as in the second word, the primary stress falls on the final or the second syllable and secondary stress on the first.

Listen to the words on the CD and notice how they are stressed.

thirty	THIRty	/ˈθɜːti/ or /ˈθɜːrti/
thirteen	thirTEEN	/ˌθɜːˈtiːn/ or /ˌθɜːrˈtiːn/
forty	FORty	/ˈfɔːti/ or /ˈfɔːrti/
fourteen	fourTEEN	/ˌfɔːˈtiːn/ or /ˌfɔːrˈtiːn/
fifty	FIFty	/ˈfɪfti/
fifteen	fifTEEN	/ˌfɪfˈtiːn/
sixty	SIXty	/ˈsɪksti/
sixteen	sixTEEN	/ˌsɪksˈtiːn/
seventy	SEVenty	/ˈsevnti/
seventeen	sevenTEEN	/ˌsevnˈtiːn/
eighty	EIGHty	/ˈeɪti/
eighteen	eighTEEN	/ˌeɪˈtiːn/
ninety	NINEty	/ˈnaɪnti/
nineteen	nineTEEN	/ˌnaɪnˈtiːn/

(3) Abbreviations of compound words that are spoken as two, three or more individual letters such as PC, CD, BBC, and USA are pronounced with the primary stress on the last letter and secondary stress on the first.

Listen to these abbreviations on the CD and notice how they are stressed.

ATM	/ˌeɪ tiː ˈem/
EU	/ˌiː ˈjuː/
UNO	/ˌjuː en ˈəʊ/ or /ˌjuː en ˈoʊ/
WHO	/ˌdʌbljuː eɪtʃ ˈəʊ/ or /ˌdʌbljuː eɪtʃ ˈoʊ/
UAE	/ˌjuː eɪ ˈiː/
CEO	/ˌsiː iː ˈəʊ/ or /ˌsiː iː ˈoʊ/
OHP	/ˌəʊ eɪtʃ ˈpiː/ or /ˌoʊ eɪtʃ ˈpiː/
DVD	/ˌdiː viː ˈdiː/
CV	/ˌsiː ˈviː/
UFO	/ˌjuː ef ˈəʊ/ or /ˌjuː ef ˈoʊ/
IT	/ˌaɪ ˈtiː/

Exercises

1. Fill in the blanks with the appropriate reflexive pronoun. Repeat the sentences taking care to pronounce the chosen reflexive pronoun with the right stress pattern.
   - (i) The students said that they would paint the school building by ____________.
   - (ii) The little girl was crying because she hurt ________________ badly when she fell.
   - (iii) I will write to the manager ________________.
   - (iv) Did he enjoy ____________________ at the party?
   - (v) I would like to know if you wrote the story by ________________.
   - (vi) My friends came home and we had the house to ____________.
   - (vii) You children have to do everything ________________ today.
   - (viii) The TV turns ________________ off at the specified time.

2. Choose the right word from those given to fill in the blanks.
   Repeat the sentences taking care to pronounce the words chosen to fill in the blanks with the right stress pattern.
   - (i) Our apartment is on the ______________ floor.
     (*fourteen, forty, fourteenth*)
   - (ii) Her daughter is in her teens. She's only ______________
     (*seventy, seventeenth, seventeen*)
   - (iii) Gates 1-20 are on the right. You have to go to Gate ____________
     (*eighteenth, eighteen, eighty)*
   - (iv) Many people believe that ________________
     (*thirty, thirteenth, thirteen*) is an unlucky number.
   - (v) The two brothers live together with thir families; one has six children and the other five. The house is too small for ________________ people.
     (*fifty, fifteen, fifteenth*)

3. Write the expansions of the abbreviations given. If you do not know what an abbreviation means, look it up in a dictionary.
   Practise the pronunciation of the abbreviations.

   BPO ....

   CNN ....

   DNA ....

DTH ....

DVD ....

ECG ....

ECS ....

FTP ....

GDP ....

GIS ....

GMT ....

GRE ....

HIV ....

HTML ....

IMF ....

ITO ....

LCD ....

MBA ....

MMS ....

MOU ....

NGO ....

NPT ....

SLV ....

SOS ....

SUV ....

UFO ....

VOA ....

WHO ....

WTO ....

YWCA ....

We have seen that there are specific types of words and specific features of words, which sometimes determine where the stress falls in these words. But there are always exceptions and these rules may not always be followed. It is only practice with a large number of words, which will help a foreign learner of English to learn the word stress patterns in English correctly. Again, we have to keep in mind that spelling does not help in finding out the stress pattern in most of the words and that we need to check the pronunciation of words given in phonetic transcription in dictionaries and also voice recordings on the CDs that come with most of the dictionaries, if we have to learn the correct pronunciation of words.

There are a number of words in English that are pronounced differently in British English and American English mainly because of differences in word stress.

(1) Many two-syllable verbs that end in *-ate* are pronounced with stress on the second syllable in British English and on the first syllable in American English.

British English		American English	
dicTATE	/dɪkˈteɪt/	DICtate	/ˈdɪkteɪt/
gesTATE	/dʒesˈteɪt/	GEState	/ˈdʒesteɪt/
loCATE	/ləʊˈkeɪt/	LOcate	/ˈloʊkeɪt/
miGRATE	/maɪˈgreɪt/	MIgrate	/ˈmaɪgreɪt/

(2) In many five syllable words ending in *-ily*, mostly the primary stress falls on the first syllable in British English and on the third syllable in American English. American English speakers place secondary stress on the first syllable in these words.

British English		American English	
MOmentarily	/ˈməʊmənt(ə)rəli/	MOMENTArily	/ˌmoʊmənˈterəli/
NEcessarily	/ˈnesəs(ə)rəli/	NECESSArily	/ˌnesəˈserəli/
ORdinarily	/ˈɔːdɪn(ə)rəli/	ORDINArily	/ˌɔːrdɪˈnerəli/
TEMporarily	/ˈtemp(ə)rərəli/	TEMPORArily	/ˌtempəˈrerəli/

(3) Words ending in *-ary, -ery, -ory,* and *-mony* are pronounced differently in British and American English. The difference is noticeable in the pronunciation of the penultimate syllable in these words, which seems to get some stress and therefore has a different vowel in American English.

British English		American English	
ARbitrary	/ˈɑːbɪtrəri/	ARbitrary	/ˈɑːrbɪtreri/
CONtrary	/ˈkɒntrəri/	CONtrary	/ˈkɑːntreri/
CEMetery	/ˈsemətri/	CEMetery	/ˈsemәteri/
MONastery	/ˈmɒnəstri/	MONastery	/ˈmɑːnəsteri/
INventory	/ˈɪnvəntri/	INventory	/ˈɪnvəntɔːri/
MANdatory	/ˈmændətəri/	MANdatory	/ˈmændətɔːri/
CERemony	/ˈserəməni/	CERemony	/ˈserəmoʊni/
TEStimony	/ˈtestɪməni/	TEStimony	/ˈtestɪmoʊni/

(4) In words of French origin, American English tends to stress the final syllable (as in French) whereas British English has the stress on the first syllable.

British English		American English	
GARage	/ˈgærɑːʒ/	gaRAGE	/gəˈrɑːʒ/
CABaret	/ˈkæbəreɪ/	cabaRET	/ˌkæbəˈreɪ/
BOURgeois	/ˈbʊəʒwɑː/	bourGEOIS	/ˌbʊrˈʒwɑː/
FRONtier	/ˈfrʌntɪə/	fronTIER	/frʌnˈtɪr/

(5) There are other words that show a difference in stress pattern in British English and American English.

British English		American English	
laBOrarory	/ləˈbɒrətri/	LAboratory	/ˈlæbrətɔːri/
adVERtisement	/ədˈvɜːtɪsmənt/	ADverTISEment	/ˌædvərˈtaɪzmənt/
coROLLary	/kəˈrɒlərɪ/	COrollary	/ˈkɔːrəlerɪ/
ARistocrat	/ˈærɪstəkræt/	aRIStocrat	/əˈrɪstəkræt/

In many multisyllabic words such as those above, apart from different stress patterns, there is a general tendency in British English to reduce the number of syllables whereas American English is more likely to retain all the syllables.

L6.12. Listen to the following words, first in British English and then in Americcan English. Notice the difference in the stress pattern used.

1. Depending on whether you wish to learn British or American pronunciation, practise the pronunciation of these words with appropriate stress patterns

donate	frustrate	mutate	pulsate		
stagnate	rotate	vibrate	castrate		
extraordinarily	honorarily	voluntarily	temporarily	contemporarily	
monetary	secondary	planetary	signatory	explanatory	territory
articulatory	solitary	obligatory	revolutionary	observatory	dormitory
acrimony	matrimony	hegemony	alimony		

It is essential that Indian speakers understand what word stress is and develop an awareness of how it works in spoken English because Indian languages in this respect are different from English. Indian languages are mostly ***syllable-timed***, which means that they have a rhythm characterized by the occurrence of syllables at regular intervals. English, in contrast, is ***stress-timed***, which means that it has a different rhythm, which is characterized by the occurrence of stressed syllables at regular intervals. Indian speakers of English, therefore, are not familiar with word stress as a distinctive feature of speech. When they speak English, they tend to stress syllables mainly for emphasis and produce strong vowels in all positions and are mainly guided by the spelling of words. It is important for them to understand that learning the correct pronunciation of English words means learning to produce the sequence of sounds in the words with

(a) the right stress pattern and
(b) the right manner of producing the different vowels in a word, strong or reduced as necessary.

Since word stress has a very important function in English speech, they should make an effort to learn this distinctive feature of English pronunciation if they are to be able to speak English correctly.

L6.13. Listen to two jokes read by a British English speaker, an American English speaker and an Indian speaker.

First listen without looking at the texts given below and then listen again following the texts.

(i) Tech Support to customer 'I need you to right-click on the Open Desktop.' 'Okay', says the customer. Tech Support 'Did you get a pop-up menu?' 'No,' replies the customer. Tech Support, 'Okay. Right-click again. Do you see a pop-up menu?' 'Not at all,' replies the customer. Tech Support, 'Okay, sir. Can you tell me what you have done up until this point?' 'Sure,' replies the customer. 'You told me to write "click" so I wrote down "click".' (*Man walks into a bar* The Ultimate Collection of Jokes and One-liners Stephen Arnott and Mike Haskins p. 276)

(ii) Someday, the people who know how to use computers will rule over those who don't. And there will be a special name for them – secretaries. (*Man walks into a bar* The Ultimate Collection of Jokes and One-liners Stephen Arnott and Mike Haskins p. 276)

1. (a) Read the two jokes and record your readings on a tape or CD and (b) play them to your teacher or friend/s and get their feedback on your readings.

L6.14. (i) Listen to another joke read by a British English speaker, an American English speaker and an Indian speaker.

First listen without looking at the text given below and then listen again following the text.

At **a recent software engineering management course in the US, the participants** were given **an awkward question** to answer. 'If you had just boarded **an airliner** and discovered that your team of **programmers** were responsible for **the flight control software**, how many of you would **disembark immediately**?' Among **the forest of raised hands**, only one man sat motionless. When asked what he would do, he replied that he would be **quite content** to stay **onboard**. **With his team's software**, he said, the plane was unlikely to even taxi as far as the **runway**, let alone **take off**. (*Man walks into a bar* The Ultimate Collection of Jokes and One-liners Stephen Arnott and Mike Haskins p. 275)

(ii) Listen again focusing on how the words and expressions in bold are stressed.

1. (a) Read the joke and record your reading on a tape or CD and (b) play it to your teacher or friend/s and get their feedback on your reading.

L6.15. (i) Listen to a passage on Digital cameras read by a British English speaker, an American English speaker and an Indian speaker.

First listen without looking at the text given below and then listen again following the text.

In the past twenty years, most of the major technological breakthroughs in consumer electronics have really been part of one larger breakthrough. When you get down to it, CDs, DVDs, HDTV, MP3s and DVRs are all built around the same basic process: converting conventional analog information (represented by a fluctuating wave) into digital information (represented by ones and zeros, or bits). This fundamental shift in technology totally changed how we handle visual and audio information – it completely redefined what is possible.

The digital camera is one of the most remarkable instances of this shift because it is so truly different from its predecessor. Conventional cameras depend entirely on chemical and mechanical processes – you don't even need electricity to operate them. On the other hand, all digital cameras have a built-in computer and all of them record images electronically. Just like a conventional camera, a digital camera has a series of lenses that focus light to create an image of a scene. But instead of focusing this light onto a piece of film, it focuses it onto a semiconductor device that records light electronically. A computer then breaks this electronic information down into digital data. All the fun and interesting features of digital cameras come as a direct result of this process. (213 words)

http://electronics.howstuffworks.com/digital-camera.htm

(ii) Listen again focusing on how these different types of words and expressions are pronounced and stressed.

Multisyllabic words with syllabic consonants	***Abbreviations***
technological	CDs
conventional	DVDs

digital	HDTV
fundamental	MP3s
chemical	DVRs
mechanical	
Derived words	***Compounds – Noun + Noun***
technology – technological	consumer electronics
electronic – electronics – electronically	semiconductor device
Compounds – Adjective + Noun	
technological breakthrough	basic process
digital information	a fluctuating wave
fundamental shift	digital camera
most remarkable instances	conventional camera
mechanical processes	a built-in computer
electronic information	digital data
interesting features	direct result

1. (a) Read the passage and record your reading on a tape or CD and (b) play it to your teacher or friend/s and get their feedback on your reading.

Chapter summary

1. In words of two and more syllables, there is generally one syllable that is pronounced more prominently than others and this syllable is said to be ***stressed*** or ***accented***.

   A stressed syllable can be distinguished from unstressed syllables in terms of one or more of the following features: (i) length, (ii) loudness, (iii) pitch movement and (iv) vowel quality.

2. ***Word Stress*** is a feature of speech that is studied taking into account the way words are pronounced in isolation, though in speech we generally combine words into longer sequences.

   We often find that, in words of three or more syllables, in addition to a strong type of stress that falls on one syllable, a weaker stress falls on another syllable, both of which can be distinguished from other unstressed syllables, as in *specification* /ˌspesɪfɪˈkeɪʃn/. In terms of ***degrees of stress***, therefore, we can distinguish three types of syllables, namely, (a) syllables that get ***primary or strong stress***, (b) syllables that get ***secondary or weak stress*** and (c) syllables that get no stress.

3. In English, stress does not fall on a specific syllable in all words; it falls on different syllables in different words. It is therefore difficult to predict correctly where the stress

falls in a given word. But a detailed study of stress placement in a large number of words has shown that there are five features of words that largely determine where the stress falls:

(i) the number of syllables in the word. Words with one syllable are stressed, if they are nouns (*link*), full verbs (*give*), adjectives (*short*) or adverbs (*quickly*) and are unstressed, if they are grammatical words like articles (*the*), pronouns (*we*), prepositions (*for*) or auxiliary verbs (*have*).

(ii) the phonological structure of the syllables that make up a word. In many words of two or three syllables, the stress falls on the syllable that has a long vowel or a diphthong (*deceive, compile*) or the syllable that ends with more than one consonant (*collect*). There are many exceptions to this rule, especially with words that have come into English from other languages and words with more than three or four syllables.

(iii) the grammatical category that the word belongs to i.e., whether the word is a noun, adjective or a verb or whether it is a phrasal verb etc. English has many pairs of words that have the same form but function differently. In such words, the stress falls on the first syllable, if the word functions as a noun or adjective, but on the second syllable, if it functions as a verb (*protest, absent*).

In phrasal verbs that have a verb and an adverb, the verb gets secondary stress and the adverb gets primary stress (*call up*) and in phrasal verbs that have a verb and a preposition, the verb gets primary stress and the preposition is unstressed (*call for*). In three word phrasal verbs, the verb gets secondary stress, the adverb in the middle gets primary stress and the final preposition is unstressed (*look down on*). In nouns derived from phrasal verbs with an adverb, the stress pattern changes and only the verb gets primary stress (*cutback*).

(iv) the morphological structure of the word i.e., whether the word is ***simple***, or whether it is ***complex*** because it contains prefixes or suffixes or both, or whether it is ***compound***, formed by combining two, three or more words.

In complex words with a prefix, the first syllable of the ***root*** or the ***stem*** (the word to which a prefix or a suffix or both are added) is strongly stressed and the prefix is unstressed or sometimes weakly stressed. When some of these complex words with a prefix function as nouns, the stress falls on the prefix and not the root or the stem.

In complex words with a suffix, the stress placement depends on the type of suffix added. There are three types of suffixes, (a) suffixes that do not affect stress placement (*season-seasonal, collect-collective*), (b) suffixes that affect stress placement (*combine-combination, possible-possibility*) and (c) suffixes that carry the stress themselves (*refuge-refugee*). Further, the addition of a suffix sometimes changes the pronunciation of a vowel or a consonant or both in the root of a word (*resign-resignation*).

In compound words, stress placement largely depends on the grammatical category to which the two parts belong and also what grammatical function the compound word has (*checkpost, short temper, headhunt*).

(v) whether the word is of a specific type like reflexive pronouns with *self/selves*, numbers such as *thirty* and *thirteen* or abbreviations such as *PC* and *USA*. In reflexive pronouns, primary stress falls on the final *self/selves*. In numbers such as *thirty*, primary stress falls on the first syllable, where as in numbers such as *thirteen*, primary stress falls on the second syllable and secondary stress on the first. In abbreviations such as BBC, the first letter has secondary stress and the last letter, primary stress.

These general rules do not always apply and there are many exceptions. It is therefore necessary for foreign learners of English to practise stress placement in a large number of words, if they are to get the stress patterns of English correctly.

7

Connected speech – I
Rhythm and adjustments in pronunciation

(word stress, sentence stress, rhythm, and adjustments in connected speech) allow the speaker to turn the basic building blocks of the sound systems (i.e., the vowel and consonant phonemes) into words, meaningful utterances, and extended discourse. Command of these features is therefore as critical as command of the segmental features ... in achieving successful communication for second language learners.
Stress, rhythm, and adjustments in connected speech can be easily overlooked in the language classroom. Nonetheless, these invisible signals are among the main clues used by listeners to process incoming speech and are thus of primary importance in the speech communication process.

Celce-Murcia M, Brinton D.M & Goodwin J.M *Teaching Pronunciation* 1996 p. 172

English has a characteristic rhythm and listeners expect to hear all speakers use this rhythm. It is therefore absolutely vital that learners use this rhythm that is characteristic of English. There must be an alternation of stressed and unstressed syllables, with the stressed syllables occurring on a regular beat, and the unstressed syllables must have a less-than-full vowel.

Joanne Kenworthy *Teaching English Pronunciation* 1987 p. 19

Learners often attempt to pronounce each word so clearly that they fail to blend words within a single thought group smoothly. This can cause their speech to sound choppy. All languages have some rules concerning adjustments in connected speech; however, no other language has exactly the same rules as English, and teaching the conventions specific to English is the pedagogical challenge.

Celce-Murcia M, Brinton D.M & Goodwin J.M *Teaching Pronunciation* 1996 p. 172

PREVIEW

In the previous units we have seen (a) how it is necessary to learn the pronunciation of individual sounds as well as the changes in their pronunciation when they occur in combination with other sounds and (b) how stress placement in words is crucial in learning their correct pronunciation and also how it changes the pronunciation of some sounds in a word. In speech we combine words into longer stretches of language following the rules of grammar to convey different meanings and perform different functions. When we consider the manner in which these longer stretches are spoken, we find that connected speech is characterized by two strking features (i) rhythm and (ii) certain adjustments in pronunciation. These form a very important aspect of English pronunciation, particularly in fluent speech and therefore we should learn to use them appropriately to be able to speak English fluently and naturally. An understanding of these features is also essential to understand fluent English speech.

In this chapter we'll first consider what kind of rhythm English has and how it is different from the rhythm of other languages. Then we'll examine the five types of adjustments in pronunciation that we make in connected speech, namely, Linking, Assimilation, Elision, Contraction and use of Weak forms.

There are six units in this chapter.

7.1 How rhythm works in English

In our study of word stress, we saw how multisyllabic words often have a combination of unstressed, weakly stressed, and strongly stressed syllables. (It is, however, important to remember that there is only one strongly stressed syllable in a word.) For example, in *possibility*, the first syllable is weakly stressed and the third syllable is strongly stressed, whereas the second, fourth and fifth are unstressed. Similarly in *qualification*, the first syllable is weakly stressed and the fourth syllable is strogly stressed, whereas the second, third and fifth syllables are unstressed. The stress patterns in the two words are ooOoo and oooOo. This means that in each of these words, two syllables stand out from the other syllables, one more strongly than the other.

When we examine stretches of speech longer than a word, we notice that these stretches of connected speech also have combinations of unstressed, weakly stressed and strongly stressed syllables. Here too, some syllables stand out from other syllables, one of them more strongly than others. For example, if we consider strtches of connected speech such as *What's your remedy?* and *What's her intention?*, we find that they have patterns of stress similar to those in *possibility* and *qualification*.

o o O o o
possibility

o o o O o
qualification

o o O o o
What's your remedy?

o o o O o
What's her intention?

English speech is characterized by such patterns of stressed and unstressed syllables. A few other examples are

o O o o o O o
He didn't want to leave her.

o o O o o O
He had to call them at eight.

o o o O o o O o O o o.
Dev has decided to see the manager.

In each of them, we notice there are some syllables that stand out from the others, one of them more strongly than the others. In the first two, there are three syllables that are stressed, one of which is more strongly stressed than the other two. In the third, there are four syllables that are stressed, one of them more strongly than the other three.

A characteristic feature of these patterns of stressed and unstressed syllables in English speech, which gives it its ***rhythm***, is that stressed syllables occur at fairly regular intervals of time, irrespective of the number of unstressed syllables between them. This type of rhythm is called ***stress-timed rhythm.*** In this respect, English is different from many other languages, which have what is called ***syllable-timed rhythm***. In languages with syllable-timed rhythm, all syllables occur at regular intervals of time, whereas in English, which has stress-timed rhythm, stressed syllables occur at regular intervals of time. In other words, the length of an utterance in English depends on the number of stressed syllables, irrespective of the number of unstressed syllables between them, whereas in syllable-timed languages, the length of an utterance depends on the number of syllables.

The stress-timed nature of English speech can be clearly seen when we compare the following sentences.

CHILdren	LEARN	POEMS
CHILdren	will LEARN	POEMS
CHILdren	will be LEARNing	POEMS
The CHILdren	have been LEARNing	POEMS
The CHILdren	might have been LEARNing	POEMS
The CHILdren	could have been LEARNing	the POEMS.

The number of syllables in these six sentences varies, but the number of stressed syllables is the same in all of them. The time needed to say each of them is therefore roughly the same. What happens is that the length of the syllables will vary depending on the number of syllables in each sentence. In the first, which has the fewest number of syllables, each syllable is longer than the syllables in the other sentences. As we move from the first to the second, third, fourth, fifth and sixth sentences, the number of unstressed syllables increases and these unstressed syllables are much shorter than the stressed ones. Also, the stressed syllables in these sentences are slightly shorter than the stressed syllables in the first sentence. These adjustments are made in such a way that the extra unstressed syllables do not affect the time taken to say the sentences. But the speed of speech changes from slow and deliberate to rapid as we move from the first to the last of these sentences.

An important question that arises when we consider the pattern of unstressed and stressed syllables that occur in English speech is which words (syllables) in an utterance are likely to be stressed and which unstressed. Words are generally divided into two categories, (1) ***content words***, (i.e., words that carry information) and (2) ***function words*** (i.e., words that indicate grammatical relationships). Content words – generally nouns, main verbs, and adjectives in an utterance are stressed. Other words that are stressed are *wh-* words that begin questions seeking information, demonstrative pronouns, *this, that, these*, and *those*, possessive pronouns, *mine, ours, yours, theirs* etc., adverbs, *always, almost* etc., contracted negative forms *can't, aren't* etc., and *not* when it is not contracted. Function or grammatical words such as articles, auxiliary verbs, personal and relative pronouns, prepositions and conjunctions are not generally stressed.

Stress timing and regular rhythms are most noticeable in contexts where speakers deliberately try to produce rhetorical effects as in reciting or reading poems, particularly nursery rhymes and limericks and in public speeches.

Exercises

L7.1. Listen to two nursery rhymes and two limericks read by a British English speaker and an American English speaker.
Notice the rhythm.

(i) Star light Star bright
The first star I see tonight,
I wish I may, I wish I might,
Have the wish I wish tonight.

(ii) Hickory dickory dock
The mouse ran up the clock
The clock struck one
The mouse ran down
Hickory dickory dock

(iii) An artistic young man called Bo,
To an art class decided to go.
The teacher said, "Not right
Your page is all white!"
Bo said, "It is a polar bear in snow".

(iv) A tutor who tooted a flute
Tried to teach two young tooters to toot.
Said the two to the tutor,
"Is it harder to toot, or
To tutor two tooters to toot?"

Practise reading them with the right rhythm.

L7.2. You'll hear three sets of sentences below. In each set the sentences have the same rhythmic pattern.

(i) The lady wants to buy the dress.
Athletes should train to win a medal.
A student needs a lot of help.
She wondered when her son would come.
Who did the boy admire in school?

(ii) He works as a clerk in a bank.
The girl will be back in a day.
Policemen can ask for your pass.
The doctor may give you a shot.
Her book on computers is good.

(iii) Their children have been playing in the park.
Our teachers will be coming to the show.
These travellers will spend some of their cash.
Her father may be telling her to go.
My friend could be returning in a day.

Practise saying the sentences with the right rhythmic pattern.

7.2 Adjustments in connected speech – Linking

Here we will focus on five important processes of adjustment in pronunciation that occur in connected speech.

(a) Linking
(b) Assimilation
(c) Elision
(d) Contraction
(e) Use of Weak forms

Linking

In connected speech, it is possible to identify a unit of speech longer than a syllable (or word). This unit is called ***a tone unit*** or ***a speech unit*** and one of its distinctive features is that it is usually spoken without a break. (Though we imagine that there are breaks between words in speech, this is not true.) The words that make up a tone unit are connected in speech, which means that the sound at the end of one word is linked to the sound at the beginning of the next in a way that gives a smooth quality to speech. English like other languages has its own ways of connecting words in speech.

There are five kinds of linking between words in English depending on the final sound of one word and the initial sound of the next.

(1) When a word ends with a vowel and the next word begins with a vowel, a /w/ or /j/ sound is inserted between the two words to link them. Whether we use /w/ or /j/ will depend on the type of vowel that ends the first word. If /iː/, /eɪ/, /aɪ/, or /ɔɪ/ occurs at the end of the first word, the linking sound will be /j/. If the vowel at the end of the first word is /uː/, /aʊ/, or /əʊ/ or /oʊ/, the linking sound will be /w/.

I can't see‿anything.
/j/

Why don't you say‿it?
/j/

We don't like high‿interest rates.
/j/

They need a boy‿actor.
/j/

It is due‿on the first.
/w/

Now‿is your chance.
/w/

There are no‿oranges.
/w/

(2) When a word ends with a consonant and the next word begins with a vowel, the consonant is smoothly linked to the following vowel as if it belonged to both the syllables, the last in the first word and the first in the next.

What is the right‿answer?
It'll be a fine‿evening.
The story has a surprise‿ending.
It's a brief‿outline.

(3) When a word ends with a consonant cluster and the next word begins with a vowel, the final consonant of the cluster is often pronounced as part of the following syllable.

Do you know the correc/t‿address?
Hol/d‿on tight.
Take the nex/t‿exit.
This is the fif/th‿entry.

(4) When a word ends with a consonant and the next begins with another consonant, there is no break between the two consonants, though the pronunciation of the consonant at the end of the first word may change a little to make it easier to move to the next consonant.

It's a love‿song.
I'm going‿today.
It was a dream‿team.
Leave‿something for the children.

(5) When a word ends with a consonant and the next begins with the same consonant, only one lengthened consonant sound is made. (The consonant sound is not produced twice.)

There was no team‿management.
She's a big‿girl now.
Stop‿pulling my hair.
Don't make‿comments.

(6) When a word ends with one of the plosives /p/, /b/, /t/, /d/, /k/, or /g/ and the next begins with a different one of these or /m/ or /n/, no air is released at the end of the first consonant in order to make a smooth change to the second.

It's a fat‿book.
Give me a sharp‿knife.
Did you hear the loud‿bang?
Don't hike‿prices.

(7) In British English the /r/ sound is not pronounced in the final position in words such as *car, door, river, more,* and *sure*. When a word like this is followed by a word that begins with a vowel, the sound /r/ is inserted between the two words.

I must pay my car‿insurance.
/r/
The door‿is open.
/r/
This is where the river‿enters the sea.
/r/
She wants more‿oil.
/r/

Exercises

L7.3. Listen to the following question-answer sequences. Identify the type of link between the vowels in the underlined words in the answers. Practise saying the answers, linking the words underlined appropriately.

(i) What do you want to do?
Grow oranges

(ii) What do you want me to do?
Keep the tray in the fridge.

(iii) Did you hear the news?
Yes, how awful it must be for the victims!

(iv) How are you feeling?
I am a little weak, but ok otherwise.

(v) Who do you think has done it?
We think it could be a young man but don't have any clue about his identity.

(vi) Are you fond of travelling?
Yes, I want to see interesting places and meet different kinds of people.

(vii) How did they arrive at the decision?
By examining all the evidence.

(viii) Why do you always go to this restaurant?
Because the coffee is excellent here.

(ix) What will I do with these rotten fruits?
Throw all of them away.

L7.4. Listen to the following expressions. Identify the sounds that end the first word and those that begin the second and notice how the two words are linked.

gold ornaments
direct answers
test announcements
gift items
false evidence
second experiment
fifth example
last August
spent energy
present intention
send it
hold exhibitions
find engagements
connect everything
print invitations
think alike
count idioms
sift information
post instructions
punch umpires

Practise saying the expressions, linking the words appropriately.

1. Combine a word from column A with one in column B and practice saying the resulting phrases, linking the words appropriately.

A	B
brave	estimate
hot	ideal
right	understanding
noble	items
quick	Indian
mean	assignment

wide	hour
brief	intelligence
tough	entrance
rush	engagement

L7.5. Listen to the following expressions. Identify the type of sounds that end the first word and those that begin the second and notice how the two words are linked.

big garden	top person
thick carpet	foam mattress
thin notebook	tough fight
red drum	tall lad
wet towel	English shoes

Practise saying the expressions, linking the words appropriately.

L7.6. Listen to the following expressions. Identify the type of sounds that end the first word and those that begin the second and notice how the two words are linked.

proud parents	rib cage
dark night	job notice
nut cracker	ripe mangoes
dog biscuits	white paper
click button	

Practise saying the expressions, linking the words appropriately.

L7.7. Listen to the words in column A and the sentences in column B. What is the difference in the pronunciation of the word in column A when it is used in the sentence in column B?

A	B
Flower	The flower in the middle is beautiful.
Door	There is a door at the back.
Enter	Press enter and it will work.
Hair	Her hair is grey.
Tear	The tear on the sleeve can be stitched up.
River	The river is our source of water.
Chair	Sit in the chair on the other side.
Manager	I want to see the manager in charge of this store.

7.3 Assimilation

A second type of adjustment in connected speech is the process of assimilation. In this process, the pronunciation of a sound in a word changes because of the influence of another sound in a neighbouring word, which results in the two sounds becoming alike or identical. For example, in a sentence like *I don't like this shoe,* if we consider the way the expression *this shoe* is pronounced, we notice that the final /s/ in *this* is pronounced /ʃ/, because of the influence of the initial /ʃ/ in *shoe*. The result of this change is that the final sound of *this* and the initial sound of *shoe* become alike or identical.

In English, assimilation is found mostly to affect consonants. There are three types of assimilation, which are identifiable with consonants. They are (1) Regressive assimilation, (2) Progressive assimilation, and (3) Coalescent assimilation.

(1) *Regressive assimilation*

In regressive assimilation, the final consonant ending a word changes to become like the initial consonant that begins the next word as in *this shoe*.

We have seen that consonants are distinguished in terms of three features, namely the place of articulation, the manner of articulation and the presence or absence of voicing. When one consonant becomes like another, it may be with reference to any of these three features and therefore, there are three ways in which the assimilation of consonants takes place.

(a) Assimilation of place

this shoe — the final /s/ in *this*, which is alveolar, changes to post- alveolar /ʃ/ because of the influence of the following /ʃ/ in *shoe*.

that pen — the final /t/ in *that*, which is alveolar, changes to bilabial /p/ because of the influence of the following /p/ in *pen.*

that cap — the final /t/ in *that*, which is alveolar, changes to velar /k/ because of the influence of /k/ in *cap*.

bright kid — the final /t/ in *bright,* which is alveolar, changes to velar /k/ because of the influence of /k/ in *kid*.

light green — the final /t/ in *light*, which is alveolar, changes to velar /g/ because of the influence of /g/ in *green*.

In all these examples, assimilation changes one sound to another, where the two sounds are different only in terms of the place of production. There are other instances where assimilation changes one form of a sound to another form of the same sound, the two forms being different only in terms of the place of production. For example, *that thing* the final /t/ in *that*, which is alveolar, changes to dental /t/ because of the influence of *thing*.

cut those the final /t/ in *cut*, which is alveolar, changes to dental /t/ because of the influence of /ð/ in those.

Thus assimilation may be ***phonemic***, when it changes one sound to another, or ***allophonic***, when it changes one form of the sound to another form.

(b) Assimilation of manner

that soap the final /t/ in *that*, which is a plosive, changes to fricative /s/ because of the influence of /s/ in *soap*.

good night the final /d/ in *good*, which is a plosive, changes to nasal /n/ because the influence of /n/ in *night*.

In these examples, we notice that a final plosive changes to a fricative or nasal, which means that the change here is towards an 'easier' consonant or a consonant which is marked by less obstruction to the air flow. Such instances of assimilation, however, are noticeable only in very rapid speech.

(c) Assimilation of voice

good tea the final /d/ in *good,* which is voiced, changes to voiceless /t/ because of the influence of /t/ in *tea*.

big cop the final /g/ in *big,* which is voiced, changes to voiceless /k/ because of the influence of /k/ in *cop*.

This type of assimilation is much less noticeable because in final and initial positions consonants are hardly voiced.

(2) *Progressive assimilation*

In progressive assimilation, the pronunciation of a sound is influenced by a preceding sound. Progressive assimilation in English occurs at morpheme boundaries rather than word boundaries. Examples are plural nouns and third person singular forms of verbs.

bats where the final 's' is pronounced /s/ under the influence of the preceding /t/, which is voiceless.

caps where the final 's' is pronounced /s/ under the influence of the preceding/p/, which is voiceless.

laughs where the final 's' is pronounced /s/ under the influence of the preceding /f/, which is voiceless.

rods where the final 's' is pronounced /z/ under the influence of the preceding /d/, which is voiced.

pubs where the final 's' is pronounced /z/ under the influence of the preceding /b/, which is voiced.

loves where the final 's' is pronounced /z/ under the influence of the preceding /v/, which is voiced.

In these examples, we have plural nouns or third person singular forms of verbs, where the plural suffix, *–s*, or the third person singular suffix of verbs, *–s,* is influenced by the preceding consonant in terms of voicing. If the preceding consonant is voiceless, the suffix, *–s*, is pronounced as voiceless /s/ and, if the preceding consonant is voiced, it is pronounced as voiced /z/.

Another example of this type of assimilation occurs in the alternation between /t/ and /d/ in the regular past tense forms of verbs. (See page 85)

(3) *Coalescent assimilation*

In coalescent assimilation the first sound (the final consonant at the end of a word) and second sound (the initial consonant at the beginning of the next word) in a sequence coalesce or come together to create a third sound that has features from both the original sounds.

Is it this year?	where /s/ and /j/ coalesce to create /ʃ/
Has your brother come?	where /z/ and /j/ coalesce to create /ʒ/
Is that your book?	where /t/ and /j/ coalesce to create /tʃ/
Could you help me?	where /d/ and /j/ coalesce to create /dʒ/

This type of assimilation is also called ***palatalization***. When assimilation occurs between words, it is important to note that the consonant that undergoes assimilation does not disappear, but changes under the influence of another consonant in the neighbouring word.

T

We have so far seen examples of assimilation at word or morpheme boundaries, i.e., examples where the final sound in a word or morpheme is influenced by the initial sound of the following word or morpheme. But, when we consider the phonological structure of many syllables and words in English, we see that assimilation has often brought about changes in the pronunciation of sounds even within morphemes.

(1) *bank* where 'n' is pronounced /ŋ/ because of the influence of the following /k/.
link where 'n' is pronounced /ŋ/ because of the influence of the following /k/.
tenth where 'n' is pronounced as dental /n̪/ under the influence of the following /θ/.

In these examples, a nasal consonant like /n/, which precedes a plosive or a fricative like /k/ or /θ/ in a syllable final consonant cluster, is influenced by the following consonant in terms of its place of articulation and changes to velar /ŋ/ or dental /n̪/.

(2) Earlier, it was pointed out that, in English, assimilation mostly affects consonants. But there is a noticeable instance of vowel assimilation, which also occurs within morphemes.

moon where the vowel /uː/ is nasalized under the influence of the following /n/.
mean where the vowel /iː/ is nasalized under the influence of the following /n/.
name where the vowel /eɪ/ is nasalized under the influence of the following /m/.

In these examples, the vowel, which precedes a nasal consonant is influenced by the following consonant in terms of its manner of production and is nasalized.

This type of assimilation within morphemes has become 'fixed' and is a characteristic feature of the phonological structure of English syllables.

Assimilation within morphemes and at morpheme boundaries within words is part of the phonological structure of English, where as assimilation between words is a feature of rapid and casual speech.

Exercises

L7.8. Listen to the following sentences and identify the instances of assimilation in the underlined expressions.

(i) She's a smart girl.
(ii) Show me that thing.
(iii) Could you come home tomorrow?
(iv) That car is great.
(v) Is she a dancer?
(vi) Would you talk to him about it?
(vii) We can cut through the tangle of bushes.
(viii) Get those for me.
(ix) Don't you like mangoes?
(x) She doesn't know French, does she?
(xi) Did you see her going out?
(xii) The two roads meet at that point.
(xiii) I like short comedies.
(xiv) He wants bright colours.
(xv) Haven't you heard him sing?

Practise saying these sentences with appropriate assimilation of sounds.

7.4 Elision

Another more striking form of adjustment in connected speech is omitting sounds or not pronouncing them clearly in certain environments. As we saw in Chapter 5, a strategy that English speakers use in words that end with three consonant clusters such as *scripts, bumps,* and *pacts* is to leave out the middle consonant so that we hear /skrɪps/, /bʌms/, and /pæks/ and not /skrɪpts/, /bʌmps/, and /pækts/ when these words are spoken. This kind of omission of sounds is called ***elision***.

Some of the most typical instances of elision are given here.

(1) As mentioned above, in words ending in consonant clusters of three consonants with two plosives followed by a fricative, the second plosive disappears as in *attempts* or *predicts*, where the second syllable will be pronounced as /temps/ and/dɪks/.

(2) Similarly, in connected speech, when three plosives occur together, the middle plosive is left out as in *kept quiet* or *looked back*, which may be pronounced as /kepkwaɪət/ and /lʊkbæk/.

(3) When a word ends with a two consonant cluster with a final /t/ or /d/ and is followed by another word beginning with a consonant, the final /t/ or /d/ in the first word is left out.

Was it *last month*?	/lɑːsmʌnθ/ or /læsmʌnθ/
She's a *bold girl*.	/bəʊlgɜːl/ or /boʊlgɜːrl/
It's the *left button*.	/lefbʌtn/
It's a *kind gesture*.	/kaɪndʒestʃə/ or /kaɪndʒestʃər/

But if the following word begins with a vowel or /h/, there is no omission of /t/ or /d/.

It's the *left hand*.	/lefthænd/
It's a *kind action*.	/kaɪndækʃn/

Further, /d/ is not omitted if the following word begins with /l/, /w/, /r/, or /s/.

Find references	/faɪndrefrənsɪz/
Send watches	/sendwɒtʃɪz/ or /sendwɑːtʃɪz/

(4) The sound /h/ is often left out at the beginning of

(a) pronouns *he, her, his* and *him*

Who is *he*?

It's *his* turn.

Did you ask *her*?

What about *him*?

(b) the auxiliary verbs *have, has* and *had*

We ***have*** seen it.
She ***has*** left.
They ***had*** come.

(c) the question word *who*

Did you find out ***who*** it was?

But /h/ is not left out if it occurs at the beginning of an utterance or if the word beginning with it is stressed.

Have they left?

(5) The weak vowel following an initial plosive, /p/, /t/, or /k/ in words such as *perform, today* and *canal* is often left out, as the aspiration of the initial plosive becomes the most noticeable feature of the first syllable.

A weak vowel that is followed by /n/, /l/ or /r/ frequently disappears as the following consonant becomes a syllabic consonant as in *connect, collect* and *correct*. These words will then be pronounced /knekt/, /klekt/ and/krekt/.

Exercises

L7.9. Listen to the following sentences and identify and describe the elisions.

(i) They played some soft music.
(ii) He sells gold jewelry.
(iii) It was a grand function.
(iv) He looks very handsome in that dress.
(v) I've got the manuscripts.
(vi) Do you have cold coffee?
(vii) She has already left.
(viii) You dropped your handkerchief.
(ix) The children have gone home.
(x) They know the facts.
(xi) Is this your first project?

Practise saying the sentences with appropriate elisions.

7.5 Contraction

A typical feature of connected speech is the use of contracted forms, particularly of auxiliary verbs and their negative forms.

(1) Auxiliary verbs such as *is, are, am, has, have, had, will* and *would* have contracted forms *'s, 're, 'm, 's, 've, 'd, 'll* and *'d*. Some of these contracted forms have different pronunciations depending on the sound preceding them. For example, *'s* is pronounced /s/ after voiceless consonants and /z/ after voiced consonants and *'ve* is pronounced /v/ after vowels and /əv/ after consonants.

These contracted forms are generally used after *wh-* words, nouns, *this, that, these, those,* and *there*. But they are not used at the end of a sentence.

*Who**'s*** coming?
*Players**'ve*** left.
*This**'ll*** be good.
*Those**'re*** necessary.
*There**'s*** nothing here.
*There**'ll*** be many people.

(2) Contraction is frequent with negative forms of auxiliary verbs too. For example, *cannot* becomes *can't*, *do not* becomes *don't* and *will not* becomes *won't*. In these cases, along with contraction, there is also a change of vowel.

Exercises

L7.10. Listen to the following sentences and practise saying them with the appropriate contractions.

(i) What's happening? Didn't I tell you to be careful with that bowl?
(ii) She's very happy because her son's come home.
(iii) They'll call us when they reach there.
(iv) Can't you come early today?
(v) I'd already cleaned the room before they came.
(vi) Won't you be tired by the time you come home?
(vii) I don't understand how he could've done such a thing.
(viii) I'm not unhappy but I wish that she'd told me about it.
(ix) Aren't they inviting us? I thought they would.

(A)

1. Decide where contractions are appropriate in the following sentences and practise saying them with or without contractions as you think appropriate.
   - (i) I thought I would go and buy a gift for you but could not because I had no time.
   - (ii) She would not have taken up this job if she had known about these problems.
   - (iii) You should have found out the fares before you booked the tickets.
   - (iv) They will not come unless they are invited.
   - (v) He is not leaving if he cannot finish the report this evening.
   - (vi) We do not wish to offend you but we have to follow the rules.
   - (vii) She has applied for a scholarship but we do not know if she will get it.
   - (viii) You cannot be serious! I cannot believe what you are saying!
   - (ix) Did they not tell you to come early?
   - (x) Why did we not plan what we were going to do?

7.6 Use of weak forms

There are certain words that we pronounce in different ways in different contexts i.e., in different combinations of words in different environments. For example, let us consider how the word *for* is pronounced in the following sentences:

There is a letter *for* you.

Who is the letter *for*?

In the first sentence, it is pronounced /fə/, whereas in the second, it is pronounced /fɔː/. Thus the word *for* has two forms, one /fɔː(r)/ and the other /fə(r)/. The first is called the ***Strong form*** and the other the ***Weak form***. In English, there are a number of words that have two forms, strong and weak, like *for*. Almost all these words are those that we call grammatical words, i.e., words that do not have a dictionary meaning, but only a grammatical function, like conjunctions, articles, prepositions, pronouns, and auxiliary verbs. These grammatical words are generally pronounced in their weak forms. But there are certain contexts in which they are pronounced in their strong forms. It is necessary to know the contexts in which the strong forms of these words are appropriate and acceptable, and when the weak forms are more appropriate. If we use the strong forms in all contexts, our speech will sound unnatural and foreign.

Use of strong forms

Strong forms are used in the following contexts:

(1) When a weak-form word occurs at the end of a sentence;

For example, in

She works *for* a newspaper.

The word *for* is pronounced in its weak form /fər/ but in

It is a newspaper that she works *for*.

The word *for* is pronounced in its strong form /fɔː(r)/

(2) When a weak-form word is being contrasted with another;

In

Is this the train *from* Mysore?

It is not the train *from* Mysore, it is the train *to* Mysore.

the preposition *from* is used in its weak form, /frəm/ in the question, but in the answer which follows, both *from* and *to* are used in their strong forms, /frɒm/ or /frʌm/ and /tuː/ because they are in contrast.

Another instance where prepositions like *to* and *from* are used in their strong forms is when they are co-ordinated as in

The trains *from* and *to* Mysore are always crowded.

(3) When a weak-form word is stressed for the purpose of emphasis;

I'm telling you, we *can* finish the job in a week.

Here the word *can* is used in its strong form, /kæn/ because it is stressed.

(4) When a weak-form word is 'quoted' or 'cited' in contrast to being 'used';

For example, in a sentence like

She ordered for *a* book and *the* book has been sent to her.

both the articles *the* and *a* are used and therefore, are used in their weak forms, /ðə/ and /ə/. But in

Let us study how *'the'* and *'a'* are used in English.

both *the* and *a* are being quoted and therefore, require the use of strong forms, /ðiː/and/ eɪ/.

The most common of the words that have strong and weak forms are given below with their different pronunciations in different contexts.

			Strong form	Weak form
Articles	*the*		/ðiː/	
		before consonants		/ðə/
		before vowels		/ðɪ/

	a, an	before consonants	/eɪ/	/ə/
		before vowels	/æn/	/ən/
Conjunctions	*and*		/ænd/	/ənd/ or /ən/
	but		/bʌt/	/bət/
	that		/ðæt/	/ðət/
Prepositions	*at*		/æt/	/ət/
	for	before consonants	/fɔː(r)/	/fə(r)/
		before vowels	/fɔːr/	/fər/
	from		/frɒm/ or /frʌm/	/frəm/
	of		/ɒv/ or /ʌv/	/əv/
	to		/tuː/	
		before consonants		/tə/
		before vowels		/tu/
	as		/æz/	/əz/
	than		/ðæn/	/ðən/
Pronouns	*his*		/hɪz/	/ɪz/
	her	before consonants	/hɜː(r)/	/hə(r)/ or /ə(r)/
		before vowels	/hɜːr/	/hər/ or /ər/
	your	before consonants	/jɔː(r)/	/jə(r)/
		before vowels	/jɔːr/	/jər/
	she		/ʃiː/	/ʃi/
	he		/hiː/	/hi/ or /i/
	we		/wiː/	/wi/
	you		/juː/	/ju/
	him		/hɪm/	/ɪm/
	them		/ðem/	/ðəm/
	us		/ʌs/	/əs/
Auxiliaries	*can*		/kæn/	/kən/
	could		/kʊd/	/kəd/
	have		/hæv/	/həv/ or /əv/
	has		/hæz/	/həz/ or /əz/
	had		/hæd/	/həd/ or /əd/
	shall		/ʃæl/	/ʃəl/
	should		/ʃʊd/	/ʃəd/
	must		/mʌst/	/məst/
	do		/duː/	
		before consonants		/də/
		before vowels		/du/
	does		/dʌz/	/dəz/
	am		/æm/	/əm/

			Strong form	Weak form
	are	before consonants	/ɑː(r)/	/ə(r)/
		before vowels	/ɑːr/	/ər/
	was		/wɒz/	/wəz/
			or /wɑːz/	
	were	before consonants	/wɜː(r)/	/wə(r)/
		before vowels	/wɜːr/	/wər/
Other words				
	some		/sʌm/	/səm/
	there	before consonants	/ðeə/	/ðə(r)/
			or /ðer/	
		before vowels	/ðeər/	/ðər/
			or /ðer/	

There are two points to be noted here: (a) some words like the articles *the*, *a* and *an,* words like *to* and *do* and others like *her, your, are, were* which end in '*r*' have different forms depending on whether they occur before consonants or vowels, and (b) words that begin with *h* like *his, her, have* begin with initial /h/ only at the beginning of sentences.

Exercises

L7.11. Listen to the following sentences and identify the weak-form words in them. Notice whether they are used in their strong or weak forms.

(i) We shall let you know when we decide.
(ii) He asked her to stay at home. I think she should.
(iii) I asked him for some paper. He gave me some paper and a pen too.
(iv) She deals with all the letters to and from this office.
(v) Who can translate this? I can.
(vi) I will come with you whatever you may say.
(vii) What are you looking at?
(viii) That report is biased.
(ix) How much did she pay for her new car?
(x) Is there anything that you care for?
(xi) Look at that tall building there.
(xii) It was too late for me to call you.
(xiii) I thought you would be in college. Where are you now?
(xiv) They want her to wait for the taxi here.
(xv) Why don't you come over for lunch?

(xvi) When you want to use a neutral pronoun, use 'they' instead of 'he' or 'she'.
(xvii) Where do these birds come from?
(xviii) We don't eat fish, but many people do.
(xix) He is not as rich as you are.
(xx) Students must always come half an hour early for the examination
(xxi) How am I to know what happened to her?
(xxii) They don't want me to go; they want you to go.

Practise saying the sentences using the strong and weak forms appropriately.

1. Practise saying these sentences pronouncing the underlined words in their weak or strong forms as you think appropriate.

(i) I have given <u>your</u> books <u>to</u> Sheela.
(ii) Thank you <u>for</u> coming.
(iii) <u>There</u> is a magic show this evening.
(iv) What <u>are</u> you hinting <u>at</u>?
(v) <u>The</u> doctor has not yet come.
(vi) She bought <u>an</u> armchair.
(vii) What <u>do</u> they want?
(viii) You <u>have</u> to understand this.
(ix) The papers <u>are</u> in the briefcase.
(x) They liked <u>her</u> presentation.
(xi) <u>Your</u> organization is helping many people.
(xii) Where <u>were</u> you last night?
(xiii) She spoke <u>to</u> everybody at the party.
(xiv) I don't know who <u>she</u> <u>is</u>.
(xv) These apples <u>are</u> very tasty.
(xvi) <u>Her</u> interests <u>are</u> elsewhere.
(xvii) I <u>will</u> come, that's a promise.
(xviii) <u>There</u> can be no doubt about his guilt.
(xix) <u>The</u> example she gave was appropriate.
(xx) <u>There</u> is the party to look forward <u>to</u>.
(xxi) <u>The</u> reporters who <u>were</u> in the hall heard the sound of explosion.
(xxii) We did it <u>for</u> <u>a</u> lark.
(xxiii) What <u>do</u> I tell <u>her</u>?
(xxiv) We got <u>your</u> card.
(xxv) <u>For</u> information about our holiday offers, call 8345218.

The features of connected speech described above, namely rhythm and the various adjustments made in longer stretches of speech are specific to English language. The rhythm of Indian languages is different from that of English and it is necessary for Indian speakers to develop an awareness of these rhythmic differences, especially the stress timed nature of English if they are to be able to understand fluent English speech. They should also be aware of the features of linking, assimilation and elision that characterize rapid and casual English speech and learn to use them appropriately if they wish to speak naturally.

Indian speakers often use full forms of auxiliary verbs such as *is, are, have* etc. and strong forms of grammatical words such as *for, of, her,* etc. in all contexts because of a lack of awareness of the use of contractions and weak forms that are essential features of natural English speech. They need to practice the appropriate use of contractions and weak forms so that they become natural components of their English speech.

L7.13. Listen to two jokes read by a British English speaker, an American English speaker and an Indian speaker.

First listen without looking at the texts given below and then listen again following the texts.

(i) A little boy is doing his homework. He says to himself, 'Two plus five, the son of a bitch is seven. Three plus six, the son of a bitch is nine.' His mother hears this and gasps, 'What are you saying?' The little boy answers, 'I'm doing my homework. This is how my teacher taught me to do it.' Infuriated, the mother confronts the teacher the next day. 'What are you teaching my son in arithmetic? He's been saying two plus two, the son of a bitch is four?' The teacher replies, 'Oh dear, What I taught them was, two plus two "the sum of which" is four!' (*Man walks into a bar* The Ultimate Collection of Jokes and One-liners Stephen Arnott and Mike Haskins p. 154)

(ii) Tom is trying to get his new computer working. He's having trouble so he calls over Harry to give him a hand. Harry switches on the computer then asks Tom if he wants it password protected. 'Oh yes, I read about that in the manual. I think the password I'll have is "DaffyDuckBugsBunnyTomandJerry".' 'That's a very long password,' says Harry. 'Yes,' replies Tom. 'But the manual says it has to be at least four characters.' (*Man walks into a bar* The Ultimate Collection of Jokes and One-liners Stephen Arnott and Mike Haskins p. 276)

1. (a) Read the two jokes and record your readings on a tape or CD and (b) play them to your teacher or friend/s and get their feedback on your readings.

L7.14. Listen to a passage on computers read by a British English speaker, an American English speaker and an Indian speaker.

First listen without looking at the text given below and then listen again following the text.

Why computers are male: 1 – **In order** to get **their attention**, you have to **turn them on**. 2 – They have a **lot of data**, but are **still clueless**. 3 – They are supposed to help you solve your problems, but **half the time** they are the problem. 4 – **As soon as** you **commit to one**, you realize that, if you **had waited a little longer**, you might have had **a better model**. Why computers are female: 1 – No one but **their creator** understands **their internal logic**. 2 – The **native language** they use to **communicate with other computers** is incomprehensible to **everyone else**. 3 – Even your **smallest mistakes** are stored in **long-term memory** for **later retrieval**. 4 – As soon as you make a commitment to one, you **find yourself** spending half your monthly salary **on accessories** for it. (*Man walks into a bar* The Ultimate Collection of Jokes and One-liners Stephen Arnott and Mike Haskins p. 276)

(ii) Listen again focusing on how the expressions in bold are pronounced, particularly on how certain words in these expressions are linked.

(iii) Listen once again to locate where the full and contracted forms of ***'are'*** are used.

1. (a) Read the passage and record your reading on a tape or CD and (b) play it to your teacher or friend/s and get their feedback on your reading.

Chapter summary

1. In English speech, like words, stretches longer than a word too have stressed and unstressed syllables. Of the stressed syllables, one is more strongly stressed than others. A characteristic feature of English that contributes to its ***rhythm*** is that stressed syllables occur at regular intervals in speech, irrespective of the number of unstressed syllables that occur between them. This means that the length of an utterance in English depends on the number of stressed syllables it has. Generally in an utterance, content words, nouns, main verbs and adjectives are stressed and most grammatical words are unstressed.

2. In connected speech, we make various types of adjustments in pronunciation, the most important of which are ***Linking, Assimilation, Elision, Contraction***, and ***Use of weak forms***.

Words are linked with certain changes in pronunciation (i) when a word ends with a vowel and the next word begins with a vowel, (ii) when a word ends with a consonant and the next word begins with a vowel, (iii) when a word ends with a consonant cluster and the next word begins with a consonant, (iv) when a word ends with a consonant and the next word begins with a consonant, (v) when a word ends with a consonant and the next word begins with the same consonant, (vi) when a word ends with a plosive and the next word begins with a different plosive or with /m/ or /n/, and (vii) when a word ends with the sound /r/ and the next word begins with a vowel (in British English).

3. In casual and rapid speech, we often find that the initial sound of the second word and the final sound of the first word influence each other in such a way that the sounds from the two words become alike or identical. This is called ***Assimilation*** and is found in expressions like *his shop, hot soup, bad tactics,* etc. In English, it is mainly consonants that are affected by assimilation. There are three types of assimilation, ***Regressive assimilation***, ***Progressive assimilation***, and ***Coalescent assimilation***. In the case of regressive assimilation where the initial sound of the second word influences the final sound of the first word, consonants assimilate with reference to (a) place of articulation as in *that corner*, (b) manner of articulation as in *that soap*, or (c) presence or absence of voicing as in *good tea*. Progressive assimilation where the final sound of the first word influences the initial sound of the following word is generally found more at morpheme rather than word boundaries and plural forms of nouns such *dots, heads,* and *judges* are examples of progressive assimilation. Coalescent assimilation where the final consonant of the first word and the initial consonant of the second word coalesce into a third sound that shares the features of the two sounds is found in sentences such as *don't you know?* and *shouldn't you call him?*

4. Another adjustment in pronunciation that we make is that we often leave out certain sounds in some words, especially when these words are combined with other words. This is called ***Elision***. Some noticeable examples of elision occur when (i) words end with consonant clusters of two plosives and a fricative as in *contacts* and *attempts*, where the second plosive is left out, (ii) three plosives occur together in connected speech as in expressions like *booked tickets* and *kept cool*, where again the second plosive is left out, (iii) a word ends with a two consonant cluster with a final /t/ or /d/ and is followed by another word beginning with a consonant as in *bold gesture* and *hot coffee,* where the final /t/ or /d/ in the first word is left out, (iv) weak vowels follow plosives as in *tomorrow* and *perfect* or precede /n/, /l/ or /r/ as in *connect*, *collect* and *correct/*, where these weak vowels are left out, (v) pronouns and auxiliary verbs begin with /h/ as in *his, her, have, has* etc., where /h/ is left out.

5. Contraction occurs with auxiliary verbs and their negative forms in connected speech. Auxiliary verbs *is*, *are*, *am*, *has*, *have*, *had*, *will* and *would* have contracted forms *'s, 're, 'm, 's, 've, 'd, 'll* and *'d*, which are used after *wh-* words, nouns, *this, that, these,*

those, and *there* but not at the end of a sentence. Contracted negative forms of auxiliary verbs such as *can't, don't, won't* show a change of vowel too.

6. In English, many grammatical words like articles, prepositions, conjunctions, pronouns and auxiliary verbs are pronounced in two different ways, depending on the context in which they occur in speech. Words such as *a, an, the, to, for, of, from, and, you, we, he, his, she, her, can, will, shall,* etc have two forms in speech, namely, (1) ***Strong forms*** and (2) ***Weak forms***, e.g., *a* is pronounced /eɪ/ or /ə/ and *from*, /frɒm/ or /frəm/. Generally, these words are pronounced in their weak forms. There are four special contexts in which they are pronounced in their strong forms, namely,

    (a) when they occur at the end of a sentence
    (b) when one of them is used to contrast with another
    (c) when they are stressed for emphasis
    (d) when they are 'quoted' or 'cited'

8

Connected speech – II Prominence and intonation

Intonation is the melody of speech. In studying intonation we study how the pitch of the voice rises and falls, and how speakers use this pitch variation to convey linguistic and pragmatic meaning...
If we had no intonation, our speech would be – in the literal sense of the word – monotonous. Either it would remain on one pitch throughout, or every utterance would employ exactly the same stereotyped tune at all times. But speakers do neither of those things; they make the pitch of their voice rise, fall, jump and swoop, in all sorts of ways.
This is true both for the broadcaster, lecturer, preacher, politician or businessman addressing a public audience and for the participant in an ordinary everyday conversational interchange or informal chat.

J.C.Wells *English Intonation: An Introduction* 2006 p. 1

...ask ourselves what would be lost if we were to speak without intonation; you should try to imagine speech in which every syllable was said on the same level pitch, with no pauses and no changes in speed or loudness. This is the sort of speech that would be produced by a " mechanical speech " device that made sentences by putting together recordings of isolated words. To put it in the broadest possible terms, we can see that intonation makes it easier for a listener to understand what a speaher is trying to convey.

Peter Roach *English Phonetics and Phonology* 1991 2nd Edition p. 163

Intonation is important for intelligibility, because it is used to express intentions. A speaker can show that he or she is asking for information, or asking for confirmation, seeking agreement, or simply making a remark that is indisputable or 'common knowledge', through the intonation of the voice. Even though pitch rarely causes problems with the identification of words, an inappropriate intonation pattern can lead to misunderstanding just as a mispronounced sound can...Furthermore, the effect of intonation can be ***cumulative****; the misunderstandings may be minor, but if they occur constantly then they may result in judgments about the attitudes, character, ways of behaving, etc. of a particular speaker. For example, if a foreign speaker always uses low pitch, without much variation in the melody of the voice, listeners may get the impression that they are 'bored' or 'uninterested' when this is really not the case.*

Joanne Kenworthy *Teaching English Pronunciation* 1987 p. 19

PREVIEW

We saw in the previous chapter how rhythm and certain adjustments in pronunciation characterize connected speech and how crucial they are for understanding as well as producing fluent speech. Intonation is another essential feature of connected speech because no natural speech is possible without intonation, i.e., without variation in pitch and tone. Intonation is what makes speech meaningful as it helps speakers to convey their intentions, attitudes, and emotions as well as negotiate their roles in dialogues and conversations. English like other languages has unique intonation patterns with specific meanings and functions and it is essential for learners of English to be able to identify and distinguish between the intonation patterns they hear as well as to use appropriate intonation patterns in their speech.

In this chapter we will consider (a) how connected speech is divided into units longer than syllables called tone units, (b) which syllable in a tone unit get prominence or strong stress, and (c) what tones or intonation patterns are used in English to convey specific meanings.

This chapter has 8 Units.

8.1 How we divide speech into tone units
8.2 How we decide to place prominence or tonic stress in a tone unit
8.3 What is Intonation and what are the Tones used in English
8.4 Intonation and Grammar
8.5 Intonation and Emotions and Attitudes of the speaker
8.6 Intonation and Information Management
8.7 Intonation and Conversation Management
8.8 Step-ups and Step-downs in pitch

8.1 How we divide speech into tone units

As mentioned in the previous chapter, in connected speech we can identify a unit longer than a syllable (or word), which is called ***a tone unit***. A tone unit is a stretch of speech that forms a coherent part of an utterance in terms of meaning and grammar. A tone unit is also called ***a thought group***.

As a unit of speech, it is distinguished by three important phonological features:

(a) It is spoken without a break i.e., it has a pause before and after
(b) It has one syllable that is strongly stressed, and
(c) It has a distinctive pattern of ***intonation***.

In producing a long utterance, we pause for breath now and then. Generally, the points where we pause in an utterance depends on the way we divide the utterance in terms of the meaning we wish to convey. For example,

Please close the door
Please close the door, when you leave the room.

The first utterance is generally produced without a pause. The second may have a pause between the two clauses indicated by the comma.

She went to Bombay on Saturday.
On Saturday, she went to Bombay.

Here too, the first is generally spoken without a pause, where as in the second, there is a pause after *Saturday* to indicate a difference in emphasis.

Sometimes the presence or absence of a pause may change the meaning of an utterance.

Young people like modern cars which are fuel-efficient.
Young people like modern cars, which are fuel-efficient.

In this example, the same sentence can be said with or without a pause depending on the meaning the speaker wishes to convey. The first without a pause refers only to those modern cars which are fuel-efficient. The second with a pause means that all modern cars are fuel-efficient and therefore, young people like them.

In these examples, we identify one or two tone units depending on whether there is a pause or not.

Generally, the tone units are marked with //.

//please close the door //when you leave the room//
//on Saturday//she went to Bombay//
//young people like modern cars//which are fuel-efficient//

Although there are are no rules about how we divide utterances into tone units, some words are more likely to go together to form tone units than others, when we consider how we make sense of an utterance.

//it was very late // when I woke up//

is more likely than

//it was very // late when I woke up//

or

//it was very late when // I woke up//

Similarly

//luckily // it didn't rain // before we reached home//

is more likely than

//luckily it // didn't rain before // we reached home//

or

//luckily it didn't //rain before we //reached home//

Where tone unit boundaries occur

Normally tone unit boundaries occur

(1) between clauses connected by *and* or *but*,

e.g. *//They have practiced hard //and will try to win the match//*

//We tried our best to complete the work//but the unexpected power shut down caused this delay//

(2) before and after adverbial clauses, i.e., clauses that give information about how, where, when, and why,

e.g. *//After the meeting gets over//I'll be going to see the bank manager//*

//She had to take a loan from the bank//to send her daughter to study abroad//

(3) before and after non-defining relative clauses,

e.g. *//The flowering plants, //which we planted two months ago//, are in full bloom//*

//They want you to speak in English, //which everyone understands//

(4) after a clause that functions as the subject of a sentence,

e.g. *//What you do to reach here on time//is not my problem//*

//How you can download music from these sites//is not explained//

In some cases, where tone unit boundaries occur makes for a difference in meaning. For example, the sentence

The young girl who answered all the questions easily impressed everyone.

can mean either

The young girl answered all the questions easily and thus impressed everyone

or

The young girl answered all the questions and thus easily impressed everyone.

When spoken, however, the location of tone unit boundaries will make clear which meaning is intended.

//The young girl who answered all the questions easily // impressed everyone.

//The young girl who answered all the questions // easily impressed everyone.

Here, the tone unit boundary or the place where the speaker pauses signals whether the adverb *easily* qualifies the verb *answered* or *impressed.*

It is often the context that determines how a speaker divides an utterance into tone units and how many pauses he or she makes. Public speakers tend to pause frequently in order to create certain effects, whereas speakers communicating a sense of urgency may make their tone units longer and produce fewer pauses.

Exercises

L8.1. Listen to the following sentences and identify where the tone unit boundaries occur. Mark the boundaries with //.

(i) Naturally the children behaved very well.

(ii) The children sat quietly in the room which surprised everybody.

(iii) Fifteen years ago he left home looking for adventure and excitement.

(iv) We enjoyed the cultural show which was very lively and entertaining.

(v) Young people if they work hard have plenty of opportunities.

(vi) You can talk to your friend in America sitting here comfortably simply by pressing a few buttons.

(vii) He can have breakfast in Bangalore lunch in Bombay and be in Calcutta for dinner.

(viii) Her daughter did not like the Maths teacher but the English teacher she liked very much.

(ix) Every bookshop is full of computer books which are in great demand these days.

(x) What is more they lost their luggage too.

(xi) If you like everybody else believe that money is all important this job is not for you.

(xii) Because her father did not like it she did not go to Australia.

(xiii) Students of literature should have an awareness of the structure of language which is essential if they are to respond to literature critically and objectively.

(xiv) To tell you the truth I did not like it at all.

(xv) Since he left the job nobody has been happy.

(xvi) Computer scientists many of them do not have communicative skills.

(xvii) A word represents an idea in the same way as a traffic signal represents a direction.

(xviii) Tennis players who earn a lot of money travel in their own planes.

A

1. Read one of the following paragraphs aloud, record yourself and listen to the recording. Locate where the tone unit boundaries occur and see if you put the boundaries at the appropriate places. Play the recording to your friends/teacher and get their feedback.

Ours is not a drive for power, but purely a non-violent fight for India's independence. In a violent struggle, a successful general has been often known to effect a military coup and to set up a dictatorship. But under the Congress scheme of things, essentially non-violent as it is, there can be no room for dictatorship. A non-violent soldier of freedom will covet nothing for himself, he fights only for the freedom of his country.

Quit India Speech by Mahatma Gandhi August 8, 1942

One of the ways in which big companies borrow money is to sell bonds. If you buy a bond from a company, you get a contract which tells you that the company will pay you a fixed rate of interest at regular intervals and that you'll be able to get your money back at a fixed date in the future – if the company still exists of course (if the company goes bankrupt before this date, you normally get nothing!). But what happens if you want your money back before this fixed date? No problem – you simply sell the bond to someone else.

Decisionmaker David Evans CUP 1997 p.60

8.2 How we decide to place prominence or tonic stress in a tone unit

We saw in the previous chapter that English speech is characterized by patterns of stressed and unstressed syllables in such a way that stressed syllables occur at regular intervals of time, which gives it a distinctive rhythm. We also saw that some syllables in an utterance are stressed and others are unstressed and one of the stressed syllables is more strongly stressed than others.

o O o O o O o
He didn't want to leave her.

o O o O o o O
He had to call them at eight.

O o o O o o O o O o o
Dev has decided to see the manager.

A tone unit too (whether forming the whole or part of an utterance) has unstressed and stressed syllables and one of these stressed syllables is more strongly stressed than others. When we say that one of the stressed syllables is more strongly stressed than others in a tone unit, we mean that this syllable is given ***prominence***. ***Stress*** and ***prominence*** are different terms. The term ***stress*** is used in the context of words when we speak of how a syllable has primary or secondary stress in a word and how it contrasts with other unstressed syllables in the word. The term ***prominence*** is used in the context of connected speech when we speak of how a stressed syllable is made prominent or given prominence in a tone unit, i.e., given a special emphasis and how it contrasts with other stressed syllables in the tone unit.

The syllable that is given prominence in a tone unit is called ***the tonic syllable*** or ***the nucleus*** and the prominence or special emphasis that is given to this syllable is also called ***tonic or nuclear stress***.

In the three utterances above, each of which consists of one tone unit, prominence is given to *leave, eight,* and the first syllable of *manager*. These syllables stand out from the other stressed syllables in the respective utterances. When we consider utterances such as these three, by themselves without the discourse context in which they might occur, it is the stressed syllable in the last content word that is made prominent. But when we take discourse context into account, prominence may be placed on different words/syllables depending on what the speaker wishes to highlight.

There are three factors that influence the placement of prominence in a tone unit.

(1) New information, in contrast with information that is already known or is predictable, tends to receive prominence and generally occurs towards the end of an utterance (as in the three utterances above).

(2) If a speaker wishes to place special emphasis on a particular element in a tone unit, this element receives emphatic stress and is made prominent.

(3) When a speaker intends to make a contrast either in a single utterance or in response to a previous utterance, prominence is given to either both or one of the contrasting terms.

In the examples given below, lower case letters are used for unstressed syllables, small capital letters for stressed syllables and large capital letters for prominent syllables or syllables with tonic stress

(1) In connected speech speakers place prominence on words (syllables) that give important or interesting information.

(a) A: Where's Kumar working now?
B: He's got a JOB in LONdon.

A: Why are you late?
B: We had a PARty in COLLege.

A: I'm learning Japanese.
B: It must be DIFFicult.

These three examples clearly show how B makes prominent the stressed syllables in those words that convey the required information in response to the questions asked by A.

(b) Connected discourse does not merely convey new and important information; it also repeats information already given and sometimes gives information already understood in the context. Words that repeat information or give information obvious in the context are not made prominent.

For example, in the second example above, B can add *A farewell party* to the response given. If B does this, the first syllable of the word *party* is not made prominent when it is repeated. It is the second syllable of *farewell* that will be made prominent (the second syllable gets the primary stress in *farewell*)

A: Why are you late?
B: We had a PARty in COLLege. A FAREWELL party.

Thus whenever a speaker adds more specific information to what has already been said, the words/syllables that give new information are given prominence and not those that are repeated.

A good example of this is described by Hewings (2004:142). He points out how James Bond often introduces himself in films saying

The NAME'S BOND. JAMES bond.

When *Bond* is said first, it is made prominent, but when it is repeated, it is not. *James* is made prominent because it adds new information.

A few more examples are given below.

A: Where's Bangalore?
B: It's in INDIA. SOUTH India.

A: What does she do?
B: She is a TEACHer. An ENGlish teacher.

The RING is exPENsive. TERRibly expensive.

We want to BUY a TV. A FLAT tv.

Celce-Murcia et al (1996:176) give this example from Allen (1971:77) to show "how prominence marks new versus old information".

X: I've lost an umBRELla.
Y: A LAdy's umbrella?
X: Yes. A lady's umbrella with STARS on it. GREEN stars.

Here *umbrella* is new information in X's first utterance and is made prominent. In Y's response, it is *lady's* that is new information, which is made prominent. In X's second utterance, however, both *umbrella* and *lady's* are old information, whereas *stars* and *green* are new information and therefore get prominence.

Another interesting example from (Grant:2000:97) shows how a speaker uses prominence to highlight new and important information.

Let's CONTINUE our discussion of polLUtion. YEsterday we deFINED pollution. TODAY we'll talk about the IMpact of pollution….its FAR-REACHING efFECTS. MANY PEOPLE THINK that polLUtion is just a PROBlem for SCIentists but it's NOT just a problem for scientists. It's a PROBlem that afFECTS EVeryone. Because it afFECTS HUman LIVES it's a HEALTH problem. Because it afFECTS PROperty it's an ecoNOmic problem. And because it afFECTS our appreciAtion of NAture it's an aesTHEtic problem.

(c) Since it is the discourse context that determines which information is new, it is possible that within a tone unit, different words/syllables can be given prominence depending on context. For example, if we consider the utterance *I went to Canada last year*, the prominence falls on different words in different contexts.

A: Who went to Canada last year, you or your brother?
B: **I** went to Canada last year.
('I' is shown in bold here to show that it gets prominence)

A: Where did you go last year?
B: I went to CANada last year.

A: Which year did you go to Canada?
B: I went to Canada LAST year.

(2) Speakers give prominence to those words/syllables on which they want to place special emphasis. This type of prominence that is given for purposes of emphasis is called ***emphatic stress***.

A: I don't think you're interested in music.
B: I AM interested in music.

A: How do you like your boss?
B: I like her VERY much.

After describing the unpleasant experience she had in a place, the speaker might say

"I'll NEVer go there again.

The two dialogues below show how speakers give prominence to words that convey new information or elements that they wish to emphasize.

A: How's the tea?
B: It's TOO STRONG.

A: Is the tea strong?
B: It's TOO strong.

In both, B says the same thing. But in the first *strong* is new information and therefore gets prominence (*too* gets stress as a content word). But in the seond *strong* is repeated and conveys old information and therefore does not get prominence. Here the speaker wishes to emphasize how she finds the tea excessively strong and therefore places emphatic stress on *too*.

(3) Speakers give prominence to words/syllables that they wish to contrast. This may be in a single utterance or in response to something said previously.

A: Is it a GREY or a BLACK DRESS?

A: Is it a GREY DRESS?
B: No, it's a BLACK dress.

A: Are you MEETing her AFter or beFORE LUNCH?

A: Are you MEETing her after LUNCH?
B: No, we're meeting her beFORE lunch.

A: Is the MATCH on MONday or TUESday?

A: Is the MATCH on MONday?

B: No, it's on TUESday.

Speakers also give prominence to words/syllables they use to correct something previously said.

A: You had a GREY PUPPy.

B: No, it was a WHITE puppy.

A: She's learning FRENCH.

B: No, she's learning GERman

Exercises

1. Match the initiating utterances (either questions or comments) on the left with the appropriate responses on the right depending on the word/syllable shown to be prominent. Practise the initiating and responding utterances with appropriate placement of prominence.

Example:

What has she bought? → She has bought a red CAR

What color car has she bought? → She has bought a RED car

(i) Where did you meet Mr Singh?

I met Mr Singh at the PARty

I met Mr SINGH at the party

Who did you meet at the party?

(ii) Why has he gone to California?

He found a JOB in California.

He found a job in CAlifornia.

Where did he find a job?

(iii) Where has Ravi gone for training?

RAvi has gone to Germany for training.

Ravi has gone to GERmany for training.

Who has gone to Germany for training?

(iv) Here is my new mobile.

I thought YOU had an I-phone.

I thought you had an I-phone.

This I-phone, it is my brother's.

(v) What made you go to the Delhi book fair?

They offered me a free AIR ticket.

They offered me a FREE air ticket.

I thought you didn't like to travel by train.

(vi) Which poet are we studying today?

The proFEssor is going to speak on Yeats.

The professor is going to speak on YEATS.

Are you presenting your paper on Yeats?

(vii) How did Gandhi use non-violence?

Gandhi used non-violence as a political WEApon.

Gandhi used NON-violence as a political weapon.

What weapon did Gandhi use?

(viii) Doesn't their daughter play badminton?

Their DAUGHter plays tennis.

Their daughter plays TENnis.

Doesn't their son play tennis?

(ix) Are you giving a twenty dollar discount?

You'll get a TWENty percent discount.

You'll get a twenty perCENT discount.

I thought you were giving a twenty-five percent discount.

(x) What does the old lady teach?

The old lady TEACHes music.

The old lady teaches MUsic.

I hear the old lady is learning music.

2. Match the initiating and responding utterances and practise them giving prominence to the appropriate words/syllables.

Could I use your laptop please?	Is it an audio CD?
I would like to check my email.	Yes, on paying a small fee.

She wants to see what is there on this CD.	I have only a desktop.
Can you download e-books from this site?	I want a phone not a computer.
You can send and receive email with this phone.	There are no computers here.

3. Indicate which word in these sentences gets prominence if the meaning given is to be conveyed. Practise saying the sentences giving prominence to the right word.

(i) Her brother is a chemical engineer.
(*not a mechanical engineer*)
(*not her sister*)
(*not my brother*)

(ii) Our neighbor has gone to Japan on business.
(*not on vacation*)
(*not to Germany*)
(*not our manager*)

(iii) We were living in Bangalore. (*not in Delhi*)
(*are not living now*)
(*not working*)

(iv) He is angry with his son.
(*not with his daughter*)
(*not unhappy*)
(*not with our son*)

(v) They will visit us next week.
(*not call us*)
(*not this week*)
(*not next month*)

4. What will be the questions/comments to which the following sentences will be answers/ responses?
(i) Your keys are ON the desk.
(ii) This letter is FROM the Bank.
(iii) She IS happy here.
(iv) The weather WAS good.
(v) MY car needs servicing.

5. Read this transcript of a short talk and decide which words/syllables should be given prominence. Practise reading it and record yourself and listen to the recording or play it to your friends/teacher and get their feedback.

I'd like to welcome you all to the fourth annual poet's brunch. In just a few minutes a server will be around to offer you coffee or tea. Please take a moment to fill out your name tag and introduce yourself to the other artists at your table. Lunch will be served at 11:00 am sharp, followed by a reading from last year's prize winner. If any of you did not receive your free gift at the door, please make sure to pick it up on your way out. This year's gift is a poetry anthology from local youth writers. You will be amazed at the emerging talent in our town. In fact, a group of young writers meet once a month around this very table. (www.englishclub.com)

8.3 What is intonation and what are the tones used in English?

In addition to prominence, intonation pattern is another phonological feature of a tone unit that is used by a speaker to highlight specific items of information.

Intonation is to do with the pitch of the voice. The pitch of our voice is constantly changing when we speak. Very rarely do we speak with a fixed unvarying pitch. Pitch is closely related to the frequency of vibration of the vocal cords and is an auditory feature of speech i.e., a feature which is perceived by the hearer. Generally, we describe pitch in terms of high or low and can perceive variations between the high and the low. The over-all behaviour of the pitch is called ***the tone*** and ***intonation*** is to do with tones or patterns in the variations of pitch levels.

Intonation does not take into account all kinds of pitch variations in a speaker's voice. It is only those variations that convey some linguistic information that are important here. Variations in pitch that are not linguistic in nature i.e., those that are due to non-linguistic but maybe physical factors are not considered important. For example, if a person is running or riding a horse or is engaged in any activity which involves irregular movement and tries to speak at the same time, her voice will show many sudden rises and falls in pitch. These pitch variations are caused by the irregular physical movements of the speaker and are therefore not under the control of the speaker. Such variations are not linguistically significant. Similarly we know that there are typical pitch variations between one speaker and another. Women's voices, for example, are generally higher in pitch than men's. These differences are due to differences in physical structure and are also not linguistically significant. But a speaker does have control over the pitch of her voice in that she can choose to speak at a higher or lower pitch or vary the pitch in different ways to convey different meanings and emotions. It is these variations of pitch that are under the control of a speaker that are considered to be linguistically significant.

A second condition for pitch variations to be linguistically significant is that they must be perceptible i.e., the hearer must be able to perceive these differences in pitch.

A third requirement is that it must be possible to identify and describe contrasts between different patterns in pitch variation or different tones. This means that it must be possible to associate different meanings with different tones so that they can be distinguished from one another.

Thus, intonation deals with those variations in pitch that are (a) linguistically meaningful, (b) perceptible, and (c) contrastive.

Intonation is important in any study of the spoken form of a language because

(i) it is meaningful, i.e., it signals differences in meaning,

(ii) it is systematic, i.e., every language uses a specific number of pitch patterns or tones to convey certain largely predictable meanings, and

(iii) it is language specific, i.e., different languages use intonation patterns in different ways.

To be able to speak English naturally and fluently and to follow natural English speech without difficulty, it is useful if we can identify the distinctive patterns of intonation or tones that are used in English and understand the specific meanings they convey and the specific functions they perform.

There are four main intonation patterns or tones that are used in English speech. They are ***Fall, Rise, Fall-Rise***, and ***Rise-Fall***. The first three, fall, rise, and fall-rise are more frequently used than the fourth, rise-fall.

These four tones are ***moving tones*** as they are marked by a movement of pitch. ***The level tone***, in contrast, is one in which the pitch does not vary but remains steady at a particular level. This tone is not frequently used in English.

↘ indicates a fall and ↗ a rise.

↘↗ indicates a fall-rise and ↗↘ a rise-fall.

We can understand the distinctive nature of the frequently used tones and their specific meanings and functions by examining how contrasting tones, for example, fall in contrast to rise or fall-rise are used to convey contrasting meanings or perform contrasting functions. The meanings and functions of the different tones can be described in terms of

1. Grammar
2. Emotions and Attitudes of the speaker
3. Information management, and
4. Conversation management

8.4 Intonation and grammar

(1) Declarative sentences such as

The match is tomorrow
The train is gone
She is a doctor
can be used either to make statements or ask questions.

When we use them as statements, we use a falling tone with them.

The match is toMORrow↘
The train is GONE↘
She is a DOCtor↘

But when we use them to ask questions, we use a rising tone.

The match is toMORrow ↗
The train is GONE ↗
She is a DOCtor ↗

The only way we can indicate that we are asking questions and not making statements in these cases is to use a rising tone, since grammatically these sentences are declarative in form.

There are situations where we use single words either to answer questions or to ask questions. For example, *coffee, pass, science*. Here again a falling tone on the word indicates that the speaker is answering a question, whereas a rising tone marks the word as a question.

A: What would you like to have? Coffee or Tea?
B: TEA ↘

A:CoFFEE ↗
B:No, thank you.

A:PASS ↗
B:Yes, here it is

A: Do you have a pass or ticket?
B:PASS ↘

A:What do you like?
B:SCIENCE ↘

A:SCIENCE ↗
B:No, engineering.

Thus grammatically a fall indicates a statement and a rise, a question.

(2) Relative clauses that modify a noun or a noun phrase are of two types, (a) defining and (b) non-defining.

For example,
My sister who lives in California works as an engineer. (Defining relative clause)
My sister, who lives in California, works as an engineer. (Non-defining relative clause)

The first sentence means that the speaker has more than one sister, whereas the second means that the speaker has only one sister.

Flowers which are fragrant and colorful always cheer us up. (Defining relative clause)
Flowers, which are fragrant and colorful, always cheer us up. (Non-defining relative clause)

The first sentence means that some flowers are fragrant and colorful but others are not, whereas the second means that all flowers are fragrant and colorful.

In writing we use commas to separate the non-defining relative clause from the main clause but not the defining relative clause. In speech the non-defining relative clause forms a separate tone unit but the defining relative clause does not. Further, the non-defining relative clause is said with a fall, whereas the defining relative clause is said with a slight fall-rise.

My sister who lives in CAlifornia ↘ ↗ works as an engiNEER ↘
My sister ↗ who lives in CAlifornia ↘ works as an engiNEER ↘
Flowers which are fragrant and COlorful ↘ ↗ always cheer us UP ↘
Flowers ↗ which are fragrant and COlorful ↘ always cheer us UP ↘

> The ways in which grammatical differences are indicated by intonation are summed up here.
>
> | | | |
> |---|---|---|
> | Single words and Declarative sentences | Statement ↘ | Question ↗ |
> | Defining Relative clauses | ↘ ↗ | Not a separate tone unit |
> | Non-defining Relative clauses | ↘ | Separate tone unit |

Exercises

L8.2. Listen to the following sentences and decide whether they have a rising or falling tone, i.e., whether they are questions or statements. Practise the sentences with the tone you hear.

(i) This store is open 24 hours
(ii) You have a cold
(iii) The doctor is here
(iv) You found her
(v) They are gone
(vi) The show is over
(vii) Exams are next week
(viii) The book isn't available
(ix) Tea is ok
(x) The engine isn't working

1. **Practise the following words/phrases/sentences with a rising tone to ask questions.**
   (i) Tomorrow
   (ii) You are busy
   (iii) On the shelf
   (iv) You are driving
   (v) Pizzas

2. **Practise the following words/phrases/sentences with a falling tone to make statements/to answer questions.**
   (i) Sunglasses
   (ii) Two years ago
   (iii) They lost the match
   (iv) Totally free
   (v) He's going out

3. **Decide whether A's utterances are said with a rise or fall. Practise the exchanges with the right intonation patterns.**
   (i) A: You bought this watch recently
   B: Yes, yesterday in a sale

   (ii) A: She is working now
   B: Is she? Where?

   (iii) A: He likes coffee
   B: I knew that

   (iv) A: You have a pen to spare
   B: Yes, you can have it

   (v) A: She had her breakfast
   B: No, she left in a hurry

   (vi) A: They had a flat tyre.
   B: Oh, that's why they were late

   (vii) A: You have an interview tomorrow
   B:Yes, I'm putting all my papers together

   (viii) A: You speak English
   B: Yes

   (ix) A: It is a blue van
   B: No, it is a green van

(x) A: The weather will be good this weekend
B: Let's us go for a picnic

4. Decide whether the relative clauses in the following sentences are defining or non-defining and practise saying them with the right intonation pattern.
   (i) Men love dogs which are known for their loyalty.
   (ii) TV channels which make a lot of money from advertisements do not bother much about their viewers.
   (iii) Shops, which offer big discounts, would have hiked their prices earlier.
   (iv) It is difficult to silence politicians who love to talk.
   (v) Students, who take loans for their studies, are under great pressure.
   (vi) We should eat more fruits and vegetables which are good for health.

8.5 Intonation and emotions and attitudes of the speaker

The tone we use often tells the listener (1) how we feel about what we are talking about, i.e. whether we are interested or enthusiastic, whether we are exaggerating or playing something down, whether we are surprised, unbelieving or critical and (2) what our attitude is, i.e. whether we are being polite or not. It is therefore very important for learners of English to know which type of tone signals which feeling or attitude. Lack of awareness of these aspects of intonation will affect both our listening and speaking abilities. We may misunderstand a speaker's intentions if we do not know what his or her tone indicates and similarly we may signal the wrong attitude when we use an inappropriate tone.

(1) (a) The level tone in contrast to the moving tones, the fall, the rise, the fall-rise and the rise-fall is used in highly restricted contexts to indicate that the speaker is saying something routine, uninteresting or boring. A typical example is when a teacher calls the names of students from a register and the students answer the roll call, both the teacher and the students will generally use the level tone. Similarly, if someone is answering a number of routine questions for administrative purposes like *Have you* ever *been convicted of a crime? Have you been deported from any country? Do you suffer from any incurable diseases?* etc., she is likely to use a level tone in saying *no* to each of these questions.

(b) In order to show interest in what a speaker is telling us and to encourage her to continue (especially when the speaker is narrating something that has happened), we use short questions or the word *really* with a rising or a fall-rising tone

A: Saw Beena yesterday in British Library.
B: Did YOU ↗ OR ↘ ↗?

A: She said she's going to Colombo on an assignment. She didn't say much about it.

B: Didn't SHE ↗ OR ↘ ↗?

A: Apparently it is something very hush-hush.

B: REAlly ↗ OR ↘ ↗?

In such situations if the voice is flat and a level tone is used, it signals lack of interest or boredom.

(c) Questions are sometimes used neither to find out nor to make sure, but to make a comment, to express surprise, pleasure or criticism.

(i) Negative Yes-No questions are often used to express surprise, pleasure, etc. These have a falling tone, particularly when we wish the hearers to agree with us.

Doesn't she look BEAUtiful ↘?

Wasn't it HORRible ↘?

(ii) Positive Yes-No questions can be used to express criticism and these generally have a rising tone.

Are you CRAzy ↗?

Is he MAD ↗?

(iii) Wh-questions are also used to make a comment and these also have a falling tone.

HOW could I tell her ↘?

WHAT could he say ↘?

(2) (a) In English it is very often intonation that helps us to sound polite and friendly. Use of an inappropriate tone will make us sound abrupt and rude. Some of the most frequently used words/expressions that we use are *hello*, *excuse me*, and names such as Sheela or Anil (when we call out to them to tell them something). We can use either a fall or a fall-rise with these words. A fall makes our utterance sound abrupt or even curt, whereas a fall-rise will make the utterance more polite and friendly.

Hello ↘? OR Hello ↘ ↗ ?

Excuse me ↘ OR Excuse me ↘ ↗ ?

Sheela ↘ OR Sheela ↘ ↗ ?

(b) When we use imperative sentences either to make a request/a suggestion or to give a command, we add a question tag at the end in order to make it more polite. These question tags are said with a rising tone. (The imperative sentences themselves are said with a falling tone)

Let's go out for dinner, SHALL we↗?
Let's wait for some more time, SHALL we↗?
Keep these papers in the locker, WOULD you↗?
Buy some stamps for me, WOULD you↗?

(c) In response a listener may say *Okay*. If the listener uses a fall, it signals that it is not an enthusiastic acceptance, whereas the use of a fall-rise indicates an enthusiastic acceptance.

A: Let us have a party at home
B: Okay ↘
OR
B: Okay ↘↗

(d) When we make requests using modals like *could* or *would*, use of a fall-rise makes them more polite.

Could you help me with this report ↘↗?
Do you think you could get me some stamps ↘↗?
Would you come with me to the court tomorrow ↘↗?

In response if the listener agrees to the request, starting at a high pitch and then using a fall it sounds more polite than using a low fall.

(e) In contrast when we offer to do something for someone, it is more polite to use a fall rather than a rise or a fall-rise. A fall makes the offer sound more sincere and genuine.

Shall I get the cup for you ↘?
Would you like me to tie it ↘?
Would you like me to drive you to the station ↘?
Shall I water the plants ↘?

(f) As mentioned earlier, compared to fall, rise, and fall-rise, rise-fall is not frequently used in English. It is mainly used in exclamations, where we express surprise, enthusiasm, disappointment, or criticism.

How WONderful↗↘!

A: It's great, isn't it?
B: FanTAStic↗↘!

A: He's bougfht a new laptop. It's purple.
B: PURple↗↘!

A: She says they'll make a huge profit.
B: Nonsense↗↘!

The uses of different tones to express various emotions and attitudes are summed up below.

Routine or Bored responses — Level tone

Responses showing interest and understanding and encouraging speaker to continue — ↗ OR ↘↗

Negative Yes No questions showing surprise, pleasure etc. ↘ — Positive Yes No questions indicating criticism ↗

Wh questions that make a comment — ↘

Hello, Excuse me etc. Friendly and Polite ↘↗ — Abrupt or Curt ↘

Question tags following Imperative sentences used as requests, suggestions or commands — Friendly and Polite ↗

Okay in response to such requests, suggestions or commands — Enthusiastic acceptance ↘↗; Lack of enthusiasm ↘

Requests using the modals *Could, Would* etc. — Polite ↘↗

Offers — Polite ↘

Exclamations — Surprise, Enthusiasm, Disappointment and Criticism ↗↘

Exercises

L8.3. Listen and decide what emotion or attitude the speaker conveys in these sentences. Discuss with your friends/teacher.

(i) Why are you laughing at him?
(ii) Could you tell the manager that I came to see him?
(iii) Shall I help you with the paper work?
(iv) Has he told you everything?
(v) Wasn't she home?
(vi) How delightful the children are!
(vii) Do you mind moving to the front seat?
(viii) Write down the address for me, will you?
(ix) What could I have done?
(x) Haven't you renewed your licence?
(xi) Why did you call him?

Practise saying these sentences to convey the same emotion or attitude. Record yourself and listen to the recording or play it to your friends/teacher and get their feedback.

L8.4. Listen and decide whether B uses a fall or a rise/fall-rise in the responses in the following exchanges.

(i) A: They sold their old house and moved into an apartment last year.
B: Did they?
A: They were not at all happy living there. But their son thought that it'd be better for them.
B: Did he?
A: Now they are thinking of moving to the village.
B: Really?

(ii) A: Let us take a second opinion, shall we?
B: OK
A: You don't think it's a good idea.
B: No

(iii) A: My daughter did very well in school. She always topped the class.
B: Did she?
A: But I don't know what has happened to her now. She says she is bored with everything.
B: Does she?
A: Her mother wants to take her to a psychiatrist.
B: Really?

8.6 Intonation and information management

Intonation helps us to indicate what type of information we are conveying or asking for.

(1) We use a fall when we convey something *new*, and a rise or fall-rise for something that is *already known to* or *shared by* both the speaker and the hearer.

In the example below the expression *credit card* is said with a falling tone the first time when it conveys new information but with a rising tone when it is used the second time (when it is part of shared information).

You can pay online if you have a credit card ↘. If you don't have a credit card ↗, please send us a cheque.

Similarly in the exchanges below, the first part of B's response answers A's question and thus gives new information, whereas the second part is what is already known or understood by both A and B.

A: Could you call me in the morning?
B: //YES ↘ // if you WANT me to ↗ //

A: How will you pay?
B: //By CHEQUE ↘ // if it's OK ↗ //

Similarly when a speaker corrects what another speaker has said, the correction giving new information is marked by a falling tone, whereas old information, which is corrected, is marked by a rising tone.

A: I think there's a stop-over in London.
B: //There's a stop-over in PAris ↘ // not in LONdon ↗ //

(2) We find a similar contrast between the use of falling and fall-rising tones in cleft sentences, where the clause that gives new information has a falling tone and the clause that gives information that is not new has a fall-rising tone.

(a) Cleft sentences with an *It*-clause

A: This ice cream is delicious.
B: It was LEEla ↘ who gave me the RECipe ↘ ↗.

I called Chaya but it was LEEla ↘ who answered the PHONE ↘ ↗.

He had three daughters. It was LEEla ↘ who became a DOCtor ↘.

(b) Cleft sentences with *What*-clause

What you should DO ↘ ↗ is to check the PRESSure ↘.

What I couldn't beLIEVE ↘ ↗ was how she managed to get his aPPROval ↘.

(3) In making comparisons and contrasts again, we use a falling tone for information that is news to the hearer and a fall-rising tone for what is not news (for what is probably shared by the speaker and the hearer).

A: Are you attending the seminar in the afternoon?
B: The seminar is toMORrow ↘, not toDAY ↘ ↗.

I like listening to the RAdio ↘ much more than watching TV ↘ ↗.

(4) We use a fall with Wh-questions, which we generally use to find out information that we don't know and a rise or a fall-rise with Yes-No questions, which we mostly use to make sure of some information that we think we know.

When is the INTERview ↘?
How will you get to the AIRport ↘?
Where are they staying in LONdon ↘?
What does this watch COST ↘?

Do you speak ENGlish ↗?
Have your friends LEFT ↗?
Are you at WORK ↗?
Will she COME ↗?

Wh-questions are not always used to find out information and similarly Yes-No questions are not always used to make sure of some information. Wh-questions can be used to make sure of some information and Yes-No questions can be used to find out information.

When Wh-questions are used to make sure, thay can have a rising or a fall-rising tone.

This often happens when a speaker wishes to check some information that has already been given or is considered known.

A: WHY is she coming ↗?
B: I told you, to help me.

A: WHEN are they leaving ↗?
B: I told you, tomorrow morning.

When Yes-No questions are used to find out information that the speaker doesn't know, they have a falling tone.

A: Have you read her LAtest novel ↘?
B: No, I haven't been able to get it.

A: Did you go to the CONcert ↘?
B: No, I was not well.

Thus it is the function that the question performs (whether it is asked to find out information or to make sure of some information) and not its grammatical structure (whether it is a Wh-question or an Yes-No question) that determines the tone used.

(5) When we wish to get people to repeat either part or whole of what they have said, i.e. when we wish to make sure of what they have said, we use questions or some common phrases or repeat either part or whole of what was said. We do this because either we want to check that we heard correctly or we found what we heard surprising. These questions, phrases or repetitions generally have a rising tone.

A: Ravi's become a doctor.
B: WHAT ↗?
become WHAT ↗?
Ravi's become WHAT ↗?

A: She paid ten thousand rupees for the ring.
B: HOW much ↗?
HOW much did she pay ↗?

A: He's resigned his job again.
B: He's reSIGNED his job again ↗?

A: We went to see the Raos.
B: You went to see WHO ↗?

A: Sheela's bought a new cell phone.
B: SORRy ↗?
PARdon ↗?
WHAT did you say ↗?
WHAT ↗? *(Not very polite)*

(6) When we wish people to respond to something that we say, we usually add a question tag at the end of the statement we make.

(a) When we give our opinion on something and expect our hearer to agree with what we have just said, we use a falling tone with the question tag.

It's a great book, ISN'T it ↘?
They danced very well, DIDN'T they ↘?
He's not very bright, IS he ↘?

(b) When we are not certain that something is true and want to ask the hearer to say whether what we have just said is correct or not, we use a rising tone with the question tag.

You are open on Sundays, AREN'T you ↗?
This is silk, ISN'T it ↗?
It isn't dangerous, IS it ↗?

(7) Yes-No questions are those that require Yes/No answers. These Yes/No answers can indicate definiteness or reservation. When they indicate definiteness, they have a falling tone and when they indicate reservation, they have a fall-rising tone.

A: Do you like driving?
B: YES/NO ↘.
YES ↘ ↗, but not very much.

A: Are you tired?
B: YES/NO ↘.
YES ↘ ↗, but I don't mind another game.

Similarly, when we do not completely agree with something, we use a fall-rising tone to indicate our reservation.

A: Is it a good movie?
B: It has an interesting PLOT ↘ ↗, but…

A: I hear that she is a good singer.
B: She has a good VOICE ↘ ↗, but…

(8) When we list two or more items in an utterance, we use a rising tone on each of the items till the final one, on which we use a falling tone. The rising tone indicates there is more to come (incompleteness) and the falling tone, the end (completeness).

She wants to buy a comPUter ↗, a PRINter ↗ and a SCANNer ↘.
These workers get good WAges ↗, attractive BOnuses ↗, and paid HOLidays ↘.

(9) In alternative questions too, where we list two or more choices, we use a rising tone on each of the choices till the final one, on which we use a falling tone.

Are you paying by CREDit ↗ card or CHEQUE ↘?
Will you have COFFee ↗, TEA ↗ or JUICE ↘?

The contrasting uses of the fall and the rise or the fall-rise in information management are summed up below.

New information	↘	Shared or known information	↗ OR ↘ ↗
Finding out information not known	↘	Making sure of information considered to be true	↗ OR ↘ ↗
Inviting agreement	↘	Asking for confirmation	↗
Definiteness	↘	Reservation	↘ ↗
Indicating completeness	↘	Indicating incompleteness	↗

Exercises

1. Decide where the underlined expressions are said with a fall and where with a rise or a fall-rise. Practise saying the sentences with appropriate tones.
   - (i) If you have a complaint, call our toll-free number. When you call our toll-free number, a customer care executive will speak to you and register your complaint.
   - (ii) When you install a new programme, click the restart button. When you click the restart button, the computer will shut down and start again.
   - (iii) When you see an email in the Spam folder, do not open it. If you open it, there is a likelihood of a virus attacking your computer.
   - (iv) When you delete a file, you send it to the recycle bin. When you send a file to the recycle bin, it is still retrievable.
   - (v) If you want to reach the airport in time, leave early. If you don't leave early, you may be caught in the traffic and may miss your flight.

L8.5. Decide which part in B's response has a falling tone and which a rising tone. Listen and check your answers.

(i) A: I thought the book would sell well.
B: //It might not make as much money// as you expect//

(ii) A: Could we meet tomorrow?
B: //I have these two meetings// as you know//

(iii) A: Aren't you giving me a discount?
B: //As the coupon says// the discount was only till yesterday//

L8.6. Decide which part in B's response has a falling tone and which a rising tone. Listen and check your answers.

(i) A: She's leaving on Saturday.
B: //She's leaving on Sunday// not on Saturday//

(ii) A: I think he likes coffee.
B: //He likes tea// not coffee//

(iii) A: Is it a pre-paid account?
B: //No// it is not pre-paid// it is post-paid//

(iv) A: Do you have to take an oral test?
B: //Not an oral test// but a written one//

(v) A: Was she wearing a blue silk dress?
B: //It wasn't silk// it was actually cotton// but looked like silk//

(A)

2. (a) Decide which part in B's response has a falling tone and which a rising tone and practise saying them with the right intonation.

(i) A: What do they need?
B: //What they need now// is more staff//

(ii) A: They have overcharged me for two items.
B: //What you can do// is to ask them to refund you the excess amount//

(iii) A: What kind of job do you want?
B: //What I am looking for// is a job that will be interesting as well as challenging//

(iv) A: What would you like for lunch?
B: //All that I want //is a sandwich and some coffee//

(v) A: Many companies are running under huge losses.
B: //What they should do is //diversify their business //and not depend only on western markets//

(vi) A: What did you do this weekend?
B: //All that I did //was to sit at home and read for my exam//.

(b) Reverse the order of the clauses in B's responses and say them. Notice how the intonation pattern changes.

Example

The response in the first exchange will be

More staff is what they need now.

3. Using the information given, make cleft sentences and decide what intonation patterns they will have. Practise saying the sentences you make with the right intonation patterns.

Example

A: Who spoke to you when you called the supervisor?
B: The secretary answered the phone and gave me the instructions.

It was the secretary who answered the phone and gave me the instructions.

(i) A: When did you buy this dress?
B: We bought this two weeks ago.

(ii) A: How did she manage to get the tickets?
B: She managed to get the tickets by getting someone to wait at the ticket counter overnight.

(iii) A: Why have they sent a nurse and not a doctor?
B: Because he specifically asked for a nurse.

(iv) A: Who wrote this poem?
B: Keats wrote this poem, not Shelley.

(v) A: Where did you get this clock?
B: I found it in an antique shop in a small town.

(A)

L8.7. Decide which part in B's response is said with a falling tone and which a rising tone.
Listen to the sentences to check your answers.
Practise the sentences with the right intonation patterns.

(i) A: He looked to be in great pain.
B: //Though he had hurt his ankle// he played very well to win the match//

(ii) A: What time did you go? I think they said 6-30.
B: //We were there exactly at 6-30// but nobody else had come//

(iii) A: Your children must have been happy to see you.
B: //My daughter was excited // but my son had gone out of town//

(iv) A: I think I'll buy a desktop.
B: //You'd be better off with a laptop// rather than a desktop//

(v) A: It looks bright and sunny.
B: //It is now //but later it may rain//

4. Using the information given, complete B's utterances in response to what A says and decide what intonation patterns they will have. Practise saying these sentences with the right intonation patterns.

Example

A: Will you call them to make the booking?
B: (booking online easier)
//It may be easier to book online ↘//than to call them↗//

(i) A: Is she wearing the blue dress for the reception?
B: (look better in pink)

(ii) A: Did they lose because they chose to bat first?
B: (choosing to field better)

(iii) A: Could I use my credit card?
B: (using your debit card better)

(iv) A: Don't they have cold coffee?
B: (hot coffee sells better)

(v) A: Is she visiting Europe in March?
B: (May better)

5. Practise asking these questions with a falling tone.
   (i) Why do you want to go there?
   (ii) What did they do?
   (iii) Where was she teaching?
   (iv) How does he go to school?
   (v) When has the manager asked him to come?

6. Practise asking these questions with a rising tone.
   (i) Did you meet her yesterday?
   (ii) Are they open on Sundays?
   (iii) Have the children gone to bed?
   (iv) Has she registered for this course?
   (v) Does he play Hockey?

L8.8. **Listen and decide which of these questions have a falling tone and which a rising tone. Depending on the tone decide whether each of the questions is a finding out question or making sure question. Write FO or MS.**

(i) Can you hear me at the back? ----------------------

(ii) When did you last see her? ----------------------

(iii) Where is she working? ----------------------

(iv) What did he say? ----------------------

(v) Will they give you a refund? ----------------------

(vi) Has he gone home? ----------------------

(vii) Who will tell him? ----------------------

(viii) Did you see the young lady? ----------------------

(ix) Have you been shopping? ----------------------

(x) Which actor will agree to do this role? ----------------------

7. Do you think the questions in the following exchanges will have a falling or a rising tone?

(i) A: Where were you born?
B: Bangalore, India.

(ii) A: Are you hungry?
B: No

(iii) A: Are they buying the car?
B: I don't know.

(iv) A: Isn't this hot?
B: Yes, it is.

(v) A: What did the minister say?
B: I told you; he only made promises.

(vi) A: Is your daughter going to school?
B: Yes, to a nursery.

(vii) A: When can you come?
B: At eight in the evening.

(viii) A: Are you teaching Maths?
B: No, I'm teaching Physics.

(ix) A: Is your sister working?
B: Yes, she's an accountant.

(x) A: Has this tree been hit by lightning?
B: Looks like it.

8. Complete the following exchanges by filling in B's responses. What tone will these responses have?

Example

A: It cost me four thousand rupees.
B: *How much?*..................................
A: Four thousand rupees.

(i) A: He added some lime juice to the cocktail.
B: ....
A: To the cocktail.

(ii) A: She has an apartment in London.
B: ....
A: In London.

(iii) A: The prize is 120 thousand dollars.
B: ....
A: Dollars

(iv) A: I gave a new proposal for opening two more branches.
B: ....
A: Because the old one needed revision.

(v) A: There was an announcement about the hike in bus fares.
B: ....
A: Bus fares.

(A)

L8.9 Decide whether B's responses will have a falling or a rising tone. Listen to the exchanges to check your answers.

(i) A: She went to Australia last year
B: When?
A: Last year

A: She went to Australia
B: When?
A: Last year

(ii) A: The conference is in Singapore
B: Where?
A: In Singapore

A: The conference is in Singapore
B: When?
A: Next January

(iii) A: He's studying music
B: What?
A: Music

A: He's studying music
B: Where?
A: In Paris

(iv) A: There is a party this weekend
B: When?
A: This weekend

A: There is a party this weekend
B: When?
A: On Sunday

(v) A: The chidren had ice cream last evening
B: When?
A: Last evening

A: The chidren had ice cream last evening.
B: Where?
A: At the mall

(A)

L8.10. Decide whether B's responses will have a falling or a rising tone. Listen to the exchanges to check your answers.

(i) A: I'm going to a lecture on Online learning.
B: A lecture on what?
A: Online learning.

(ii) A: The managing director is going to Bejing next month.
B: What is the purpose?
A: To explore the possibility of opening a subsidiary there.

(iii) A: The concert's at six in the evening.
B: What time?
A: Six in the evening.

(iv) A: He's a sociologist and has made a deep study of tribal customs.
B: Has he written any books?
A: Yes, two books on Tribal customs.

(v) A: My nephew has bought a cell phone for twelve thousand rupees.
B: For how much?
A: Twelve thousand rupees.

9. Practise these sentences using a falling tone on the question tags.
   (i) It's a beautiful picture, isn't it?
   (ii) You are from India, aren't you?
   (iii) She writes very well, doesn't she?
   (iv) It was a delightful party, wasn't it?
   (v) He wasn't hopeful, was he?

10. Pracise these sentences using a rising tone on the question tags.
   (i) They have bought a new house, haven't they?
   (ii) She has written two novels, hasn't she?
   (iii) The workers called off the strike, didn't they?
   (iv) You are staying with your friends, aren't you?
   (v) It's a 24 hour channel, isn't it?

(A)

L8.11 Decide which question tags are likely to have a falling tone and which, a rising tone.
Listen and check your answers.
Practise the exchanges with the right intonation patterns.

(i) A: The flower arrangement is beautiful, isn't it?
B: Yes, I particularly like the lilies.

(ii) A: Your brother can give you a ride from the airport, can't he?
B: No, he has an appointment with his lawyer tomorrow evening.

(iii) A: The test results have come, haven't they?
B: Yes, of course.

(iv) A: She studied Sociology, didn't she?
B: No, she did Economics.

(v) A: It was very windy in the morning, wasn't it?
B: Yes and drizzling too.

(vi) A: You have had your lunch, haven't you?
B: Yes, I'm going back to the cash counter.

(vii) A: He has won an award for his acting in his latest movie.
B: The movie is about teaching dyslexic children, isn't it?

(viii) A: The food is very good at this restaurant.
B: They serve both vegetarian and nonvegetarian food, don't they?

(ix) A: Their house is kept very clean; it's spotless.
B: It is a big house, isn't it?

(x) A: My friends want me to go to the party tomorrow.
B: They will give you a ride, won't they?

(A)

L8.12. Listen and identify where B agrees with A completely or only partially. How is the tone different in the two types of responses?
Practise the exchanges with the correct intonation patterns.

(i) A: He made a good presentation, didn't he?
B: He spoke well ….

(ii) A: The price is reasonable, isn't it?
B: Yes, it is.

(iii) A: I like this bag, don't you?
B: Well, the color is a bit bright.

(iv) A: The roses have grown very well, haven't they?
B: Yes, but we should water them adequately.

(v) A: They say the school is very good.
B: It is, but the fees are high.

(vi) A: The book is selling well, isn't it?
B: It's doing well in southern states.

(vii) A: The car gives good mileage, doesn't it?
B: Yes, it is very fuel efficient.

(viii) A: He has a good job, doesn't he?
B: Yes, but the pay is not very good.

L8.13. Listen to the following sentences and decide which items in the lists have a falling tone and which a rising tone.
Practise saying the sentences with the right intonation patterns.

(i) During our European tour we visited Belgium, Switzerland, Netherlands, Germany, Italy and France.

(ii) She has written books on Abraham Lincoln, Mahatma Gandhi, Martin Luther King and Nelson Mandela.

(iii) He knows Sanskrit, Hindi, Chinese, Japanese, and English.

(iv) A: What ice creams do you have?
B: We have vanilla, chocolate, strawberry, mango, and orange.

(v) A: Which poets have you studied?
B: Milton, Wordsworth, Keats, Shelley and Yeats

11. Decide which items in the lists in these questions have a falling tone and which a rising tone. Practise saying the questions with the right intonation patterns.

(i) Would you like a motorbike, a moped, or a scooter?

(ii) Do you have Firefox, Internet Explorer or Crome?

(iii) Are they going by taxi, bus or train?

(iv) Is the dress green, blue or grey?

(v) Shall I give you fruits, biscuits, or nuts?

8.7 Intonation and conversation management

When we take part in a conversation, we use various strategies to keep the conversation going smoothly. We use a number of sounds, words and phrases for these purposes. It is intonation, particularly the tone used with these sounds, words and phrases that signals what we wish to convey as speakers or as listeners.

(1) As speakers we often wish to check that something we have said has been understood or accepted. For this purpose we use expressions such as *you see, you know, alright, okay, right* with a rising tone.

She had to be there by 8 in the morning, you SEE↗?
Don't open your gift till tomorrow morning, oKAY↗?
He hasn't been well, you KNOW↗?
There will be fifty people for dinner, RIGHT↗?

(2) As listeners we show the speakers that we are following what they are saying and we indicate either (a) that we want them to go on or (b) that we want to take a turn in the conversation ourselves.

(a) A: I'll tell you how to start a programme from the Start button.
You can find the Start button easily. It is in the bottom left corner.
B: YES↗.
A: Slide the mouse across your desktop till the arrow points at the Start button.
B: oKAY↗.
A: Click the left mouse button. A menu listing various items will appear.
B: RIGHT↗.
A: Click on the word Programs. Another menu will appear listing all the programs you can start from here.
B: YES↗.
A: Click on the name of the program you want to use. The program you want will appear on the screen.
B: YES↘.

This exchange shows how the rising tone is used to signal an invitation to continue when a listener responds to a series of instructions or directions. Here B responds with words in a rising tone to A's instructions as she signals to A that she understands what has been said and that she wishes A to continue after each new instruction. Only the response to the last instruction will be in a falling tone as this marks the end of the task. It indicates that the listener thinks the speaker has finished speaking.

(3) As speakers, we sometimes add information to a sentence that could be left out, which is spoken as an aside. The expressions we use for this purpose are called ***parenthetical expressions*** and in writing, they are inserted between commas, dashes or brackets. In speech, they are said in a separate tone unit and with a fall-rising tone.

The main reason for my coming, as you KNOW↘↗, is to find out what these children need.

Professor David Crystal, the famous LINGuist↘↗, is giving a talk tomorrow.

Learning to use a computer, particularly to surf the INternet↘↗, is a fascinating experience.

If there are job losses, as we fear there WILL be↘↗, nobody knows what to do help the unemployed.

The ways in which intonation is used for conversation management are summed up below.

Checking if something we said has been understood and accepted	↗
Indicating to the speaker that we have understood and would like him/her to go on	↗
Indicating to the speaker that we would like to take a turn in the conversation	↘
Parenthetical expressions	↘↗

Exercises

1. Decide whether the underlined expressions in the following sentences have a rising or a falling-rising tone.
   (i) The seminar is next Saturday, Right
   (ii) You will pick up the photos from the studio, Okay
   (iii) This young man, as you all know, has cycled more than 10000 miles to collect funds for flood relief.
   (iv) She isn't accepting the offer, you know
   (v) The situation in some countries has, as you predicted, improved a lot from last two years.
   (vi) The stock market, as we hoped, has recovered quite substantially.

8.8 Step-ups and step-downs in pitch

The five tones, namely the fall, the rise, the fall-rise, the rise-fall and the level are the basic tones used in normal unemphatic speech in English. But in situations where speakers either wish to emphasize certain items of information or to express strong emotions, other complications arise. In order to explain some of these complications, two important concepts are used. One is that of ***pitch range*** and the other is that of ***pitch height***. Every speaker is said to have his/her own normal ***pitch range*** which means that for every speaker there is a top pitch level which is the highest pitch normally used by the speaker and a bottom pitch level below which the speaker's pitch normally does not go. In normal speech, a speaker generally uses the lower part of his/her pitch range and the intonation patterns occur within this lower part. But when a speaker wants to emphasize something or to express strong emotions, he/she uses extra ***pitch height*** i.e., uses the higher part of his/her pitch range also. In such cases there is a ***step-up*** in pitch and the voice rises to a level higher than before. Like step-ups, ***step-downs*** to a lower pitch are also used for specific purposes.

↑ indicates a step-up and ↑ a step-down

(1) When we contradict what someone has just said either because we wish to correct it or to disagree with it, we emphasize the word/expression that focuses on the difference between the speaker's and our views by stepping up the pitch level on that word.

A: You were sleeping
B: I ↑ WASN'T sleeping ↘. I was meditating.

A: She is going to Paris.
B: No, she is going to ↑ London ↘

(2) Similarly when we present information that contrasts with what has been previously said or what is expected, we use a step-up to highlight the word that introduces the contrast.

Instead of brooding on past mistakes, you should plan for the ↑ future ↘

(3) In speeches and other types of prepared spoken discourse such as presentations and newscasts, step-ups are used to indicate the beginning of a new topic and step-downs to mark the end of a topic.

I would like to describe three ways of reducing pollution in our ↓ cities. ↑ First is to protect our parks and gardens by cleaning them up and by educating our citizens how to keep them ↓ clean. ↑ Second, we need to overhaul our garbage disposal ↓ system. ↑ Finally, industries should be made to comply with laws controlling emission of harmful ↓ chemicals. ↑ Now I'll deal with each of them in some ↓ detail.

A

Exercises

1. Mark the word where you think a step-up will occur with ↑ in the following sentences and practice saying them with the step-ups you have marked.

   (i) We were sure they would come right on time, but they were late by fifteen minutes.

(ii) This dish takes long to prepare, but it tastes really great.
(iii) We thought the boy was asleep, but actually he was wide awake.
(iv) The book was praised by all the critics, but readers hated it.
(v) Everyone thought he would have put on weight, but he looked thin and weak when he returned.

L8.14. Listen and mark where you think there are step-ups and step-downs.

As you know I am very interested in psychology and today I'll speak about hypnosis. This topic is of special interest to me, but I think it's also a subject of general interest to many people.

Whenever the word hypnosis is mentioned, it seems to get varied reactions from people. These range from disbelief to fear, and even laughter. But there are some people who believe that hypnosis can work miracles. All these reactions are based on inaccurate information about hypnosis.

I'll try to answer five important questions about hypnosis.

The first question is 'What is hypnosis?' The second, Who can be hypnotized? Third, What about hypnosis used for "fun"? Fourth, What are the legitimate uses of hypnosis? And fifth, Is hypnosis dangerous?

Adapted from *Extempore Speaking Practice* Joan Morley The University of Michigan Press

The differences between British and American English pronunciation have been described in some detail with reference to the articulation of consonants and vowels and word stress, as these have been studied quite extensively. But very little research has been done on the differences in intonation between the two varieties of English. There are only a few scattered observations on how the British and the Americans perceive each other's intonation. According to Celce-Murcia et al. (1996: 370), Americans consider the British "pretentious and mannered", whereas the British think that the Americans are "monotonous and negative".

When we study the descriptions of English intonation in British and American textbooks, however, we find a few differences in approach.

(1) The British mainly talk about two levels of pitch, namely low and high and describe the different tones in terms of movements in pitch between these two levels. They acknowledge the possibility of speakers using the higher part of their pitch range for emphatic or emotional speech and also the occurrence of step-ups and step-downs for specific purposes. American textbooks, in contrast, describe four pitch levels termed low, middle, high and extra high and say that normal conversation moves between middle and high pitch, adding that low pitch generally signals the end of an utterance and that extra high pitch is used for emphatic or emotional speech.

(2) The British books describe the contrasting uses of the falling and rising tones whereas in American textbooks, the main contrast is between the rising-falling tone and the rising tone.

	British	American
Declarative statements	Fall	Rise-Fall
Wh Questions	Fall	Rise-Fall
Commands	Fall	Rise-Fall
Tag questions that seek agreement	Fall	Rise-Fall
Declarative Questions	Rise	Rise
Yes-No Questions	Rise	Rise
Echo Questions	Rise	Rise
Repetition Questions	Rise	Rise
Tag questions that express uncertainty	Rise	Rise

The Rise-Fall in American books is described as the intonation that begins at the middle level, rises to the high level and then falls either to the middle or the low level.

Indian speakers have to pay particular attention to the features of spoken English described in this chapter, namely division of speech into tone units, placement of prominence and use of different intonation patterns or tones to convey different meanings, since these are specific features of English and it is essential to learn to use them appropriately if they are to be able to speak English well.

It is not very difficult to learn how speech is divided and where prominence is placed if the general rules are followed, but mastering English intonation is very difficult for most learners of English. The first problem is to be able to distinguish between different tones and then learn to produce these tones correctly.

It is very important to bear in mind that intonation patterns or tones, the meanings they convey and the functions they perform are language-specific and that English tones are different from the tones they use in their own languages. Not only do we need to develop an ability to recognize and distinguish between the different tones and the meanings they convey, but also learn to use them appropriately in our own speech. Though the description given above does not cover all the complexities of English intonation, the contrasts between the tones and their meanings described above offer useful guidelines for practice in listening as well as speaking. The best way is to listen to as much English speech as possible carefully noticing the various tones used for different purposes and try to produce the different tones in such a way that the appropriate contrasts are made in order to convey specific meanings.

L8.15. Listen to two jokes read by a British English speaker, an American English speaker and an Indian speaker.

First listen without looking at the texts given below and then listen again following the texts.

(i) An English professor writes the sentence, 'A woman without her man is nothing' on the blackboard and tells his students to punctuate it. A male student writes, 'A woman, without her man, is nothing.' A female student writes, 'A woman: without her, man is nothing'. (*Man walks into a bar* The Ultimate Collection of Jokes and One-liners Stephen Arnott and Mike Haskins p. 278)

(ii) A woman worked for a psychiatrist but in the end she had to give the job up. If she was late, he said she was hostile. If she was early, he said she had an anxiety complex. And if she was on time, he called her a compulsive. (*Man walks into a bar* The Ultimate Collection of Jokes and One-liners Stephen Arnott and Mike Haskins p. 348)

1. (a) Read the two jokes and record your readings on a tape or CD and (b) play them to your teacher or friend/s and get their feedback on your readings.

L8.16. (i) Listen to another joke read by a British English speaker, an American English speaker and an Indian speaker.

First listen without looking at the texts given below and then listen again following the texts.

A young man's parents were trying to figure out what their son's future career would be so they decided to give him a test.

They took a twenty dollar bill, a Bible, and a bottle of whiskey, and put them on the front hall table. Then they hid, hoping he would think they weren't at home. The father told the mother, "If he takes the money he will be a businessman, if he takes the Bible he will be a clergyman but if he takes the bottle of whiskey, I'm afraid our son will be a drunkard."

So the parents took their place in the nearby closet and waited nervously. Peeping through the keyhole they saw their son arrive home. He saw the note they had left, saying they'd be home later. Then, he took the twenty dollar bill, looked at it against the light, and slid it in his pocket. After that, he took the Bible, flicked through it, and took it also. Finally, he grabbed the bottle, opened it, and took a whiff to be assured of the quality. Then he left for his room, carrying all the three items.

The father slapped his forehead and said, " Darn, it's even worse than I could ever have imagined…"

" What do you mean?" his wife asked.

" Our son is going to be a politician!" replied the unhappy father. http://politicaljokes.resourcesforattorneys.com/index.php

(ii) Listen again to locate where tone unit boundaries occur.

(iii) Listen once again to locate which words are made prominent.

(iv) Listen once again focusing on the tones used by the father and the mother.

1. (a) Read the joke and record your reading on a tape or CD and (b) play it to your teacher or friend/s and get their feedback on your reading.

L8.17. (i) Listen to a fable read by a British English speaker, an American English speaker and an Indian speaker.

First listen without looking at the text given below and then listen again following the text.

A HIGHWAYMAN confronted a Traveller, and covering him with a firearm, shouted: "Your money or your life!"

"My good friend," said the Traveller, "according to the terms of your demand my money will save my life, my life my money; you imply you will take one or the other, but not both. If that is what you mean, please be good enough to take my life."

"That is not what I mean," said the Highwayman; "you cannot save your money by giving up your life."

"Then take it, anyhow," the Traveller said. "If it will not save my money, it is good for nothing."

The Highwayman was so pleased with the Traveller's philosophy and wit that he took him into partnership, and this splendid combination of talent started a newspaper.

http://aesopfables.com/cgi/aesop1.cgi?ab&TheHighwaymanandtheTraveller

(ii) Listen again to locate which words are made prominent.

(iii) Listen once again focusing on the tones used by the Highwayman and the Traveller.

1. (a) Read the fable and record your reading on a tape or CD and (b) play it to your teacher or friend/s and get their feedback on your reading.

Chapter summary

In speech we can identify a unit longer than a syllable, which is called ***a tone unit***. It has three important features, (a) it is spoken without a break, (b) it has one syllable that is strogly stressed, and (c) it has a distinctive ***intonation pattern*** or ***tone***.

1. We divide an utterance into tone units depending on the meaning we wish to convey. A tone unit generally forms a coherent stretch of speech in terms of meaning and grammar. Context also plays an important role in deciding where a speaker pauses and whether he/she makes a few or many pauses. Sometimes the meaning of sentences that are ambiguous in writing can be made clear in speech by the way they are divided into tone units

2. A tone unit has unstressed and stressed syllables and of the stressed syllables one is given stronger stress or ***prominence***. Prominence is also called ***tonic*** or ***nuclear stress*** and the syllable that receives prominence is called ***the tonic syllable***.

   Prominence may be placed on different words/syllables depending on what the speaker wishes to highlight. There are three factors that influence the placement of prominence in a tone unit. (i) New information, in contrast with information that is already known or is predictable, tends to receive prominence and generally occurs towards the end of an utterance (ii) The element that a speaker wishes to emphasize is made prominent and receives emphatic stress. (iii) When a speaker intends to make a contrast either in a single utterance or in response to a previous utterance, prominence is given to either both or one of the contrasting terms.

3. Intonation deals with patterns in the variations of pitch. In describing a language linguistically, only those variations which are meaningful, perceptible and contrastive are studied.

   Intonation is an important feature of spoken language because (a) it conveys meanings, (b) it is used systematically and (c) it is language-specific.

   English has mainly five tones, namely, ***Fall***, ***Rise***, ***Fall-Rise***, ***Rise-Fall*** and ***Level***. The meanings and functions of these different tones can be described in terms of (1) grammar, (2) attitudes and emotions of the speaker, (3) information management and (4) conversation management and are summed up below.

(1)	Single words and Declarative sentences	Statement ↘ Question ↗
	Defining Relative clauses ↘↗	Not a separate tone unit
	Non-defining Relative clauses ↘	Separate tone unit

(2) Routine or Bored responses Level tone

Responses showing interest and understanding
and encouraging speaker to continue ↗ OR ↘↗

Negative Yes No questions
showing surprise, pleasure etc. ↘

Positive Yes No questions
indicating criticism ↗

Wh questions that make a comment ↘

Hello, Excuse me etc. Friendly and Polite ↘↗ Abrupt or Curt ↘

Question tags following Imperative sentences
used as requests, suggestions or commands Friendly and Polite ↗

Okay in response to such requests, suggestions
or commands Enthusiastic acceptance ↘↗ Lack of enthusiasm ↘

Requests using the modals *Could, Would* etc. Polite ↘↗

Offers Polite ↘

Exclamations Surprise, Enthusiasm Disappointment and Criticism ↗↘

(3) New information ↘ Shared or known information ↗ OR ↘↗

Finding out information
not known ↘

Making sure of information
considered to be true ↗ OR ↘↗

Inviting agreement ↘ Asking for confirmation ↗

Definiteness ↘ Reservation ↘↗

Indicating completeness ↘ Indicating incompleteness ↗

(4) Checking if something we said has been understood and accepted ↗

Indicating to the speaker that we have understood and would like him/her to go on ↗

Indicating to the speaker that we would like to take a turn in the conversation ↘

Parenthetical expressions ↘ ↗

When speakers wish to emphasize any items of information strongly or to express strong emotions, they tend to step up the pitch of their voice to a higher level. Such ***step-ups*** are used in (a) contradictions when speakers want to correct or disagree with something that has been said and (b) contrasts when speakers present information that differs from what has been said or expected.

Speakers use ***step-downs*** too by lowering the pitch of their voice for specific purposes. In speeches and other types of prepared spoken discourse, step-ups are used to introduce new topics and step-downs to end topics.

I1- I154 on the Audio CD

In each chapter you have listened to jokes, fables and other passages read by three speakers, a British English speaker, an American English speaker, and an Indian speaker. These readings give you plenty of opportunities to develop an awareness of the important features of English pronunciation such as

(i) the way in which words with consonant clusters and syllabic consonants are pronounced
(ii) the placement of word stress in different types of words
(iii) the ways in which words are linked in connected speech
(iv) the use of contractions, elision and strong and weak forms
(v) the division of speech into tone units
(vi) the placement of prominence, and
(vii) the appropriate use of intonation.

They also help you to see the important differences between British and American pronunciation.

To help you focus exclusively on some of these features, individual words, phrases, and sentences illustrating a particular feature have been taken from each of these readings and combined into separate audio files I1 to I154. The file's name tells you what feature is focused on. You can listen to all the files from a particular passage, e.g., 'coffee' or all the files focusing on a particular feature e.g., word stress from all the passages. After listening to words and expressions separately, you can go back to the full reading to see how they sound in connected speech. A word of caution is necessary here. You'll notice that when we listen separately to words and phrases taken from a reading, they sound different from what they would sound like, if they were said individually and carefully.

9

Speaking activities focusing on overall ability

These activities are designed to help you integrate all the pronunciaqtion features – individual sounds, word stress and features of connected speech and incorporate them into contextualized speech.

[Though a few hints/points are given regarding the content you could use in these activities, you can change them or add to them]

1. *You are preparing for a job interview. You know you will be asked to make a brief statement on your educational background and your experience in your field of study/ work. Prepare the statement and practise it, focusing first on what you have studied and then on your experience using the words and expressions given below. Record yourself making the statement.*

   Play the tape or the CD to your friends and discuss with them your pronunciation and/or give the tape or the CD to your teacher for feedback.

Your educational background:

- Interested in being with and helping people,
- Chose to study sociology and public administration for my first degree,
- Graduated in 2006,
- Decided to do my masters in social work specializing in community development,
- Completed the masters in one and half years,
- Participated in workshops on the best ways to utilize community resources for setting up health, sports and recreational facilities for teenagers and elderly people, and
- Researched and wrote a dissertation on state policies and laws regarding social service organizations and workers

Your experience in your field of study:

- Did voluntary work in three non-governmental organizations working for the elderly,
- Planned and managed two short programmes to counsel the elderly patients on what kinds of help they could get from social workers, and

- Conducted seminars for senior students in high schools to introduce them to social work and public service and tell them about the jobs available in these fields.

(*All the consonants are used in the different words above and there are different stress patterns in these words*)

2. *Imagine you have to give a short talk on what computers are and what they are mainly used for by most people. Organize your points under three headings, Description, Word-processing, and the Internet. Using the words and expressions given below prepare your talk and give the talk to a group of elders or rural students who may not be familiar with computers.*

   Record the talk and listen to it with your friends and discuss with them your pronunciation and/or give the tape or the CD to your teacher for feedback.

Description – electronic device, hardware, software, mouse, keyboard, printer, monitor, add and remove programmes, applications

Word processing – enter text, create, save, copy, move and store files, use fonts and styles, insert pictures, select options from menus, select, click, scroll, send, cut and paste texts or parts of texts, change format and design, scan and print

Internet – use browsers, access websites, download and upload documents, photos, audios, and videos, send and receive emails, chat with friends

(*All the vowels are used in the different words above and there are different stress patterns in these words*)

3. *One of the most important decisions you had to make was to decide which college you should go to. Prepare a short talk to a group of school-leaving students on how they should choose the best college for them using the hints given below. Give the talk to a group of students.*

   Record the talk and play the tape or the CD to your friends and discuss with them your pronunciation and/or give the tape or the CD to your teacher for feedback.

   - A crucial decision that will affect your prospects,
   - Not just how a college is ranked, but the one best for you,
   - First select the colleges that offer the subjects of interest to you, the particular combination that you wish to study,
   - Consider the reputation they have
   - Get the prospectuses
   - Examine important factors – available educational facilities such as library, computer access and guidance, financial assistance such as scholarships and grants, recreational centre for sports and games and cultural activities, medical centre for emergency

help, student transport, cafeteria and the food and drinks served, location and physical environment

- Calculate the total cost for three years till graduation taking into account tuition and other fees, and various expenses
- Find out from old students what kind of teaching and counselling is provided and whether any job placement assistance is given
- A good strategy would be to visit the college and spend some time looking over the available facilities and meeting students and faculty members
- Decide on the college that is most suitable for you keeping in mind your priorities

(*A number of words above have consonant clusters and syllabic consonants*)

4. *Your teacher has asked you to give a short talk on what you think is an ideal job. Organize your points under four headings, Work, People, Benefits, and Facilities. Using the words and expressions given below, prepare your talk and give the talk to your class.*

   Record the talk and listen to it. You can discuss your pronunciation with your friends and your teacher.

Work – Opportunities to use and develop your skills, to learn, to be creative, to make useful contributions, and to participate in decision making

People – Interaction with professionals, Team of friendly and cooperative colleagues, Intelligent and understanding boss

Benefits – Good salary, motivational incentives for good performance, opportunities for promotions, vacation/holiday benefits, and attractive health insurance

Facilities – Comfortable workplace environment, convenient and flexible working hours, recreational facilities, and easy to commute location

(*Many of the words above are multisyllabic and have different stress patterns*)

Appendix

Some Problems of Indian Pronunciation

Some of the most noticeable instances where Indian speakers simply follow the spelling of words and use a strong vowel or a diphthong in place of a reduced vowel are found in

(i) words ending in *-age*, *-ace*, and *-ature* e.g., *damage, surface,* and *literature*
(ii) words ending in *-ial* and *-ious*, e.g., *partial* and *cautious* and
(iii) words ending in *-logy* e.g., *technology*

In all these words the stress falls on a previous syllable and the final syllable is unstressed and therefore pronounced with a reduced vowel.

(i) (a) In these words *-age* at the end is pronounced /ɪdʒ/ and not /eɪdʒ/.

J1

average
baggage
bandage
cabbage
carriage
cottage
courage
damage
dosage
drainage
footage
garbage
heritage
homage
hostage
language
leakage
marriage

manage
mortgage
package
percentage
pilgrimage
ravage
rampage
rummage
salvage
savage
seepage
shortage
storage
village
voyage
wastage
wreckage

(b) In these words *-ace* at the end is pronounced /ɪs/ and not /eɪs/.

J2
furnace
menace
necklace
palace
preface
solace
surface
terrace

(c) In these words *-ature* at the end is pronounced /ətʃə(r)/ and not /eɪtʃə(r)/.

J3
candidature
curvature
implicature
literature
miniature

signature
temperature

(ii) (a) In these words *-cial* or *-tial* at the end is pronounced /ʃ(ə)l/ and not /ʃɪəl/.

J4
artificial
beneficial
circumstantial
commercial
consequential
controversial
crucial
differential
essential
existential
exponential
impartial
influential
judicial
preferential
prejudicial
presidential
providential
sacrificial
superficial
tangential

(b) In these words *-ious* at the end is pronounced /əs/ and not /ɪəs/.

J5
auspicious
cautious
contagious
delicious
gracious
judicious
infectious

luscious
malicious
nutritious
officious
precious
superstitious
suspicious
vicious

(iii) In these words *-logy* at the end is pronounced /lədʒi/ and not /lɒdʒi/. But when the suffix *-cal* is added to such words as *technology*, *-logical* at the end of *technological* is pronounced /ˈlɒdʒɪkl/ because of the change in stress placement.

J6

biology	biological
chronology	chronological
cosmology	cosmological
ecology	ecological
etymology	etymological
geology	geological
gynaecology	gynaecological
ideology	ideological
lexicology	lexicological
morphology	morphological
mythology	mythological
neurology	neurological
pathology	pathological
psychology	psychological
radiology	radiological
sociology	sociological
technology	technological
theology	theological
zoology	zoological

Glossary

abbreviation – a short form of a phrase or name with only the first letter of each word in it, e.g., UNO is an abbreviation of United Nations Organization.

abutting consonants – two or more **consonants** that occur together within a word but belong to different **syllables**, e.g., '*n*' and '*t*' in the word *contest* where '*n*' occurs at the end of the first syllable and '*t*' occurs at the beginning of the second syllable. (Compare **consonant clusters**)

accent – (1) the type of pronunciation in speaking a language that identifies a person regionally or socially, e.g., an accent in speaking English that identifies the speaker as coming from India or America or Australia. (2) **Stress** or emphasis that makes a **syllable** or word stand out in speech, e.g., the second syllable in *believe* gets the stress or accent, whereas it is the first syllable in *common* that is stressed or accented.

acoustic phonetics – the branch of phonetics that studies the physical features of speech sounds in their transmission. (Compare **articulatory phonetics** and **auditory phonetics**)

active – a term that refers to any construction that has a **verb** followed by an **object**, e.g., *She writes poems, They are playing tennis*, and *He opened the door*. (Compare **passive**)

adjective – a word that describes a quality of a person, place, thing etc., occurs either before a **noun** or immediately after a **verb** such as *be, seem, look, become* etc and has comparative and superlative forms, e.g., *smart* as in either *the smart girl* or *The girl is smart* with comparative and superlative forms *smarter* and *smartest*. (Compare **noun, verb,** and **adverb**)

adverb – a word that modifies (adds information about) an **adjective**, a **noun** or a **verb** or makes a comment on the information in a **clause**/sentence and occurs in the beginning, middle or end of a clause, e.g., *highly* as in *a highly sensitive issue*, where *highly* modifies the adjective *sensitive, here* as in *The children here are very quiet*, where *here* modifies the noun *the children*, *frankly* as in *She spoke frankly*, where *frankly* modifies the verb *spoke* or *Frankly, she doesn't trust anyone*, where *frankly* makes a comment on the information conveyed in the sentence. (Compare **noun, adjective,** and **verb**)

adverbial – an element of **clause** structure that gives information about when, where, why and under what condition the event described in the clause took place or makes a comment on the information conveyed in the clause, e.g., *They will leave tomorrow/next week/when their work is done* where a word *tomorrow*, a phrase *next week* or a clause *when their work* *is done* can be used as an adverbial and *Surprisingly, she agreed to come with us* where the adverbial *surprisingly* makes a comment on the information conveyed in the clause. (Compare **subject, verb, object** and **complement**)

adverbial clause – a **clause** that has an adverbial function in a sentence, i.e. gives information about when, where, why, or under what condition the event described in the sentence took place or makes a comment on the information conveyed in the sentence, e.g., *She did not attend the meeting because she was not in town,* where *because she was not in town* is the adverbial clause that answers the question why or *If I can speak frankly, you should not do anything in a hurry*, where *if I can speak frankly* is the adverbial clause that makes a comment.

affricate – a term used in the classification of **consonant** sounds on the basis of their manner of **articulation** to refer to a **consonant** sound that begins as a **plosive** but ends as a **fricative**, i.e. a consonant sound that begins with a complete **closure** in the **vocal tract** but ends with a slow release of air with **friction**. The initial sounds of *cheap* and *jeep*, /tʃ/ and /dʒ/ are the two affricates used in English. (Compare **plosive, fricative, nasal, lateral** and **approximant**)

allophone – a particular **phonetic** realization of a **phoneme** (distinct sound of a language) in speech depending on its position in relation to other sounds in an utterance, (phonemic symbols are written between oblique brackets, whereas allophones or the phonetic realizations of a phoneme are written between square brackets) e.g., the phoneme /p/ is pronounced [pʰ] with **aspiration** in the initial position in words such as *poster* and *passive*, whereas it is pronounced [p] without aspiration in the middle or final positions as in *supply* and *group* and therefore we can say that [pʰ] and [p] are allophones of the phoneme /p/.

alternative questions – questions that mention two or more alternatives and expect in answer one of the alternatives mentioned, e.g., *Would you like coffee or tea? Do you travel by car, bus or train?*

alveolar – a term used in the classification of **consonant** sounds on the basis of their place of **articulation** to refer to a **consonant** sound made by the blade of the tongue in contact against the **alveolar ridge** immediately behind the top front teeth. In English we have six alveolar consonants, two **plosives**, /t/ and /d/, two **fricatives**, /s/ and /ʃ/, one **nasal**, /n/ and one **lateral**, /l/. (Compare **bilabial, labio-dental, dental, palate-alveolar, palatal, velar** and **glottal**)

alveolar ridge – the bony part of the roof of the mouth immediately behind the top front teeth.

approximant/semivowel – a term used in the classification of **consonant** sounds on the basis of their manner of **articulation** to refer to a **consonant** sound produced with the **articulators** approaching each other but not close enough to produce a **closure** or **friction** so that the air escapes freely through the gap between the articulators, e.g., the initial sounds of *red, wet,* and *yet*, namely /r/, /w/, and /j/.

arresting consonants – **consonants** that follow the **central vowel** or the **nucleus** in a **syllable**, e.g., /g/ in *egg*, /ŋk/ in *ink*, and /kts/ in *acts*. (Compare **releasing consonants**)

articles – the words *a/an* and *the*, which are used to indicate whether a noun has a particular or general meaning, e.g., *They have a cat and a dog, The dog they have is huge*, where 'a' and 'the' show that the nouns they are used with have particular meanings and *A dog/the dog is a faithful animal*, where 'a' and 'the' show that the noun 'dog' has a general meaning referring to the species and not to a particular animal.

articulation – the general term for the movements of the vocal organs or **articulators** in order to modify the air stream in the **vocal tract** to produce various types of speech sounds.

articulators – the organs in the **vocal tract** that alter the shape and character of the air stream by modifying it to produce various types of speech sounds, e.g., the lips, the tongue and the lower jaw.

articulatory phonetics – the branch of **phonetics** that studies the physical features of speech sounds in their production. (Compare **acoustic phonetics** and **auditory phonetics**)

aspiration – the audible puff of air sounding like 'h', which accompanies the production of some sounds such as /p/, /t/, and /k/ when they occur in the initial position. When a sound like /p/ is aspirated, it is symbolized as [p^h].

assimilation – a process of adjustment in pronunciation that occurs in connected speech where a sound in a word influences the pronunciation of another sound in a neighbouring word in a way that the two sounds become alike or identical, e.g., in *that parcel* the pronunciation of /t/ is influenced by /p/ in the next word in such a way that it becomes /p/. (See also **progressive assimilation, regressive assimilation** and **coalescent assimilation**)

auditory phonetics – the branch of **phonetics** that studies the physical features of speech sounds in their perception. (Compare **acoustic phonetics** and **articulatory phonetics**)

auxiliary verbs – the words *be, have, do, can/could, may/might, shall/should, will/would,* and *must,* which are used as helping verbs with **main verbs/lexical verbs** such as *come, eat, play* etc., to form **verb phrases,** e.g., *has gone* in *She has gone home, are not coming* in *They are not coming, didn't see* in *I didn't see him, may go* in *He may go to Germany,* and *should listen* in *You should listen to music*.

back vowels – **vowels** that are **articulated** by raising the back part of the tongue, e.g., the vowels in *fool, farm,* and *fall*, /uː/, /ɑː/, and /ɔː/. (Compare **front vowels** and **central vowels**)

bilabial – a term used in the classification of **consonant** sounds on the basis of their place of **articulation** to refer to a consonant sound made by the coming together of both lips, e.g., the initial sounds of *post* and *most*, /p/ and /m/.

central vowels – **vowels** that are **articulated** by raising the central part of the tongue, e.g., the vowels in *cut* and *curt*, /ʌ/ and /ɜː/. (Compare **front vowels** and **back vowels**)

centre/peak/nucleus – the central element of a **syllable**, which is mostly a **vowel** is called the centre, the peak or the nucleus, e.g., the vowel /iː/ in *seat* or the vowel /æ/ in *tramp*.

centring diphthongs – **diphthongs** that end in /ə/, a **central vowel**, i.e., the diphthongs in *fear, fare,* and *tour*, /ɪə/, /eə/, and /ʊə/. (Compare **closing diphthongs**)

clause – a term used in grammar to refer to a stretch of language that has at least a **subject** and a **verb** in most cases and may have an **object**, a **complement** and/or an **adverbial** following the verb, e.g., *The train has left*, which has a subject *the train* and a verb *has left*, *She bought fruits*, which has *she* as subject, *bought* as verb and *fruits* as object, *The book is interesting*, which has *the book* as subject, *is* as verb and *interesting* as complement and *I left the book on the table*, which has *I* as subject, *left* as verb, *the book* as object and *on the table* as adverbial.

A clause may be **independent** as in the examples above or **dependent** on or **subordinated** to another clause as in *We reached home after they had left*, where the second clause *after they had left* is subordinated to the first, *we reached home*.

close/high vowels – **vowels** that are **articulated** with the tongue raised very high so that the surface of the tongue is very close to the roof of the mouth, e.g., the vowels in *beat* and *boot*, /iː/ and /uː/. (Compare **open/low vowels** and **mid vowels**)

closed syllable – a **syllable** in which the **vowel** at the centre is followed by one or more than one **consonant** but is not preceded by any other sound, e.g., *us, ink,* and *art*. (Compare **open syllable**)

closing diphthongs – **diphthongs** that end in /ɪ/ or /ʊ/, a **close vowel**, e.g., the diphthongs in *hay* and *how*, /eɪ/ and /aʊ/. (Compare **centring diphthongs**)

closure – a term used to refer to the movement of one **articulator** against another so that there is an obstruction to the flow of air in the **vocal tract** and no air is allowed to escape through the mouth and/or nose, e.g., the two lips come together to block the flow of air in producing the initial sounds of *pat, bat,* and *mat*, /p/, /b/, and /m/.

coalescent assimilation – a type of **assimilation** where the final **consonant** of the first word and the initial consonant of the second word occurring in a sequence coalesce to create a third consonant that has features of both coalescing consonants, e.g., *Was that your brother?* where /t/ at the end of *that* and /j/ at the beginning of *your* coalesce to create /tʃ/. (Compare **regressive assimilation** and **progressive assimilation**)

complement – an element of **clause** structure that follows **verbs** such as *be, become, appear, seem* and *look* in a clause and is a **noun, pronoun** or an **adjective**, which gives information about the **subject**, e.g., *She is a teacher, She is brilliant, This bag is hers*, where *a teacher*, *brilliant* and *hers* are complements. A complement can also give information about the **object** as in *I consider her an expert/brilliant* where *an expert* and *brilliant* describe the object *her*. When a complement describes the subject, it is called subject complement and when it describes the object, it is called object complement. (Compare **subject, verb, object** and **adverbial**)

complex words – words that have **prefixes** and/or **suffixes**, e.g., *upload* and *overheat* with prefixes, *hopeful* and *darkness* with suffixes, and *unhelpful* and *invalidity* with both prefixes and suffixes. (Compare **simple words** and **compound words**)

compound words – words that are made up of two or more independent words, e.g., *sunglasses, red-hot, brainstorm,* and *customer care centre*. (Compare **simple words** and **complex words**)

conjunctions – words that link together two parts of a sentence, e.g., *The exams were over and the children are very happy*, where *and* links the two clauses and *If he gives up smoking, his health will improve*, where *if* links the two clauses. Conjunctions are of two types, coordinating such as *and* and subordinating such as *if*.

consonant clusters – two or more **consonants** that occur together initially or finally in a **syllable**, e.g., *place* and *spring*, where consonant clusters occur initially in the syllable and *gulf, tempt,* and *texts*, where consonant clusters occur finally in the syllable. (Compare **abutting consonants**)

consonants – sounds that are produced with a **closure** or a narrowing in the **vocal tract**, which causes an obstruction or a **friction** to the flow of air as it passes through the vocal tract, e.g., the initial sounds in *pass, fun, chip, loss,* and *yes*. (Compare **vowels**)

content/full words – words that have a definite meaning that can be stated (as in a dictionary), e.g., nouns such as *tree, fish,* and *anger,* verbs such as *play, travel,* and *think,* adjectives such as *afraid, tall,* and *fast* and adverbs such as *now, quickly,* and *never* (Compare **grammatical/function words**)

continuants – sounds produced with an incomplete closure in the vocal tract that we can continue making without interruption as long as we have air in our lungs, e.g., **fricatives** such as /s/, /ʃ/, /z/ and /ʒ/ and also **vowels** such as /iː/, /uː/, /ɑː/, and /e/.

contraction – a process of adjustment in pronunciation that occurs in connected speech where a word is reduced or contracted so that it gets attached to an adjacent word, e.g., *'ve* the reduced or contracted form of *have* that gets attached to *I* in *I've* or to *they* in *they've* and *n't* the reduced or contracted form of *not* that gets attached to *have* in *haven't* or to *did* in *didn't*.

declarative sentence – a sentence in which the **subject** is present and occurs before the **verb**, which is mostly used to make a statement, e.g., *The train leaves early, Apples are expensive,* and *She got married last year*. (Compare **interrogative sentence, imperative sentence** and **exclamatory sentence**)

defining relative clause – a **relative clause** that gives information essential to identify the **noun** that it modifies, e.g., *The book that you ordered hasn't yet come*, where the relative clause *that you ordered* gives the information necessary to identify which book is being talked about. (Compare **non-defining relative clause**)

demonstrative pronouns – **pronouns** that point to something in the situation, namely *this, that, these* and *those* as in *This is what I found* or *Do you want these or those*? (Compare **personal pronouns, possessive pronouns, reflexive pronouns,** and **relative pronouns)**

dental – a term used in the classification of **consonant** sounds on the basis of their place of **articulation** to refer to a consonant sound made by the tip of the tongue against the teeth, e.g., the initial sounds in *thank* and *there*, /θ/ and /ð/. (Compare **bilabial, labio-dental, alveolar, palate-alveolar, palatal, velar and glottal)**

digraph – any sequence of two letters pronounced as a single sound, e.g., 'ph' in *photo*, 'ea' in *seat*, 'sh' and 'oe' in *shoe*.

diphthong – a **vowel** sound characterized by a glide or movement from one vowel to another, e.g., the vowel /aɪ/ in *five*, the vowel /aʊ/ in *foul*, and the vowel /eɪ/ in *fail*. (Compare **monophthong**) (See also **centring diphthongs** and **closing diphthongs)**

elision – a process of adjustment in pronunciation that occurs in connected speech where certain sounds are omitted, e.g., *scripts* pronounced /skrɪps/ where /t/ is omitted, and *Who's he*? where *he* is pronounced without /h/.

emphatic stress – the type of **prominence** that a speaker gives to a word/syllable for purposes of special emphasis, e.g., *He HAS given up smoking*, where *has* gets emphatic stress when the speaker responds to a comment such as *I don't think he can give up smoking*.

exclamation/exclamatory sentence – an utterance that expresses strong emotion such as surprise, disappointment, admiration or criticism, which can be in the form of a word, a phrase or a sentence, e.g., *Wonderful*! *Fantastic*! *or How wonderful*! *Isn't it fantastic*! *or How wonderful she looks*! *What a fantastic movie it is*!

fall – a type of **intonation** pattern or **tone** in which the **pitch** moves from relatively high to relatively low, e.g., the tone used in statements such as *They won the match* and in questions such as *When will you come*? (Compare **rise, fall-rise, rise-fall,** and **level tone)**

fall-rise – a type of **intonation** pattern or **tone** in which the **pitch** moves from relatively high to relatively low and then again moves to relatively high, e.g., the tone used in making statements with reservation as opposed to definite ones as in *It has an interesting story but is not written very well*, where the first clause is said with a fall-rise. (Compare **fall, rise, rise-fall,** and **level tone)**

fortis – a term used in the classification of **consonant** sounds on the basis of their manner of **articulation** to refer to a **consonant** sound that is made with relatively great muscular effort and force of breath and is **voiceless**, e.g., the initial sounds in *pan, tan, can,* and *fan*, /p/, /t/, /k/, and /f/. (Compare **lenis)**

fricative – a term used in the classification of **consonant** sounds on the basis of their manner of **articulation** to refer to a **consonant** sound that is made when two articulators come so close together that the air passing through the narrow passage produces audible **friction**, e.g., the initial sounds in *thump, fun, sun, shun,* and *hum*, /θ/, /f/, /s/, /ʃ/ and /h/. (Compare **plosive, affricate, nasal, lateral,** and **approximant)**

friction – a term that refers to the sound produced when air passes through a very narrow passage in the **vocal tract**, e.g., the hissing sound heard in producing the initial sounds in *see, zoo,* and *sheep*, /s/, /z/, and /ʃ/.

front vowels – **vowels** that are **articulated** by raising the front part of the tongue, e.g., the vowels in *keep*, *cat*, and *bet*, /iː/, /æ/, and /e/. (Compare **back vowels** and **central vowels**)

glottal – a term used in the classification of **consonant** sounds on the basis of their place of **articulation** to refer to a consonant sound made with the air from the lungs passing through a narrow passage in the **glottis** (between the **vocal cords**), namely the initial sound in *hit*, /h/. (Compare **bilabial, dental, labio-dental, alveolar, palate-alveolar, palatal,** and **velar**)

glottis – a term that refers to the opening between the **vocal cords.**

grammatical/function words – words that do not have a dictionary meaning, but only a grammatical function, e.g., **conjunctions** like *and, or, if,* and *because*, **articles**, *the* and *a/an*, **auxiliary verbs** such as *have, be, can,* and *shall*, **pronouns** such as *we, they, he,* and *she,* and **prepositions** such as *for, to, from, on* and *in*.

hard palate – the smooth curved surface of the roof of the mouth from behind the **alveolar ridge** to the **velum** or the **soft palate**. (Compare **soft palate or velum**)

imperative/imperative sentence – a sentence that does not have a subject and begins with a verb, which is mostly in the base form and is used to ask someone to do something e.g., *Call the police, Drink some water, Let us go out this evening*. (Compare **declarative sentence**, **exclamatory sentence** and **interrogative sentence**)

International Phonetic Alphabet – the most widely used writing system to represent the sounds of a language.

interrogative sentence – a sentence that has an **auxiliary verb** before the **subject** or a question word such as *what, who, where,* or *when* at the beginning or both, which is mostly used to ask a question, e.g., *Have the shops opened? Who are these people? When were the shops closed?* (Compare **declarative sentence, exclamatory sentence** and **imperative sentence**)

intonation – a term that refers to the use of distinctive patterns of **pitch** or **tones** in speech, e.g., the use of a **fall** in statements such as *She has bought a new cell phone* and a **rise** in Yes-no questions such as *Do you work here*?

labio-dental – a term used in the classification of **consonant** sounds on the basis of their place of **articulation** to refer to a consonant sound made with the lower lip coming into contact with the upper teeth to from a narrow passage through which air escapes, e.g., the initial sounds in *fine* and *vine*, /f/ and /v/.

larynx – the part of the windpipe or trachea that contains the **vocal cords**, which is also called 'voice box'.

lateral – a term used in the classification of **consonant** sounds on the basis of their manner of **articulation** to refer to a consonant sound made with a complete **closure** between the front of the tongue and some part of the **hard palate** and the air escaping along the sides of the tongue, namely the initial sound in *like*, /l/. (Compare **plosive, fricative, affricate, nasal** and **approximant)**

lenis – a term used in the classification of **consonant** sounds on the basis of their manner of **articulation** to refer to a **consonant** sound that is made with relatively weak muscular effort and force of breath and is **voiced**, e.g., the initial sounds in *bone, done, gone* and *van,* /b/, /d/, /g/, and /v/. (Compare **fortis)**

level tone – a **tone** in which there is no **pitch** movement, neither a **fall** nor a **rise** with the pitch remaining steady at a particular level, e.g., the tone we use to show boredom and lack of interest. (Compare **moving tones)**

linking – a process of adjustment in pronunciation that occurs in connected speech where the sound at the end of a word is connected to the sound at the beginning of the next in a way that gives a smooth quality to speech, e.g., *good evening*, where /d/ at the end of the first word is smoothly linked to the following vowel /iː/ as if it belonged to both the **syllables**/ words. (Compare **assimilation, elision, contraction** and **weak forms)**

long vowels – a term used in the classification of **vowels** in terms of the duration of the sound to refer to a vowel sound that is relatively long, e.g., the vowels in *beat, pool,* and *part*, /iː/, /uː/, and /ɑː/. (Compare **short vowels)**

main verbs/lexical verbs – **verbs** such as *come, eat, help* etc. that have a definite meaning, which can combine with **auxiliary verbs** to form **verb phrases** such as *may come, has eaten,* and *are helping*. (Compare **auxiliary verbs)**

mid vowels – **vowels** that are **articulated** with the tongue neither raised high as in **close/high vowels** nor kept low as in **open/low vowels** but in a mid position between these two extreme positions, e.g., the vowels in *tall, term,* and *tell*, /ɔː/, /ɜː/, and /e/. (Compare **close/high vowels** and **open/low vowels)**

minimal pair – a pair of words with different meanings that differ only in one sound, e.g., *bet* and *bit*, *put* and *pat*, *feel* and *fool*, *chip* and *ship*, *ten* and *hen*, and *night* and *fight*.

modal auxiliaries/modals – auxiliaries *can/could, may/might, will/would, shall/should,* and *must*, which convey meanings such as permission, obligation, possibility or necessity, e.g., *May/ can we come in? It may rain today, We should leave early*, and *You must be careful*.

monophthong – a **vowel** that is constant and not marked by a glide or movement, e.g., the vowels in *tap*, *get*, and *cut*, /æ/, /e/, and /ʌ/. (Compare **diphthong)**

monosyllabic words – words that consist of only one **syllable**, e.g., *red, ink, eye, ball* and *go*. (Compare **multisyllabic words)**

morpheme – a term that refers to the smallest constituent of a word with a distinct function and meaning, e.g., *un-, interest,* and *-ing* in *uninteresting* and *dis-, respect, -ful* in *disrespectful*.

moving tones – **tones** that are marked by a movement of **pitch**, e.g., **fall, rise, fall-rise** and **rise-fall**. (Compare **level tone**)

multisyllabic words – words that consist of more than one **syllable**, e.g., *mother, transfer, tomato, president, technology* and *information*. (Compare **monosyllabic words**)

nasal – a term used in the classification of speech sounds on the basis of their manner of **articulation** to refer to a sound produced with the **soft palate** or the **velum** lowered to allow the air to escape through the nose, e.g., the final sounds in *jam, tan,* and *bang*, /m/, /n/, and /ŋ/.

nasal consonants – a term used in the classification of **consonant** sounds on the basis of their manner of **articulation** to refer to a consonant sound made when there is a complete **closure** in the mouth and all the air is allowed to escape through the nose with the **soft palate or the velum** being lowered, e.g., the initial sounds in *matter* and *name*, /m/ and /n/, and the final sound in *strong*, /ŋ/. (Compare **plosive, affricate, fricative, lateral** and **approximant)**

non-defining relative clause – a **relative clause** that gives additional information that is not essential for identifying the **noun** it modifies, e.g., *Our maths teacher, who has a Ph.D., has written a very interesting book on Numbers*, where the relative clause *who has a Ph.D.* gives additional information about *our maths teacher,* who is identified independently. (Compare **defining relative clause**)

non-sibilants – **fricatives** that are produced with less **friction** and energy than those produced with a high pitched hissing sound, e.g., the initial sounds in *fat, value, thin,* and *thus*, /f/, /v/, /θ/, and /ð/ are produced without the high pitched hissing sound that is heard in the production of the initial sounds in *some, shine,* and *zip*, /s/, /ʃ/, and /z/. (Compare **sibilants**)

noun – a word that has singular and plural forms, occurs with **articles** *the* and *a/an* and words such as *this/these* and *that/those* and functions as **subject, object** or **complement** in a **clause**/sentence, e.g., *project/projects, foot/feet, the bravery they showed, this/that example you gave, Music helps me relax, She hired a cook,* and *They are fools*. (Compare **adjective, adverb,** and **verb)**

noun phrase – a phrase that has a **noun** at the centre and functions as **subject, object** or **complement** in a **clause**/sentence, e.g., *The girls there are very pretty, I bought new books,* and *He is a good teacher.*

noun clause – a **clause** that functions as **subject, object** or **complement** in another clause or a sentence, e.g., *That he came home surprised me, I didn't know that she got a new job*, and *The story is that the company has gone bankrupt.*

nuclear stress/tonic stress – the **prominence** or special emphasis that is given to a **stressed syllable** in a **tone unit** in connected speech so that this **syllable** contrasts with the other stressed syllables in the tone unit, e.g., *The child ate an APPLE* where *apple* gets the nuclear or tonic stress and *I bought a SKIRT yesterday* in response to the question *What did you buy yesterday*? where *skirt* gets the nuclear or tonic stress.

number – a term that refers to the contrast between singular and plural forms of **nouns**, e.g., *book* and *books*, *tooth* and *teeth*, and *dog* and *dogs*.

object – an element of **clause** structure that follows the **verb**, is either a **noun** or a **pronoun**, and can become the **subject** in a corresponding **passive** construction, e.g., *Ravi has started a company* and *Leela invited us*, where *a company* and *us* function as object, with the corresponding passive constructions being *A company has been started by Ravi* and *We were invited by Leela*, where *a company* and *we* function as subject. (Compare **subject, verb, complement,** and **adverbial**)

onset – a term that refers to the **consonant** sounds that occur before the **vowel** at the centre in a **syllable**, e.g., /f/ in *fee*, /tr/ in *tree* and /spr/ in *spree*. (Compare **termination**)

open/low vowels – **vowels** that are **articulated** with the tongue in the lowest possible position, i.e., with the mouth wide open, e.g., the vowels in *bark* and *hat*, /ɑː/ and /æ/. (Compare **close/high vowels** and **mid vowels**)

open syllable – a **syllable** in which the **vowel** at the centre is preceded by one or more than one **consonant** but is not followed by any other sound, e.g., *pay, play,* and *spray*. (Compare **closed syllable**)

oral – a term used in the classification of speech sounds on the basis of their manner of **articulation** to refer to a sound produced with the **soft palate** or the **velum** raised to block the passage of air through the nose and to allow the air to pass only through the mouth, e.g., the vowels in English and consonants such as the initial sounds in *pit, bit, tip, dip, come, gum, lip* and *sip*, /p/, /b/, /t/, /d/, /k/, /g/, /l/, and /s/. (Compare **nasal**)

palatal – a term used in the classification of **consonant** sounds on the basis of their place of **articulation** to refer to a consonant sound made with the front of the tongue raised to approach the **hard palate**, e.g., the initial sound in *young* and *yet*, /j/. (Compare **bilabial, labio-dental, dental, alveolar, palato-alveolar, velar,** and **glottal**)

palato-alveolar – a term used in the classification of **consonant** sounds on the basis of their place of **articulation** to refer to a consonant sound made with the tip and the blade of the tongue moving near the **alveolar** and the front of the tongue moving near the **hard palate** and the air escaping through the narrow passage between the tongue and the hard palate just behind the alveolar, e.g., the initial sound in *shoot* and *shine*, /ʃ/. (Compare **bilabial, labio-dental, dental, alveolar, velar,** and **glottal**)

parenthetical expressions – expressions that add extra information, which could be left out of a sentence and which are spoken as an aside, e.g., *They will only make promises, as we all know, but will not do anything to help the people*, where *as we all know* is a parenthetical expression.

particle – a term used to refer to the word/s that occur with a **verb** to form a **phrasal verb**, e.g., *by* in *go by*, *out* in *make out*, *down* in *turn down*, and *up* and *with* in *put up with*.

passive – a term that refers to a construction with *be* plus **past participle** in which the **subject** is what would be the **object** in a corresponding **active** construction, e.g., *Accessories are sold in these shops* and *The exams were cancelled by the university*, which have the corresponding active constructions *They sell accessories in these shops* and *The university cancelled the exams*. (Compare **active**)

past participle – *-ed/-en* form of a verb, e.g., *walked, made, gone,* and *known*. In contrast, *-ing* form of a verb such as *walking, making, going* or *knowing* is called the present participle.

person – a term that refers to the nature of the participants in a situation, first person referring to the speakers, second person referring to those addressed by the speakers and third person referring to others, e.g., *I, we, you, he, she, they* and *it*.

personal pronouns – **pronouns** that are used to identify speakers, addressees and others showing contrasts in person, gender, and number, e.g., *I, we, you, he, she, they* and *it*. (Compare **demonstrative pronouns, possessive pronouns, reflexive pronouns,** and **relative pronouns)**

pharynx – a tube that begins just above the **larynx** through which the air stream from the larynx passes into the **vocal tract**.

phoneme – a term that refers to the minimal unit of sound in a language, i.e., a distinct sound of a language, e.g., the initial sounds of *cheap* and *jeep*, /tʃ/ and /dʒ/. (Compare **allophone**)

phonetics – the study of the physical features of speech sounds that deals with methods of their description, classification and transcription. (See also **acoustic phonetics, articulatory phonetics** and **auditory phonetics**) (Compare **phonology**)

phonology – the study of the sound system of a language that deals with the distinctive sounds and their patterns that characterize speech in that language, e.g., the sounds of English, the patterns in which they combine and the features of **stress** and **intonation** that characterize English speech. (Compare **phonetics**)

phrasal verb – a term that refers to a **verb** that is followed by one or two **particles (adverb** or **preposition)**, e.g., *turn up, look into,* and *take care of.*

pitch – an auditory feature of speech that is closely related to the frequency of vibration of **vocal cords**, which is described in terms of high or low and in which variations between high and low can be perceived and described.

plosive/stop – a term used in the classification of **consonant** sounds on the basis of their manner of **articulation** to refer to a consonant sound made with a complete **closure** in the mouth followed by a sudden of release of air resulting in an explosive sound, the initial sounds in *pin, tin,* and *kin*, /p/, /t/, and /k/. (Compare **affricate, fricative, nasal, lateral** and **approximant**)

possessive pronouns – **pronouns** that are used to indicate ownership, which are used before **nouns** or on their own, e.g., *This is her book, This book is hers,* and *Our house is small, theirs is big*, where the possessive pronouns *her* and *our* are used with the nouns *book* and *house*, whereas hers and *theirs* are used independently. (Compare **demonstrative pronouns, personal pronouns, reflexive pronouns,** and **relative pronouns**).

prefix – a **morpheme** that is added at the beginning of a word, which cannot be used independently but has a distinct meaning and function when added to a word, e.g., *un-* in *unhurt*, *over-* in *overshoot*, and *dis-* in *disjoin*. (Compare **suffix**)

preposition – a word that typically occurs before a **noun/noun phrase/noun clause** e.g., *on* in *on the river*, *for* in *for my children*, *at* in *at the party*, *from* in *from the government*, and *with* in *with all the documents*. It can follow a **verb** to form a **phrasal verb**, e.g., *on* in *depend on*, *for* in *pay for*, *at* in *look at*, and *with* in *speak with*.

primary/strong stress – the greater degree of **stress** that is given to a **syllable** in a word with three or more syllables so that it is heard as being the most emphatic of all the syllables in the word, e.g., the third syllable in *gene'ration* and the fourth in *accommo'dation* get the primary stress. Primary stress is indicated by the symbol ' just before the syllable. (Compare **secondary/weak stress**)

progressive assimilation – a type of **assimilation** where the pronunciation of a sound is influenced by a preceding sound, e.g., '*s*' in *logs* is pronounced /z/ because of the influence of /g/, but in *locks* it is pronounced /s/ because of the influence of /k/. (Compare **coalescent assimilation** and **regressive assimilation**)

prominence – the special emphasis given to a **stressed syllable** in a **tone unit** so that it stands out from other stressed syllables in the tone unit, e.g., in *RAO has deCIded to STUdy CHEmistry*, the first syllable in *chemistry* is given prominence so that it stands out from the other stressed syllables, *Rao*, the second syllable in *decided* and the first syllable in *study*. (Compare **stress**)

pronoun – a word that can be used to substitute for a **noun/noun phrase**, e.g., *He* can substitute for *The goalkeeper* in *The goalkeeper fell down* and *this* can substitute for *the latest gadget* in *Let me show you the latest gadget*. (See also **demonstrative pronouns, personal pronouns, possessive pronouns, reflexive pronouns,** and **relative pronouns**)

question tag – a small question consisting of an **auxiliary verb** and a **pronoun** attached to the end of a statement, e.g., *She hasn't come back, has she? You are coming, aren't you?* where *has she?* and *aren't you?* are the question tags.

reduced vowels – **vowels** that are found in **unstressed syllables** where they are pronounced either /ə/ or /ɪ/, e.g., in *context*, the vowel in the first syllable is pronounced /ɒ/ or /ɑː/ because this syllable is stressed, whereas in *contextual*, this vowel is pronounced /ə/ because here the first syllable is unstressed and it is the second syllable that is stressed.

reflexive pronouns – **pronouns** that end in *–self/-selves* and refer back to a **noun/pronoun** in the same **clause**, e.g., *herself* in *She hurt herself* and *themselves* in *They enjoyed themselves during the trip*. (Compare **demonstrative pronouns, personal pronouns, possessive pronouns,** and **relative pronouns**)

regressive assimilation – a type of **assimilation** where the pronunciation of a sound is influenced by a following sound, e.g., the alveolar /t/ changes to the velar /k/ because of the influence of the following /g/ in *bright girl* and the alveolar /d/ changes to the nasal /n/ because of the following /n/ in *good news*. (Compare **coalescent assimilation** and **progressive assimilation**)

relative clause – a **clause** that occurs immediately following the **noun** about which it gives essential or additional information, e.g., *that she has written* in *I like the poem that she has written* and *who scored the first goal* in *The captain, who scored the first goal, was cheered by all his teammates*. (See also **defining relative clause** and **non-defining relative clause**) (Compare **adverbial clause** and **noun clause**)

relative pronouns – **pronouns** that introduce **relative clauses**, namely *who, whom, whose, which* and *that* as in *Have you finished reading the book that I gave you?* or *My friend, whom you haven't seen, works in this school.* (Compare **demonstrative pronouns, personal pronouns, possessive pronouns,** and **reflexive pronouns**)

releasing consonants – **consonants** that precede the **central vowel** or the **nucleus** in a **syllable,** e.g., /b/ in *bee,* /pl/ in *plea,* and /skr/ in *screw*. (Compare **arresting consonants**)

retroflex – a term used in the classification of **consonant** sounds on the basis of their place of **articulation** to refer to a consonant sound made with the tip of the tongue turned back in the direction of the front part of the **hard palate**, e.g., the initial sound in *room* and *rain*, /r/.

rhythm – a term used to refer to the regularity of patterns of **stressed** and **unstressed syllables** in connected speech. (See also **stress-timed rhythm** and **syllable-timed rhythm**)

rise – a type of **intonation** pattern or **tone** in which the **pitch** moves from relatively low to relatively high, e.g., the tone used in **yes-no questions** such as *Are the children sleeping*? and *Has the train left*?

rise-fall – a type of **intonation** pattern or **tone** in which the **pitch** moves from relatively low to relatively high and then again moves to relatively low, e.g., the tone used in **exclamations** such as *How wonderful*! and *What a surprise*!

root/stem – the base form of a word that cannot be analysed further without loss of identity, i.e., that part of the word that is left after the **prefixes** and **suffixes** are removed, e.g., *industry* in contrast to *industrialist* or *industrialization*, or *honour* in contrast to *honourable* or *dishonour*.

rounded vowels – **vowels** that are **articulated** with the rounding of the lips, e.g., the vowels in *mood, wood, dot,* and *call*, /uː/, /ʊ/, /ɒ/, and /ɔː/. (Compare **unrounded vowels**)

secondary/weak stress – the lesser degree of **stress** that is given to a **syllable** in a word with three or more syllables so that it is heard as being less emphatic than the syllable with **primary stress** but more emphatic than the other syllables in the word, e.g., the first syllable in *ˌgeneration* and the second in *aˌccommodation* get the secondary stress. Secondary stress is indicated by the symbol ˌ just before the syllable. (Compare **primary/strong stress)**

short vowels – a term used in the classification of **vowels** in terms of the duration of the sound to refer to a vowel sound that is relatively short, e.g., the vowels in *sit, foot,* and *hot,* /ɪ/, /ʊ/, and /ɒ/. (Compare **long vowels)**

sibilants – **fricatives** that are produced with a high pitched hissing sound, e.g., the initial sounds in *song, shine,* and *zest*, /s/, /ʃ/, and /z/. (Compare **sibilants)**

silent letter – a consonant letter that is not pronounced in a word, e.g., 'k' in *know*, 'p' in *psychology*, 'g' in *gnat*, and 'w' in *write*.

simple words – words consisting of only one **morpheme**, e.g., *hope, green, table,* and *sample*. (Compare **complex words** and **compound words)**

soft palate/velum – the soft and fleshy part of the roof of the mouth at the back. (Compare **hard palate)**

step-down – a term that refers to the voice moving down to a noticeably lower **pitch** than before for a specific purpose, e.g., the voice goes down to a lower pitch in speeches to mark the end of a topic. (Compare **step-up)**

step-up – a term that refers to the voice moving up to a noticeably higher **pitch** than before for a specific purpose, e.g., when we correct or contradict someone, the voice moves up to a higher pitch on the word/expression that focuses on the difference between our views and also when we wish to indicate the beginning of a new topic in a speech, we move the voice up to a higher pitch. (Compare **step-down)**

stress/word stress – a term used to refer to the degree of force used in producing a **syllable** so that it is heard as being more emphatic than the other syllables in a word, e.g., the first syllable in *basket* and the second in *combine* get stress. (Compare **prominence)** (See also **primary or strong stress** and **secondary or weak stress)**

stressed syllable – a **syllable** that gets **stress** so that it stands out more than the other syllables in a word, e.g., the first syllable in *future* and the second in *mature* are stressed.

stress-timed rhythm – a type of **rhythm** that is characterized by the occurrence of **stressed syllables** at fairly regular intervals of time, irrespective of the number of **unstressed syllables** between them, where the length of an utterance depends on the number of stressed syllables in it, e.g., the rhythm of English speech. (Compare **syllable-timed rhythm)**

strong form – the form of **grammatical words** such as **conjunctions** and **prepositions** when they are **stressed** in connected speech, which contrasts with the other form that is **unstressed**, e.g., *and* /ænd/ in the exchange *A: Did she buy VCDs or DVDs? B: She bought VCDs and DVDs*. (Compare **weak form)**

subject – an element of **clause** structure that comes before the **verb** and is a **noun/pronoun**, **noun phrase** or **noun clause**, which agrees with the verb in **person** and **number**, e.g., *The girl/She* in *The girl/She has bought oranges*, and *The tall boy next door* in *The tall boy next door plays tennis*. (Compare **verb, object, complement** and **adverbial**)

suffix – a **morpheme** that is added at the end of a word, which cannot be used independently but has a distinct meaning and function when added to a word, e.g., *-ness* in *weakness*, *-ity* in *security*, *-ish* in *feverish*, and *-able* in *honourable*. (Compare **prefix**)

syllabic consonant – a **consonant** like /l/ or /n/ that functions as the **centre/nucleus** of a **syllable** that is without a **vowel** and is **unstressed**, e.g., /l/ in *bottle* and /n/ in *button.*

syllable – a unit of speech that is typically larger than a sound but smaller than a word, which consists of a **vowel** at the **centre** that can be preceded by one or more **consonants** and/or followed by one or more consonants, e.g., *con-* and *-test* in *contest*, *fa-*, *-mil*, and *-iar* in *familiar*, and *in-*, *-di*, *-ca*, and *-tion* in *indication*.

syllable-timed rhythm – a type of **rhythm** that is characterized by the occurrence of **syllables** at regular intervals of time, where the length of an utterance depends on the number of syllables in it. (Compare **stress-timed rhythm**)

tempo – a term that refers to the speed of speaking.

termination – a term that refers to the **consonant** sounds that occur after the **vowel** at the centre in a **syllable**, e.g., /t/ in *eat*, /kt/ in *act*, and /lvz/ in *elves*. (Compare **onset**)

tone – a term that refers to the pattern of variation in **pitch**, e.g., the pattern where the pitch moves from relatively high to relatively low is called a falling tone or a **fall** and the pattern where the pitch moves from relatively low to relatively high is called a rising tone or a **rise**.

tone unit/speech unit/thought group – a stretch of speech in which there is one main **tone** and in which words are spoken together without pauses, e.g., *She didn't go to work* has one tone unit, and *Though she was ok, she didn't go to work* has two tone units.

tonic syllable – the **stressed syllable** that gets special emphasis or **prominence** in a **tone unit** so that it stands out from the other stressed syllables in the tone unit, e.g., the first syllable of *party* in *She went to a party* and *He* and *I* in *He didn't do it, I did.*

trachea – the windpipe

transcription – a method of writing down speech sounds systematically and consistently using the **International Phonetic Alphabet**, e.g., the word *feel* is transcribed /fi:l/ and *chip* /tʃɪp/.

unrounded vowels – **vowels** that are **articulated** without the rounding of the lips but with the lips spread, e.g., the vowels in *heat* and *hat*, /i:/ and /æ/. (Compare **rounded vowels**)

unstressed syllable – a **syllable** that does not get **stress** so that it contrasts with a **stressed syllable**, e.g., the second syllable in *future* and the first syllable in *mature* are unstressed in contrast to the first syllable in *future* and the second syllable in *mature*, which are stressed. (Compare **stressed syllable**)

velar – a term used in the classification of **consonant** sounds on the basis of their place of **articulation** to refer to a consonant sound made with the back of the tongue against the **soft palate** or the **velum**, e.g., the initial sounds in *cot* and *got*, /k/ and /g/.

verb – (1) a word that has present and past tense forms, e.g., *uses* and *used, sells* and *sold*, and *does* and *did*. (Compare **adjective, adverb** and **noun**) (See also **main verb/lexical verb** and **auxiliary verb**) (2) an element of **clause** structure that typically follows the **subject** and is a **verb/verb phrase**, which agrees with the subject in **person** and **number** e.g., *travel* in *They travel by train* and *has been teaching* in *She has been teaching for more than twenty years*. (Compare **subject, object, complement** and **adverbial)**

verb phrase – a **main verb/lexical verb** with one or more **auxiliary verbs** before it that functions as the verbal element in a **clause**, e.g., *were sleeping* in *The children were sleeping* and *should have called* in *I should have called the doctor*.

vocal cords – two thick flaps of muscle in the **larynx**, which can produce a faint sound by vibrating.

vocal tract – a term that refers to the whole of the air passage above the **larynx** ending in the mouth or the nose, the shape of which affects the quality of speech sounds.

voiced sounds – sounds produced when the **vocal cords** vibrate making a faint sound, e.g., the initial **consonants** in *bun, gun, joy,* and *zap*, /b/, /g/, /dʒ/, and /z/ and all the **vowel** sounds in English. (Compare **voiceless sounds)**

voiceless sounds – sounds produced without the **vocal cords** vibrating, e.g., the initial **consonants** in *pun, come, chin,* and *son*. /p/, /k/, /tʃ/, and /s/, (Compare **voiced sounds)**

vowels – sounds that are produced without any obstruction or **friction** to the flow of air as it passes from the **larynx** through the **vocal tract** and escapes through the mouth or the nose, e.g., the initial sounds in *art, ill, end,* and *ant*, /ɑː/, /ɪ/, /e/, and /æ/. (Compare **consonants)**

weak form – the form of **grammatical words** such as **conjunctions** and **prepositions** when they are **unstressed** as they are normally in connected speech, which contrasts with the other form that is **stressed**, e.g., *to* /tə/ in *She's going to Paris* and *for* /fə(r)/ in *This is for my daughter*. (Compare **strong form)**

wh-question – a question beginning with a question word such as *what, who, why, where* or *how*, e.g., *What does he do? Where is my phone?* (Compare **yes-no question)**

yes-no question – a question beginning with an **auxiliary verb** followed by the **subject**, which can be answered with *yes* or *no*, e.g., *Are they leaving tomorrow? Have you read his latest book?* (Compare **wh-question)**

Further reading

Most of the course books given here come with audio CDs and cassettes, which you can listen to as you study the different features of English pronunciation.

Arnold, Gordon Frederick, and J.D. O'Connor. (1973) *Intonation of Colloquial English* New York: Prentice Hall Press

Baker, Ann. (2007) *Ship or Sheep? An Intermediate Pronunciation Course* New York: Cambridge University Press 3rd Edition

Baker, Ann. (2007) *Tree or Three? An Elementary Pronunciation Course* New York: Cambridge University Press 2nd Edition

Balasubramanian, T. (1981) *A Textbook of English Phonetics for Indian Students* Madras: Macmillan India Limited

Bowler, Bill, Sarah Cunningham, Peter Moor, Sue Parminter, John Soars, and Liz Soars. (2002) *New Headway Pronunciation Course: Pre-intermediate level (New Headway English Course)* London: Oxford UniversityPress

Bowler, Bill, Sarah Cunningham, Peter Moor, and Sue Parminter. (1999) *New Headway Pronunciation Course: Intermediate level (New Headway English Course)* London: Oxford University Press

Bradford, Barbara. (1989) *Intonation in Context: Intonation Practice for Upper-intermediate and Advanced Learners of English*
New York: Cambridge University Press

Childs, Charlsie. (2004) *Improve Your American English Accent*
New York: McGraw-hill Companies

Cunningham, Sarah, Peter Moor, John Soars, and Liz Soars (2002) *New Headway Pronunciation Course: Elementary*
(*New Headway English Course*)
London: Oxford University Press

Dale, Paulette, and Lillian Poms. (2004) *English Pronunciation Made Simple*
London: Pearson ESL
2nd Edition

Gilbert, Judy B. (2005) *Clear Speech from the Start Basic Pronunciation and Listening Comprehension in North American English*
New York: Cambridge University Press

Gillett, Amy. (2004) *Speak English like an American*
Ann Arbor: Language Success Press

Grant, Linda. (2009) *Well Said: Pronunciation for Clear Communication*.
Boston: Heinle & Heinle
3rd Edition

Hancock, Mark. (2003) *English Pronunciation in Use*
Cambridge: Cambridge University Press

Hancock, Mark. (1996) *Pronunciation Games (Cambridge Copy Collection)*
Cambridge: Cambridge University Press

Hewings, Martin. (2007) *English Pronunciation in Use-Advanced (English Pronunciation in Use)*
Cambridge: Cambridge University Press

Jones, Daniel. (2006) *English Pronouncing Dictionary* Cambridge: Cambridge University Press 17th Edition

Kenworthy, Joanne. (2000) *Pronunciation of English: A Workbook* London: Arnold

Kreidler, Charles W. (2004) *The Pronunciation of English: A Course Book.* Malden, MA: Wiley-Blackwell 2nd Edition

Marks, Jonathan. (2007) *English Pronunciation in Use Elementary* Cambridge: Cambridge University Press

Morley, Joan. (1991) *Extempore Speaking Practice: Improving Spoken English* Ann Arbor: University of Michigan Press

Mortimer, Colin. (1985) *Elements of Pronunciation: Intensive Practice for Intermediate and More Advanced Students* Cambridge: Cambridge University Press

O'Connor, J. D. (1981) *Better English Pronunciation (Cambridge English Language Learning)* New York: Cambridge University Press 2nd Edition

Roach, Peter. (1991) *English Phonetics and Phonology: A Practical Course* Cambridge: Cambridge University Press 2nd Edition

Trim, John. (1975) *English Pronunciation Illustrated.* Cambridge: Cambridge University Press 2nd Edition

Underhill, Adrian. (2005) *Sound Foundations: Learning and Teaching Pronunciation* London: Macmillan ELT 2nd Edition

Wells, J. C. (2006) *English Intonation: An Introduction* Cambridge: Cambridge University Pres

General Books on Language and Pronunciation

Crystal, David. (1988) *The English Language* Harmondsworth: Penguin Books Ltd.

Crystal, David. (2003) *The Cambridge Encyclopaedia of the English Language* Cambridge: Cambridge University Press 2nd Edition

Fromkin, Victoria and Robert Rodman (1993) *An Introduction to Language* New York: Harcourt Brace Jovanovich College Publishers 5th Edition

Gimson, A.C. (1980) *An Introduction to the Pronunciation of English* London: Edward Arnold

Books on Teaching Pronunciation

Brinton, Donna M., Marianne Celce-Murcia, and Janet M. Goodwin. (1996) *Teaching Pronunciation: A Reference for Teachers of English to Speakers of Other Languages* New York: Cambridge University Press

Gilbert, Judy B. (2008) *Teaching Pronunciation Using the Prosody Pyramid* Cambridge: Cambridge University Press

Hewings, Martin. (2004) *Pronunciation Practice Activities: A Resource Book for Teaching English Pronunciation* Cambridge: Cambridge University Press

Kelly, Gerald. (2001) *How to Teach Pronunciation* London: Pearson ESL

Kenworthy, Joanne. (1987) *Teaching English Pronunciation (Longman Handbooks for Language Teachers)* White Plains, NY: Longman Publishing Group

Pennington, Martha C. (1996) *Phonology in English Language Teaching: An International Approach (Applied Linguistics and Language Study)* London: Longman

Online Resources

The Introduction gave you information about (a) a few very useful websites, where you can learn how individual sounds of English are pronounced and (b) two online dictionaries that give you the correct pronunciation of words.

(a)

http://www.teachingenglish.org.uk/try/resources/pronunciation/phonemic-chart-0
http://www.bbc.co.uk/worldservice/learningenglish/grammar/pron/sounds/index.shtml
www.uiowa.edu/~acadtech/phonetics/**english**/frameset.html

(b)

http://www.macmillandictionary.com/
www.howjsay.

There are several other websites that can help you in your study of English pronunciation and help you speak English better. Some of them are given here. Try them out.

www.fonetiks.org
www.rong-chang.com/pronunciation.htm
www.soundsof**english**.org/**pronunciation**/index.htm
www.manythings.org/pp
www.shiporsheep.com
www.international.ouc.bc.ca/**pronunciation**
www.rachels**english**.com
www.**english**club.com
www.youtube.com/user/JenniferESL
www.pronuncian.com/podcast.aspx

www.**english**medialab.com/**pronunciation**.html
http://www.focusenglish.com/dialogues/conversation.html
www.isabelperez.com/tesllinks.htm
www.englishconversations.org
www.englishcentral.com
www.englishspeak.com
www.podcastsinenglish.com

Key

2.2

2. Consonants
   Voiced sounds
   Nasal sounds
   Vowels
   Velar sounds
   Oral sounds
   Alveolar sounds
   Voiceless sounds

2.3

1.

fig	bag	bit
broom	grim	group
toss	less	lot
ditch	patch	pick
odd	ass	ash
pad	feed	fat
gate	doubt	daze
with	moth	miss
size	rouse	right
sin	din	thick
pup	keep	cut
back	knock	nag
ate	ease	eel
tent	saint	send
boy	jay	toy

post	haste	most
ship	chap	chill
on	oaf	in
burn	torn	turf
charm	hard	heart

2.4

2. (i) *food* and *mood* are pronounced with /uː/ but *good* and *hood* are pronounced with /ʊ/.

(ii)

heed	heat
been	bean
see	sea

(iii) *cheap, chore, church* and *chimp* are pronounced with /tʃ/ and *chord, chorus* and *chronic* are pronounced with /k/.

(iv)

cede	seed
cent	sent
cereal	serial

(v) 'w' in *wrong*
'p' in *psychology*
'l' in *palm*
'g' in *align*
'k' in *knowledge*
'b' in *tomb*
'b' in *doubt*
'd' in *Wednesday*

(vi) /w/ in *queen* and *one* and /j/ in *uniform, curious, computer* and *mutual*.

(vii)

ball - 3	seed - 3	free - 3	butter - 4 or 5(if 'r' is pronounced)
thumb - 3	ring - 3	trunk - 5	simple - 5
carry - 4	kindle - 5	bury - 4	phone - 3
neat - 3	beauty - 5	wheat - 3	fear - 2 or 3(if 'r' is pronounced)

3. (i) (1) /dʒ/ (2) /d/ (3) /tʃ/ (4) /f/ (5) /z/ (6) /s/ (7) /g/ (8) /k/ (9) /m/ (10) /ŋ/ (11) /l/ (12) /h/ (13) /n/ (14) /v/ (15) /f/ (16) /θ/ (17) /ð/ (18) /ʃ/ (19) /z/ (20) /ʒ/ (21) /j/ (22) /w// (23) /θ/ (24) /b/ (25) /p/ (26) /ð/ (27) /t/

(ii)

/z/	**z**ip	i**s**	ha**z**e	**z**ombie	cra**z**e	free**z**e	lo**s**e
/ʒ/	lei**su**re						
/tʃ/	**ch**eap	**ch**ip	tou**ch**	bea**ch**	**ch**at	bun**ch**	
	pic**t**ure	clin**ch**	ma**tch**	**ch**ime	crun**ch**		
/s/	**s**eep	bo**ss**	le**ss**	**s**eat	ki**ss**	lo**ss**	mer**c**y
/ʃ/	**sh**eep	i**ss**ue	**sh**ine	**sh**ut	gu**sh**	hu**sh**	
	ma**ch**ine	**sh**iver	fre**sh**	har**sh**			
/dʒ/	**j**eep	he**dg**e	**j**am	**g**em	**g**entle	grud**g**e	ma**j**or
	June	**j**acket	crin**g**e	**g**ene	ma**g**ic		

L2.2

/tʃ/	/w/
/l/	/z/
/h/	/s/
/dʒ/	/b/
/j/	/θ/
/d/	/t/
/n/	/p/
/f/	/ð/
/g/	/r/
/k/	/m/
/ʃ/	/v/

4. (i) (1) /ɪ/ (2) /ə/ (3) /ɑː/ (4) /æ/ (5) /iː/ (6) /ʌ/ (7) /e/ (8) /ɒ/ or /ɑː/ (9) /uː/ (10) /ɔː/ (11) /ʊ/ (12) /ɜː/ (13) /aɪ/ (14) /æ/ (15) /ʌ/ (16) /aʊ/ (17) /eɪ/ (18) /ɔɪ/ (19) /ɪə/ or /ɪ/ (20) /ʊə/ or /ʊ/ (21) /ɒ/ or /ɑː/ (22) /eə/ or /e/ (23) /əʊ/or/oʊ/ (24) /eɪ/ (25) /ʊə/ or /ʊ/ (26) /eə/ or /e/ (27) /əʊ/or/oʊ/

(ii)

/e/	**e**ditor	**e**mpty	s**e**t	p**e**n	**e**gg
/aɪ/	**i**tem	**i**dea	n**igh**t	n**i**nth	**i**dentity
/iː/	**e**qual	**e**vil	b**ea**t	tr**ea**t	**ea**gle
/ɑː/	**ar**my	**ar**gue	p**ar**k	c**ar**d	**au**nt
/æ/	**a**ngry	**a**bsent	h**a**nd	p**a**ck	**a**dd
/ɒ/ or /ɑː/	**o**x	**o**ffice	p**o**t	c**o**t	**o**bject

/uː/	**cool**	**soon**	**mood**					
/ʊ/	**good**	**put**	**wood**					
/ʌ/	**gun**	**umbrella**	**love**	**understand**	**money**			
/ə/	**polite**	**account**	**about**	**collect**	**afraid**	**affair**	**obtain**	**material**
/ɜː/	**turn**	**earn**	**bird**	**urgent**	**search**			
/ɔː/	**lord**	**author**	**organ**	**short**	**orbit**	**score**		
/ɪə/ or /ɪ/	**ear**	**dear**	**tear**	**near**				
/eɪ/	**aim**	**same**	**day**	**aid**	**gate**			
/aɪ/	**ice**	**time**	**kind**	**idea**	**ivory**	**kite**		
/aʊ/	**owl**	**loud**	**sound**	**down**				
/ɔɪ/	**oil**	**boil**	**poison**	**oyster**	**join**			
/əʊ/or/oʊ/	**old**	**coach**	**load**	**own**	**open**	**gold**		

L2.3

/e/	/ʊə/ or /ʊ/
/ɜː/	/ɒ/ or /ɑː/
/uː/	/ɪə/ or /ɪ/
/ʌ/	/eə/ or /e/
/aɪ/	/ɑː/
/iː/	/ɔɪ/
/ɪ/	/æ/
/ɔː/	/eɪ/
/aʊ/	/ə/ /ɔː/
/ʊ/	/əʊ/ or /oʊ/

3.1

Focusing on description and classification of English consonants

2. (i) (a)

market	merit
normal	knowledge
politics	pencil
unity	yellow
begin	beautiful
kitchen	canal
gallant	government
challenge	cheerful
generous	jewelry
welcome	warmth

terror	telephone
dynamic	determine
shortage	shiver
thesis	thought
vehement	variety
certain	science
them	therefore
feminine	phenomenon
heredity	humour
little	lovely
writing	remember
zoom	zest

(b) /ʒ/ and /ŋ/

(ii) (a)

board	rub
violet	derive
magic	room
charming	teach
lazy	bottle
temple	permit
citizen	notice
kneel	certain
genuine	damage
pattern	soap
philosophy	safe
diversion	solid
theme	south
careful	trick
thus	breathe
gaudy	league
shooting	polish
zip	browse

(b) /ʒ/ at the end of 'beige' and /ŋ/ at the end of 'long'.

(c) /r/ in 'rain', /w/ in 'wish', /j/ in 'usual', and /h/ in 'hungry'.

(iii)

youth	theory
model	luxury
tribe	balance
captain	knife
lodge	gentle

	zip	patient			
	poem	mother			
	phrase	zenith			
	cherish	shield			
	soothe	there			
	batch	choice			
	knock	kindness			
	wig	gate			
	grief	feast			
	dominate	table			
	justice	sensitive			
	valid	deceive			
	shave	vacation			

(iv)	Plosive	desire	dominant	primary	grateful	terrible
		character	chemistry	gaudy	pleasure	chord
		cancel	charismatic	question	qualify	kingdom
		tremendous	breakable			
	Fricative	physics	thread	circle	showman	sacrifice
		variety	vegetable	pseudonym	psychology	therefore
		hurricane	phenomenon	chivalry		
	Affricate	jubilant	generous	charge	general	judicious
		chafe				
	Nasal	manager	number	knowledge	material	knife
	Approximant	wisdom	yesterday	wonderful	wings	yellow
		round	writing			
(v)	Bilabial	bottom	bomb	egotism	morpheme	
	Labio-dental	positive	triumph	belief	achieve	tough
		housewife				
	Dental	mouth	strength	breathe		
	Alveolar	bottle	reflect	content	ideal	contrast
		elephant	inspect	complex	civilize	attract
		division	excess	disguise	devise	wise
		prize	house	spice		
	Palato-alveolar	sandwich	language	hostage	insecure	
		divulge	exchange	arrange	polish	
		package	fanfare	teach		

Velar	dialog	magic	belong	bank
	drawing	hanging	flag	monarch
	unique	graphic	long	plastic

(vi) /p/ is bilabial whereas /t/ is alveolar. Both are voiceless plosives.
/b/ is bilabial whereas /g/ is velar. Both are voiced plosives.
/k/ is voiceless whereas /g/ is voiced. Both are velar plosives.
/d/ is a plosive whereas /z/ is a fricative. Both are alveolar and voiced.

(vii) (a) /ŋ/ is a velar nasal whereas /n/ is an alveolar nasal.
/ŋ/ is a velar nasal whereas /g/ is a velar plosive.

(b) /dʒ/ is a palate-alveolar affricate whereas /d/ is an alveolar plosive
/dʒ/ is an affricate whereas /ʒ/ is a fricative.

(c) /f/ is a labiodental fricative whereas /p/ is a bilabial plosive.
/f/ is a labiodental fricative whereas /h/ is a glottal fricative.

(viii) (a) /p/ is similar to /m/ in the same way as /t/ is to /n/ and /k/ to /ŋ/.
(b) /t/ is different from /s/ in the same way as /d/ is from /z/.
(c) The difference between /tʃ/and /dʒ/ is the same as that between /θ/ and /ð/, /ʃ/ and /ʒ/, and /k/ and /g/.

Focusing on correct pronunciation of English consonants

1. (i) /s/ or /z/
(ii) /m/
(iii) /k/ or /g/
(iv) /θ/ or /ð/
(v) /r/
(vi) /h/
(vii) /l/
(viii) /p/ or /b/
(ix) /n/
(x) /f/ or /v/
(xi) /t/ or /d/
(xii) /ŋ/

L3.1

SOUND	**1**	**2**	**3**	**4**	**5**	**6**	**7**	**8**	**9**
/p/	M	B	E	B	E	M	E	M	B
/b/	M	B	E	B	M	M	E	E	B
/t/	B	E	M	E	B	M	M	B	B
/d/	M	E	M	E	B	E	B	M	B
/k/	B	M	E	M	B	B	E	E	M
/g/	E	M	M	B	E	E	M	B	B
/tʃ/	E	E	E	B	M	B	M	B	M
/dʒ/	B	M	B	E	B	E	M	E	B
/θ/	B	E	E	M	M	B	E	B	M
/f/	E	M	M	M	B	B	B	E	E
/v/	B	M	E	M	B	M	E	E	B
/s/	M	M	B	B	E	E	E	B	M
/ʃ/	B	E	M	E	M	B	M	B	E
/l/	B	M	B	M	E	M	E	B	E

L3.2 tool pool pop top tan pan pub tub pale tale teach peach

/p/	/t/
2	1
1	2
2	1
1	2
1	2
2	1

L3.3 (i) A (ii) A (iii) B (iv) A (v) A

5. tycoon
   tout
   pirate
   pioneer
   teller
   proprietor
   punter
   tenant
   techie
   plaintiff

L3.4 feel peel pool fool pun fun full pull fail pail fond pond

/p/	/f/
2	1
1	2
1	2
2	1
2	1
2	1

L3.5 (i) A (ii) B (iii) A (iv) B (v) A

9. folder
peripheral
pittance
fledgling
profile
franchise
format
portfolio
freeware
protocol

L3.6 dad bad bark dark bout doubt die buy day bay bump dump

/b/	/d/
2	1
1	2
1	2
2	1
2	1
1	2

L3.7 (i) B (ii) A (iii) A (iv) B (v) A

13. bandwidth
dividend
default
browser
desktop
barcode
debenture
broadband
buffer
download

L3.8	veer beer	bail veil	bole vole	very berry	vet bet	bile vile
		/b/			/v/	
		2			1	
		1			2	
		1			2	
		2			1	
		2			1	
		1			2	

L3.9 (i) B (ii) B (iii) A (iv) B (v) B

17. virus
benchmark
backup
voucher
bequest
version
Bluetooth
vendor
bubble
venture

L3.10	cheap jeep	jinx chinks	choice Joyce	Jap chap	cheese jeez	cherry jerry
		/tʃ/			/dʒ/	
		1			2	
		2			1	
		1			2	
		2			1	
		1			2	
		1			2	

L3.11 (i) A (ii) B (iii) A (iv) B (v) A

21. generation
chat
channel
Java
charter
jitters
charge
junk
chip
joystick

L3.12	through true	tin thin	therm term	thick tick	tie thigh	taught thought
		/t/			/θ/	
		2			1	
		1			2	
		2			1	
		2			1	
		1			2	
		1			2	

L3.13 (i) A (ii) A (iii) B (iv) B (v) A

25. taskbar
threshold
tab
throwaway
tariff
thrift
terminal
throughput
template
thread

L3.14	vet wet	vicar wicker	went vent	worse verse	wise vice	vile while
		/v/			/w/	
		1			2	
		1			2	
		2			1	
		2			1	
		2			1	
		1			2	

L3.15 (i) B (ii) B (iii) A (iv) B (v) A

29. webzine
videoconferencing
warranty
vacuum
windfall
watchdog
validity
watershed
venue
veteran

L3.16 veil fail volley folly focal vocal veal feel veer fear view few

/v/	/f/
1	2
1	2
2	1
1	2
1	2
1	2

L3.17 (i) A (ii) B (iii) A (iv) A (v) A

33. floppy
 vocabulary
 fiber
 veto
 fax
 volt
 flag
 verdict
 firewall
 vanguard

L3.18 thank sank saw thaw theme seem sigh thigh thought sought song thong

/θ/	/s/
1	2
2	1
1	2
2	1
1	2
2	1

L3.19 (i) A (ii) B (iii) A (iv) B (v) A

37. software
theatre
spam
theology
slump
therapy
server
thermostat
scam
throttle

L3.20	same shame	sign shine	short sort	sun shun	shoot soot	sop shop
		/ʃ/			/s/	
		2			1	
		2			1	
		1			2	
		2			1	
		1			2	
		2			1	

L3.21 (i) A (ii) B (iii) B (iv) A (v) B

41. stocks
shell
scrollbar
shareware
scrip
shift
scanner
shortcoming
stipend
showpiece

L3.22 sheaf chief cheer shear shop chop chit shit chew shoe shore chore

/ʃ/	/tʃ/
1	2
2	1
1	2
2	1
2	1
1	2

L3.23 (i) B (ii) A (iii) B (iv) A (v) B

45. changeover
sham
checkout
sheaf
charger
shrine
checkmate
shuttle
chime
sheen

L3.24 law raw ray lay lip rip lush rush road load lot rot

/l/	/r/
1	2
2	1
1	2
1	2
2	1
1	2

L3.25 (i) B (ii) A (iii) B (iv) A (v) B

49. log
ripper
lapse
router
lease
rally
levy
retail
lull
rigging

3.2

L3.26

package	…A………	topic	…A………	table	…A………
batch	…………..	coffee	…A………	danger	……………
camel	…A………	gallon	……………	bicycle	……………
kindness	…A………	public	…A………	ticket	…A………
guidance	……………	damp	……………	picture	…A………
borrow	……………	culture	…A………	custom	…A………
district	……………	beauty	……………	taxi	…A………
pension	…A………	guard	……………	target	…A………
college	…A………	budget	……………	guest	…………..
doubt	……………	paint	…A………	google	……………

L3.27

	/p/	/t/	/k/
tackle		A	
repeat	A		
contest		A	
skilful			
remote			
studio			
gallant			
colour			A
gipsy			
habit			

daughter			
sputnik			
surprise			
patient	A		
fabric			
keyboard			A
stable			
topic		A	
pencil	A		
special			
tourist		A	
detail		A	
grope			
capture			A
doubt			
direct			
subject			
mountain			
cabinet			A
happen			
focus			
pursuit			
merit			
gossip			
forest			
mistake			
palace	A		
secret			
technical		A	
polish	A		
flop			
kitchen			A
discount			
rocket			
country			A
perfect	A		
temper		A	
better			

L3.28

(i)	(ii)	(iii)	(iv)	(v)	(vi)	(vii)	(viii)	(ix)	(x)
B	A	A	B	A	B	A	B	B	A
A	B	B	A	B	A	B	A	A	B

(xi)	(xii)	(xiii)	(xiv)	(xv)	(xvi)	(xvii)	(xviii)	(xix)	(xx)
B	A	B	A	B	A	B	A	A	A
A	B	A	B	A	B	A	B	B	B

L3.29

computers	…z……	charities	…iz……	missiles	…z……
curtains	…z……	students	…s……	memos	…z……
currencies	…iz……	museums	…z……	colleges	…iz……
maps	…s……	shelves	…z……	horses	…iz……
degrees	…z……	pitches	…iz……	drugs	…z……
months	…s……	washes	…iz……	husbands	…z……
ratings	…z……	mouths	…s……	windows	…z……
breaks	…s……	surprises	…iz……	props	…s……

L3.30

promised	…t……	selected	…id……	demanded	…id……
bagged	…d……	kicked	…t……	lapped	…t……
logged	…d……	compared	…d……	sustained	…d……
survived	…d……	provided	…id……	permitted	…id……
tapped	…t……	attached	…t……	lodged	…d……
married	…id……	helped	…t……	travelled	…d……
maimed	…d……	arrested	…id……	polished	…t……
flattered	…d……	boiled	…d……	attacked	…t……

L3.31 There is /r/ in American pronunciation but not in British pronunciation.

3.3

L3.32

(i)	(ii)	(iii)	(iv)	(v)
B	B	A	B	B
A	A	B	A	A

(vi)	(vii)	(viii)	(ix)	(x)
B	A	B	B	B
A	B	A	A	A

3.4

1. quadruple
   critique
   quake
   queasy

oblique
quest
grotesque
quell
quiet
physique

L3.33

	/ks/	/gz/
excavate	......√.......	....
example	....	......√.......
exceed	......√.......	....
excellent	......√.......	....
exam	....	......√.......
except	......√.......	....
excess	......√.......	....
exact	....	......√.......
exchange	......√.......	....
excite	......√.......	....
exclaim	......√.......	....
excise	......√.......	....
exclude	......√.......	....
execute	......√.......	....
executive	....	......√.......
exercise	......√.......	....
exertion	....	......√.......
exhale	......√.......	....
excuse	......√.......	....
exemption	....	......√.......
exhaust	....	......√.......
exhibit	....	......√.......
exile	......√.......	....
exist	....	......√.......
exit	......√.......	....
exotic	....	......√.......
expand	......√.......	....
expect	......√.......	....

exorbitant	....	......√......
expel	......√......	....
expense	......√......	....
experience	......√......	....
expert	......√......	....
explain	......√......	....
explicit	......√......	....
explode	......√......	....
exploit	......√......	....
explore	......√......	....
export	......√......	....
exuberant	....	......√......
expose	......√......	....
express	......√......	....
exquisite	......√......	....
extend	......√......	....
extra	......√......	....
extinct	......√......	....
extreme	......√......	....
extricate	......√......	....

L3.34

	/n/	/ŋ/
ankle	....	......√......
answer	......√......	....
blanket	....	......√......
bland	......√......	....
bunker	....	......√......
bundle	......√......	....
drink	....	......√......
flannel	......√......	....
flank	....	......√......
hanker	....	......√......
handle	......√......	....
junk	....	......√......
junction	....	......√......
tanker	....	......√......
tangent	......√......	....

L3.35

	/ʃ/	/ʒ/
dimension	......√.......	....
admission	......√.......	....
decision	....	......√.......
revulsion	......√.......	....
extension	......√.......	....
explosion	....	......√.......
seclusion	....	......√.......
concession	......√.......	....
collision	....	......√.......
expansion	......√.......	....
evasion	....	......√.......
profession	......√.......	....
provision	....	......√.......
occasion	....	......√.......
aggression	......√.......	....
compassion	......√.......	....
corrosion	....	......√.......
commission	......√.......	....
invasion	....	......√.......
precision	....	......√.......
submission	......√.......	....
succession	......√.......	....
conclusion	....	......√.......
recession	......√.......	....
television	....	......√.......
illusion	....	......√.......
comprehension	......√.......	....
confusion	....	......√.......
revision	....	......√.......
repression	......√.......	....

L3.36

	American	***British***
excursion	....../ʒ/.......	....../ʃ/.......
expulsion	....../ʃ/.......	....../ʃ/.......
perversion	....../ʒ/.......	....../ʃ/.......

immersion	……/ʃ/……	……/ʃ/…….
intermission	……/ʃ/…….	……/ʃ/…….
inversion	……/ʒ/…….	……/ʃ/…….
aspersion	……/ʒ/…….	……/ʃ/…….
emulsion	……/ʃ/……	……/ʃ/……
diversion	……/ʒ/…….	……/ʃ/……
dissension	……/ʃ/……	……/ʃ/……
aversion	……/ʒ/…….	……/ʃ/……

L3.37

	/tʃ/	/k/	/ʃ/
chafe	……√…….	…………	…………
chameleon	…………	……√…….	…………
chancellor	……√…….	…………	…………
chandelier	…………	…………	……√…….
chagrin	…………	…………	……√…….
chaos	…………	……√…….	…………
chapter	……√…….	…………	…………
chaperone	…………	…………	……√…….
character	…………	……√…….	…………
charity	……√…….	…………	…………
charade	…………	…………	……√…….
charisma	…………	……√…….	…………
cheerful	……√…….	…………	…………
chef	…………	…………	……√…….
chemo-therapy	…………	……√…….	…………
chivalry	…………	…………	……√…….
choice	……√…….	…………	…………
chauffeur	…………	…………	……√…….
choir	…………	……√…….	…………
chore	……√…….	…………	…………
chauvinism	…………	…………	……√…….
chord	…………	……√…….	…………
choreography	…………	……√…….	…………
chronology	…………	……√…….	…………
chunk	……√…….	…………	…………
churl	……√…….	…………	…………

arch	......√.......	....	....
architect	....	......√.......	....
avalanche	....	....	......√.......
bachelor	......√.......	....	....
brochure	....	....	......√.......
echo	....	......√.......	....
achieve	......√.......	....	....
launch	......√.......	....	....
mechanic	....	......√.......	....
niche	....	....	......√.......
ochre	....	......√.......	....

7. (a)

(i) whistle	(ii) knob	(iii) campaign	(iv) budget
(v) hymn	(vi) doubt	(vii) folk	(viii) qualms
(ix) debt	(x) align	(xi) wriggle	(xii) foreigner
(xiii) salmon	(xiv) crumbs	(xv) castle	(xvi) dodge
(xvii) stalk	(xviii) diaphragm	(xix) condemn	(xx) writ
(xxi) grudge	(xxii) malign	(xxiii) balm	(xxiv) smudge
(xxv) yolk	(xxvi) baulk	(xxvii) knot	(xxviii) sovereign
(xxix) nudge	(xxx) know-how	(xxxi) wedge	(xxxii) wrinkle

L3.38

	American		***British***
accuse		no difference	
adduce	...no /j/......		...with /j/...
avenue	...no /j/......		...with /j/...
compute		no difference	
conducive	...no /j/......		...with/j/...
confuse		no difference	
deuce	...no /j/......		...with/j/...
dubious	...no /j/......		...with/j/...
dupe	...no /j/......		...with/j/...
duration		no difference	
eunuch		no difference	
euphemism		no difference	
exude		no difference	
exuberant		no difference	

feudal		no difference
fusion		no difference
humorous		no difference
illusion	…no /j/……	…with/j/...
immune		no difference
impunity		no difference
neutralize	…no /j/……	…with/j/...
newspaper	…no /j/……	…with/j/...
nutrition	…no /j/……	…with/j/...
puny		no difference
ruse		no difference
tube	…no /j/……	…with/j/...
Tuesday	…no /j/……	…with/j/...

4.1

Focusing on description and classification of English vowels

1.

	Front	**Central**	**Back**
Close (High)			
Rounded			…/uː/…fool…… …/ʊ/… full……
Unrounded	…/iː/…feet……… …/ɪ/…fit…………		
Mid			
Rounded			…/ɔː/……fall……
Unrounded	…/e/…fetch………	…/ɜː/……firm….. …/ə/……familiar..	
Open (Low)			
Rounded			…/ɒ/……fog…….
Unrounded	…/æ/……fan……	…/ʌ/……fun……	…/ɑː/……far…….

2. /iː/ is front and unrounded, whereas /uː/ is back and rounded. Both are close vowels.
   /ʌ/ is central whereas /ɑː/ is back. Both are open and unrounded.
   /ɒ/ is open whereas /ɔː/ is mid. Both are back and rounded.

3. (i) /ɜː/ is mid and central, whereas /ɑː/ is open and back. Both are unrounded.
   /ɜː/ is central and unrounded, whereas /ɔː/ is back and rounded. Both are mid.

   (ii) /ʌ/ is central and unrounded, whereas /ɒ/ is back and rounded. Both are open.
   /ʌ/ is open whereas /ə/ is mid. Both are central and unrounded.

   (iii) /e/ is mid whereas /æ/ is open. Both are front and unrounded.
   /e/ is mid whereas /ɪ/ is close. Both are front and unrounded.

4.

foot	put
dirt	pearl
park	card
bank	lax
teeth	beat
tin	live
luck	judge
box	knot
set	dead
glue	rule
torn	form

5.

Ending in /ɪ/	Ending in /ʊ/	Ending in /ə/
…/eɪ/………fame…….	…/aʊ/………how……	…/ɪə/………fear………
…/aɪ/………fine……..	…/əʊ/ or /oʊ/ ….go…….	…/eə/………fare………
…/ɔɪ/………coin……		…/ʊə/………tour……..

6. (i) /aɪ/, /eɪ/, /ɔɪ/, and /aʊ/
   (ii) /əʊ/ British and /oʊ/ American
   (iii) /ɪə/, /eə/, and /ʊə/

7.

fight	price
cow	house

noise	toy
hair	care
cake	say
beer	near
sure	poor
nose	tone
rise	buy
raise	praise

Focusing on correct pronunciation of English vowels

L4.1

(i)	√	√	×	√
(ii)	√	√	√	×
(iii)	√	×	√	√
(iv)	√	√	√	×
(v)	×	√	√	√
(vi)	√	×	√	√
(vii)	√	√	×	√
(viii)	√	√	×	√

L4.2

(i)	√	√	√	×
(ii)	√	×	√	√
(iii)	√	√	×	√
(iv)	√	×	√	√
(v)	×	√	√	√
(vi)	√	√	×	√
(vii)	√	×	√	√
(viii)	√	√	√	×

L4.3

(i)	×	√	√	√
(ii)	√	√	×	√
(iii)	√	√	√	×
(iv)	√	√	×	√
(v)	√	×	√	√
(vi)	×	√	√	√
(vii)	√	√	×	√
(viii)	√	√	×	√

L4.4

(i)	√	×	√	√
(ii)	√	√	√	×
(iii)	√	×	√	√
(iv)	√	√	√	×
(v)	√	√	×	√
(vi)	√	√	√	×
(vii)	√	√	×	√
(viii)	√	√	√	×

L4.5

(i)	√	×	√	√
(ii)	√	√	×	√
(iii)	√	√	×	√
(iv)	√	×	√	√
(v)	√	√	×	√
(vi)	√	×	√	√
(vii)	√	√	√	×
(viii)	√	×	√	√

L4.6

(i)	√	√	√	×
(ii)	√	√	×	√
(iii)	√	√	√	×
(iv)	√	×	√	√
(v)	√	√	√	×
(vi)	×	√	√	√
(vii)	√	√	×	√
(viii)	√	×	√	√

L4.7

(i)	2	1	1	2
(ii)	1	2	1	2
(iii)	2	1	2	1
(iv)	2	1	2	1
(v)	1	2	1	2
(vi)	2	1	1	2
(vii)	2	1	2	1
(viii)	2	1	2	1

L4.8

(i)	1	2	1	2
(ii)	1	2	2	1
(iii)	1	2	2	1
(iv)	2	1	1	2
(v)	1	2	1	2
(vi)	1	2	1	2
(vii)	1	2	1	2
(viii)	2	1	1	2

L4.9

(i)	1	2	1	2
(ii)	2	1	1	2
(iii)	1	2	2	1
(iv)	1	1	2	2
(v)	1	2	1	2
(vi)	2	1	1	2

L4.10

(i)	1	2	2	1
(ii)	2	1	1	2
(iii)	1	2	2	1
(iv)	2	1	1	2
(v)	1	2	2	1
(vi)	2	1	1	2
(vii)	1	2	2	1
(viii)	1	2	1	2

L4.11

(i)	1	2	1	2
(ii)	2	1	1	2
(iii)	1	2	2	1
(iv)	2	1	1	2
(v)	2	1	1	2
(vi)	1	2	1	2

L4.12	bin bean	peel pill	rid reed	teak tick	fist feast	heap hip
	(1)	/iː/		/ɪ/		
		2		1		
		1		2		
		2		1		
		1		2		
		2		1		
		1		2		

L4.13 (i) A (ii) B (iii) B (iv) A (v) A

L4.14	beg big	pick peck	hell hill	spill spell	led lid	rid red
		/ɪ/			/e/	
		2			1	
		1			2	
		2			1	
		1			2	
		2			1	
		1			2	

L4.15 (i) A (ii) B (iii) A (iv) A (v) B

L4.16	bet bat	ten tan	gas guess	had head	less lass	wreck rack
		/e/			/æ/	
		1			2	
		1			2	
		2			1	
		2			1	
		1			2	
		1			2	

L4.17 (i) B (ii) B (iii) A (iv) B (v) A

L4.18	puck perk	turn ton	curt cut	fun fern	third thud	shut shirt
		/ʌ/			/ɜː/	
		1			2	
		2			1	
		2			1	
		1			2	
		2			1	
		1			2	

L4.19 (i) A (ii) B (iii) A (iv) B (v) B

L4.20	/e/	/eɪ/
pen pain	1	2
bell bail	1	2
blade bled	2	1
fade fed	2	1
gate get	2	1
lace less	2	1

L4.21 (i) A (ii) A (iii) B (iv) B (v) A

L4.22	/ʌ/	/ɒ/ or /ɑː/
putt pot	1	2
bog bug	2	1
hut hot	1	2
mock muck	2	1
dug dog	1	2
shot shut	2	1

L4.23 (i) B (ii) B (iii) A (iv) B (v) A

L4.24	/ʌ/	/ɔː/ or /ɑː/
cull call	1	2
balk buck	2	1
mull mall	1	2
gall gull	2	1
dun dawn	1	2
sun sawn	1	2

L4.25 (i) A (ii) B (iii) B (iv) A (v) A

L4.26	/ɑː/	/ɔː/
par pore	1	2
shard shored	1	2
dork dark	2	1
court cart	2	1
bar bore	1	2
fore far	2	1

L4.27 (i) A (ii) A (iii) B (iv) A (v) B

L4.28	purr par	cart curt	hurt heart	Karl curl	lurk lark	barn burn
		/ɑː/			/ɜː/	
		2			1	
		1			2	
		2			1	
		1			2	
		2			1	
		1			2	

L4.29 (i) A (ii) B (iii) A (iv) B (v) A

L4.30	turn torn	cur core	port pert	fur fore	sore sir	pore purr
		/ɜː/			/ɔː/	
		1			2	
		1			2	
		2			1	
		1			2	
		2			1	
		2			1	

L4.31 (i) B (ii) B (iii) A (iv) A (v) B

4.2

L4.32					
support	carbon	honour	forget	garbage	author
apartment	parcel	thermal	excellent	person	humorous
alimony	exuberant	matrimony	order	formal	purpose
advertisement	ceremony	urban	exorbitant	ordinarily	doctor
monastery	arbitrary	sugar	fever	conserve	lawyer

L4.33 British pronunciation has the vowel /ɑː/ whereas American pronunciation has /æ/.

4.3

L4.34					
(i) A B	(ii) B A	(iii) B A	(iv) A B	(v) B A	(vi) A B
(vii) A B	(viii) B A	(xi) A B	(x) B A	(xi) A B	(xii) B A
(xiii) A B	(xiv) B A	(xv) B A			

2.	(i) fortunate (/ət/)	delegate (/ət/)	(ii) estimate (/ət/)	exaggerated (/eɪtɪd/)
	(iii) investigate (/eɪt/)	legitimate (/ət/)	(iv) desperate (/ət/)	coordinate (/eɪt/)
	(v) appropriate (/ət/)	dominate (/eɪt)	(vi) delicate (/ət/)	communicate (/eɪt/)
	(vii) terminate (/eɪt/)	exasperate (/eɪt/)	(viii) evaluate (eɪt)	adequate (/ət/)
	(ix) educate (/eɪt/)	graduate (/ət/)	(x) accurate (/ət/)	fabricated (/eɪtɪd/)

4.4

L4.35 The pronunciation of these words does not follow the rules described under (1) (a), (b), (c), (d) and (e).

give	live (verb)				
bold	both	host	most	post	ton
come	done	gone	glove	love	lose
move	none	some			
bush	push	put	truth		

2.

(i) proof	(ii) journey	(iii) hoax	(iv) mould	(v) food
(vi) priest	(vii) coach	(viii) wound	(ix) height	(x) deal
(xi) treat	(xii) south	(xiii) peace	(xiv) boom	(xv) deaf
(xvi) diet	(xvii) coarse	(xviii) wood	(xix) peasant	(xx) bout
(xxi) brief	(xxii) siege	(xxiii) touch	(xxiv) hood	(xxv) sweat
(xxvi) reach	(xxvii) weight	(xxviii) deceive	(xxix) beige	(xxx) foam

5.1

L5.1

national	…3…	students	…2…	umbrella	…3…	popular	…3…
saintly	…2…	angle	…2…	might	…1…	consult	…2…
idea	…2…	promise	…2…	season	…2…	smile	…1…
neither	…2…	twelfth	…1…	social	…2…	about	…2…
hastily	…3…	English	…2…	number	…2…	courtship	…2…
people	…2…	friendliness	…3…	textiles	…2…	pressurize	…3…
painfully	…3…	foreign	…2…	shrewd	…1…	attempt	…2…
occasion	…3…	baggage	…2…	eyes	…1…	stand	…1…
control	…2…	calm	…1…	pleasantly	…3…	heaven	…2…
callous	…2…	loyalty	…2…	lights	…1…	paper	…2…
flower	…1…	waterfall	…3…	college	…2…	wonderful	…3…
phonetics	…3…	history	…3…	paint	…1…	palmist	…2…

L5.2

2 syllables	3 syllables	4 syllables	5 syllables
student	numerous	magnificent	organization
degree	computer	humidity	international
passport	beautiful	stabilizer	verification
transport	temperature	comparison	argumentation
	apartment	graduation	
	prominent	certificate	
	publisher		
	programming		
	disallow		

'parliamentarian' has 6 syllables

L5.3

strike	...CCCVC...	next	...CVCCC...	both	...CVC...	true	...CCV...
height	...CVC...	texts	...CVCCCC	first	..CV(C)CC..	count	...CVCC...
joy	...CV......	church	...CV(C)C...	more	...CV(C)...	aim	...VC...
clasps	..CCVCCC..	push	...CVC...	catch	...CVC...	lamp	...CVCC...
scream	...CCCVC...	prompt	..CCVCCC..	third	...CV(C)C..	hurt	..CV(C)C..
ease	...VC......	spine	...CCVC...	queen	...CCVC...	twist	...CCVCC...
kite	...CVC......	cough	...CVC...	ought	...VC...	bike	...CVC...
swing	...CCVC...	hanged	...CVCC...	depth	...CVCC...	thirst	..CV(C)CC..
self	...CVCC...	float	...CCVC...	pure	...CV(C)...	noise	...CVC...
please	...CCVC...	child	...CVCC...	dwell	...CCVC...	warmth	..CV(C)CC..
widen	...CVCC...	theirs	...CV(C)C...	fifths	...CVCCC...	tempts	..CVCCCC..
key	......CV......	halves	...CVCC...	axe	...VCC......	judge	...CVC...

L5.4

CVC	CCVC	CVCC	CCVCC	CCCVC	CVCCC
surf (Br)	treat	surf (Am)	skirt (Am)	struck	charms (Am)
love	bloom	hurt (Am)	drips	scream	lisps
mouse	plight	dark (Am)	plant	squeeze	helps
hurt (Br)	queen	fax	sleeps		pumps
dark (Br)	crime	charms (Br)	clasp		fifths
judge	skirt (Br)	salt	drink		
king	climb		spasm		
shoes					
keys					
lock					
thief					
match					

L5.5	(i) A B	(ii) B A	(iii) B A	(iv) B A	(v) B A
	(vi) B A	(vii) B A	(viii) A B	(ix) B A	(x) B A
	(xi) B A	(xii) B A	(xiii) B A	(xiv) B A	(xv) B A
	(xvi) A B	(xvii) B A	(xviii) B A	(xix) A B	(xx) A B
L5.6	(i) A B	(ii) B A	(iii) B A	(iv) B A	(v) B A
	(vi) B A	(vii) B A	(viii) A B	(ix) B A	(x) A B
	(xi) B A	(xii) A B	(xiii) B A	(xiv) B A	(xv) B A
L5.7	(i) A B	(ii) A B	(iii) B A	(iv) B A	(v) A B
	(vi) B A	(vii) B A	(viii) A B	(ix) A B	(x) A B

L5.8
(i) global tumble
(ii) troubles rattle
(iii) considerable fiscal
(iv) tickle
(v) vehicles
(vi) disposal
(vii) communalism
(viii) *no words with syllabic consonants*
(ix) incredible channel
(x) articles liberal
(xi) arrival double
(xii) international models fumble
(xiii) final eternal
(xiv) special children
(xv) superstition
(xvi) professional beaten
(xvii) festival celebrations opened
(xviii) activism
(xix) mission impossible
(xx) enable disabled

L5.10

Qualities you'll be praised for	Qualities you'll be criticized for	Religious beliefs you may have	Social beliefs you may have
patriotism heroism magnetism pragmatism liberalism dynamism scepticism	chauvinism racism escapism casteism puritanism	agnosticism paganism atheism theism	feminism secularism

6.1

L6.1

begin	oppose	basket	structure	foolish
number	protect	organ	prepare	silent
surprise	signal	sponsor	equal	contempt
climate	teacher	sterile	erase	taboo
arrow	amuse	vacate	provoke	disturb
alarm	manage	immense	legend	become
system	harbour	promise	velvet	crusade
council	disgrace	derive	protein	mature
crystal	mistake	concern	fulfil	question
problem	polite	belief	consult	option

6.2

L6.2

ABBREViAtion	CREDiBILity
huMANiTArian	MANifesTAtion
PRODucTIVity	SENTiMENTal
COMMUniCAtion	VERisiMILitude
ZOoLOGical	PROBleMATic
inSENSiBILity	BIoGRAPHical
CONtraDICtion	DISconTINuous
PRIVatiZAtion	MEDiCAtion
ELeMENTary	CONsulTAtion
TRANSforMAtion	CONducTIVity

L6.3

Ooo	oOo
register	betrayal
citizen	portrayal
minimum	develop
bifurcate	proportion
history	phonetics
beautiful	tomorrow
calculate	companion
deputy	behaviour
prejudice	department
balcony	professor
delicate	computer
secular	demolish
suitable	survival
cinema	successful
gradual	transparent
telephone	detachment
terrible	momentum
practical	collective
chemistry	important
guardian	mechanic
formula	removal
benefit	
decorate	
molecule	
fantasy	
tentative	
feminine	
manuscript	
barrister	

6.5

L6.4

baLLOON	BARgain	BEAcon
beLIEVE	bomBARD	BOrrow
camPAIGN	caSIno	CIRcumstance

CLImax	coHEsive	coLLECT
COLLeague	coLLIDE	comBINE
comPETE	COMplex	comPUter
CONcrete	conSTRICT	conTINue
CORReSPOND	COStume	COURtesy
deCLARE	deFEND	deFINE
deGREE	DELicate	dePICT
deSPAIR	DIFFicult	diRECT
DIStrict	FACile	faTIGUE
FInance	FOcus	FUtile
GEnius	HUmour	maCHINE
MAGnet	MAjor	maNOEUvre
MArathon	maROON	MAster
miSTAKE	MONitor	NEPHew
perFORM	PERfume	PERfect
perPLEX	perSIST	perSPECtive
perSUADE	perTURB	poLICE
poLITE	preCISE	preDICT
prePARE	preTEND	proMOTE
proTECT	proVIDE	purSUE
reCEIVE	reCRUIT	reDUCE
reFLECT	reLAX	reQUEST
reSIST	reSTRICT	reTIRE
saLUTE	SCHEdule	seDUCE
seLECT	SIlence	STUpid
suBLIME	suGGEST	suPPORT
suSPECT	THOUsand	transFORM

6.6

L6.5

(i) noun verb	(ii) verb noun	(iii) verb noun	(iv) noun verb	(v) noun verb
(vi) noun verb	(vii) verb adjective	(viii) noun verb	(ix) noun verb	(x) noun verb

(xi) noun / verb (xii) noun / verb (xiii) verb / noun (xiv) adjective / noun (xv) noun / verb

(xvi) noun / verb (xvii) noun / verb (xviii) verb / noun (xix) noun / verb (xx) verb / noun

(xxi) noun / verb (xxii) verb / noun (xxiii) verb / noun (xxiv) verb / noun (xxv) noun / verb

6.7

L6.6 (i) adverb (ii) preposition (iii) adverb (iv) adverb
(v) preposition (vi) adverb (vii) preposition (viii) adverb
(ix) preposition (x) adverb (xi) preposition (xii) preposition
(xiii) adverb (xiv) preposition (xv) preposition (xvi) adverb
(xvii) adverb (xviii) preposition (xix) adverb (xx) adverb

2. (i) go in for (ii) stand up to (iii) get along with (iv) shy away from
(v) reach out to (vi) watch out for (vii) hit out at (viii) look down on
(ix) ended up with (x) catch up on

L6.7 (i) noun / phrasal verb (ii) phrasal verb / noun (iii) phrasal verb / noun (iv) noun / phrasal verb

(v) noun / phrasal verb (vi) phrasal verb / noun (vii) phrasal verb / noun (viii) noun / phrasal verb

(ix) phrasal verb / noun (x) phrasal verb / noun

6.8

1. (i) apart (ii) contain (iii) uncover (iv) outweigh
(v) undermine (vi) inactive (vii) outshine (viii) unclear
(ix) mismatch (x) alive (xi) discolour (xii) insight
(xiii) outlast (xiv) overhear (xv) misfire (xvi) disgrace
(xvii) underlie (xviii) over-ride (xix) configure (xx) uphold
(xxi) debar (xxii) beware (xxiii) devalue (xxiv) upturn
(xxv) overload

L6.8 (i) noun verb (ii) verb noun (iii) verb noun (iv) noun verb (v) verb noun (vi) noun verb

6.9

L6.9 (i) active activities (ii) recognize recognition (iii) historic history (iv) composed composition

(v) political politician (vi) analysis analytical (vii) generous generosity (viii) recommend recommendation

(ix) energetic energy (x) defective defects (xi) nationality nationalization (xii) artist artistic

(xiii) curious curiosity (xiv) declare declaration (xv) observation observed (xvi) valid validity

(xvii) economist economical economics economy (xviii) biography biographical (xix) responsible responsibilities

(xx) restored restoration (xxi) human humanity (xxii) competition compete (xxiii) dynasty dynastic

(xxiv) problems Problematic (xxv) sensitive sensitivity

3.

-aire	*-eer*	*-ee*	*-ese*
millionaire	mountaineer	trainee	legalese
doctrinaire	auctioneer	refugee	journalese
commissionaire	puppeteer	divorcee	
billionaire	commandeer	interviewee	
	musketeer	addressee	

L6.10 diSKETTE techNIQUE groTESQUE launDERETTE
physSIQUE caSSETTE burLESQUE statuETTE
mySTIQUE statuESQUE oBLIQUE bouTIQUE

L6.11

Primary stress remains on the same syllable		Primary stress doesn't remain on the same syllable	
No change in pronunciation	With change in pronunciation of a vowel or a consonant or both	No change in pronunciation	With change in pronunciation of a vowel or a consonant or both
approve-approval	absorb-absorption		able-ability
danger-dangerous	assume-assumption		academic-academician
employ-employment	Christ-Christian		acquire-acquisition
guide-guidance	collide-collision		admire-admiration
reason-reasonable	defame-defamatory		analyze-analytical
	direct-direction		benefit-beneficial
	exhaust-exhaustion		botany-botanical
	expand-expansion		central-centrality
	grave-gravity		ceremony-ceremonial
	introduce-introduction		combine-combination
	invade-invasion		condense-condensation
	permit-permission		dissolve-dissolution
	prescribe-prescription		explain-explanation
	reduce-reduction		formal-formality
	suggest-suggestion		hero-heroic
			human-humanity
			inform-information
			invite-invitation
			local-locality
			method-methodical
			resign-resignation
			technology-technological
			theme-thematic
			valid-validity

6.10

1.

WEEK day	COOL box	FILM editing	HIGH school
BRAND shop	LOW PRICED	BACKspace	fakeCURRency
WEDDing guest	bold eSCAPE	FASHion designer	BURglar alarm
HEALTH drink	easy ACcess	maCHINE stitched	FUN loving
HORRor movie	LONG LASTing	ACTing career	LUXury hotel
long COAT	WAter filter	KICKstart	TAPE recorder
light SNACK	DUty FREE	WEBsite	COOKing oil
hot SPRING	TIGHT FISted	ANswering machine	MEdium sized
VOICE mail	HARD WORKing	DRAWing board	narrowSPACE
HAND crafted	FINGer print	BULLet wound	FAST MOVing

2. (i) reALity show (ii) HIGH FLYer (iii) DOWNLOAD(verb)
(iv) MARket driven (v) CHILDproof (vi) JET lag
(vii) HARD SELL (viii) BOTTOM LINE (ix) TEXT message
(x) GREEN PARty (xi) RIGHT click (verb) (xii) HAIR raising
(xiii) LIVE MUsic (xiv) BUNgee jumping (xv) SHIFT key
(xvi) WATCH dog (xvii) PHONE tapping (xviii) SOFT COPY
(xix) WORD processor (xx) SPEAker phone

6.11

1. (i) themselves (ii) herself (iii) myself (iv) himself
(v) yourself (vi) ourselves (vii) yourselves (viii) itself

2. (i) fourteenth (ii) seventeen (iii) eighteen (iv) thirteen
(v) fifteen

7.2

L7.3 (i) /w/ link (ii) /j/ link (iii) /w/ link
(iv) /j/ link (v) /w/ link (vi) /j/ link
(vii) /j/ link (viii) /j/ link (ix) /w/ link

L7.4 The first word ends with a consonant cluster and the second word begins with a vowel.

L7.5 The first word ends with a consonant and the second word begins with the same consonant.

L7.6 The first word begins with a plosive and the second word begins with a different plosive or with /m/ or /n/.

7.4

L7.9 (i) soft music (ii) gold jewellery (iii) grand function
(iv) handsome (v) manuscripts (vi) cold coffee
(vii) She has (viii) handkerchief (ix) The children have
(x) facts (xi) first project

7.5

1. Contracted forms can be used for the underlined words and expressions.
   - (i) I thought I would go and buy you a gift but could not because I had no time.
   - (ii) She would not have taken up this job if she had known about these problems.
   - (iii) You should have found out the fares before you booked the tickets.
   - (iv) They will not come unless they are invited.
   - (v) He is not leaving if he cannot finish the report this evening.
   - (vi) We do not wish to offend you but we have to follow the rules.
   - (vii) She has applied for a scholarship but we do not know if she will get it.
   - (viii) You cannot be serious! I cannot believe what you are saying!
   - (ix) Did they not tell you to come early?
   - (x) Why did we not plan what we were going to do?

7.6

L7.11 The underlined words are weak-form words.
- (i) We shall let you know when we decide.
- (ii) He asked her to stay at home. I think she should.
- (iii) I asked him for some paper. He gave me some paper and a pen too.
- (iv) She deals with all the letters to and from this office.
- (v) Who can translate this? I can.
- (vi) I will come with you whatever you may say.
- (vii) What are you looking at?
- (viii) That report is biased.
- (ix) How much did she pay for her new car?
- (x) Is there anything that you care for?

(xi) Look at that tall building there.
(xii) It was too late for me to call you.
(xiii) I thought you would be in college. Where are you now?
(xiv) They want her to wait for the taxi here.
(xv) Why don't you come over for lunch?
(xvi) When you want to use a neutral pronoun, use 'they' instead of 'he' or 'she'.
(xvii) Where do these birds come from?
(xviii) We don't eat fish, but many people do.
(xix) He is not as rich as you are.
(xx) Students must always come half an hour early for the examination.
(xxi) How am I to know what happened to her?
(xxii) They don't want me to go; they want you to go.

1. (i) I have given your(w) books to(w) Sheela.
(ii) Thank you for(w) coming.
(iii) There(w) is a magic show this evening.
(iv) What are(w) you hinting at(s)?
(v) The(w) doctor has not yet come.
(vi) She bought an(w) armchair.
(vii) What do(w) they want?
(viii) You have(s) to understand this.
(ix) The papers are(w) in the briefcase.
(x) They liked her(w) presentation.
(xi) Your(w) organization is helping many people.
(xii) Where were(w) you last night?
(xiii) She spoke to(w) everybody at the party.
(xiv) I don't know who she(w) is(s).
(xv) These apples are(w) very tasty.
(xvi) Her(w) interests are(w) elsewhere.
(xvii) I will(s) come, that's a promise.
(xviii) There(w) can be no doubt about his guilt.
(xix) The(w) example she gave was appropriate.
(xx) There(w) is the party to look forward to(s).
(xxi) The(w) reporters who were(w) in the hall heard the sound of explosion.
(xxii) We did it for(w) a(w) lark.
(xxiii) What do(w) I tell her(s)?

(xxiv) We got your(w) card.

(xxv) For(w) information about our holiday offers, call 8345218.

8.1

L8.1 (i) Naturally // the children behaved very well.

(ii) The children sat quietly in the room // which surprised everybody.

(iii) Fifteen years ago // he left home // looking for adventure and excitement.

(iv) We enjoyed the cultural show // which was very lively and entertaining.

(v) Young people // if they work hard // have plenty of opportunities.

(vi) You can talk to your friend in America // sitting here comfortably // simply by pressing a few buttons.

(vii) He can have breakfast in Bangalore // lunch in Bombay // and be in Calcutta for dinner.

(viii) Her daughter did not like the Maths teacher // but the English teacher // she liked very much.

(ix) Every bookshop is full of computer books // which are in great demand these days.

(x) What is more // they lost their luggage too.

(xi) If you like everybody else // believe that money is all important // this job is not for you.

(xii) Because her father did not like it // she did not go to Australia.

(xiii) Students of literature should have an awareness of the structure of language // which is essential if they are to respond to literature // critically and objectively.

(xiv) To tell you the truth // I did not like it at all.

(xv) Since he left the job // nobody has been happy.

(xvi) Computer scientists // many of them do not have communicative skills.

(xvii) A word represents an idea // in the same way as a traffic signal represents a direction.

(xviii) Tennis players // who earn a lot of money // travel in their own planes.

8.2

1. (i) Where did you meet Mr Singh? → I met Mr Singh at the PARty.

Who did you meet at the party? → I met Mr SINGH at the party.

(ii) Why has he gone to California?

He found a JOB in California.

He found a job in CAlifornia.

Where did he find a job?

(iii) Where has Ravi gone for training?

RAvi has gone to Germany for training.

Ravi has gone to GERmany for training.

Who has gone to Germany for training?

(iv) Here is my new mobile.

I thought YOU had an I-phone.

I thought you had an I-phone.

This I-phone, it is my brother's.

(v) What made you go to the Delhi book fair?

They offered me a free AIR ticket.

They offered me a FREE air ticket.

I thought you didn't like to travel by train.

(vi) Which poet are we studying today?

The proFEssor is going to speak on Yeats.

The professor is going to speak on YEATS.

Are you presenting your paper on Yeats?

(vii) How did Gandhi use non-violence?

Gandhi used non-violence as a political WEApon.

Gandhi used NON-violence as a political weapon.

What political weapon did Gandhi use?

(viii) Doesn't their daughter play badminton?

Their DAUGHter plays tennis.

Their daughter plays TENnis.

Doesn't their son play tennis?

(ix) Are you giving a twenty dollar discount?

You'll get a TWENty percent discount.

You'll get a twenty perCENT discount.

I thought you were giving a twenty-five percent discount.

(x) What does the old lady teach?

The old lady TEACHes music.

The old lady teaches MUsic.

I hear the old lady is learning music.

2. Could I use your laptop please? — I have only a DESKtop.
I would like to check my email. — There are no comPUters here.
She wants to see what is there on this CD. — Is it an AUdio CD?
Can you download e-books from this site? — YES, on paying a small FEE.
You can send and receive email with this phone. — I want a PHONE not a comPUter.

3. (i) Her brother is a CHEMical engineer. *(not a mechanical engineer)*
Her BROTHer is a mechanical engineer. *(not her sister)*
HER brother is a mechanical engineer. *(not my brother)*

(ii) Our neighbour has gone to Japan on BUSIness. *(not on vacation)*
Our neighbour has gone to JaPAN on business. *(not to Germany)*
Our NEIGHbour has gone to Japan on business. *(not our manager)*

(iii) We were living in BANGalore. *(not in Delhi)*
We WERE living in Bangalore. *(are not living now)*
We were LIVing in Bangalore. *(not working)*

(iv) He is angry with his SON. *(not with his daughter)*
He is ANGry with his son. *(not unhappy)*
He is angry with HIS son. *(not with our son)*

(v) They will VISit us next week. *(not call us)*
They will visit us NEXT week. *(not this week)*
They will visit us next WEEK. *(not next month)*

4. (i) Are my keys in the desk?
(ii) Is this a letter to the Bank?
(iii) She may not be happy here.
(iv) I thought the weather wasn't good.
(v) Whose car needs servicing?

8.4

L8.2 (i) Falling tone – Statement
(ii) Rising tone – Question
(iii) Rising tone – Question
(iv) Rising tone – Question

(v) Falling tone – Statement
(vi) Falling tone – Statement
(vii) Falling tone – Statement
(viii) Falling tone – Statement
(ix) Rising tone – Question
(x) Falling tone – Statement

3. (i) Rise (ii) Fall (iii) Fall (iv) Rise (v) Rise (vi) Fall
(vii) Rise (viii) Rise (ix) Fall (x) Fall

8.5

L8.4 (i) Rise, Rise, Rise (ii) Fall, Fall (iii) Rise, Rise, Rise

8.6

L8.5 (i) first part – fall, second part – rise
(ii) first part – fall, second part – rise
(iii) first part – rise, second part – fall

L8.6 (i) first part – fall, second part – rise
(ii) first part – fall, second part – rise
(iii) first part – rise, second part – fall
(iv) first part – rise, second part – fall
(v) first part – rise, second part – fall, third part – fall

3. (i) It was two weeks ago that we bought this.
(ii) It was by getting someone to wait at the ticket counter overnight that she managed to get the tickets.
(iii) It was because he specifically asked for a nurse that they sent a nurse and not a doctor.
(iv) It was Keats who wrote this poem and not Shelley.
(v) It was in an antique shop in a small town that I found it.

L8.7 (i) first part – rise, second part – fall
(ii) first part – rise, second part – fall
(iii) first part – rise, second part – fall
(iv) first part – fall, second part – rise
(v) first part – rise, second part – fall

4. (i) She'll look better in the pink dress than in the blue one.
 (ii) It would have been better if they had chosen to field first rather than to bat.
 (iii) It may be better to use the debit card rather than the credit card.
 (iv) Hot coffee sells better than cold coffee.
 (v) It may be better for her to visit Europe in May rather than in March.

L8.8 (i) MS (ii) FO (iii) MS (iv) MS (v) MS
(vi) MS (vii) FO (viii) MS (ix) FO (x) FO

8. (i) To what? (rise) (ii) Where? (rise)
 (iii) 120 thousand what?(rise)
 (iv) Why? (fall) (v) hike in what? (rise)

L8.9 (i) Rise Fall (ii) Rise Fall (iii) Rise Fall (iv) Rise Fall (v) Rise Fall

L8.10 (i) Rise (ii) Fall (iii) Rise (iv) Rise (v) Rise

L8.11 (i) Fall (ii) Rise (iii) Rise (iv) Rise (v) Fall
(vi) Rise (vii) Rise (viii) Rise (ix) Fall (x) Rise

L8.12 (i) Fall-Rise (partial agreement) (ii) Fall (complete agreement)
(iii) Fall-Rise (partial agreement) (iv) Fall-Rise (partial agreement)
(v) Fall-Rise (partial agreement) (vi) Fall-Rise (partial agreement)
(vii) Fall (complete agreement) (viii) Fall-Rise (partial agreement)

L8.13 (i) Belgium (rise), Switzerland (rise), Netherlands (rise), Germany (rise), Italy (rise), and France (fall).
 (ii) Abraham Lincoln (rise), Mahatma Gandhi (rise), Martin Luther King (rise), and Nelson Mandela (fall).
 (iii) Sanskrit (rise), Hindi (rise), Chinese (rise), Japanese (rise), and English (fall).
 (vi) vanilla (rise), chocolate (rise), strawberry (rise), mango (rise), and orange(fall).
 (v) Milton (rise), Wordsworth (rise), Keats (rise), Shelley (rise), and Yeats (fall)

11. (i) a motorbike (rise), a moped (rise), or a scooter (fall)
 (ii) Firefox (rise), Internet Explorer (rise), or Crome (fall)
 (iii) taxi (rise), bus (rise), or train (fall)
 (iv) green (rise), blue (rise), or grey (fall)
 (v) fruits (rise), biscuits (rise), or nuts (fall)

8.7

1. (i) Rise (ii) Rise (iii) Fall-Rise
(iv) Rise (v) Fall-Rise (vi) Fall-Rise

8.8

1. (i) We were sure they would come right on time, but they were ↑ late by fifteen minutes.
(ii) This dish takes long to prepare, but it tastes really ↑ great.
(iii) We thought the boy was asleep, but actually he was wide ↑ awake.
(iv) The book was praised by all the critics, but readers ↑ hated it.
(v) Everyone thought he would have put on weight, but he looked ↑ thin and weak when he returned.